THE OFFICIAL

eBay™

BIBLE

■ The Newly Revised and Updated Version of the Most Comprehensive eBay How-To Manual for Everyone from First-Time Users to eBay Experts

SECOND EDITION

JIM "GRIFF" GRIFFITH

GOTHAM
BOOKS

GOTHAM BOOKS
Published by Penguin Group (USA) Inc.
375 Hudson Street, New York, New York 10014, U.S.A.
Penguin Group (Canada), 10 Alcorn Avenue, Toronto, Ontario, Canada M4V 3B2 (a division of Pearson
Penguin Canada Inc.); Penguin Books Ltd, 80 Strand, London WC2R 0RL, England; Penguin Ireland,
25 St Stephen's Green, Dublin 2, Ireland (a division of Penguin Books Ltd); Penguin Group (Australia), 250
Camberwell Road, Camberwell, Victoria 3124, Australia (a division of Pearson Australia Group Pty Ltd);
Penguin Books India Pvt Ltd, 11 Community Centre, Panchsheel Park, New Delhi – 110 017, India; Pen-
guin Group (NZ), cnr Airborne and Rosedale Roads, Albany, Auckland 1310, New Zealand (a division of
Pearson New Zealand Ltd); Penguin Books (South Africa) (Pty) Ltd, 24 Sturdee Avenue, Rosebank,
Johannesburg 2196, South Africa

Penguin Books Ltd, Registered Offices: 80 Strand, London WC2R 0RL, England

Published by Gotham Books, a division of Penguin Group (USA) Inc.

Gotham Books and the skyscraper logo are trademarks of Penguin Group (USA) Inc.

ISBN 1-592-40092-2

Printed in the United States of America
Set in Sabon with Frutiger
Designed by Victoria Hartman

To the millions of eBay members
who have helped make eBay what it is today

CONTENTS

ACKNOWLEDGMENTS

For their help and support, I would like to thank the following: Pierre Omidyar and Jeff Skoll for throwing me that life-saver back in 1996; my esteemed eBay colleagues Henry Gomez—whose support was crucial in getting this project off the ground—and Brett Healy for his legal guidance; Lisa Shotland and Jim Davis; Joni Evans at William Morris; Lauren Marino, Erin Moore, and William Shinker at Gotham Books for showering me with their expertise, advice, and counsel; friends Patti (Louise) Ruby, Matt England, Rodney Hill, John Tillinger, Chris Byrne, Rob Stanger, Joan Wing, Mary Lou Song, Marsha Collier, Michael Kaiser, and Josh Lewis for their support and encouragement; and of course, Mike Winslow for standing by me during the rough and lean early days.

I also would like to thank the following for their support and guidance during the revisions for the second edition: my eBay colleagues Michael Rudolph, Elisa Stern, and Sharon Guldner; Howard L. Miller, George Morgan, and Michael Johnson for their constant support and good humor during the second edition (and especially for putting up with me as I furiously finished the second edition during our weeklong vacation in Hawaii—sorry, guys); and finally the millions of eBay members who make up the eBay community, especially those I've had the honor of meeting in person at our eBay University events.

Very special thanks to the following eBay members who contributed their tips, tricks, and stories: Craig M. Keller, Sr., Craig Knouse, Tim Heidner, Tom

Reddick, Tim Burnett, Julie Douglas, Pam Withers, Heather Luce, Mike Ford, Leah Lestina, Karen Gray, Anita Leather, Melissa Fiala, Brenda Bienlein, Robert Sachs, Barry Lamb, Peter Cini, Deanna Rittel, Keri Lyn Shosted, Classic Moments Video, Dave Rayner, Mike Driscoll, Chris and Kim Hecker, Chris Spencer, Laurie Liss, and Pat Fulton.

INTRODUCTION

On the morning of May 10, 1996, a friend sent me an e-mail. At the time, I was living in Vermont, dividing my day between administrative duties for a nonprofit arts organization known as The Carving Studio, some residual mural painting left over from my once flourishing decorative painting business, and buying, building, and reselling computers.

I was going broke.

My online friend knew I was searching for a hard-to-find memory chip. He had just stumbled upon a new Web site called eBay, where he had discovered that the very part I needed was for sale there in an auction format. I immediately clicked the URL he had copied into the body of the e-mail and found myself at a plain, gray-background Web site with a logo on the top of the page that announced "AuctionWeb—eBay Internet."

With a little easy searching, I soon found the chip and put in a bid of $15. (Two days later, I would win the auction for $10—a bargain.) I had finally found the part for which I had been searching. Excited by my find, I was soon exploring the rest of the site, looking for more treasure on which to bid, when I came across a page called "The AuctionWeb Bulletin Board."

[Listings] [Buyers] [Sellers] [Search] [Contact]

The AuctionWeb Bulletin Board

This page contains messages left by AuctionWeb registered users. You can use this bulletin board to communicate with the rest of the AuctionWeb community. Only the most recent **100** messages will be kept. (This used to be higher, but this page became too slow.)

User: wgtaylor (175) **Date:** 04/04/97 **Time:** 16:47:19 PST	Dan, Just scroll up to the top of this page, right under "The Auction Web Bulletin Board" and click on user feedback forum. It will give you instructions from there.
User: antique (93) **Date:** 04/04/97 **Time:** 16:46:31 PST	Dan, there is a link to the user feedback forum just above the boxes where you just entered your question. 8^) Aunt Patti
User: dwboynton (1) **Date:** 04/04/97 **Time:** 16:43:29 PST	How do I pass feedback, positive or negative. Can't seem to find the right niche..... Dan
User: wgtaylor (175) **Date:** 04/04/97 **Time:** 16:35:09 PST	Hey Donna, You sing pretty good...I really like the "Oldies" but don't you ever do "Country"?
User: wgtaylor (175) **Date:** 04/04/97 **Time:** 16:31:25 PST	Phillip, Sounds like your server to me.. Nancy
User: qvpsv13 (4) **Date:** 04/04/97 **Time:** 16:24:05 PST	Hey out there, am I the only one who cannot contact a seller through "ask the seller a question"? Every time i try, it goes to the e-mail page, I compose the message, try to send it, but it never goes anywhere. Is the problem eBAY's or netcom (my server) Thanks for any help Phillip

The original eBay chat board was nothing fancy—just a simple message board where anyone could submit a text-only post for the rest of the world to read and to which anyone else could post a response.

I watched for a few hours as new eBay users posted their questions and a few regular eBay experts provided answers. Here were a group of friendly buyers and sellers having a grand time chatting and sharing expertise—a genuine online community! Unable to resist the fun, I jumped in and started posting my own eBay-related questions, making acquaintance with other regular posters and learning a lot about buying and selling on eBay. Within weeks and with the help of generous eBay chat denizens, I had mastered the finer points of buying and selling and started answering questions like a seasoned eBay pro.

The ultimate pro, AuctionWeb creator Pierre Omidyar, usually stopped by the chat board in the evenings to say hello and chat about new features he was considering for his "hobby" site. He would even answer a few queries about listing procedures or policies. I was immediately struck by Pierre's good-natured chatting style, encyclopedic computer knowledge, and genuine concern for eBay users.

During the next few weeks, inspired by Pierre, I slowly patched together my own online persona, "Uncle Griff"—a hybrid of Miss Manners, Dame Edna Everage, Maude from the 1971 cult film *Harold and Maude,* along with a bit of Norman Bates thrown in for "balance."

Uncle Griff's primary mission on the chat board—besides chewing the online scenery—was to establish and maintain decorum and civility by dint of his own exemplary online behavior and slightly weird sense of humor. With the torch of his perfect manners held aloft, Uncle embarked on a valiant crusade to lead the huddled eBay chat board masses out of the darkness of messy, tear-ridden misunderstandings—which often escalated into all-out flame wars—onto the lofty plateau of polite and productive eBay discussion.

For a while, it was great fun, but although the Uncle Griff avatar was outwardly a jolly and well-adjusted—if somewhat bizarre—old coot, in truth, my off-line life was coming apart, and by late September, with savings depleted and no prospect of gainful employment in sight, I sank into a severe and paralyzing depression.

I thought it was a typical male midlife crisis, but it proved to be much more serious. I would later learn that I had been suffering from regular bouts of clinical depression for most of my life, but just like many sufferers of this pernicious disease, I had proudly resisted acknowledging or addressing my condition.

Unable to rouse myself out of bed, Uncle Griff unceremoniously disappeared one day from the AW Bulletin Board.

After a few weeks, with the support of concerned friends, therapy, and medication, I was able to return one morning to my studio. My landlord, an understanding man, had been patient about the back rent, but not so the utility companies. The studio heat and electricity had been shut off.

Standing alone in my cold, dark space, I considered my options. Although technically "on the mend," I would still need a job in order to crawl out of debt and pull my life together. But who in his right mind would ever hire an undereducated, middle-aged, previously-self-employed-now-flat-broke gentleman with a very left-of-center sense of humor?

It was the low point of my life.

Then, the phone rang.

"Hello?"

"Hello, is Uncle Griff there?"

"Who wants to know?"

"This is Jeff Skoll from eBay. Pierre is here with me. We are looking for Uncle Griff."

I remember thinking that I must have not paid my AuctionWeb bill.

"Uncle? Where have you been?"

"I had, uh . . . a cold. Is something wrong?"

"No, not at all. We were concerned. We've been watching Uncle Griff's antics for the last few months. We really think he's terrific. Then he just disappeared. We don't want Uncle to disappear again, so we were wondering if we could pay you to keep him around."

". . ."

"Uncle? You still there?"

"Work for eBay?"

"Are you interested?"

Interested? Jeff and Pierre had thrown me a life preserver. I grabbed it.

"Yes!"

We settled on a fair hourly wage, worked out a schedule of sorts, and by the end of the call, I was eBay's first official customer-support rep—answering e-mails and chatting on the boards, and all from West Rutland, Vermont.

Nearly ten years, and a lot of changes, later, I am still with eBay, except that my job title has changed to "Dean of eBay Education" and I am living in California instead of Vermont. Although I now travel around the country and the world spreading the word about eBay to the experienced and the uninitiated, I am still teaching others how to use eBay every other weekend at one of our eBay University seminars. (More on eBay University later in this book.)

EBAY CHANGED MY LIFE—IT CAN CHANGE YOURS!

It sounds like a cliché, but it's absolutely true—eBay changed my life. eBay has changed or enhanced the lives of literally millions of folks who, like me, stumbled one day upon this incredible revolutionary Web site and, as either buyers or sellers or both, found themselves suddenly taking control of their lives in ways they had never imagined were possible.

Over the past nine years, through e-mail and face-to-face, literally hundreds of eBay members have shared their own awe-inspiring eBay stories with me. Some of these stories are brief tales of the "Good Samaritan" who helped someone get started with her auctions. Others border on the miraculous—how finding eBay helped salvage a career or a business on the verge of collapse and ruin. People have met on eBay and were later married. One woman bought her entire wedding on eBay.

Others who once felt they were too incompetent or just plain too dumb to ever learn how to get online were motivated by the eBay juggernaut to finally master that damnable computer their son or daughter had given them and were soon buying and selling along with the other millions of registered eBay users.

Today, over 135 million buyers and sellers around the world have jumped on the eBay train; an impressive number indeed, but by my reckoning that leaves several hundred million still unaccounted for.

Are you one of the unaccounted for?

- Your friends and relatives all use eBay and you want to join in the fun, but just the very thought of computers gives you the willies.
- You've heard the buzz and checked out eBay once or twice but are overwhelmed by the sheer numbers of items for sale on the eBay Web site.
- You are currently selling at eBay but you want to improve your eBay skills with more tips, tricks, and eBay seller secrets.

If any of the above fit your situation, then this book is for you!

By combining the eBay knowledge I have garnered since 1996, the tips and tricks of other savvy eBay experts, and the incredible tales of people whose lives have forever been changed by eBay, I've put together this comprehensive how-to manual for using eBay—one that I hope will inspire you to take those first steps toward successful eBay buying and selling, and reward you with the confidence and the satisfaction that comes from learning and applying, firsthand, a new and exciting set of skills.

Buyers: We'll take you step-by-step through the eBay registration process and show you how to effectively browse and search the eBay site; with lots of information on how to bid and buy safely both for yourselves and your families.

Sellers: You'll take better digital pictures; write professional item listings with HTML; learn how to put together a new eBay business and how to promote it effectively.

Don't think you can do it? Think again.

Over the last nine years, I've witnessed thousands of folks just like you get the "eBay knack," and all it took was encouragement, a little humor, and step-by-step instructions in plain English.

I *know* you can do it!

What are we waiting for? There's treasure to discover.

Let's get started!

HOW TO NAVIGATE *THE OFFICIAL EBAY BIBLE*

The Official eBay Bible can be read from cover to cover or used as a reference. I have tried to include a wide range of information to benefit both the brand-new computer user as well as the seasoned eBay expert.

This book is divided into two sections. Section One is primarily for eBay buyers. However, whether you want to buy or sell on eBay—if you are a brand-new computer user, start with Section One. Section Two is most definitely for eBay sellers.

Experienced computer and Internet users can start anywhere or use the index at the end of the book to look up specific topics.

The Official ebaY™ Bible

SECTION

1

Buying
the eBay Way!

Let's Get Started

You are about to enter a wondrous universe called eBay—a place where you can hunt for and buy treasure; sell the contents of your attic; or maybe finally follow that old dream of yours and start your own online business—all the while meeting and chatting with other eager eBay traders in your hometown, your state, or from halfway around the globe. But first, a little history . . .

The eBay Phenomenon

Shopping!

Whether it's at garage sales or malls, through mail-order catalogs or the Shopping Channel, in Middle Eastern souks, at auctions, bazaars, swap meets, flea markets, or even the stock market—we humans love to shop. Shopping and acquiring are basic to human nature. We can't get enough of them. Our uniquely human passion for barter and trade is what sets us apart from the rest of the animal kingdom. In fact, we've been bartering goods since before recorded history, so it's no surprise that the some of the earliest surviving examples of human writing—Sumerian cuneiform V-shaped impressions on clay tablets—are receipts.

There have been watershed moments in the history of human commerce, starting with the invention of the wheel, agriculture, water-powered mills, and currency, through the creation of the first steam engines, assembly lines, and flight, but in the 1990s a completely new conduit for commerce appeared—one so revolutionary in scope that in just a few short years, it changed forever the way that humans traded with one another.

The Internet provided anyone with a computer and a telephone line access to a rapidly growing universe of millions of Web sites from around the globe offering a staggering array of information, news, entertainment, and most important, goods.

At first, the Internet was considered suitable only for the exchange of information through e-mail and bulletin boards, but in 1993, with the creation of the graphics-capable World Wide Web, the idea of the Internet as a venue for commerce took hold, especially as the first trickle of Internet pioneers grew overnight into a virtual stampede of new users. Where there are people, there's trading.

In the early summer of 1995, the commercial and social potential of the Internet was on the mind of Pierre Omidyar, a computer programmer living and working in San Jose, California.

Most commercial Web sites up to 1995 were just online variations of the offline merchant-customer model where a single company offered merchandise for sale at a set cost. These Web sites were only slightly more exciting than mail order catalogs.

Pierre had an idea.

Why not create a Web site where buyers and sellers could trade directly with each other, much like an old-time flea market, using an auction format?

The concept was simple. The World Wide Web could provide a market "space" where sellers could list items and where buyers could browse for and buy these items, just like a flea market—except where the traditional flea market was limited to one geographical location, the Web was truly worldwide in scope. This would be real Internet trading—people trading with other people online, through their computers, from the comfort of their homes, from anywhere around the world.

Working alone and in his spare time (he had a day job after all), it took Pierre only a few weeks to complete a design and write the software that would run his new Web site.

The actual design of the site was simple.

Using a unique e-mail address as an "identifier," anyone with something to sell could, through their home computer and an Internet connection, upload an item description and title to the site. Anyone who visited the site and found the item—either by searching on keywords or by browsing the list of item titles in various categories—could then submit a bid for that item.

Bids would be accepted by a proxy system; that is, instead of having to sit on the listing to rebid every time someone outbid him, the bidder could instead submit a maximum bid amount—the highest amount he was willing to pay—and the system behind the Web site would execute his maximum bid on his behalf, protecting his interest until either the auction ended or another bidder submitted a bid amount higher than the first bidder's proxy. It was a simple but brilliant and efficient way to import the traditional auction format into this new medium.

The most brilliant aspect of all: The buyer and seller would complete the transaction without the direct involvement of the Web site! The seller would send payment instructions to the high bidder, and the high bidder would send payment. The seller would then mail or deliver the item to the high bidder.

Pierre called his new Web site "AuctionWeb—eBay Internet." The Auction-Web site went "live" on Labor Day, 1995. Pierre's only initial marketing effort was to post a simple announcement that month on Usenet:

```
From: Pierre Omidyar <pierre@shell1.best.com>
Subject: SHOPPING: Free Interactive Web Auction
Date: 1995/09/27

AuctionWeb
----------

 "The most fun buying and selling on the web!"

 * Run your own auction
 * Bid on existing auctions
 * New listings added daily!
 * Fast, fun, and FREE!

 * AuctionWeb doesn't sell anything - we just provide the service.

Try it out!

 <URL:http://www.ebay.com/aw/>


--
Pierre Omidyar    Home page: http://www.ebay.com/pierre.shtml
pierre@ebay.com   Free Web Auction:   http://www.ebay.com/aw/
```

(The *AuctionWeb* name was dropped in favor of just *eBay* in September of 1997.)

The first eBay site was totally devoid of fancy graphics, colors, icons, or logos. It was as visually thrilling as a gray paper box:

| Auction Web | | |

[Menu] [Listings] [Buyers] [Sellers] [Search] [Contact/Help] [Site Map]

Welcome to today's online
marketplace...

Welcome to our community. I'm glad you found us. AuctionWeb is dedicated to bringing together buyers and sellers in an honest and open marketplace. Here, thanks to our auction format, merchandise will always fetch its market value. And there are plenty of great deals to be found!

...the market that brings
buyers and sellers together
in an honest and open
environment...

Take a look at the listings. There are always several hundred auctions underway, so you're bound to find something interesting.

If you don't find what you like, take a look at our **Personal Shopper.** It can help you search all the listings. Or, it can keep an eye on new items as they are posted and let you know when something you want appears. If you want to let everyone know what you want, post something on our wanted page.

If you have something to **sell**, start your auction instantly.

Welcome to eBay's
AuctionWeb.

Join our community. Become a registered user. Registered users receive additional benefits such as daily updates and the right to participate in our user feedback forum and the bulletin board.

Please **read on** about the AuctionWeb vision...

What Does the Word *eBay* Mean?

Earlier on in Pierre's career, he made a trip to Sacramento to incorporate all of his current and future business endeavors under a single "holding company" using a favorite name—Echo Bay. However, much to Pierre's disappointment, the clerk at the state capital office informed him that someone else had already incorporated a California business using Echo Bay. Thinking fast, Pierre came up with e-bay.

The clerk checked. The name ebay had not yet been incorporated.

The rest is history.

In the months immediately following the launch, a few hundred people stumbled across eBay and began listing items for bid; at first mostly computer parts, used items, and a smattering of collectibles.

Throughout 1996, news about Pierre's little Web site began to spread across the Internet. Each day, more and more sellers came to eBay, liked what they saw and added their merchandise to the expanding list of items for bid. The increasing number and variety of items brought more curious buyers looking for a possible bargain. As more items were sold, even more sellers would come to

AuctionWeb and list even more items, bringing even more new buyers and so on, until the number of eBay users began to expand at a remarkable rate.

By the fall of 1996, there were close to ten thousand registered users on eBay.

In May of 1997, the one millionth item was sold on eBay (a *Sesame Street* Big Bird figure).

For the first two years, the astonishing growth in both eBay members and eBay items was due entirely to word of mouth. By the end of 1998, there were over 2 million registered eBay users. Sellers were listing 3.4 million items per month.

In 1998 eBay went public. This new American pastime—buying and selling on eBay—had attracted the attention of not only Wall Street but the general public as well. By 1999, "eBay"—the brand—was recognizable enough to be a regular feature of David Letterman's Top Ten List and a punch line in *New Yorker* cartoons. eBay was a bona fide cultural phenomenon.

The number of registered users grew to 10 million by the end of 1999, and eBay sellers were listing nearly 10 million items a month.

By the end of 2001, the number of eBay users stood at over 40 million with eBay sellers each month listing a staggering 31 million items.

Starting in earnest in early 2000 and continuing to the present, the eBay Inc. team, led by CEO Meg Whitman, has extended the eBay reach across the globe as new language and culturally distinct eBay Web sites were opened in Britain, Australia, France, Italy, South America, Korea, and mainland China.

Today, the trading statistics are astonishing. On eBay . . .

> Someone buys a Corvette every hour.
> A diamond ring is purchased every two minutes.
> Thirteen CDs are sold every minute.
> A digital camera sells every forty seconds.
> One article of clothing is sold every .75 seconds.

Looking back, given the extraordinary timing, the brilliant simplicity of the idea and the business model, and how seamlessly it fit the promise of the Internet, the birth and subsequent phenomenal success of eBay now seem to have been inevitable. Pierre's vision of a Web site for person-to-person trading was an idea whose time had clearly arrived. But that's not the entire picture.

A person-to-person trading site is nothing without the "persons" who do the trading. eBay's success and popularity are due in large part to the dedication and hard work of those individual buyers and sellers who use it every day. These folks make up the core of the eBay Community.

That's the story of eBay so far. It's most definitely not the end of the tale. From Pierre's simple idea—a Web-site trading outpost—eBay has grown into the biggest human commerce phenomenon of the last hundred years of trading.

Welcome to eBay!

Using eBay—the Basic Tools

To use eBay, you will use two basic computer tools: a Web browser and an e-mail application.

WEB BROWSERS

All computers come with at least one version of a Web browser. The two most popular models of Web browsers are Microsoft Internet Explorer and Netscape.

All of the illustrations and examples in this book use Internet Explorer (IE). However, with just a few minor adjustments you can easily adopt them to Netscape or any other Web browser.

You can start Internet Explorer on your computer by looking for the blue *E* icon on your computer desktop:

When you first start up your Web browser, the page that initially displays is the default home page set by the computer manufacturer. The first thing we are going to do with your Web browser is change the preset default home page to the eBay home page. That way, every time you connect to the Internet, the first Web page displayed will be eBay.

CHANGING YOUR WEB BROWSER'S DEFAULT HOME

Position your mouse cursor inside the Address box and highlight the text within the box by clicking the left mouse button two times.

Begin typing the address for the eBay home page, *www.ebay.com*. The old text will automatically be replaced by the text you type.

Press the Enter key on your keyboard or click the Go button to the very right of the Address window:

This will bring up the eBay home page in your browser window.

On the command menu, click on Tools, and then from the drop-down menu, Internet Options.

This will display the Internet Options box. In the top third of the box, there is a section labeled "Home page." The URL (Web address) for the current page displayed in your Web browser will show in the Address box. Click the Use Current button.

9

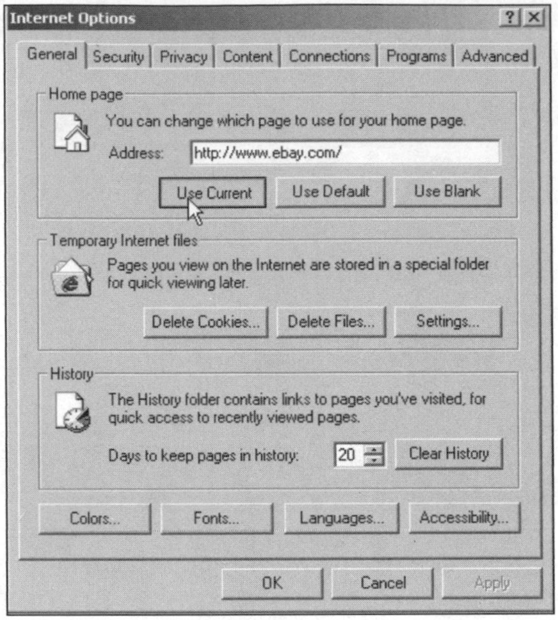

Then click the OK button on the bottom of the Internet Options window.

eBay is now your default home page! Every time you open a new browser window by clicking on the Internet Explorer icon, the first page you will see will be the eBay home page.

You can change your "home page" at any time by following the above steps.

GRIFF TIP! Throughout this book, you will see suggestions to "go to" a particular Web address such as *http://www.ebay.com.*

To "go to" any Web page address in this book, repeat step one, type in the web address (make sure to type it exactly as shown), then press the Enter key on your keyboard.

Basic Web Page Navigation

HYPERLINKS

Navigating from one Web page to another is a snap.

If you look at the eBay home page, you will notice that many of the lines of text are a blue color and underlined. If you move your mouse over this blue, underlined text, the mouse cursor will change from a little arrow to a tiny hand with a pointing index finger.

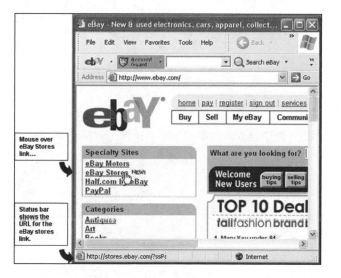

These changes indicate that the text underneath the mouse cursor is a *hyperlink*.

The task of hyperlinks is to take you to another location, either within the current Web page or to a completely different Web page. You ask the hyperlink to do its task by clicking the mouse directly on the hyperlink.

Try moving your mouse cursor over one of the hyperlinks on the eBay page. Also, when you do move your mouse over a link, watch as the Web address for the Web page to which the link leads appears in the IE status bar on the bottom of the IE window.

Once your mouse cursor is over a hyperlink, move to the Web page represented by that link by clicking the left-hand button on your mouse. Depending on the speed of your Internet connection, the page whose hyperlink you clicked will start to appear in the IE window.

BACK AND FORWARD BUTTONS

Clicking a link will move you forward to that page. To move back to the previous Web page, look for and click the Back button located on the menu bar at the top of the IE window.

To move forward again to the clicked page, click the Forward button (located directly to the right of the Back button).

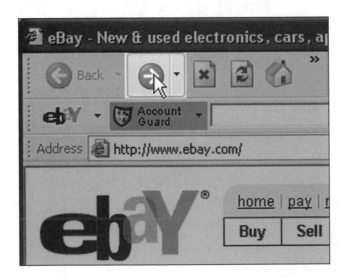

THE IE ADDRESS BOX

As I mentioned in the previous Griff Tip, if you know the address for a Web page, you can type it into the box labeled Address at the top of the IE window.

Remember that the quickest way to type text into any text entry box is to click twice anywhere inside the box to highlight the existing text and to then start typing the new text. (Many folks don't believe the highlighted text is going to disappear, so they press the Delete key on their computer keyboard before they start typing. This is unnecessary.)

CHANGING YOUR WEB BROWSER'S COOKIE SETTINGS

To use most eBay Web pages to their fullest, your Web browser needs to be able to accept cookies.

Cookies are simple text files stored on your computer to which a Web site will write your chosen preferences. For example, the first time you visit a Web site like *www.fandango.com* looking for film locations and schedules for your city, the Fandango site will "remember" your city preferences by storing them in a cookie file. On your return to Fandango, the Web site will read the contents of the cookie and immediately display the pages for your city, saving you the trouble of navigating there.

eBay's most popular features must use cookies to work properly. Two of the most important (but by no means the only) eBay features that use cookies are the Sign In feature and the eBay Picture Services feature. If your Web browser is not set to accept cookies, you will not be able to use either of these features properly.

Here are the steps for making sure that your Web browser is set up to accept cookies from eBay.

For Internet Explorer Versions 5.0 and Below

Go to the menu bar on Internet Explorer (the menu bar is the list of commands on the top of any Windows application) and look for the option for Tools. Select it, then click "Internet Options . . ."

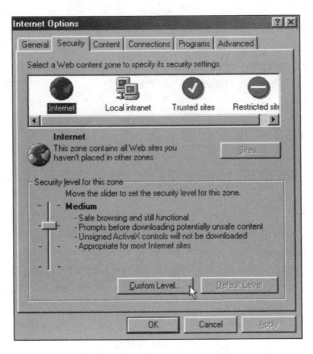

In the next window, select the top tab Security and make sure the Internet icon is highlighted. Then look for and click the button for "Custom Level . . ." at the bottom of the window.

This will bring up the Security Settings window. Scroll down and look for the section Cookies. Make sure that the Enable option is checked for both "Allow cookies that are stored on your computer" and "Allow per-session cookies (not stored)."

NOTE: Selecting Enable will allow all sites you visit to place a cookie on your computer.

Click OK (the Security Settings window will close), then click Apply and OK on the Internet Options window.

For Netscape

In a Netscape browser, select the option for "Preferences . . ." under the menu command Edit.

In the Preferences window, highlight the option Advanced in the left-hand panel. Make sure that the option for Cookies is set to either "Accept all cookies" or "Accept only cookies that get sent back to the originating server."

Click OK.

Now you can use all of eBay's time-saving features!

For Internet Explorer Versions 6.0 and Above

On the Internet Explorer toolbar, click on Tools, then click the menu item "Internet Options . . ."

In the resulting Internet Options window, select the Privacy tab and click on the button labeled "Edit . . ." in the Web Sites frame (located at the bottom of the window).

This will bring up the Per Site Privacy Actions window, where you can add Web sites by name and either Allow or Block their cookies.

NOTE: To use eBay correctly and efficiently and to have access to all of eBay's user features, you *must* allow cookies from *www.ebay.com*.

Type in *www.ebay.com* in the window marked "Address of Web site:" and click the button Allow.

Once you have added the Web sites for which you wish to allow or block cookies, click the button OK, then in the Internet Options window, click the button OK.

E-MAIL

As a form of communication, e-mail has nearly supplanted the handwritten letter. It's quick and easy to send, receive, and keep track of e-mail. E-mail is also incredibly well suited for sending out one mailing to one, two, or—curses!—several hundred people all at once.

In short, e-mail is a blessing and a curse. E-mail is also an absolutely critical tool for using eBay and the Internet. You cannot tap the Internet's fullest potential without using e-mail, and to do so, you will need an e-mail account.

E-mail is part of the service package of every ISP (Internet Service Provider). Outlook Express is the e-mail application that comes built in with all versions of Internet Explorer. It can handle all your basic e-mail needs, including your eBay e-mail.

Free Web-Based E-mail Accounts

Free Web-based e-mail accounts are one of the most popular methods of sending and receiving e-mail, mostly because, well, it's free, but also because Web-based e-mail is accessible from any place on earth with an Internet-connected computer, be it your friend's house, an Internet café in Italy, or from your laptop while on the road.

There are literally hundreds of free e-mail accounts to choose from. Two of the most popular are:

Yahoo!
Hotmail

You can find hundreds of others online at *http://www.e-mailaddresses.com/*.

AOL E-mail

AOL is popular with millions of eBay members, and their e-mail service is easy to learn and use. There is one small drawback to their service. As of this writing, AOL e-mail doesn't always display hyperlinks as active, "clickable" links. If someone sends you the address of a Web page and that address is static text, not clickable, you will have to *copy and paste* the Web page address from the e-mail body to your Web browser's address box to view the page.

My advice? If you are an AOL user and are comfortable with their e-mail service, by all means keep using it. One suggestion: Keep your AOL software updated to the latest release (as of this writing, AOL 9.0) by visiting *www.aol.com.*

Save Your E-mail!

Saving your old in and out e-mails—either as "soft copy" or printouts—is a wise habit to acquire, especially when you start buying and selling on eBay. You will receive and send many e-mails to sellers and buyers as your activity on eBay increases, and you may well need to access them sometime long after the transactions have closed.

The Internet and computers can be overwhelming at first, but with just a little perseverance, you will master Web browsers and e-mail in no time.

Just like eBay member Craig M. Keller Sr.:

Uncle Griff,

I am one of those "older farts." . . . I wanted nothing, and I mean NOTHING, to do with computers, when we first got them in at work. I fought and fought against using them. When in 1999 due to a serious illness I was forced to leave work and retire, my daughter (bless her heart) said that she was going to e-mail me a joke or cartoon every day on my wife's computer and that I had to read it.

One day, my wife came home from her job and said that if while I was reading my joke of the day, I wanted to check out the neatest site, try www.ebay.com. Well, let me tell you, my whole life changed on that day. I found a whole new world out there in cyberspace, and I have learned not only great things to buy, but I now do quite a bit of selling. . . .

Believe you me, without eBay to go to each day, I would have sooner or later went out of my mind after being forced to stay at home.

I have had an operation, in 2001, that now lets me pretty much do everything I used to do before the illness, but I'll never give up eBay.

Craig did it. So can you!
Let's get you registered on eBay.

Registering on eBay, Step by Step

THE COMPLETE PROCESS

You will need to register on eBay to bid or buy, sell, or use the other various eBay features such as feedback or chat. Even though you don't need to be registered to browse for treasure at eBay, we might as well get ourselves registered sooner rather than later.

Registering on eBay is fairly straightforward, with three simple steps:

1. Fill in your information (name, address, etc.) and choose your eBay User ID and password.
2. Agree to Terms.
3. Receive confirmation e-mail and confirm your registration.

To begin, go to the eBay home page, *www.ebay.com,* and look for the button on the top of the eBay home page labeled "register now."

If you are a first-time eBay visitor, you may see a different version of the home page. If so, look for and click the Register Now link:

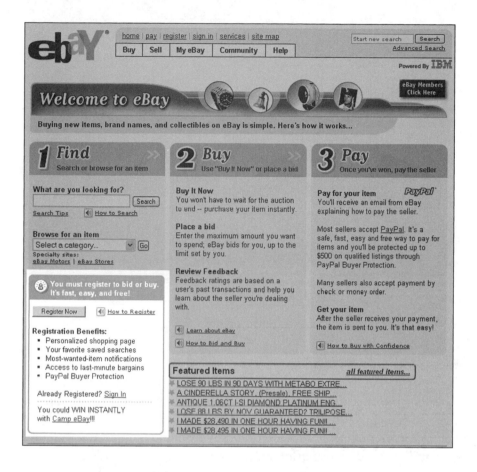

Either way will bring you to Step 1 of the three-step registration process.

Step 1—Enter Information

On this page, enter your contact information.

> First and last name
> Street address
> City
> State (from the drop-down list)
> Zip code
> Country
> Primary phone number
> Secondary phone number
> E-mail address

Registration: Enter Information ⑦ Need Help?

① Enter Information   2 Agree to Terms   3 Confirm Your Email

First name
Jim

Last name
Griffith

Street address
PO Box 819

City
Draper

State
Utah

Zip code
84020

Country
United States
Change country

Primary telephone
(801) 501-9930

Extension

Secondary telephone
(801) 545-2203

Extension

Important: To complete registration, enter a valid email address that you can check immediately.

Email address
unkiegriff@aol.com

Re-enter email address
unkiegriff@aol.com

Contact Information—Tips

As a part of registration, you agree to provide correct and valid contact information. This information is not available to anyone except the winning buyer or seller in a successful closed eBay transaction, and then, only the phone number is provided (not your name or address) and only by manual request, never automatically. In addition, the information on file is never sold or rented to another party. (View eBay's privacy policy at *http://pages.ebay.com/help/policies/privacypolicy.html.*)

You may provide a P.O. box for an address, and you may provide a dedicated voice-mail or pager number for a primary phone.

The registration form does not provide a field for entering a business name. If you are planning on running a business on eBay, supply the name that appears on your business or personal credit or debit card as well as your business checking account. This will help later when you set up your eBay Seller's Account (Section Two, chapter 1).

At the bottom of the same page, enter your valid e-mail address (twice, to make sure you type it correctly), your choice of eBay User ID and password, and select a secret question and answer. (If you forget your password, you'll be asked the secret question and you'll need to answer the question correctly to receive a new password.)

Create your eBay User ID

unkiegriff

Example: rose789 (Don't use your email address)
Your User ID identifies you to other eBay users.

Create password

6 character minimum
Enter a password that's easy for you to remember, but hard for others to guess. See tips.

Re-enter password

Secret question   **Secret answer**

What street did you grow up on?

You will be asked for the answer to your secret question if you forget your password.

Date of birth

April   05   Year 19

Continue >

Choosing an eBay User ID and Password—Tips

Your eBay User ID is the "handle" by which all other eBay members will recognize you on the site. Your User ID will show up on the pages of your items for sale, next to your bids, on your feedback profile, on your About Me page, and anywhere you chat online at eBay. Since this is your official handle (you may actually become famous by this User ID), it is crucial that you create one that is absolutely perfect for you.

If you are primarily a bidder, you may want to create an eBay User ID that reflects your buying passions. For example, if you collect balls of string, a good ID might be "ballofstringlover001" or something similar.

If you are a seller, choose something that hints at your business. If your business name were Say It With Widgets, then perhaps "sayitwithwidgets" would be a good choice. (Do not use *www.sayitwithwidgets.com,*" as the system is set to reject any User ID that is a Web site address.)

Whatever you choose, do keep it easy to remember. Complicated combinations of letters and numbers are not easy to remember. If you are a seller, this can be an obstacle for your future eBay customers. Shorter User IDs are easier to notice and recall.

Avoid punctuation. If you attempt to create a User ID and it comes back as already in use, you may find that by adding a period at the end it will go through. However, as a seller, you could end up with confused bidders who think you are someone else. Your User ID should be as identifiable and memorable as possible.

Every User ID on eBay is displayed in lowercase, regardless of how you type it in the box. Certain combinations of letters and numbers in lowercase can look ambiguous in a viewer's Web browser, so avoid User ID choices that include directly adjacent combinations of the letters *I*, *L*, and the numeral 1. Also avoid choices that include directly adjacent combinations of the letter *O* and the numeral 0.

You cannot use your e-mail address as your eBay User ID. Initially, it was possible to do so, but this policy was changed in 2001. This no-e-mail-address-for-a-User-ID policy was implemented to discourage bulk e-mail senders from using software to harvest the eBay site for new e-mail addresses to add to their spam lists. Although the policy cannot completely prevent e-mail harvesting, it has made it more difficult for harvesters to do so.

A Word About Passwords . . .

Never use an obvious word or phrase as a password! For example, don't use a common name or your eBay User ID. The best passwords are a combination of random letters and numbers. Another solution is to use a word or words that have special meaning to you, then surround them with numbers that also relate to something in your life, maybe the first phone number you can recall for your family. Either way, avoid writing the password down unless you positively cannot memorize it. If you must write it down, store it in a secure, safe place such as a safe-deposit box.

Like eBay User IDs, eBay passwords are always reduced to lower case. Therefore, to avoid confusing yourself, use only lowercase in your password.

Once you have finished entering all the requested information, click the Continue button.

If your e-mail address is through a pay service such as your ISP, you will go directly to Step 2—Agree to Terms.

However, if your e-mail address is with one of the thousands of free e-mail account services such as hotmail.com, yahoo.com (or, in our example, mail.com), you will see a Web form requesting a credit- or debit-card number, name, and billing address.

Registration: Enter Information

Since most free or Web-based e-mail services do not verify the identity of their subscribers, eBay makes this step necessary to verify that the name and address you have provided for your registration are valid (by matching the registration name and address with the name and billing address on the credit or debit card).

If you do not wish to list a credit card, and you have an e-mail address that does not come from one of the free, Web-based e-mail services, click the link for "enter a different e-mail." This will take you back one page so you can edit the e-mail address field.

NOTE: Make sure that the credit- or debit-card billing name and address match the contact information you provided for the registration. Your credit card will not be charged, nor will it be used for any future billing purposes. eBay uses the billing address and name for the card to match against the name and address you provided for your contact information. The credit card number is not kept at eBay. This is important to note because, later, if you create an eBay Seller's Account, you will be asked for a credit card again, which eBay will, at that time, store on your eBay Seller's Account.

Step 2—Agree to Terms

To use the eBay site, you must first agree to the eBay User Agreement and Privacy Policy. Take a few moments to read through them and print them out (by clicking the links Printer-friendly User Agreement and Printer-friendly Privacy Policy).

Registration: Agree to Terms   ⑦ Need Help?

1 Enter Information   ② **Agree to Terms**   3 Confirm Your Email

Please read the User Agreement and Privacy Policy below.

> User Agreement
> Welcome to the User Agreement for eBay Inc. This Agreement
> describes the terms and conditions applicable to your use of our
> services available under the domain and sub-domains of www.ebay.com
> (including half.ebay.com, ebaystores.com) and the general principles

Printer-friendly User Agreement

> Privacy Policy
> Privacy is very important to us. We want you to fully understand
> our privacy practices and therefore, in addition to this Privacy
> Policy, we have created Privacy Central
> (http://pages.ebay.com/help/privacycentral1.html) to help you fully

Printer-friendly Privacy Policy

Check the boxes and click **I Agree** to accept the User Agreement, Privacy Policy and incorporated terms.

☑ **I am 18+ years old.**
   21+ years old in some states.

☑ **I understand that eBay may email or notify me** (When I buy an item, product updates, etc.)
   I can change how eBay contacts me at any time by going to the Notification Preferences page in My eBay.

[**I Agree To These Terms >**]   I decline

If you have never registered with an online service, you may be unfamiliar with user agreements (also known on other Web sites as Terms of Service agreements).

User agreements are binding contracts. They list the dos and don'ts for you, the registered user, and for eBay. The eBay User Agreement is extensive and comprehensive. If you read it carefully, you will get a clear picture of what responsibilities, activities, and conduct eBay expects from all registered members.

GRIFF TIP! Never take a Web site's User Agreement for granted, including ours. The information contained in the User Agreement can prove invaluable later on. You can always review the text of the eBay User Agreement by clicking the Help link on the top of the eBay home page. Type the phrase "user agreement" into the Search Help box. On the next page, click the link for "User Agreement."

Read each section of the User Agreement and check off all of the boxes on this page. All of the boxes must be checked to complete your registration.

You also must check the boxes for "I am 18+ years old" and "I understand that eBay may e-mail or notify me." Once you have done so, click the button "I Agree To These Terms."

Step 3—Confirm Your E-mail

This screen informs you that you need to check your e-mail.

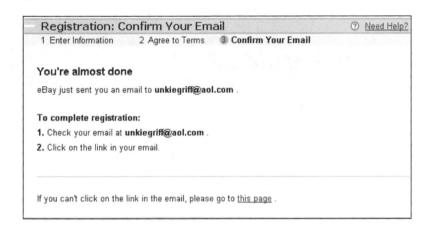

I used an AOL account to register, so I will open my AOL e-mail for *unkiegriff@ aol. com.*

Here is the eBay registration-confirmation e-mail in my AOL New Mail box:

I open it and click on the button Complete eBay Registration.

GRIFF TIP! If your e-mail doesn't display clickable links, you can go directly to the "User ID and Password" page by going to the eBay Site Map:

home	pay	register	sign in	services	site map
Buy	**Sell**	**My eBay**	**Community**		**Help**

On the Site Map, look for the link "Confirm registration" under the section Registration in the top middle column of links.

Services

- Services Overview
- eBay Education: Learn all about
- **Registration**
  Register now
  Confirm registration ◄────
  I forgot my password
  I forgot my Billpoint security key

This will take you to the following page, where you can enter your e-mail address and the confirmation code contained in the confirmation e-mail.

Registration: Confirm Your Email ⑦ Need Help?

1 Enter Information 2 Agree to Terms ③ **Confirm Your Email**

To complete registration, please enter the code provided in your registration email.

Email address

[   ]

Enter code in email

[   ]

[Continue >]

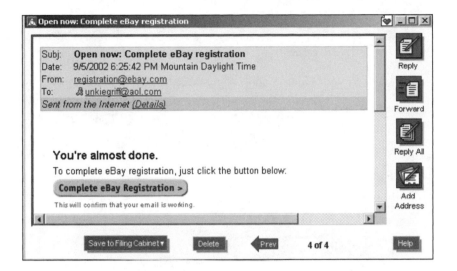

And the registration process is complete!

Changing Your Contact Information

Should you someday move to a new address, you will need to change the address for your eBay registration information.

You can change your contact information by going to your "My eBay" page. The link for "My eBay" can be found on the top of any eBay page.

Click the link. If you are not currently signed in, you will be prompted for your eBay User ID and password. Enter them and click the Sign In Securely button.

29

My eBay   Help

Already an eBay user?

View all your bidding and selling activities in one location.

eBay User ID

unkiegriff

Forgot your User ID?

Password

••••••••

Forgot your password?

Sign In Securely >

☐ Keep me signed in on this computer unless I sign out.

💡 Account protection tips

Once you are on your "My eBay" page, look on the left-hand side of the page for the link Personal Information, under My Account.

My eBay   Wholesale Lots
                                                            Buy to Resell

Hello, unkiegriff (0)

My eBay Views

My Summary

All Buying
- Watching
- Bidding
- Won
- Didn't Win

All Selling
- Scheduled
- Selling
- Sold
- Unsold

All Favorites
- Searches
- Sellers
- Categories

My Account
- Personal Information
- Manage Subscriptions
- eBay Preferences
- Feedback
- Seller Account

Item counts delayed. Refresh

Related Links

Personal Information

User ID:	**unkiegriff**	change
Password:	********	change
Password hint:	What street did you grow up on?	change
Email address:	**unkiegriff@aol.com**	change
Wireless email address:	**Not Specified**	change
About Me page:	--	change

Address Information

Billing Address:	**Jim Griffith** Ave San Jose CA 95128 United States	change
Shipping Address:	**Jim Griffith** Ave San Jose CA 95128 United States	change

Financial Information

Checking Account		change
Routing number:	Not Specified	

Here you will find three sections: Personal Information, Address Information, and Financial Information. Each component has a "change" link to the far right of its row. For example, let's change our Address Information. Under the section for Address Information, locate the link "change" to the right of the Billing Address section.

Address Information

Billing Address:	**Jim Griffith**	change
	Ave	
	San Jose CA 95128	
	United States	

On the next page, make the necessary changes and click the "change registration information" button.

Enter Your Registration Information

E-mail address	unkiegriff@aol.com	(change your e-mail address)
User ID	unkiegriff	(change your User ID)
Name	.lim Griffith	
	First Name M.I. Last Name	
Company		
Address		
City	San Jose	
State	California	
Postal Code (Zip)	95128	
Country	United States	(change your Country)
Primary telephone	(408) _ - ___ ext.: ___	
Secondary telephone (optional)	(408) ___ - ___ ext.: ___	
Gender (optional)	Unspecified	

Registration date: Sep-05-02 17:22:58 PDT

Last change to registration or feedback: Jan-22-04 13:19:58 PST

Click [change registration information] to submit your changes.

Click [clear form] to reset the form to the original values and start over.

Review the information to make sure it is accurate. If you are satisfied, click the "submit" button.

Review and confirm your contact information

Full name	Jim Griffith	OK
Address	PO Box	OK
City	D	OK
State	UT	OK
Zip Code		OK
Country	United States	OK
Primary phone #	801-	OK
Date of Birth	*Not Specified*	OK

Click the Back button on your browser if you want to change any of the listed information.

Click submit to commit your changes.

Your new contact information is now recorded.

Changing Your User ID, E-mail Address, Password, and Other Information

Use the other "change" links to change your User ID, password, password hint, e-mail addresses on file, and your About Me page.

Hello, **uncle_griff** (872 ⭐) Wholesale Lots
Buy to Resell

Personal Information		
User ID:	**uncle_griff**	change
Password:	********	change
Password hint:		change
Email address:	**jimgriff@**	change
Wireless email address:	**jimgriff@**	change
About Me page:	View	change

Changing your eBay User ID, e-mail address, or password is nearly as easy as changing your contact information. However, there are some important points you need to know about each.

Changing Your User ID—Tips

When you change your User ID, your old User ID becomes "locked" for thirty days, after which anyone can claim it. Therefore, you should give serious consideration to any changes you make to your current User ID, since once it is abandoned, you may not be able to get it back.

You can only change your eBay User ID once every thirty days.

Each time you change your eBay User ID, a special icon will appear next to your new eBay User ID for thirty days. This alerts other members that you are either a brand-new eBay member or have recently changed your User ID.

Other eBay members will still be able to locate you through a search of your old User ID anytime during the first thirty days. After that, any search on your old User ID will return a "no such user" type error message until and if such time as someone "claims" your old User ID for his or her own.

Changing Your E-mail Address

You can change the e-mail address for your registration at any time and as often as you like. However, you cannot change it to one that is currently or was previously registered at eBay. If the system rejects your choice of a new e-mail address, you probably registered it sometime in the past and forgot that you had done so.

IMPORTANT! Never register a new account in order to change your e-mail address! If you have established a good feedback profile (more on feedback later) and a noted presence as a seller or a bidder, you will not be able to move your feedback from the old account to the new account. Instead, use "My eBay" to change the e-mail address for your current, established account.

Changing Your eBay Password

Although you should not need to change your eBay password, in some cases doing so is prudent. For example, if you suspect that someone has obtained or deciphered your password, or if you believe you may unwittingly have supplied it to a stranger, you should change it immediately. Again, choose a password that is not obvious. (Don't use your pet's name.) Create a combination of random letters and numbers. Memorize it to avoid having to write it down. If you must write it down, store it somewhere safe and secure, a bank safe-deposit box, for example.

TROUBLESHOOTING

I Forgot My User ID or Password!

It happens. Maybe you registered a while back and don't recall your User ID or password. Don't panic. There is a quick and easy process for obtaining a forgotten eBay password. Click the eBay Sign In link at the top of any eBay page.

home	pay	register	sign in	services	site map
Buy	Sell	My eBay		Community	Help

On the Sign In page, look for the links "Forgot your password?" and "Forgot your User ID?"

Click either one and follow the instructions from there.

2

The eBay Web Site

Navigating the eBay Web Site—a Road Map

The eBay Web site is big. No, that's not quite accurate. The eBay Web site is "gi-mongous" (to quote Mr. Will Ferrell). Not counting the nearly 25 million-plus separate pages for each item listed on eBay, there are hundreds of other pages containing virtual warehouses of information about eBay. Finding one's way around eBay can sometimes be daunting.

But don't despair. You will find navigating eBay is a snap once you have a good grasp of how certain eBay Web pages are grouped together, what they contain, and how they are interconnected.

Let's start with the most basic navigation tool, the eBay Navigation Bar.

THE EBAY NAVIGATION BAR

The eBay Navigation Bar is found on the top of nearly every eBay Web page.

Think of the eBay Navigation Bar as your personal signpost showing you the route and direction to every single possible place on eBay you might wish to visit.

Whenever you are lost or are searching for a particular area of the eBay Web site, use the navigation bar and the various hyperlinks above it to quickly get your bearings.

These are the hyperlinks on the top of the eBay Navigation Bar:

home | pay | register | sign out | services | site map

These links point to important Web pages on eBay:

> Home (the eBay home page)
> Pay (the PayPal home page)
> Register
> Sign In/Sign Out
> Services
> Site Map

These links, and the pages to which they lead, are examined in greater detail later on in this chapter.

Below the links are the boxes that make up the eBay Navigation Bar. Each of these boxes will take you to the respective main page for Buy, Sell, My eBay, Community, and Help. In addition to taking you to the main topic page, clicking Community will expand the eBay Navigation Bar down one level to display the subnavigation bar for that topic.

The Buy link takes us to the Buy portal page. This page contains sections for Search, Browse Categories, My eBay At A Glance, Buying Resources, and Featured Items.

The Sell link leads to the Sell Hub page. From here, click the Start A New Listing button to proceed to the Sell Your Item form.

"My eBay" we've seen earlier, but let's see it again. Click the "My eBay" box on the top of the page.

The Community link is the only one with a sub-navigation bar. Each of the boxes leads to one of the four main Community pages (plus an overview page).

The link for Community directs you to the Community Overview page, which contains all the links related to community, chat, news and announcements, etc.

Subtopics for Community

Clicking Talk takes you right to the chat-board hub page, from which you can navigate to any of over one hundred separate chat areas.

The Events page contains a calendar for all upcoming eBay events, workshops, appearances, etc.

The News link takes you to a page containing links to all the news-related pages, press releases, important events, etc.

Finally, the People link brings you directly to the eBay Groups page. eBay Groups lets you connect with people with whom you share an interest, a hobby, a concern, or a location.

Finally, my favorite link, Help. This link will lead you directly to the eBay Help page portal.

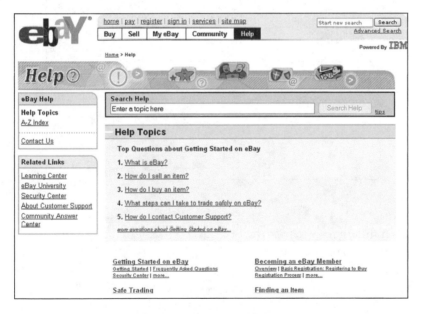

We discuss eBay Help in depth at the end of Section Two, but you should note these pages now for access later. Help contains the answer to all commonly asked eBay questions. If you are stumped for an answer, try Help first by either entering a keyword into the box provided or scanning and reading through the various Help subtopics below the Search Help section.

THE SIGN IN PAGE

Although you don't need to supply an eBay User ID and password to view current items, item categories, or to search for current items using keywords (Title Search), you will need to supply your User ID and password to bid, buy, list an item, search for a "completed listing," or visit your "My eBay" page. To reduce the need to enter your User ID and password over and over, you will need to sign in.

To sign in, just click the Sign In link on the top of any eBay page.

This will take you to the eBay Sign In page.

Sign In		Help
New to eBay?	**or**	**Already an eBay user?**
If you want to sign in, you'll need to register first.		eBay members, sign in to save time for bidding, selling, and other activities.
Registration is fast and **free.**		**eBay User ID**
		Forgot your User ID?
Register >		**Password**
		Forgot your password?
		Sign In Securely >
		☐ Keep me signed in on this computer unless I sign out.
		💡 Account protection tips

Enter your eBay User ID and password in the boxes provided. To keep yourself signed in indefinitely, check the box "Keep me signed in on this computer unless I sign out." Then click the Sign In Securely button.

Now you won't have to reenter your eBay User ID and password each time you bid on or list an item, leave feedback, or use your "My eBay" page.

GRIFF TIP! You can change your Sign In preferences using your "My eBay" page. We discuss the "My eBay" page in depth later on in this chapter.

NAVIGATING THE EBAY HOME PAGE

Go to *http://www.ebay.com*. Many eBay members make the eBay home page their browser's start or home page so that it is the first Web page they see when they start their Web browser. Instructions on how to do this are in Section One, chapter 1.

The basic layout of the eBay home page currently looks something like this:

The eBay home page includes a section for searching by keyword at the very top of the page, a link for "register" and a link to the eBay Featured Items (covered in more depth in a following chapter). At the bottom of the home page there are links to third-party services and partners.

There's also a series of text links at the bottom of the page:

> Feedback Forum | Anything Points | Downloads | Gift Certificates | PayPal | Jobs | Affiliates | Developers | The eBay Shop
> About eBay | Announcements | Security Center | Policies | Site Map | Help

These may come in handy someday, especially Security Center, so remember where you saw them. One of my favorites is the About eBay page.

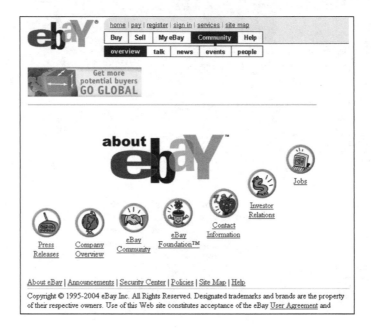

Visit this page to read recent eBay press releases as well as to learn more about eBay Inc., the eBay Foundation, the eBay Community, and current job openings at eBay.

NAVIGATING WITH THE EBAY SITE MAP

Although not the prettiest page at eBay, the eBay Site Map can be the most helpful. Nearly every page on the eBay site can be reached by a link on this page. Think of the Site Map as your eBay "index" page. If you are ever unable to find a certain eBay page using other navigation methods, don't give up! Try looking on the Site Map. If it's an eBay page, it's probably on this list.

I make it a habit to stop at this page first whenever I can't find a certain eBay Web page. I am usually able to find it again starting from the Site Map!

NAVIGATING THE EBAY CATEGORIES— CATEGORY HIERARCHY

There are over forty-five thousand separate eBay categories. To make navigating them easy, all forty-five thousand are arranged in a hierarchy structure according to topic.

There is more than one way to view the eBay category hierarchy. The most obvious and most popular method is to start from list of top categories in the left-hand column on the eBay home page.

Specialty Sites
eBay Motors
eBay Stores NEW!
Half.com by eBay
PayPal

Categories
Antiques
Art
Books
Business & Industrial
Cameras & Photo
Cars, Parts & Vehicles
Cell Phones
Clothing, Shoes & Accessories
Coins
Collectibles
Computers & Networking
Consumer Electronics
Crafts
Dolls & Bears
DVDs & Movies
Entertainment Memorabilia
Gift Certificates
Health & Beauty
Home & Garden
Jewelry & Watches
Music
Musical Instruments
Pottery & Glass
Real Estate
Sporting Goods
Sports Mem, Cards & Fan Shop
Stamps
Tickets
Toys & Hobbies
Travel
Video Games
Everything Else
see all eBay categories

Business Marketplace
Giving Works (Charity)
Live Auctions
Professional Services
Wholesale

The links listed under Categories represent the top-level categories of the eBay categories.

Navigating eBay categories is a breeze. By clicking any one of these top-level categories, you are directed to that category's "home page," where you can find a list of links for subcategories related to the top-level category. For example, here is a partial view of the home page for the "Clothing, Shoes and Accessories" category.

From here, you can navigate to any of the various Clothing, Shoes, and Accessories subcategories, related categories, or popular searches for the category. Let's click the subcategory Heels, Pumps under the category Women's Shoes.

From here, you can start browsing through the category for women's heels and pumps.

GRIFF BROWSING TIP! The Heels, Pumps subcategory page above shows that there are 24,464 items currently listed within this subcategory. It would take several hours to scroll through that many items looking for that special pair of shoes.

You can easily filter these 24,464 items by selecting one or more options from the drop-down lists in the box Women's Shoes Finder. For example, let's select "6.5" in the US Size drop-down list.

This reduces the number of displayed items to 1,779 that match your shoe size!

We'll dive deeper into the finer points of searching eBay in the next chapter.

If you plan on revisiting this or any other category, you may want to make it one of your Favorite Categories in "My eBay" (see the "My eBay" section later in this chapter for more information about "My eBay" Favorites).

View All Categories

Under each of the many main categories on the home page, there are numerous subcategories, all grouped together by type, brand name, or make. A quick way to view all top- and second-level subcategories is to go to the All Categories page.

Click Buy on the eBay Navigation Bar.

Scroll down the page and click the link for "See all categories."

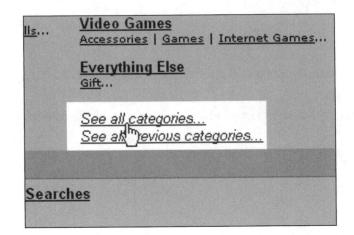

This displays the All Categories page. You can also customize the display of this page for Category, Item Type, and Item Status, as well as filter the results to show the number of items in each category or the actual category numbers.

All Categories

Search

☐ Search titles & descriptions

Browse Categories

Category | Item Type | Item Status
All Categories ▾ | All Items ▾ | Current Items ▾ | Show
◉ Show number of items in category ○ Show category numbers

Antiques (195499)
Antiquities (Classical, Amer.) (5753)
Architectural & Garden (7725)
Asian Antiques (36349)
Books, Manuscripts (3400)
Decorative Arts (37853)
Ethnographic (3139)
Furniture (9484)
Maps, Atlases, Globes (9090)
Maritime (2805)
Musical Instruments (716)
Primitives (10355)
Rugs, Carpets (17048)
Science & Medicine (1275)
Silver (27971)
Textiles, Linens (13424)
Other Antiques (9112)
See all Antiques categories...

Art (182125)
Digital Art (939)

Crafts (284292)
Basketry (430)
Bead Art (6607)
Candle & Soap Making (5852)
Ceramics, Pottery (6208)
Crocheting (8705)
Cross Stitch (26672)
Decorative, Tole Painting (5925)
Embroidery (9189)
Fabric (36780)
Fabric Embellishments (7172)
Floral Supplies (2203)
Framing, Matting (1030)
General Art & Craft Supplies (3723)
Glass Art Supplies (1238)
Handcrafted Items (4704)
Kids Crafts (1753)
Knitting (5212)
Lacemaking, Tatting (327)
Latch, Rug Hooking (1028)
Leathercraft (3181)

Pottery & Glass (300806)
Glass (105473)
Pottery & China (195333)
See all Pottery & Glass categories...

Real Estate (3678)
Commercial (403)
Land (1139)
Residential (1007)
Timeshares for Sale (920)
Other Real Estate (209)

Sporting Goods (414683)
Airsoft (7364)
Archery (7551)
Baseball & Softball (10575)
Basketball (4344)
Billiards (5304)
Bowling (4410)
Boxing (1745)
Camping, Hiking, Backpacking

You can navigate from here to any of the top-level category home pages (sometimes referred to as Category Portal pages). For example, click on the link "See all Antiques categories . . ." to display that category's portal page.

eb**Y**®   home | pay | register | sign in | services | site map   Start new search   Search

Buy   Sell   My eBay   Community   Help   Advanced Search

Powered By IBM

Home > Buy > All Categories > **Antiques**

All Categories >

New to eBay?
start here

[   ]   Search

☐ Search titles & descriptions

Browse Categories

Category   Item Type   Item Status
Antiques   ▾   All Items   ▾   Current Items   ▾   Show

◉ Show number of items in category   ○ Show category numbers

Antiques (194575)

Antiquities (Classical, Amer.) (5728)
  Egyptian (1028)
  Greek (443)
  Roman (1386)
  The Americas (1443)
  Other (1428)

Architectural & Garden (7809)
  Ceiling Tins (141)
  Chandeliers, Fixtures, Sconces (861)
  Doors (259)
  Finials (48)
  Fireplaces, Mantles (220)
  Garden (1161)
  Hardware (2353)
    Door Bells, Knockers (145)
    Hooks & Brackets (263)
    Knobs & Handles (1079)
    Locks & Keys (197)
    Plates - Doors, Lights (138)
    Other (531)
  Signs (62)
  Stained Glass (931)
  Tiles (632)
  Weathervanes, Lightning Rods (163)

Furniture (9443)
  Beds (363)
    Pre-1800 (4)
    1800-1900 (133)
    Post-1900 (226)
  Benches, Stools (282)
    Pre-1800 (4)
    1800-1900 (76)
    Post-1900 (202)
  Bookcases (246)
    Pre-1800 (1)
    1800-1900 (66)
    Post-1900 (179)
  Cabinets, Armoires, Cupboards
  (1415)
    Pre-1800 (41)
    1800-1900 (440)
    Post-1900 (934)
  Chairs (1625)
    Pre-1800 (34)
    1800-1900 (377)
    Post-1900 (1214)
  Desks (406)
    Pre-1800 (6)

Rugs, Carpets (17080)
  Small (1x2-4) (1064)
  Medium (4x2-9x6) (6726)
  Large (9x7-9x12) (2352)
  Larger than 9x12 (2505)
  Runners (2161)
  Other (2272)

Science & Medicine (1263)
  Medical (661)
  Science Instruments (519)
  Other (83)

Silver (27839)
  Coin Silver (690)
  Silverplate (8757)
    Bowls (344)
    Candlesticks, Candelabra (119)
    Cups, Goblets (187)
    Flatware (4769)
      Holmes & Edwards (224)
      International/1847 Rogers (1459)
      Oneida/Wm. A. Rogers (1419)
      Wallace (90)
      Other (1577)

The numbers in parentheses next to each category are the actual number of items currently for sale in that category. The Antiques portal page displays a vast smorgasbord of related subcategories, for example, Antiquities; Architectural & Garden; Furniture; Rugs, Carpets; etc. Some of these have one, two, and, in the case of Maps, Atlases, Globes, four subcategory levels.

```
Maps, Atlases, Globes (9184)
    Globes (184)
    Maps, Atlases (8983)
        Africa (172)
        Asia (245)
        Australia, New Zealand (87)
        Caribbean (121)
        Continental Europe, Russia (1072)
        India (35)
        Middle East (96)
        North America (3860)
            Canada (117)
            Mexico (29)
            United States (3714)
                AK, HI (36)
                AL, FL, GA, MS, NC, SC (156)
                AR, IA, KS, LA, MO, NE (193)
                AZ, CA, CO, NM, NV, UT (250)
                CT, MA, ME, NH, RI, VT (185)
                DE, MD, NJ, NY, PA (470)
                ID, OR, WA (169)
                IL, IN, MI, OH, WI (276)
                MN, MT, ND, SD, WY (140)
                OK, TX (157)
                VA, WV, KY, TN (91)
                Entire US (1591)
        South America (148)
        United Kingdom (629)
        World & Hemisphere Maps (2121)
        Mixed Lots (76)
        Other (321)
Maps on CD (17)
```

The All Categories page is an excellent way to search for those sublevels in the category hierarchy that contain items of interest to you.

NAVIGATING THE EBAY ITEM DESCRIPTION PAGE

We've seen how browsing through categories can take us to specific subcategories where we can more easily find particular treasure that piques our interest. On eBay, all items are displayed in a list. In the next screen shot, we are looking at a category list for Antiques > Rugs, Carpets.

(Later we will cover search lists that look almost exactly like category lists. Item titles are displayed the same way in both.)

Each item title in a category list is a clickable link. To view an individual item, you simply click on the item title wherever it appears in a category or search list. I searched through the Rugs, Carpets category pages and found this intriguing gallery picture and title:

Clicking on the title will open up the Item Description page for that particular item.

A typical Item Description page looks like this:

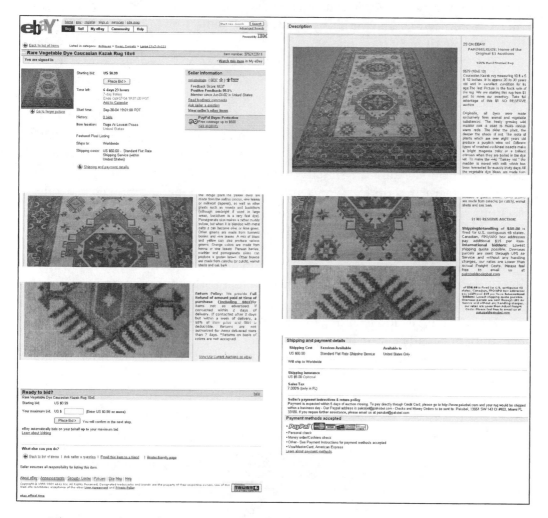

There are six sections to every Item Description page:

Title
Seller information
Description
Shipping and payment details
Payment methods accepted
Ready to bid?/Ready to buy?

The Title section of the Item Description page, directly under the bar containing the item's title, is where you find the basic information about the item, such as the current high bid, time and date of the listing's closing, bid history, and the seller's location. The title may also contain a subtitle if the seller opted for this feature. If applicable, it may also show a Buy It Now button and the quantity available (if more than one).

The "Seller information" section displays the seller's feedback stats. It may also show a link to the seller's eBay Store (if she has one) and an indication of PayPal Buyer Protection (if the seller is offering it).

The Description section is just below the Title section. The seller provides everything that appears in this section, including text, pictures, and any fancy layout or graphics. There is no limit to how much text or how many pictures a seller can include within the Description section.

Underneath Description, you will find the "Shipping and payment details" section, which displays the shipping terms (carriers, fees, and times) the seller offers for this item. Note that most experienced sellers on eBay restate this information within their item description.

The "Payment methods accepted" section outlines exactly what types of payment the seller accepts. Again, smart sellers repeat this information within their item description.

Finally, the "Ready to bid?" or "Ready to buy?" section is where you enter the amount of either your bid or, if the seller provided a Buy It Now option for instant purchase and you decide to simply buy the item outright without bidding, the Buy It Now price.

I think I might want to bid on this item later, so I am going to add it to my Watch list. The link for adding the item to my Watch list is toward the top of the Item Description page.

I click the link and the display changes to:

Where is the item actually being "watched"?

"My eBay"

No other page on eBay provides such a fantastic array of services for the eBay buyer or seller as "My eBay."

From your "My eBay" page, you can keep track of all your current and recent bidding and selling; your feedback; your eBay favorite searches, sellers, and stores as well as your eBay e-mail notice preferences, your account setup, your contact information, and the custom "My eBay" preferences as well.

To go to your "My eBay" page, simply click the link for "My eBay" located on the top of any eBay page.

(If you have not signed in yet, you will be prompted to do so.)

Your "My eBay" page will look something like mine (minus the item-listing details of course!):

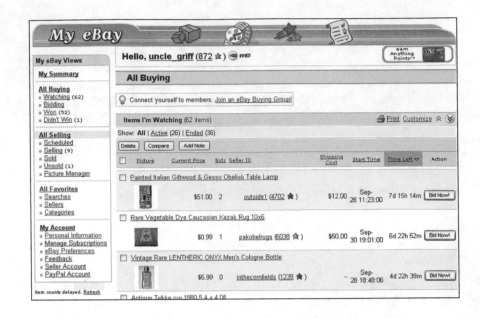

(Note the listing for the Rare Vegetable Dye Caucasian Kazak Rug that I just added to my Watch list. More on this later . . .)

The important "My eBay" navigation links are located under the section My eBay Views on the left-hand side of the page. They include My Summary, All Buying, All Selling, All Favorites, and My Account.

NOTE: Remember these links! You will need to access the information and procedures to which they link. Do you need to change your e-mail address or User ID? Have you moved and now need to change your contact information? Every aspect of all your eBay activity or information can be accessed, viewed, and, if applicable, edited, augmented, or deleted from your "My eBay" page.

Since I am primarily a buyer (who regularly sells), I tend to use the All Buying, All Favorites, and My Account sections of "My eBay" the most.

Let's explore the various sections of the All Buying page. (Note: You can customize the display of your page and shuffle each section's place on the page.)

Buying Reminders

This summarizes all your buying activity, including how many items you need to pay for, how many items you are watching, and how many feedbacks you need to leave. This is a helpful tool for keeping up with all your buying obligations.

Items I'm Bidding On

All of your current bids will show in this section, with each item on a separate row. One of the best uses of this section is to check your maximum bid amounts.

In addition, any auctions where you are a bidder but have been outbid will show the bid amount in red as an alert so that you can consider a new bid.

Buying Totals

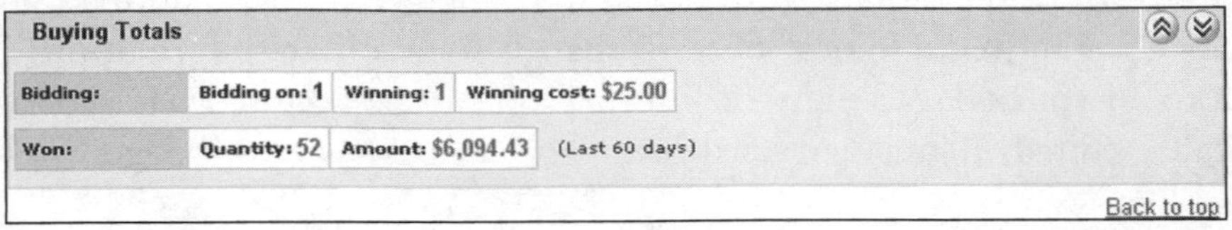
Buying Totals
Bidding:
Bidding on: 1
Winning: 1
Winning cost: $25.00
Won:
Quantity: 52
Amount: $6,094.43
(Last 60 days)
Back to top

Shows all your current bidding activity, including which ones are currently high bids, and the cost of all your current winning bids. This section also shows the quantity and the total of all your won bids.

Items I've Won

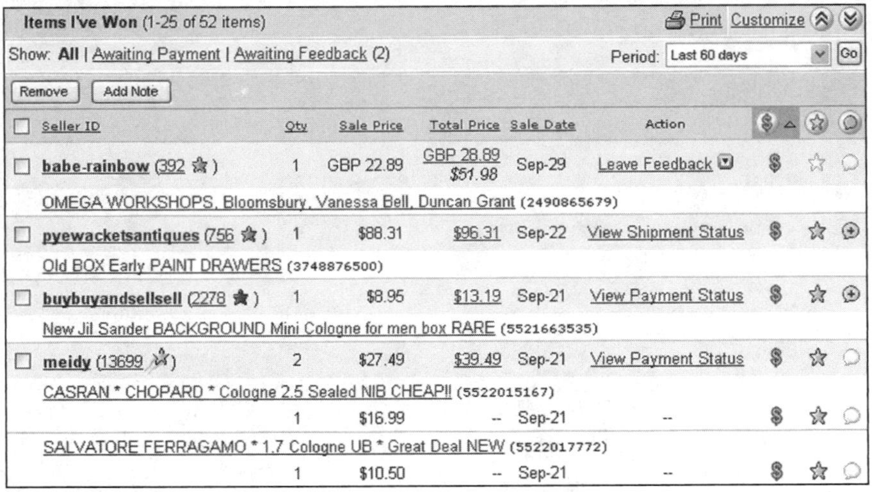
Items I've Won (1-25 of 52 items)
Print Customize
Show: All | Awaiting Payment | Awaiting Feedback (2)
Period: Last 60 days Go
Remove Add Note
Seller ID Qty Sale Price Total Price Sale Date Action
babe-rainbow (392) 1 GBP 22.89 GBP 28.89 $51.98 Sep-29 Leave Feedback
OMEGA WORKSHOPS, Bloomsbury, Vanessa Bell, Duncan Grant (2490865679)
pyewacketsantiques (756) 1 $88.31 $96.31 Sep-22 View Shipment Status
Old BOX Early PAINT DRAWERS (3748876500)
buybuyandsellsell (2278) 1 $8.95 $13.19 Sep-21 View Payment Status
New Jil Sander BACKGROUND Mini Cologne for men box RARE (5521663535)
meidy (13699) 2 $27.49 $39.49 Sep-21 View Payment Status
CASRAN * CHOPARD * Cologne 2.5 Sealed NIB CHEAP!! (5522015167)
1 $16.99 -- Sep-21 --
SALVATORE FERRAGAMO * 1.7 Cologne UB * Great Deal NEW (5522017772)
1 $10.50 -- Sep-21 --

GRIFF TIP! You have powerful display customization options for "My eBay" right at your fingertips. Just locate the section's Customize link.

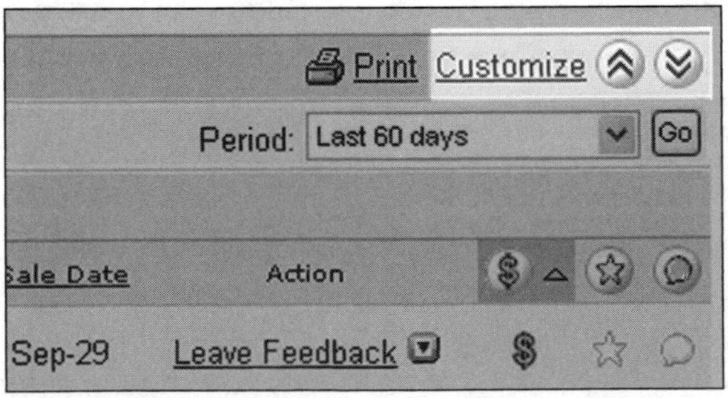
Print Customize
Period: Last 60 days Go
Sale Date Action
Sep-29 Leave Feedback

Clicking it allows you to add or subtract fields to the current section as well as change the way the section is displayed.

Select from the list of available column headers to delete or add columns to your view. You can also alter the way the section displays.

I have customized "My eBay" to show the fields for the quantity, the sale price, the total price (with shipping), and the sale date for each item I have won. In addition, there is the field Action, which, when clicked, displays a drop-down list of available actions that the buyer can take. In this case, I can either leave feedback or view the payment status for the listing.

Notice the icons on the right side of the row. These icons indicate payment and feedback status for that listing (depending on the type of icon or whether it is grayed out or full black).

Items I Didn't Win

The saddest place on the whole page, this section displays items where you were a bidder but were outbid and subsequently the auction closed. (I really, really, really wanted those sconces but I forgot to rebid. Curses!) This section is helpful in that you can use the links to the right of the item title to view that seller's other current items or view similar items.

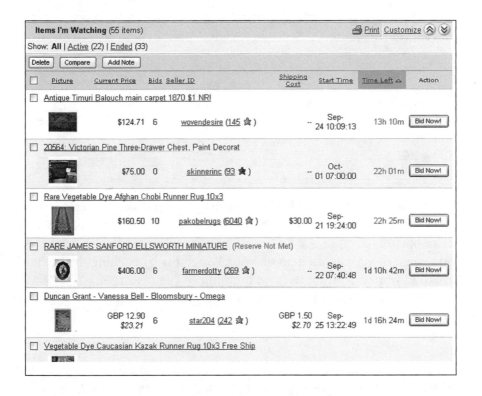

Items I'm Watching

Finally, we reach one of my favorite features, the Items I'm Watching section of "My eBay," All Buying.

Now you have a better idea of what type of treasure I hunt on eBay.

When I find intriguing items that I may wish to bid on later, I add the item to my "My eBay" Watch list by clicking the "Watch this item in My eBay" link on the right side of the item Title bar.

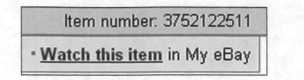

Once clicked, the "Watch this item" text changes to "This item is being watched in My eBay."

Email to a friend | This item is being watched in My eBay

Now my Watch list shows the watched item:

	Picture	Current Price	Bids	Seller ID	Shipping Cost	Start Time	Time Left △	Action
Items I'm Watching (55 items)							Print Customize ⊗ ⊗	
Show: **All** | Active (22) | Ended (33)								
Delete Compare Add Note								
☐ Rare Vegetable Dye Caucasian Kazak Rug 10x6								
		$0.99	1	pakobelrugs (6040 ☆)	$50.00	Sep-30 19:01:00	6d 22h 02m	Bid Now!
☐ 20564: Victorian Pine Three-Drawer Chest, Paint Decorat								
		$75.00	0	skinnerinc (93 ★)	--	Oct-01 07:00:00	22h 01m	Bid Now!

You can watch up to one hundred items. You can delete items from your Watch list by checking the box to the left of the item number and then clicking the Delete button.

You can go directly to an item on your Watch list by clicking the item title or the Bid Now! button for that item on the right of the item title.

The other columns display the current bid amount for the item and the start time and time left.

GRIFF TIP! Worried you might forget to bid on an item you are watching? Have no fear! eBay will remind you that a watched item is about to end. Go to My eBay > My Account > eBay Preferences.

Click the link for "view/change" for "Notification preferences" under the "eBay Preferences" bar.

Check the box for "Watch notice" located under Status E-mails.

63

You will now receive an e-mail three hours before any watched item is set to end so you can go make a bid before it's too late!

As a constant eBay bidder, I would be lost without the "My eBay" All Buying page. If you are primarily a bidder, I urge you to make this page one of your favorite places and visit it every time you come to eBay.

ALL SELLING

The "My eBay" All Selling page is similar to the All Buying page except that instead of tracking bids and purchases, it tracks an eBay seller's pending, current, and completed selling.

We cover the "My eBay" all Selling page in greater depth in Section Two of the book. For now, just keep it in mind.

ALL FAVORITES

The next "My eBay" page is All Favorites, which is definitely my favorite!

On this page, you can:

- Select up to four favorite categories to display.
- Save up to one hundred favorite title searches for easy access.
- Have eBay automatically run these searches for you and notify you by e-mail when new matching items have been listed.
- Create a list of your favorite sellers or stores.

Since my "My eBay" Favorites page is rather full, I have broken it up into separate screens to better illustrate each section:

Favorite Categories
You can add categories to your Favorite Categories list by clicking the "Add new Category" link.

All Favorites

My Favorite Categories (3 categories)   Add new Category ⌃ ⌄

☐ My Favorite Categories

☐ Art:Folk Art
  Current | Starting Today | Ending Today | Ending Within 5 Hours

☐ Collectibles:Vanity, Perfume & Shaving:Perfumes:Decorative Glass/Crystal

Select the category from the series of boxes.

Add or modify your favorite categories

If you prefer to use the old-style method of choosing a category, click here.

Favorite category 1

eBay Category   required You have chosen category # 37981

Just click in the boxes below from left to right until you have found the appropriate category for your item.
The chosen category number will appear in the small box to indicate that you have made a valid selection.

① Antiques ->	② Musical Instruments ->	③ Small (1x2-4)
Art->	Primitives	Medium (4x2-9x6)
Books ->	Rugs, Carpets->	Large (9x7-9x12)
Business & Industrial ->	Science & Medicine ->	Larger than 9x12
Cameras & Photo ->	Silver->	Runners
Cell Phones ->	Textiles, Linens ->	Other
Clothing, Shoes & Accessories ->	Other Antiques	------------------
Coins ->		next line...

To delete categories from the list, check the box next to the category you wish to delete and click the Delete button.

All Favorites

My Favorite Categories (4 categorie

☐ My Favorite Categories

☐ Antiques:Rugs, Carpets:Large (9x7-
  Current | Starting Today | Ending To

☐ Art:Folk Art
  Current | Starting Today | Ending To

☑ Collectibles:Vanity, Perfume & Sha
  Current | Starting Today | Ending To

☐ Collectibles:Vanity, Perfume & Sha
  Current | Starting Today | Ending To

Delete

To add a Favorite Search to your list, click on the link "Add new Search" on the top right-hand side of the table.

My Favorite Searches (32 searches; 3 emails)			Add new Search ⊗ ⊗
Delete			
☐ Name of Search ▽	Search Criteria	Email Settings	Action
☐ Woodhue	**Woodhue men** Sort: Newly Listed		Edit Preferences ▾
☐ Windows #1	**window* (round, light, architectural, antique, old, arch, arched, lead, leaded, "half round", halfround) -(stain, stained, trompe, pulls, mounts, pull, mount, lock, locks, bevel, beveled, box, planter, hook)** Category: Antiques		Edit Preferences ▾
☐ tommy bahama (xl,xxl) - polo	**tommy bahama (xl, xxl) -polo** Category: No longer valid, Sort: Newly Listed		Edit Preferences ▾

To delete a search, check the box next to it and click the Delete button.

Favorite Sellers and Stores

My Favorite Sellers (25 sellers)		Add new Seller or Store ⊗ ⊗
Delete		
☐ Seller △	View Seller's Store	View Seller's Other Items
☐ agvgera (646 ⭐) 🏆Power Seller	--	View
☐ antiqueaday (2173 ⭐) 🏆Power Seller	--	View
☐ benimor (231 ⭐)	--	View
☐ bhara (4578 ⭐) 🏆Power Seller me	--	View
☐ eliza500 (8243 ⭐) 🏆Power Seller me	Eliza500	View

To add up to thirty new favorite sellers or eBay Store IDs to this list, click the link for "Add new Seller or Store" and follow the instructions.

We delve deeper into the intricacies of Search (both creating and saving) in a later chapter.

MY ACCOUNT

Make special note of this section of My eBay. If you ever have to change anything about your eBay registration, go to this page. This includes your User ID, password, e-mail address, contact information, credit card on file, and About Me page.

The top-level My Account link displays a quick access portal to a seller's PayPal and eBay account information.

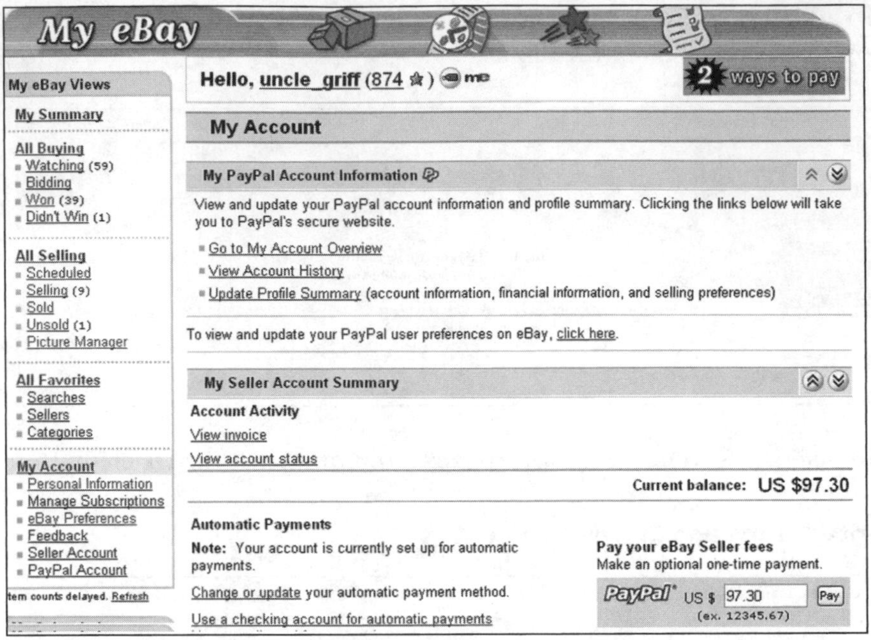

We explore these pages in greater detail in Section Two of this book, "Selling the eBay Way." Below the My Account link are links for:

> Personal Information
> Manage Subscriptions
> eBay Preferences
> Feedback
> Seller Account
> PayPal Account

Personal Information
Clicking this link displays the Personal Information page, which contains sections for your personal, address, and financial information.

Under the section labeled Personal Information, you will find links for editing the main components of your eBay Registration, including your User ID (which you can change once every thirty days), Password, Password hint, E-mail addresses, Wireless e-mail address, and your About Me page.

The next section of the Personal Information page—Address Information—contains links for changing your billing or shipping addresses.

The last section of the Personal Information page—Financial Information—provides links for adding or changing your checking and credit/debit card on file for your eBay Seller's Account.

eBay Preferences

The eBay Preferences page contains five sections: eBay Preferences, eBay Sign In Preferences, Seller Preferences, My eBay Preferences, and Authorization Settings.

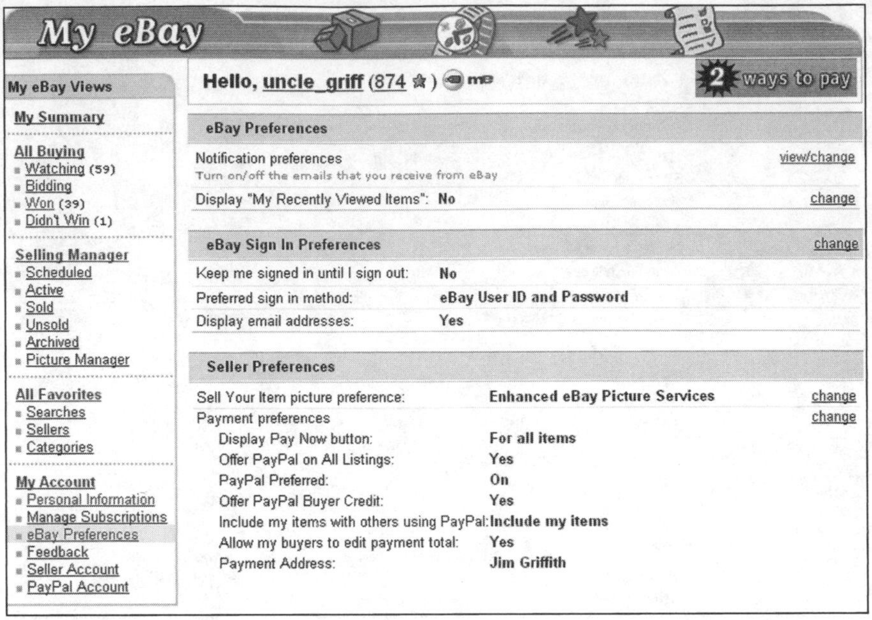
My eBay
Hello, uncle_griff (874 ☆) me
2 ways to pay
My eBay Views
My Summary
All Buying
Watching (59)
Bidding
Won (39)
Didn't Win (1)
Selling Manager
Scheduled
Active
Sold
Unsold
Archived
Picture Manager
All Favorites
Searches
Sellers
Categories
My Account
Personal Information
Manage Subscriptions
eBay Preferences
Feedback
Seller Account
PayPal Account
eBay Preferences
Notification preferences view/change
Turn on/off the emails that you receive from eBay
Display "My Recently Viewed Items": No change
eBay Sign In Preferences change
Keep me signed in until I sign out: No
Preferred sign in method: eBay User ID and Password
Display email addresses: Yes
Seller Preferences
Sell Your Item picture preference: Enhanced eBay Picture Services change
Payment preferences change
Display Pay Now button: For all items
Offer PayPal on All Listings: Yes
PayPal Preferred: On
Offer PayPal Buyer Credit: Yes
Include my items with others using PayPal: Include my items
Allow my buyers to edit payment total: Yes
Payment Address: Jim Griffith

Under eBay Preferences, you can turn off or on types of e-mails that you receive from eBay, and you can select Yes or No for viewing recently viewed items on the bottom of certain eBay pages.

The "change" link for eBay Sign In Preferences lets you change your sign-in options and User ID display settings.

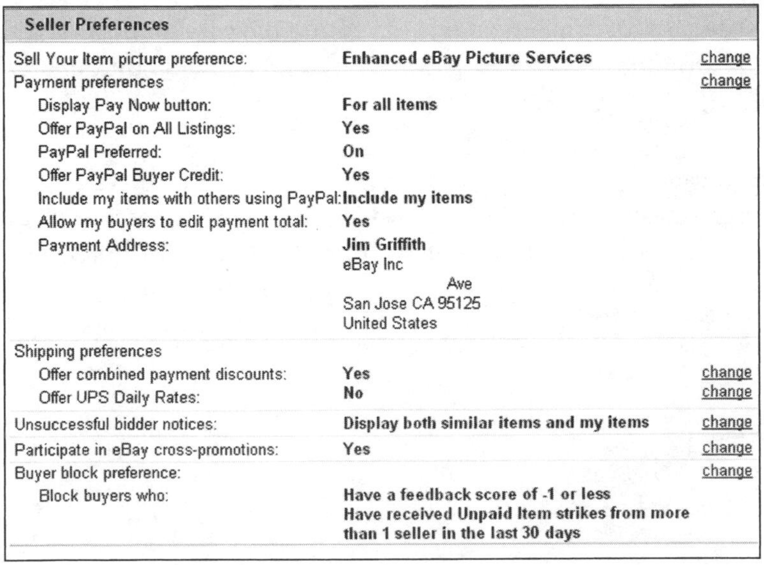
Seller Preferences
Sell Your Item picture preference: Enhanced eBay Picture Services change
Payment preferences change
Display Pay Now button: For all items
Offer PayPal on All Listings: Yes
PayPal Preferred: On
Offer PayPal Buyer Credit: Yes
Include my items with others using PayPal: Include my items
Allow my buyers to edit payment total: Yes
Payment Address: Jim Griffith
eBay Inc
Ave
San Jose CA 95125
United States
Shipping preferences
Offer combined payment discounts: Yes change
Offer UPS Daily Rates: No change
Unsuccessful bidder notices: Display both similar items and my items change
Participate in eBay cross-promotions: Yes change
Buyer block preference: change
Block buyers who: Have a feedback score of -1 or less
Have received Unpaid Item strikes from more than 1 seller in the last 30 days

From Seller Preferences, you can change critical components for selling on eBay, including your picture, payment, and shipping preferences, as well as what shows up in the unsuccessful bidder notices eBay sends to your buyers. You can also change your cross-promotion preferences and block buyers from bidding on your listing based on buyer location, feedback score, or current Unpaid Item standing.

With My eBay Preferences, you can change the default opening "My eBay" page, change the display time and help content, and even retrieve items that you have removed from sections of your other "My eBay" pages.

Finally, Authorization Settings lets you revoke all your current authorizations for certain third parties (such as SquareTrade) or special eBay Features (eBay Picture Manager).

Feedback

Whenever two people trade with each other on eBay, either or both can leave a short, public, indelible comment for the other person indicating their satisfaction (or lack thereof) with their trading partner.

These comments are called feedback. All eBay members have a Feedback Profile, which can easily be viewed simply by clicking the number in parentheses next to their eBay User ID.

We discuss the intricacies of eBay Feedback in a later section. For now, note that the "My eBay" Feedback page displays recent feedback left for you with the most recent on the top of the list. (You will be so proud the day you get your first feedback. I have heard from new members who wept with joy when they got theirs. We have some very emotional members.)

My eBay

My eBay Views	Hello, **uncle_griff** (874 ⭐) 👁 me			**2** ways to pay

My Summary

All Buying
- Watching (59)
- Bidding
- Won (39)
- Didn't Win (1)

Selling Manager
- Scheduled
- Active
- Sold
- Unsold
- Archived
- Picture Manager

All Favorites
- Searches
- Sellers
- Categories

My Account
- Personal Information
- Manage Subscriptions
- eBay Preferences
- Feedback

Would you like to leave feedback for **all** your items at once?

[Leave Feedback] | Go to Feedback Forum to reply or follow up on feedback.

Recent Feedback (View all feedback) ⌃ ⌄

	Comment	From	Date/Time	Item #
⊕	fast payment, good transaction,Thank you very much .A+++++	Seller: tenikiti (1682 ⭐)	Oct-04-04 07:14	6710197952
⊕	Quick response and fast payment. Perfect! THANKS!!	Seller: babe-rainbow (399 ⭐)	Oct-03-04 15:35	2490865679
⊕	We enjoy serving wonderful customers like you! You make everything so nice!	Seller: buybuyandsellsell (2312 ⭐)	Sep-29-04 16:53	5521663535
⊕	EXCELLENT EBAYER....EXCELLENT COMMUNICATIONS!!!!!!!!!!!!!!!!!!!!!!	Seller: pyewacketsantiques (757 ⭐)	Sep-29-04 14:38	3748876500
⊕	Thanks , you are the best, fast payment, excellent deal.	Seller: junglegreen (379 ⭐)	Sep-25-04 00:49	3732107182

Back to top

Items Awaiting Feedback (15 items) ⌃ ⌄

On this same page, you can view the feedback you need to leave by individual transaction.

Items Awaiting Feedback (15 items) ⌃ ⌄

Title	User ID	Sale Date ▽	Action	☆	💬
IBM ThinkPad X40 X31 semi hard pouch/ case /inner case (6710197952)	**tenikiti** (1682 ⭐)	Oct-01-04 06:19:21	Leave Feedback	☆	⊕
OMEGA WORKSHOPS, Bloomsbury, Vanessa Bell, Duncan Grant (2490865679)	**babe-rainbow** (399 ⭐)	Sep-29-04 12:00:00	Leave Feedback	☆	⊕
SALVATORE FERRAGAMO * 1.7 Cologne UB * Great Deal NEW (5522017772)	**meidy** (13778 ⭐)	Sep-21-04 17:24:03	--	☆	○
CASRAN * CHOPARD * Cologne 2.5 Sealed NIB CHEAP!!	**meidy** (13778 ⭐)	Sep-21-		☆	○

GRIFF TIP! One extremely important tool on this page bears highlighting. Click the Leave Feedback button on the top of the "My eBay" Feedback page to leave feedback in bulk.

On the Feedback Forum: Leave Feedback page, you can find an individual feedback comment by searching on a User ID or item number. In addition, you can view all of your recent transactions from the past ninety days where you are either the buyer or the seller and have not yet left the other party feedback.

Just scroll down this page and enter feedback comments for each completed transaction.

This little-known and little-used feature not only makes leaving feedback an easy task as opposed to a confusing chore, it also prevents your forgetting to leave feedback for a deserving buyer or seller.

Do make a note of this feature for later reference. This and the fine art of leaving and receiving feedback are examined in depth later in this chapter.

Seller Account

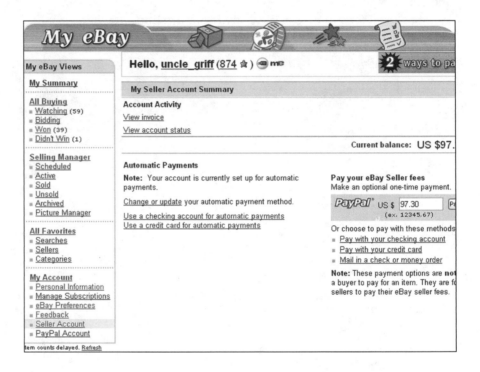

From here, you can view your most recent eBay invoice and your account status as well as change the settings for your automatic monthly invoice payment method (credit/debit card, bank account, or manual). If you elect to pay your monthly invoices manually and you have a PayPal account (as well you should!), you can pay your current balance with PayPal at any time by clicking the button provided.

PayPal Account

This link provides a handy and fast way to access your PayPal account.

My PayPal Account Information 🗗

View and update your PayPal account information and profile summary. Clicking the links below will take you to PayPal's secure website.

- Go to My Account Overview
- View Account History
- Update Profile Summary (account information, financial information, and selling preferences)

To view and update your PayPal user preferences on eBay, click here.

Edit your sign in options

Sign in options

☑ Bidding and buying – Remember my User ID and password for bidding and buying

☑ Selling – Remember my User ID and password for selling

☑ Keep me signed in on this computer until I sign out (Available only when you select the eBay preferred sign in method below.)

Note: For your protection, updating personal information or financial information will always require that you enter your User ID and password.

Display Settings

☑ See email addresses when viewing User IDs – if you are involved in a transaction. Learn more

Preferred sign in method

I prefer to sign-in to eBay using:

⦿ eBay User ID and password

○ Microsoft Passport

[Save changes]

[Cancel]

Notifications and emails from eBay:

Change my notification preferences
(Turn on/off the emails that you receive from eBay)

Change Your Notification Preferences

A checked box means you will receive a notification, and you can click on the checkbox to turn the notification off. We do not sell or rent your personally identifiable information to third parties for marketing purposes, and only use your information in accordance with our privacy policy.

Transaction Emails

Note: You cannot opt out of some notifications because they are necessary to provide our services(✔).

☑ **Outbid Notice**
Notify me when I have been outbid.
  ☑ .Net Alerts
  ☑ Receive Wireless Email

✔ **End of Auction Notice**
Notify me at the end of an auction in which I am the seller or winning bidder.
  ☑ .Net Alerts
  ☐ Receive Wireless Email

☐ **End of Item Notice**
Notify me when an item ends if I did not win the item.

☑ **Personal Offer Notice**
Send me seller offers through eBay for items that I have bid on but did not win.
Note: Only purchases completed on eBay are covered by eBay services.

☐ **Bid Notice**
Notify me when eBay has received a bid I have placed on an item.

☐ **Bidding and Selling Daily Status**
Send me a daily status email of auctions on which I am a bidder or seller.

☑ **Item Watch Reminder**
Send me daily lists of all items in my watch list that will end within 36 hours.

☐ **Listing Confirmation**
Send me a confirmation for each of my new listings.

Transaction Emails Delivery Format
○ Get Text-Only Email
◉ Get HTML Email

Microsoft© .NET Alerts
.net You are now receiving alerts through the Microsoft© .Net Alerts service!
Click here to change your delivery settings. **Wireless Email Alerts**
You currently have a wireless email address: **jimgriff@omnisk y.com**. You can change this address!

The Feedback Forum

To the first pioneering eBay buyers and sellers back in late 1995 and early 1996, the infant eBay Web site proved to be a nearly perfect trading platform where individuals could trade with each other directly through the age-old tradition of the auction format.

An enterprising new eBay seller could set up listings in a matter of minutes, and within days that seller would be completing successful transactions, usually with a buyer whom she had never met. As eBay's founder, Pierre Omidyar, stated on the old Web site, it was all truly based on trust. A seller trusted that a high bidder would honor her bid and send payment, and a buyer trusted a seller to send him the merchandise.

The system had one glaring deficiency: After an eBay sale was completed, the buyer and seller had no mechanism for telling the world how the transaction had gone. You could complete many transactions, but no one else at eBay would know that you were someone who could be trusted based on your prior successful transactions.

And so it was that within about six months after the introduction of eBay/AuctionWeb, Pierre created a system where members could leave comments about other eBay members from whom they had bought or sold.

READING FEEDBACK

Simply put, the eBay Feedback Forum is a mechanism whereby a registered eBay member can leave a public comment about any other registered eBay member. All feedback left for a member can be viewed by clicking the number in parentheses next to that member's User ID wherever the User ID appears.

uncle_griff (874 ☆) me

You can also view feedback for a member by clicking on the Advanced Search link on the upper right-hand corner of any eBay page

Start new search   Search
Advanced Search

and then clicking the link "Find a Member."

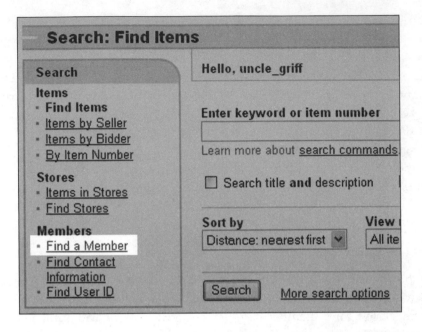

Enter that member's User ID in the box provided and select the radio option button "Feedback profile."

Either way will take you to that member's Feedback Profile. Here is my Feedback Profile:

Member Profile: uncle_griff (874 ⭐) me ⊜

| Feedback Score: | 874 | Recent Ratings: | | | | Member since: May-20-96 |
| Positive Feedback: | 99.9% | | Past Month | Past 6 Months | Past 12 Months | Location: United States |

Members who left a positive:	874	⊕ positive	24	104	210	• ID History
Members who left a negative:	1	⊜ neutral	0	0	0	• Items for Sale
All positive feedback received:	1042	⊖ negative	0	0	0	• Visit my Store
						• Learn more About Me
Learn about what these numbers mean.		Bid Retractions (Past 6 months): 0				[Contact Member]

All Feedback Received | From Buyers | From Sellers | Left for Others
1053 feedback received by uncle_griff (0 mutually withdrawn) — Page 1 of 43

Comment	From	Date / Time	Item #
⊕ fast payment, good transaction,Thank you very much .A+++++	Seller tenikiti (1683 ⭐)	Oct-04-04 07:14	6710197952
⊕ Quick response and fast payment. Perfect! THANKS!!	Seller babe-rainbow (399 ⭐)	Oct-03-04 15:35	2490865679
⊕ We enjoy serving wonderful customers like you! You make everything so nice!	Seller buybuyandsellsell (2313 ⭐)	Sep-29-04 16:53	5521663535
⊕ EXCELLENT EBAYER....EXCELLENT COMMUNICATIONS!!!!!!!!!!!!!!!!!!!!!!!!!	Seller pyewacketsantiques (757 ⭐)	Sep-29-04 14:38	3748876500
⊕ Thanks, you are the best, fast payment, excellent deal		Sep-25-04 09:48	3732107192

The Feedback Profile page consists of two parts: Member Profile and a paginated list of all the comments ever left for that member. The list of left comments can be sorted by All Feedback Received, From Buyers, From Sellers, and Left for Others.

Three important facts about eBay Feedback:

1. From the beginning of the Feedback Forum, there have been three types of comments from which a member can select: positive, neutral, and negative. A colored icon to the left of the feedback comment indicates the comment type: green for positive, gray for neutral, and red for negative. Besides the type of comment, a member can also type a comment of up to eighty characters.

2. Everyone starts out at eBay with a feedback rating of zero. Each positive feedback comment left for another member increases his feedback rating (the number in parentheses) one point. Each negative decreases his rating one point. A neutral comment does not count for or against a person's feedback rating.

3. The same user can increase or decrease another user's feedback score only one point in either direction. A user can leave successive comments for the same user (if he has future transactions with that person), and those comments could be a combination of positive and negative, but they will not move the other user's feedback score up or down more than one point.

HOW TO READ A MEMBER'S FEEDBACK PROFILE

Here is the Member Profile for my eBay registration:

Member Profile: uncle_griff (874 ☆) me

| Feedback Score: | 874 | Recent Ratings: | | | | Member since: May-20-96 |
| Positive Feedback: | 99.9% | | Past Month | Past 6 Months | Past 12 Months | Location: United States |

Members who left a positive: 874
Members who left a negative: 1

		Past Month	Past 6 Months	Past 12 Months
⊕ positive		24	104	210
⊘ neutral		0	0	0
⊖ negative		0	0	0

All positive feedback received: 1042

- ID History
- Items for Sale
- Visit my Store
- Learn more About Me

Contact Member

Learn about what these numbers mean. **Bid Retractions (Past 6 months): 0**

Since May 20, 1996, I have received a total of 1,042 positive comments in my feedback profile, but my actual feedback score is only 874. How is that? Though it is possible to leave multiple comments for each transaction one has with a specific member, an eBay member can only increase another eBay member's feedback score once. Any subsequent feedback left for that member will not raise that member's score. Thus the difference between the total received and the actual feedback score shown is the sum of positive comments left by repeat buyers or sellers. I have about 150 comments that were left by repeat buyers or sellers. Though the comments for these 150 positive feedbacks are displayed chronologically within the long list of feedback comments, they do not count toward my total score.

I received one negative (way back in 1996).

A member's Feedback Profile tells you many things about that member. For example, when she became an eBay member, if she used ID Verify*, and the country from which she registered.

Also, the Recent Ratings section breaks down how many of what type of comment the member has received in the past one, six, and twelve months.

Notice the mention of Bid Retractions. Any bids retracted in the last six months will be listed on a page accessible via the Bid Retraction link. If the member has not retracted bids in the last six months, the text will be static (nonlinking).

On the right-hand side of the Profile section, there are four links: ID History (where you can view any previous User IDs used for this account); Items for Sale; Visit my Store; and Learn more About Me (which leads to my About Me page if I have previously created one).

---

*ID Verify is an eBay feature that uses a third party to cross-check the information a user provides and verifies its accuracy. The ID Verify feature is covered in Section Two.

Finally, there is a button for sending the member an e-mail through the eBay e-mail system.

A Little eBay Feedback History Trivia

In its original incarnation, the ability to leave a comment for another eBay member was unrestricted. You could leave a comment for anyone just to tell the rest of the world just how wonderful he or she was. Unfortunately, it was also possible to leave unlimited negative comments for another eBay member, deserved or not. Although the majority of community members maintained only the highest standards of conduct on the Feedback Forum, a few bad apples did cause innocent eBay members some major headaches.

For a short time, a remedy to this problem was implemented that effectively wiped out all scores by any suspended eBay member. The comments remained but the type was changed from negative or positive to neutral.

Still, this remedy proved to be only a partial panacea. Since fairness dictated that *all* of the feedback, both positive and negative, left by a suspended member be changed to neutral, many eBay members would wake up one day to find their feedback score had *decreased* overnight.

eBay members came up with the best solution: limit the ability to leave feedback to only the buyer and the seller of a closed listing.

Feedback Comments

Below the Member Profile section, one finds all of the feedback comments left for that member.

By default, comments are displayed twenty-five per page. You can change the number of comments displayed per page by scrolling down to the bottom of the first page of comments and selecting from the options provided:

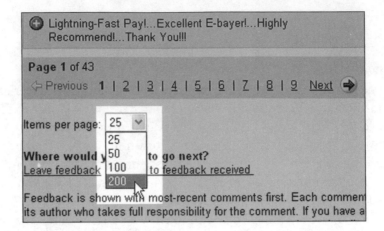

The numbers in parentheses are the individual pages of twenty-five comments each. You can navigate to any of these pages by clicking the page number.

In addition, there are links here for "Leave feedback" and "Reply to feedback received."

Let's break down the information contained within one feedback comment:

The comment above was left by har1986 on April 3, 2002, at 8:12 Pacific standard time. The comment was about item 707217972. You can view the item itself by clicking the item number, but the link is clickable for only ninety days from the close of the listing. "Seller" indicates that the person leaving the comment was, well . . . the seller for this transaction.

Another feature of the feedback system allows members to follow up on feedback left for them or that they left originally. Here's an example of a feedback in my profile where the seller posted a follow-up:

☺ .:⌒⁓:.WOW!~GREAT BUYER~PD. IMMED~FRIENDLY~GRATEFUL~CANT SAY ENUFF!.:⌒⁓:.	Seller **badcatnap** (badcatnap@yahoo.com) (1455 ⭐)	Aug-12-04 20:32	5511693951
Follow-up by badcatnap: Thanx again for bein a SUPERB E-BAYER! »(⌒v⌒)-» E N J O Y!~Come back ANYTIME!		Aug-15-04 17:30	
Follow-up by badcatnap: Thanx again for bein a SUPERB E-BAYER! »(⌒v⌒)-» E N J O Y!~Come back ANYTIME!		Aug-15-04 17:30	

In addition, the person who left the comment can also respond to the recipient's response. This allows for some back-and-forth between two parties.

☺ Item was shipped in record time! I am EXTREMELY pleased! Thanks!	Seller **88mic** (667 ⭐)	Jan-30-04 12:16	2982173069
Reply by 88mic: Thanks. I had moved all nutrition products to www.stores.ebay.com/uugiftshop		Feb-24-04 16:43	
☺ VERY pleased with item. Nice packing too! Thanks!	Seller **decoduck** (1356 ⭐)	Jan-30-04 12:16	2590204551
Reply by decoduck: My Pleasure, uncle_griff!!!		Jan-30-04 12:54	

LEAVING FEEDBACK

A buyer or seller can leave feedback for any eBay member with whom he has a closed eBay transaction. There are two ways to begin: from the Closed Item page and from "My eBay." How to leave feedback using "My eBay" is described earlier in this chapter in the "My eBay" section.

Leaving Feedback from the Closed Item Page

The Closed Item page is simply the item page for a closed listing. You can reach a Closed Item page via the item number, from your completed item list in Search as Bidder or Seller, or from your "My eBay" All Buying page.

The Title section of every eBay Closed Item page has a link to leave feedback for the other party in the closed transaction:

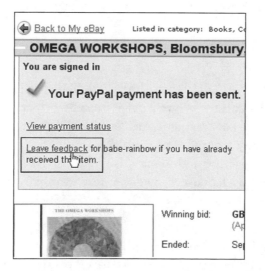

The link will only appear if you are the signed-in buyer or seller of the item.

THE IMPORTANCE OF FEEDBACK

All eBay members place enormous importance on their feedback. At eBay, feedback is considered by most to be the currency of an eBay member's reputation. Feedback promotes accountability and good trading ethics among all eBay members, buyers and sellers alike.

Feedback Protocol—Who Goes First?

For most members, leaving feedback is a crucial duty. However, there is no set protocol regarding who should leave feedback first. Normally, the seller leaves it for the buyer once the seller has received the buyer's payment. The buyer never leaves feedback until she has received the item. Over the past few years, I have noticed that many sellers will not leave feedback for a buyer until the buyer has done so for them. It really doesn't matter who leaves feedback first as long as someone does so.

Keep a Civil Tongue

The vast majority of all eBay transactions end with satisfied buyers and sellers. However, if by some chance you need to leave a less-than-positive comment, don't do so in anger. Remember that feedback left cannot be removed (except under specific, severely defined, and limited circumstances outlined later). It never pays to leave a belligerent comment. State your case clearly and concisely. A good rule of thumb: Never post a feedback comment you would be ashamed to show your mother.

Positive Feedback

If you do your homework and bid with trusted eBay sellers who provide professional, easy-to-understand, comprehensive item descriptions, payment/shipping terms, secure methods of payment such as PayPal, and clear photos of their items, all of your eBay transactions should be flawless. Let the world know by leaving your trading partner a glowing positive feedback.

eBay member Craig Knouse provided a few examples of simple but concise positive comments:

"Item was even better than described. I'm very pleased with this deal."

"Thanks again, I'll be happy to refer more eBay customers to you in the future."

"Thanks for the opportunity to buy this outstanding item. You really
made my day!"

"I was very impressed by this seller's professionalism and commitment.
Thanks!"

And I love this comment someone left for me:

> ⊕ MY MAILMAN HAD FLAMES COMING OUT OF THE BACK OF HIS SHOES. FASTEST PAYMENT EVER!

And if I may, I believe that the following comment I left for a seller (who sold
me a wonderful Timex Indiglo wristwatch) may be the only palindrome feedback
ever left on eBay (prove me wrong!):

> ⊕ Look ma! I won! Olga's Timex emits a 'glo!' Now I am 'kool!'

A few tips:

- Use all of the eighty character spaces. With a little ingenuity, you can get a
  lot of praise and information into eighty spaces. Try abbreviating wherever
  possible.
- Leave out punctuation. It takes up valuable space from the 80-character-
  limit-space that is better served with actual words.
- Avoid using any part of a member's contact information, such as their
  name or phone number.
- Never post an e-mail address or Web address in a feedback comment.

Negative Feedback—the Last Resort

Your eBay transaction didn't go as smoothly as you hoped. The item arrived broken or was not as described. The seller used soiled packing materials. The bidder
or seller hasn't responded to your e-mails. The item or payment is late in arriv-
ing. The receipt shows that the shipping cost was a lot less than what the seller
charged you.

Stop. Take a deep breath. The world is not a perfect place. Sometimes things
go awry. Sometimes, sellers make mistakes.

Only leave negative feedback as a last resort. Communication is crucial.
E-mail the other party and, using all the diplomatic skills you possess, try to
work out a solution. Let her know your concerns.

The item arrived broken? Many sellers buy insurance as a habit. Contact the seller via e-mail. Let him know, in a polite, nonaccusing manner, that the item arrived damaged.

The item isn't as described? Even those sellers who state "no returns" will exhibit more flexibility if you state your case with respect and with no aggression.

The packing materials were soiled or the packing was imperfect? Let the seller know your feelings in a polite and helpful e-mail.

Your bidder or seller hasn't responded? A faulty e-mail system or address could be the culprit. Request the contact information (phone number) of the other party and give him a call.

The item or payment has not yet arrived? E-mail the seller or buyer and let her know. No delivery system is perfect.

You feel you were overcharged for shipping? Let the seller know (again, in a polite e-mail) and perhaps suggest that she state her shipping terms more explicitly in her descriptions so that bidders will not be unpleasantly surprised by the higher-than-necessary shipping costs. (And of course, in the future, you will always determine shipping costs *before* you bid.)

As always, be polite. Nine times out of ten, you will find that diplomacy, civility, and tact are more effective at resolving difficulties than a hasty negative comment.

If all of the above fail and you have to leave negative feedback as a last resort, keep in mind what longtime eBay member Tim Heidner (just_ducky) has to say about leaving negative feedback:

1. Never, under any circumstances, leave feedback when you are angry. Take a break and think about what you want to say. Don't be a hothead. It can scare away future users.
2. Don't embellish. Stick to the facts.
3. Keep it within your transaction. Don't bring up other problems this person has had. You don't know the circumstances regarding other feedback left for this person. It might not be true.
4. Don't use profanity. We are adults. Profanity only shows how immaturely you react in a situation.
5. Be respectful. Remember this is still a person. It is possible to leave negative feedback in a respecful way.

Communication is a two-way street. How you say something may tell a story about someone else, but it could speak volumes about you.

The majority of feedback left at eBay is positive, but occasionally a buyer or seller may not be pleased with his trading partner's behavior and will let the world know with a neutral or negative comment. In most cases where someone has left a negative comment, the other party will usually respond in kind.

Over the past five years, I have fielded many an e-mail from an unhappy eBay member who is distraught to have received what he believes to be an undeserved negative comment. A "retaliatory" negative feedback may sting at first, but it is a necessary risk that all eBay members must assume if feedback is to work as originally and currently intended.

Feedback is a public record between you and your trading partner. If you are a good eBay buyer or seller, your feedback will reflect that clearly to all who view it, even if your feedback contains the occasional negative comment. That one recent negative may glare out at you, but in the eyes of other eBay members, it doesn't change your previous string of positive comments, and that is what counts: the sum total of all your comments.

I hear from many eBay members who flatly tell me they will never leave a negative comment, no matter how well deserved, for fear of receiving a negative in kind. These eBay members are more concerned with keeping their feedback unblemished. On first consideration, who could blame them? However, there is a dangerous flaw in this strategy.

Feedback is not a beauty contest. If you have an unpleasant experience with another eBay member and you do not leave appropriate feedback for fear of retaliation, you may keep your own feedback lily-white, but you are doing a grave disservice to the rest of the eBay Community. There are two important reasons for always leaving appropriate feedback.

One: You could be the victim. You read a feedback profile of another eBay member and decide, based on their total lack of negatives, to go ahead and bid on her item. Subsequently, you discover that the seller is not very customer-oriented and is prone to anger and rudeness in her e-mails to you. Wouldn't you have appreciated a warning about this seller's rudeness? Why did no one leave a previous feedback alerting you to this seller's lack of good business manners? Because people were afraid that if they did, the seller would leave a negative in kind for them. The outcome? This seller's bad business practices go unmentioned, and you are unaware of them until it is too late.

Two: Appropriate feedback is corrective. People really are basically good. It's true. Still, sometimes it is up to us to help bring out this innate goodness, especially for those buyers or sellers whose eBay activity could use some gentle correction. By leaving constructive critical feedback in the form of a neutral or, when necessary, a negative, you help educate and, hopefully, reform the buyer or seller so that she can learn from the experience.

EBAY MEMBER TIP! Not all sticky situations call for negative feedback. You have to use common sense and good judgment. Tom Reddick, (treddick), an eBay member since 1998, makes a good point regarding when not to leave negative feedback:

"As a buyer I have received a few things that were not as described but the losses were small and I did not leave a negative feedback. And I did not get any in return. It is important to leave feedback to warn others in serious situations, but it is also smart to consider the long-term consequences of racking up lots of negatives because you 'negged' someone over a small oversight or a misunderstanding over a three-dollar item."

EBAY INC. AND FEEDBACK

eBay will not edit or change a feedback comment under any circumstances. No exceptions. Don't even think about it. That's why it is so important to make sure you leave comments carefully, especially negative comments.

eBay will, however, remove a feedback comment, but only under very specific circumstances.

In addition, if the two parties in a transaction agree, they can have feedback withdrawn. Withdrawn feedback comments remain in view, but their point count is neutralized. An eBay notation explaining that the feedback was mutually withdrawn will be displayed with the comment.

To view the Feedback Removal and Withdrawal policies and instructions, click on the Help link on the top of any eBay Web page. Then click the link Help Topics. Scroll down to the eBay Policies link, click the Feedback link, and click the link for Feedback Removal Policy.

There are some important detailed rules and guidelines regarding how to properly leave feedback in the Trust and Safety chapters of this book.

ANOTHER AMAZING EBAY TESTIMONIAL

Before we move on, take a look at this post to one of the eBay chat boards, eBay member auntiem:

Sincere Gratitude and Heartfelt Thanks

auntiem71 (176)
1:53 P.M. June 16, 2001

I just wanted to tell you how thankful I am for eBay. My husband had a severe stroke seven years ago, at age forty-four. It left him with aphasia/apraxia and comprehension difficulties. He had all but closed himself off to the world. He was afraid people would laugh at him and think he was stupid. I bought a computer a few years ago, hoping he would try to use it. Well, after months of failed attempts, he finally mastered the basics. In the meantime, I had gotten "hooked" on eBay thru my brother-in-law. I started selling some of my dolls to make some extra money. My husband eventually learned to navigate eBay also, a slow process for him. It has been many months now and he has become quite a pro! He had been an automotive machinist, so naturally our house is packed with car parts. He decided he wanted to start selling his "treasures" on eBay! He gets the parts ready and gives me the information and I type up the auctions for him.

Here is the part I am grateful for. He has started talking to people, is more outgoing, and has confidence in himself! He realizes that he is not worthless just because he cannot get the words out of his mouth or that he takes a long time to do something that other people finish in a short time. He has always been excellent where cars are concerned, and now knows he still has this knowledge and always will. Thank you, everyone, for listening to me. I just needed to express my thanks.

3

Shopping on eBay—
Find it!

What Can I Buy on eBay?

Well, what are you looking for?

eBay seller Linda Huffman (eBay User ID lindyfrommindy) found a small wooden beer sign at a local yard sale. After she dragged it home, her husband nixed her plan to hang it in their family room. She put it aside in her "to be eBayed" pile.

"I finally got around to photographing it and listing it and I was surprised at the interest in this corny Pabst Blue Ribbon sign."

She was most pleased when the winning bidder contacted her with profuse thanks. He had been searching everywhere (Internet, yard sales, flea markets, etc.) for a long time for this particular sign.

"His dad had owned one just like it and for years it had decorated their family's basement until it was destroyed in a fire. His dad had passed away, and being able to have this memento of his childhood in his own home now was very important to him. The money I made selling this item was small, but knowing I had reunited someone with an item they valued more than money was priceless."

Just about anything you can imagine is probably available right now, this very minute, on eBay. From the old stalwarts, collectibles and computers, to clothing, jewelry, cameras, and farm machinery, to real estate, houses, cars, planes, boats, event tickets, services, etc. . . . you can find it on eBay.

In just a few minutes of random browsing on eBay, I found all the items shown on these two pages.

A 1960 Cadillac

A new men's Armani suit

A new Black & Decker miter saw

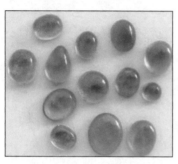

13 Colombian emeralds

A complete computer system

A new cello

A John Deere bucket loader

A used ten-burner commercial Garland restaurant stove

A new glass chess set

A Lalique vase

Lucille Ball's childhood home in upstate New York

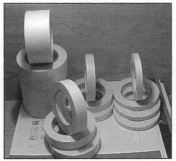

A box of brand new masking-tape rolls

A pet-door kit

A new Pierre Cardin luggage set

A fifties pink poodle suitcase

If you can think of it (and it's legal), you can probably find it on eBay.

Last year I received an e-mail from an eBay member named Julie who actually found most everything for her wedding on eBay!

Let me tell you a little about myself. I am a working mom. My fiancé works and has two kids and so do I. . . . I started going to eBay because of the great deals my fiancé and I got on computer parts for my whole family. . . . I want this day to be so special. I plan to keep everything for the girls when they get married. We even found real champagne glasses on eBay. . . . Most of what I bought I got from eBay. . . . I bought a wedding topper on eBay that cost $25 including shipping. It was completely custom-made . . . the prettiest cake topper I have ever seen. The seller runs her business off of eBay. . . . My wedding is going to be totally elegant. I owe my thanks to all the people who I have purchased things from. . . . One deal early in the game changed everything about the wedding. . . . I was bidding on four bridesmaid dresses . . . in the auction [the seller] stated that they were a pastel blue. Well, when I got them, they were a pastel green. She did offer to take them back. I had already bid on some other high-dollar things in dark blue based off of *the dresses. Anyway, my fiancé and I discussed this problem and I was busy sending out e-mails frantically the next day to the auctioneers. I didn't know if I was going to be able to have these good people change the color from blue to green but I had to try. . . . Our wedding colors are now emerald-green and white. . . . I have met some wonderful friends . . . on eBay. . . . eBay has been very good to me and my fiancé is impressed with the deals that I have made.*

Of course, the trick is, like Julie, to know how to find what you are looking for. With over 25 million items up for bid or sale at any given moment, finding that special object (like an entire wedding) can seem a formidable task. However, by utilizing some or all of the following helpful tips, you'll be an expert eBay searcher in no time!

To begin, there are two primary methods of finding items on eBay—browsing and searching.

Browsing eBay

By "browsing," I mean the Internet equivalent of old-fashioned "window-shopping," much like taking a leisurely stroll through a mall or the old downtown of your hometown, scanning the windows of the shops, not exactly sure what it is you are looking for but hoping that something will catch your eye. Or maybe you have a pretty good idea of the type of item you want, so you focus on specific stores offering this type of item.

Browsing on eBay is much the same thing. A buyer can browse on eBay two ways: through

eBay Categories
eBay Stores

BROWSING THE EBAY CATEGORIES

All items on eBay are placed somewhere in the eBay category hierarchy (see chapter 2). As of this writing, there are thirty-one top-level categories (and five specialty categories). The folks at eBay don't usually add more top-level categories, but new subcategories are always showing up based primarily on eBay buyer and seller requests.

Let's say you are looking to buy something old and rare. You can start your search from the eBay home page by clicking on the link Antiques in the category list.

This will bring you to the Antiques category home page.

By starting your browsing on the Antiques home page, you have reduced the number of items to browse from the 25 million–plus total items available on eBay to about two hundred thousand items that were specifically listed by sellers in the Antiques categories. Note: The seller determines under which category her item will appear when she lists the item.

The Antiques home page contains subcategories for specific types of antiques. Select and click on a link for a subcategory of your choice and you will be directed to "page one" for all items that are currently listed under that subcategory. For example, I like to search for Oriental rugs so I would click on the Rugs, Carpets link and start my browsing from there.

Let's dissect this page.

The most prominent features are the three tabs on the top of the page: "All Items, Auctions, and Buy It Now. The default view is for All Items. Clicking the Auctions tab will display only those listings that are listed as auctions. Clicking the Buy It Now tab will display only those listings where the seller has listed the item as either an auction with a Buy It Now option or a straight, no-auction, fixed-price listing.

All Items	Auctions	Buy It Now
		Rugs, Carpets

This feature is a boon to the many eBay buyers who prefer to skip the auction listings and shop only for those items that they can buy immediately.

Over the tabs are a series of links showing the location of the subcategory Rugs, Carpets in the overall category hierarchy.

Home > All Categories > Antiques > **Rugs, Carpets**

You can move up the hierarchy by clicking any of the links. We'll stay with Rugs, Carpets for now.

Directly under the subcategory name you will find a search box where you can enter keywords to search within the category. (The mechanics of a search are discussed in depth in the next section of this chapter.) Under that is the number of total items currently listed in this category. When this screen shot was captured, the number of New Today items was 2,332.

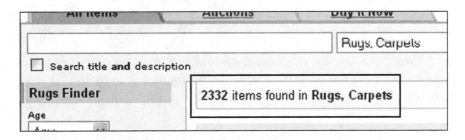

To the right of the page is a drop-down box for selecting one of six sort options, four for time and two for price. The time sort options are the default, "ending soonest" followed by "newly listed," "ending today," and "new today." The price sorts are "lowest first" and "highest first."

arpets   Add to My Favorite Categories

Sort by: Time: ending soonest ▾   Customize Display

	Time: ending soonest	Bids	Time Left
em Title	Time: newly listed		
	Time: ending today		
	Time: new today		
ME 1920S RARA	Price: lowest first	-	6d 23h 20m
N PERSIAN RUG	Price: highest first		

The default "ending soonest" shows the category sorted by the chronological order of their listing, with those about to end on the top.

"Newly listed" shows all items in the category, sorted by newest items first.

"Ending today" displays only those items that are slated to end in the next twenty-four hours, sorted by the oldest first.

"New today" shows only those items listed in the last twenty-four hours with the newest first.

The two price sorts order the items by either lowest price or highest price. Note that the price used is either the current bid or, if there are no bids on the item, the starting bid.

Scroll down to the bottom of this category list page. In the right-hand corner under the "Go to page . . ." box, you'll find an important bit of information in tiny text.

> Note: Bid counts and amounts may be slightly out of date.
> This page was last updated: Oct-09 15:56

This indicates the date and time that this category was last updated. When items are listed on eBay, they do not immediately appear in their categories. Instead, they are held aside until the eBay system updates that particular category, at which time all items in the "holding pen" are added. This process, called indexing, occurs once every five to ten minutes.

On the left-hand side of the page you will find other tools for sorting and filtering the contents of a category. Many categories now have what is called a Finder, which provides a precision filtering tool using item attributes specific to the category. For example, the Rugs Finder section contains selectable attributes for age, shape, size, style, and background color. In addition, there is a box for entering search keywords.

The next section is called Categories. You can view a list of the subcategories one level down. For Rugs, Carpets, they are Small (1x2–4), Medium (4x2–9x6), Large (9x7–9x12), Larger than 9x12, Runners, and Other.

Below this, the Search Options section contains some limiting factors for your search. These are "Items listed with PayPal," "Buy It Now items," "Gift items," "Completed listings," "Listings Starting today," "Ending today," "Ending within 5 hours," and "Items priced from x to y."

Note the small link for "customize options displayed above." This link lets you alert the options appearing for Search Options. For example, click the link, select the option "Multiple item listings," and click the little blue arrow that points to the right.

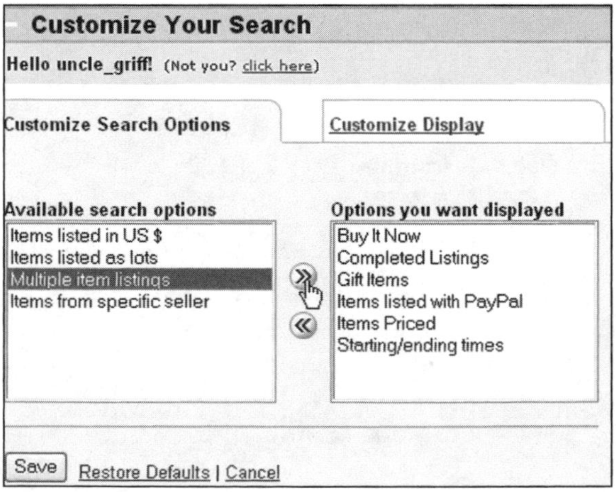

Now the option "Multiple item listings" appears in the right-hand window. Click the Save button.

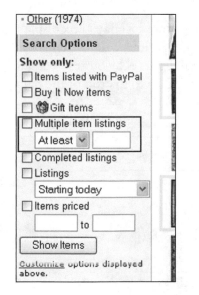

Now the option for viewing Multiple Item Listings is inserted into the Search Options section.

GRIFF TIP! Look for the "customize" links on eBay to customize just about any feature to suit your particular shopping and selling needs.

In the "More on eBay" box, you will find links to Popular Searches. Popular Searches are the actual most popular keyword searches that other browsers use in this category.

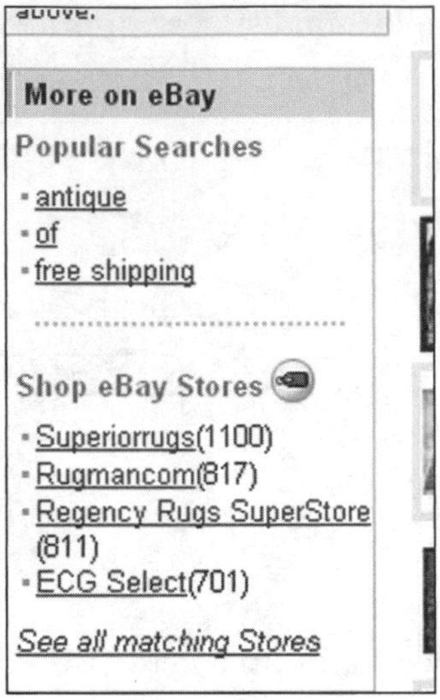

The last section of the "More on eBay" box displays a random selection of eBay Stores for sellers offering items similar to the items in the category. eBay stores are listed by Store Name. We'll discus eBay Stores in greater detail later in this section.

For now, let's move back up to the top of the page, to the actual item titles as shown in the category itself.

Directly under the bar containing the last update information is a bar labeled Featured Items:

Featured Items

When the sellers of these items listed them to eBay, they selected a special option, Featured Plus. It costs the seller $19.95 to have an item appear as a Featured Plus. The benefit of Featured Plus is that these items will always appear on the top of page one of their category as well as within the category pages themselves.

The Featured Items section usually fits on the first page of the category, but for the more populated categories, it can extend two or three pages into the list of category pages. At the end of the Featured Items, the All Items section begins.

NOTE: An item that appears in the Featured Items section of a category will also appear in the All Items section.

Each time eBay updates a category, items that were listed after the previous update are added to the top of both the Featured and All Items sections in chronological order according to the actual time that the seller submitted them. Items are added to the top of each list and are scrolled down and onto the next page as new items are added after them. Think of it as a tall stack of plates with new plates constantly added to the top of the stack.

You can probably see why sellers who list their items so that they appear in the Featured Items section are at an advantage over those who do not. Those items are always on the first or second page of every category for current view, and on eBay, where there are sometimes hundreds of item pages, it pays to be on the top of the stack!

On the left-hand side of the category list, you should see Gallery thumbnail images for those items where the seller opted to employ a Gallery picture.

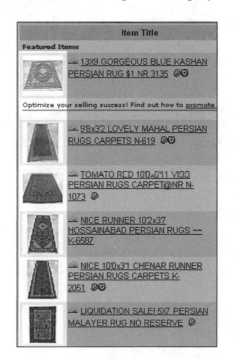

Gallery pictures allow browsers to scan through the category items more efficiently. It's also an excellent way for sellers to promote their items. A title may be descriptive and enticing, but as we all know, a picture is worth a thousand title keywords.

Not all the items in the category list will have Gallery thumbnails. For those items where the seller did not opt for a Gallery image but supplied photos, there will be a camera icon.

If there is no Gallery thumbnail and no green camera icon to the left of an item title, then the seller may not have provided a picture for the item. This is not always the case. The only way to tell for sure is to click the item title to open the item description page.

To the right of the Gallery thumbnail or the camera icon is the item title as provided by the seller.

Item Title	Price*	Bids	Time Left ▲
98x32 LOVELY MAHAL PERSIAN RUGS CARPETS N-619	$5.00	2	6d 23h 54m

You may have noticed that there are many different styles of composition for titles. Some sellers use all caps, some use long strings of punctuation to create eye-catching designs, others use words of enticement like "L@@K," "Must See," or the ever-popular "Best on eBay." (In Section Two of this book, we describe the pros and cons of different title composition styles and provide tips for creating the most effective item titles.)

NOTE: The small "pp" icon indicates that the seller accepts PayPal for payments, and the "shield" icon means the seller provides PayPal Buyer Protection.

The next column, Price, shows the current price of the item as of the last category index update.

The next column, Bids, indicates the number of bids received as of the last category index update. A Buy It Now (BIN) icon indicates the seller listed the item with a Buy It Now format. If someone bids on the item (and the reserve, if any, has been met), the BIN icon will disappear and the number of bids will show in the space.

The final column, "Time left," displays the absolute closing time for the item in Pacific Standard Time.

If you find an item that interests you, you can click either the Gallery image or the item title to open up the Item Description Page.

The Product "Finder"

eBay recently enhanced the ability to locate specific items with a new tool called Finder. With Finder, you can filter the items in the category using an expanded range of item attributes. Currently, this feature extends to most eBay categories.

In the Art, Sculpture, Carvings category, the box Sculpture Finder is on the left-hand side:

This box contains a long list of attributes, such as Medium, Subject, Longest Dimension, Date of Creation, and Country/Region.

Use any of these links in any combination to target only those items in which you are interested. For example, if you were seeking nineteenth-century bronze, you could spend a few hours browsing the over nine thousand items currently listed in the Art > Sculpture, Carvings category or simply click the link for Bronze under the Sculpture Finder.

And then click the link Pre-1900, under Date of Creation.

Results: from over nine thousand items down to thirty-six items, all of which are for nineteenth-century or earlier bronze sculptures.

Below the Finder list is the same Search Options section we saw in Antiques > Rugs & Carpets. Above the Finder list you'll always find a text entry box for keyword searches. You can combine the Finder links, keyword search, and Search Options to focus your browsing and searching on only those items that interest you most.

107

BROWSING BY EBAY STORES

eBay Stores are a way for sellers to offer their customers both auction and fixed-price merchandise on eBay through an online storefront. To browse, search, and buy at the eBay Stores home page, go to the eBay home page and click the link at the top of the left-hand column marked eBay Stores (under Specialty Sites).

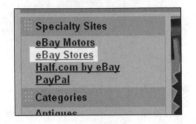

This will take you to the eBay Stores home page:

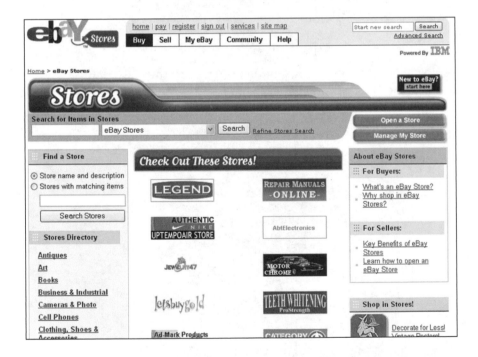

The eBay Stores home page looks similar to the eBay home page except that, instead of a Categories box, there is a box for Stores Directory sorted by the same category list as for the eBay main home page. The eBay Stores browsing experience is entirely different from the main eBay site. The focus is on individual eBay Stores as opposed to items. For example, we'll start with a top-level category, Antiques.

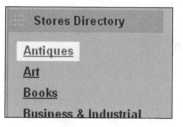

This brings us to a page that looks a bit like the Antiques portal page for the main eBay site, except that no individual items are listed on the page.

Click a subcategory on the left, for example, Architectural & Garden.

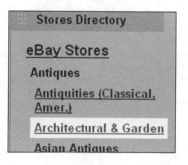

Now the page shows individual eBay Stores including a matching item count for each. Note that eBay Stores are ordered by amount of matching items in each store, with those with the most matching items on the top of the list.

You can either click down another level or select an individual eBay Store from the list. Let's drill down one more level to the subcategory Chandeliers, Fixtures, Sconces:

This brings us to a page of eBay Stores.

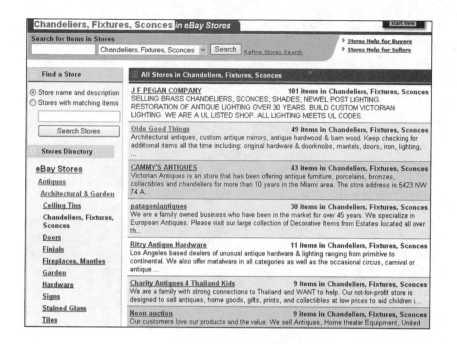

Each one has at least one item in the selected category. Let's visit one of these eBay Stores. Cammy's Antiques looks intriguing:

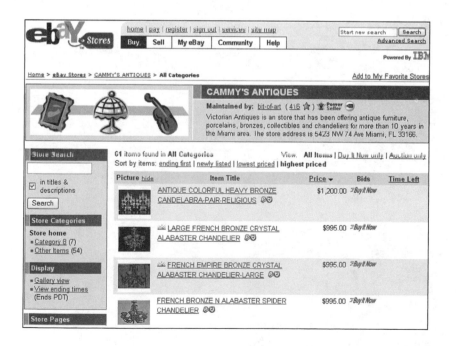

Another way to browse eBay Stores containing items matching a specific category (for example, Antiques > Architectural & Garden > Chandeliers, Fixtures, Sconces) is to navigate to the first page of that category. Then, look for the random selection of a few matching eBay Stores as well as the Shop eBay Stores link in the "More on eBay" box for that category.

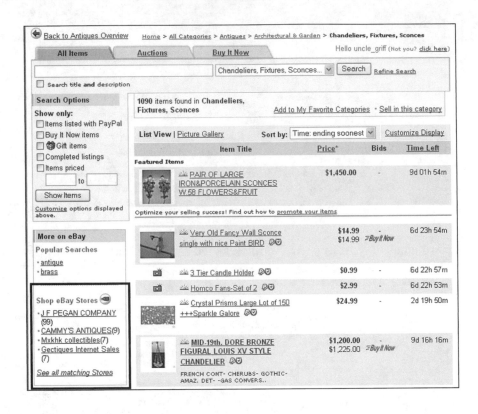

You can also get to an individual eBay Store by clicking on the red Stores icon next to a seller's User ID or by clicking the link for "Visit my eBay Store!" found in that seller's eBay listings. (Only those sellers who have set up an eBay Store will display the Stores icon.)

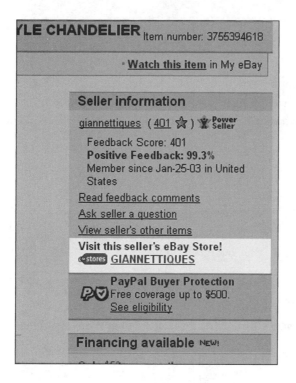

Although the default sort lists all eBay Stores starting with the store containing the highest number of items at the top, you can switch to an alphabetical sort of eBay Stores by clicking the appropriate link located at the bottom of the Stores Directory section.

Browsing is one-half of the eBay shopping picture. When it comes to serious treasure hunting, most eBay shoppers rely on Search.

Searching eBay

Although casually browsing eBay Categories and eBay Stores can be a fun and often rewarding way to hunt down treasure, it's not the most efficient option, in that it takes time and effort to scan through so many items. However, if you have a specific type of item in mind, an efficient and popular method for locating those items is Search.

There are five basic ways to search for items on eBay:

Search using Title Keywords
Search using Item number
Search by Seller
Search by Bidder
Items in Store

In addition, you can use the Search page to:

Find Stores
Find a member
Find Contact Information
Find User ID

All of these search options are quickly accessible by the link Advanced Search on the upper right-hand corner of any eBay page.

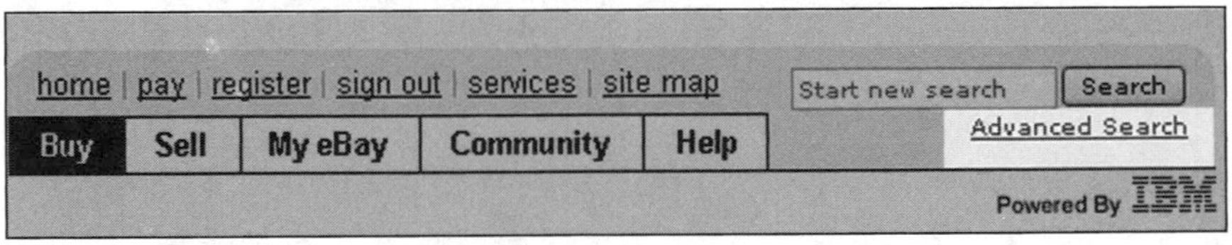

This will take you to the Search: Find Items page, showing the default (and most popular) search method, "keyword or item number."

Let's start with Title Search.

SEARCHING BY TITLE—TITLE SEARCH

Searching by keyword (Title Search) is by far the most popular method for finding items on eBay.

Title Search searches for keyword matches in the titles created by sellers for their items. To use Title Search, you type one or more keywords into any keyword search box. (The keywords used should relate to the type of item for which you are searching.)

The system then searches all listed item titles (depending on your choice, within a single category or all of eBay) and returns those that match your search.

Title searches can be as simple as typing one word and as complex as a long list of words and special commands. Let's explore the default search view for Search: Find Items.

Besides the text entry box, the Search: Find Items page provides six other filters to help you tailor or restrict the returned results of your Title Search.

In This Category

This feature limits the selected search to only one top-level category, an effective way to reduce large numbers of items to a targeted few.

Search Title and Description

Searches the contents of all item descriptions as well as titles. This is a great tool for increasing the number of returned results in cases where certain keywords may not appear in the title (such as a model number or name), but it can also dramatically increase the returned results, sometimes by tens of thousands.

Completed Listings Only

This filter is a popular and valuable tool for viewing matching items that have closed within the last twenty-one days. If you are a seller, you will want to start using this tool for market research.

"Sort by," "View results," and "Results per page" change the display and layout for returned results.

Sort By

Select an option here to sort the returned list of items by one of the five following options: "Time: ending soonest," "Time: newly listed," "Price: lowest first," "Price: highest first," and "Distance: nearest first."

Note: The "Distance: nearest first" option replaces the old "Search by region" feature, but don't despair: This is an improvement. Items in the sorted list will show those nearest to you first. The sort is based on the distance in miles between your zip code and the zip code of the seller.

View Results

There are three possible choices: "All items" (displays all items—Gallery and non-Gallery alike), "Picture Gallery" (displays only those items for which the seller has added a Gallery image), and "Show item numbers" (displays the item number in a column to the left of item title).

Results per Page

Select from twenty-five, fifty, one hundred, or two hundred results per page.

We will use some of these options in a later example. For now, let's focus on the nuances of and tricks for creating effective Title Searches.

A Simple Title Search

Let's say you are looking for certain types of Beatles-related items. One way to find all the Beatles items at eBay is to type in the word *beatles* in the Title Search text entry box and then click the Search button.

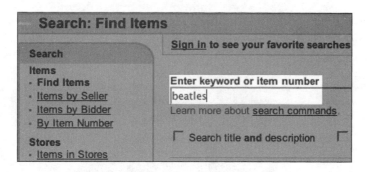

This Title Search will return a list of all items that have the word *beatles* in their title. At the time of this writing, there were 16,192 such items on eBay.

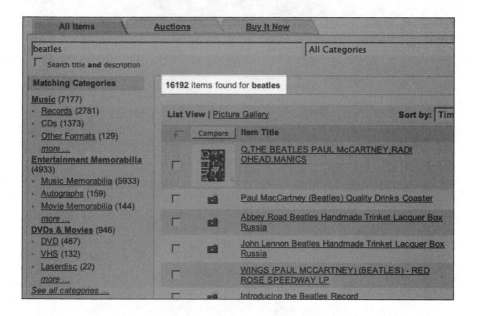

This page is called a Search Results page.

On the left-hand side of the page is the box Matching Categories, which shows the entire list of returned results sorted by category. For searches that return a high volume of results, the Matching Categories feature can help narrow the range of your title keyword search to specific types of items. For example, you may be looking to add to your collection of Beatles movie memorabilia and not be interested in perusing Beatles recordings. In this case, the matching category link for Movie Memorabilia reduces the amount of items you would otherwise need to scan from an overwhelming 16,192 down to a manageable 144.

If the matching category you seek doesn't appear in the Matching Categories box, try clicking the link "more . . ." under any of the top level matching categories. For example, click the link "more . . ." under Entertainment Memorabilia to expand the section with other matching subcategories.

Now we view all of the matching subcategories for Entertainment Memorabilia.

The Matching Categories box is a handy tool for most Title Searches. But when you are looking for something specific, you can use some simple Title Search tips to focus the scope of your searches down to a few, or even just one item.

Tailoring a Simple Title Search

Many of these 16,192 Beatles-related items may not be on your treasure hunt list. For example, say you are looking for only old vinyl Beatles albums, not CDs or CD-ROMS or songbooks or videos. You can tailor your search by going back to the Search page and clicking the "More search options" link.

Search: Find Items

Sign in to see your favorite searches

Search

Items
- Find Items
- Items by Seller
- Items by Bidder
- By Item Number

Stores
- Items in Stores
- Find Stores

Members
- Find a Member
- Find Contact Information
- Find User ID

Enter keyword or item number

Learn more about search commands.

☐ Search title **and** description   ☐ Completed listings only

Sort by   View results   Results per
Time: ending soonest ▾   All items   ▾   50 ▾

Search   More search options

About eBay | Announcements | Security Center | Policies | Site Map | Help

Copyright © 1995-2004 eBay Inc. All Rights Reserved. Designated trademarks and brands are the property of their respec...

This displays several new search options, one of which is "Exclude these words." Type in words like *CD* and *CD-ROM*. Type each word with a space between them.

Search: Find Items

Sign in to see your favorite searches

Search

Items
- Find Items
- Items by Seller
- Items by Bidder
- By Item Number

Stores
- Items in Stores
- Find Stores

Members
- Find a Member
- Find Contact Information
- Find User ID

Enter keyword or item number

beatles

Learn more about search commands.

☐ Search title **and** description   ☐ Complete

All of these words ▾

Exclude these words

CD CD-ROM

Exclude words from your search

Items Priced

Min: US $ Max: US $

This reduces the number of items to 14,439 items—

—still too many items to browse quickly. Let's add *book* and *poster* to the exclusion list:

This trims the number of returned results to 12,916.

We show fewer items, but still too many to browse efficiently. We need to narrow this search down even more.

Let's add some other words to include, instead of exclude. We know we are looking for Beatles albums. What other words besides *album* would a seller use to describe such an item? *LP* and vinyl come to mind. But how do we add them?

Go back to the Search page and type in the following: *beatles (lp,vinyl,album)*.

This is a more advanced search method. The words in parentheses form an "OR search." This search looks for all items that have *beatles* and *lp* OR *beatles* and *vinyl* OR *beatles* and *album*. Note the syntax:

word [space] (word[comma]word[comma]word)

There are no spaces between the words and commas inside the parentheses.

Add to this Title Search the following excluded words: *CD CD-ROM songbook video book poster*. Any item titles that contain one of these excluded words will be filtered out of the search.

The results for this more detailed Title Search number 2,055 items.

This is a much easier list to scroll through. Still, we could continue to tweak this search by adding keywords to the OR list or the excluded list and reduce the results to an even more manageable number.

Once you have tailored a Title Search to your liking, you can save it on your "My eBay" Favorites page by looking on the top of the first page of returned results for the link "Add to Favorites."

Effective Title Search Tips from eBay

- Try as many related keywords words as possible.

  What keywords would you use to describe the item if you were selling it?

- Use more than one specific keyword to target your search.

  As we have seen above, *beatles poster* will return fewer and more targeted listings than a search for *beatles*.

- Use conjunctions and articles *(and, or, the, a)* carefully.

  Use *and, or, the,* and *a* only if you're searching for items containing these words. For example, "*Tommy James and the Shondells* or *Truth or Dare* or *A Beautiful Mind.*" If the number of returned matches is too high, try the search minus the conjunction or article.

- **Use punctuation only when required.**

  For example, you'll be successful if you search for *Elvis T-shirt* (correct punctuation with hyphen) or *Elvis tee shirt* (correct wording without hyphen). But don't try *Elvis: T-shirt* (unnecessary colon) or *Elvis-tee-shirt* (incorrect hyphen).

- **Use an asterisk (wildcard) to include plural forms of nouns and alternate endings.**

  If searching for *diamond rings* doesn't return enough matches, find more items with little overlap by entering *diamond ring**.

  Using the asterisk, you can also search for items with multiple endings. For example: *Beatles man** would return items such as *Beatles manager, Beatles mania, Beatles Nowhere Man,* etc.

- **Increase your results by selecting the "Search *titles* and *descriptions*" option.**

  Search always looks in the *title* of the items for sale to find the keywords that you specify. You can find many more items by searching both the *title* and the *description* for each item. Just click on the option to "search titles *and* descriptions" under the search box.

- **Search for exact phrases using quotation marks (" ").**

  Typing "*Statue of Liberty*" or "*Gone with the Wind*" inside quotes will find items with *those exact words in sequence.* Without the quotation marks, you could wind up with many other listings containing the words *statue* or *liberty.*

- **Use the minus sign (–) to narrow your search.**

  antique –lamp tells the search engine to include the word antique but not lamp. Remember there's no space after the sign (e.g., *–card, –teddy*).

- **Sort your results by starting date, ending date, or price.**
  After you see the results of your search, you can use the sort menu to rank these items by starting date, ending date, or bid price. The drop-down sort menu is right above your search results.
- **For the closest matches, specify a date, color, or brand.**
  For example, to find a particular *Barbie* item, don't just type *Barbie* in the search box. If you are looking for a Barbie dress made in the 1960s, enter *Barbie dress 196**. If you want only red dresses, type *Barbie red dress*. The trick is to be specific and use a narrowly defined search!

SEARCH COMMAND CHART

The following advanced search commands will work for any eBay Title Search.

To Search For	Use the Command	Example
One word **AND** another	Use space between words	**baseball autograph** Returns items with the words *baseball* **and** *autograph* in the title.
One word **OR** another	(word 1,word 2) *Attention: No spaces after the comma!*	**(baseball,autograph)** Returns all items with the words *baseball* **or** *autograph* in the title.
EXACTLY these words	"word 1 word 2 "	**"baseball autograph"** Returns items with **exactly** the words *baseball* and *autograph,* in that specific order, separated by a space, in the title.
One word **BUT NOT** another	– (minus symbol) *Attention: No spaces after the minus sign!*	**baseball –autograph** Returns items containing the word *baseball* and will **exclude** all items containing the word autograph in the title.
One word **BUT NOT SEVERAL** others	–(word 1,word 2,word 3) *Attention: No spaces after the minus sign or the comma!*	**baseball –autograph,card, star)** Returns items containing word *baseball* and will **exclude all** items containing the words *autograph, card,* and *star* in the title.

SEARCH COMMAND CHART *(continued)*

To Search For	Use the Command	Example
Any words starting with a **SPECIFIC SEQUENCE OF LETTERS**	* (asterisk)	**base*** Returns items with **words starting** with *base* such as *baseball card, baseball cap,* and *iron bases.*
Words **OUT OF A GROUP**	@1 word 1 word 2 word 3	**@1 baseball autograph card** Returns all items containing **two out of the three words** specified. This example will return items containing the words *baseball* and *autograph, baseball* and *card,* or *autograph* and *card* in the title. You can try searching for 3 words out of 4 by using *@2* in the beginning of the command.
One word **ALONG WITH AN ADVANCED SEARCH**	+ (plus symbol) *Attention: No spaces after the plus sign!*	**@1 baseball autograph card +star** Returns items containing two out of the three words specified **plus** the word *star* in the title.

You can also use any of these commands to search item descriptions by clicking on the option to "Search titles and descriptions" under the search box.

TITLE SEARCHING TIPS (SMART SEARCH)

Misspellings

Most sellers take great pains to insure that their title keywords are spelled correctly. Then there are those sellers for whom spelling has always been a challenge. These sellers often spell keywords incorrectly. This can decrease the potential for a high price for that item since the misspelling will prevent the item from appearing in most Title Search results—bad news for the seller but good news for the crafty eBay treasure hunter (that's you!).

An effective way to take advantage of these unfortunate spelling errors is to regularly run Title Searches using the most common misspellings of the appropriate keywords—for example, singular versus plural.

Sellers may list many types of items as plural or singular. As shown above in "Effective Title Search Tips from eBay," above, the use of the singular root of a word along with the wildcard asterisk in place of the *s* or *es* for the plural will return both singular and plural forms of a specific keyword.

Creating a Custom-Tailored Title Search—
Another Example Using Item Location

Let's explore how to custom-tailor a title search to find only those items that are located near me.

Let's say I was looking to purchase a good, used grand piano (preferably from a local seller here in San Jose, California). I start by going to the Search page, clicking the "More search options" link. Next I enter the words *grand piano* in the Search Title box. Then I scroll down toward the bottom of the page, type my

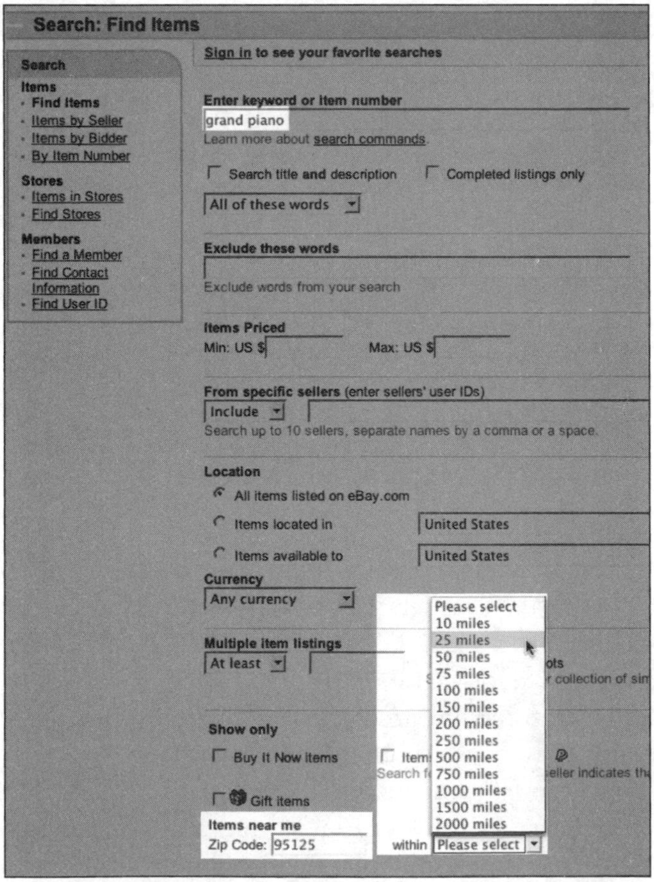

Search: Find Items

Sign in to see your favorite searches

Search
Items
· Find Items
· Items by Seller
· Items by Bidder
· By Item Number
Stores
· Items in Stores
· Find Stores
Members
· Find a Member
· Find Contact Information
· Find User ID

Enter keyword or item number

grand piano

Learn more about search commands.

☐ Search title and description   ☐ Completed listings only

All of these words ▾

Exclude these words

Exclude words from your search

Items Priced
Min: US $ Max: US $

From specific sellers (enter sellers' user IDs)
Include ▾
Search up to 10 sellers, separate names by a comma or a space.

Location
◉ All items listed on eBay.com
○ Items located in   United States
○ Items available to   United States

Currency
Any currency ▾

Multiple item listings
At least ▾

Please select
10 miles
25 miles
50 miles
75 miles
100 miles
150 miles
200 miles
250 miles
500 miles
750 miles
1000 miles
1500 miles
2000 miles

collection of sim

Show only
☐ Buy It Now Items   ☐ Item   eller indicates th
                      Search f
☐ 🎁 Gift Items

Items near me
Zip Code: 95125   within Please select ▾

zip code in the "Items near me" box, and select an acceptable distance from my zip code (twenty-five miles—I am not willing to travel too far from home).

After I clicked the Search button, the eBay search engine returned the following results:

In the San Jose area at the time I ran this search, 743 items had the words *grand piano*. Some of the items are actual pianos, but a few are not; for example, the clock in the shape of a grand piano. I can filter out all the nonmusical instruments by clicking the link to the left for Keyboard, Piano, under Matching Categories. The "(427)" next to the link gives the number of items within that category that contain the words *grand piano* in their title.

Saving a Search with "My eBay"

Instead of running this search manually every day, I can save it in my "My eBay" favorites page and elect for the eBay e-mail system to alert me when a seller within a twenty-five-mile radius of my zip code lists an item matching my title search criteria. To do so, I click the link "Add to Favorites" (found in the upper right-hand side of the page).

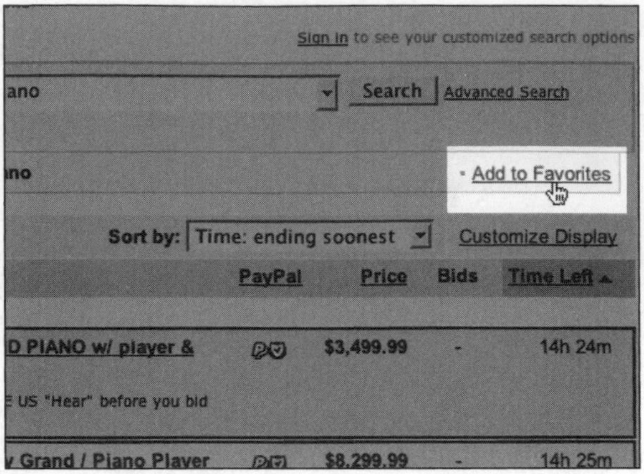

This takes us to a page for setting the options for the saved search:

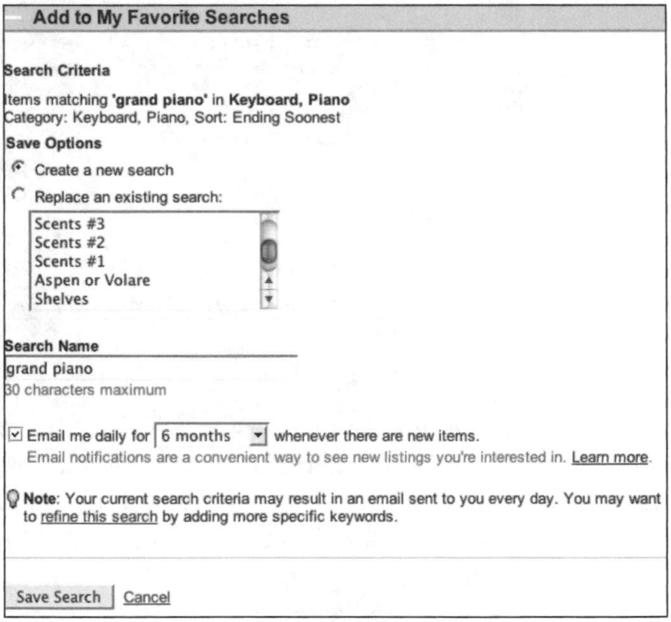

We can make this a new search or replace an existing search in the drop-down list. Let's give this search a new name, "grand piano," and we'll check the box for "e-mail me daily for . . ." selecting a duration from the drop-down list. Then, with a click of the Save Search button, this new search will be inserted into my My eBay: My Favorite Searches page in alphabetical order.

For the next 180 days, eBay will automatically send me an e-mail alert (once a day) when new items matching my search criteria are added to the site.

NOTE: You can save up to one hundred separate Favorite Searches in "My eBay." You can have up to six Favorite Searches checked for e-mail alerts.

There are other ways of searching using the eBay Search page. Some of them may come in handy for you in the future.

Advanced Searching—"More Search Options"

Besides the "Exclude the words" and "Items near me" options, the expanded search option page provides several other advanced filters for Title Search. For keyword searches, the drop-down box returns three options:

- "All these words" (returns listings with all the provided keywords in their title in any order)
- "Any of these words" (returns listings with at least one of the provided keywords)
- "Exact phrase" (only returns listings with all of the keywords in the exact order provided)

"Items Priced" lets you filter results by a price range.

"From specific sellers" lets you include or exclude up to ten seller IDs.

"Location" lets you select one of three options:

- Item on eBay.com
- Items located in a specific country (based on seller location)
- Items available to a specific country (based on the shipping preferences selected by the seller when listing the item)

Select a specific currency using the Currency drop-down list. By selecting the default, "Any currency," your search will cover all eBay global sites including the United States. If you select a currency from the drop-down box, your search will be limited to the eBay Country site for that currency. This option replaces the old International Search option.

"Multiple item listings" is a new option. It helps you pinpoint multiple quantities by number as well as those items listed as lots.

What is a "lot"?

A lot is a group of similar or identical items that are sold together to one buyer (a case of batteries, three dresses, a CD collection, etc.).

"Show only" filters returned item results by format (Buy It Now or Auction), payment method ("Items listed with PayPal"), and "Gift items" (items for which the seller will provide or offer extra services such as gift wrapping, gift card, and expedited shipping directly to the gift recipient).

Show only

☐ Buy It Now items

☐ Items listed with PayPal 🅿
Search for items where the seller indicates that they accept PayPal.
Learn more.

☐ 🎁 Gift items

Items near me
Zip Code: 95125   within Please select ▾

Try our new filters!

☐ Items offering Anything Points

☐ eBay Giving Works Items for Charity
Find all items listed to benefit nonprofit organizations.

Sort by
Distance: nearest first ▾

View results
Picture Gallery ▾

Results per page
200 ▾

[Search]   Clear search | Fewer search options

In addition, a new filter was recently added for the eBay Giving Works, which will limit the results to only those items benefiting nonprofit organizations.

Searching by Item Number

If you know an item's number, you can reach it quickly by typing it into the same keyword text box used for typing in keywords.

Hello, uncle_griff   Favorite Searches:

Enter keyword or item number
5338377917

Learn more about search commands.

Click the Search button to go directly to that item page.

Items by Seller

To search for items listed by a specific seller, click the link "Items by Seller."

Include completed listings. Selecting one of the options here will limit the results to closed listings from a specific period from the Last Day to Last 30 Days.

Include bidder's e-mail addresses. This option is restricted to a seller searching on her own User ID for a list of her listings. This is a useful tool for garnering e-mail addresses for the high bidders of each closed listing in order to send e-mail notices or invoices.

Results per page. If you have a slow dial-up Internet connection, set this option to "50" or lower since anything higher may take longer to display, especially if the seller has hundreds of items listed. If, however, you have a quick connection through DSL, cable, or some other high-speed or broadband connection, you may want to select a higher amount of items displayed per page. Choose the amount per page from the drop-down box.

Searching by Bidder

Just as you can search items by seller, you can also search for items by bidder.

The options are for including completed listings (last thirty days) by any bidder or high bidder only, and for the number of results displayed on one page. Note the "Results per page" option of "All items on one page."

Items in Stores

This search is identical to the Find Items search with one added filter: Items in Stores.

NOTE: The items that are specifically listed in eBay Stores are not included in a regular Find Items search. Use this Title Search to find store items.

As more and more eBay shoppers spend more and more time shopping eBay Stores for great items at good value, they are relying more and more on this option.

Find Stores

This is a versatile tool for using keywords or a store name to look for stores with matching items or store name and descriptions.

Want It Now

What if you know what you want but cannot find it on eBay, even after searching entire categories? You can use a recently introduced tool called Want It Now.

With Want It Now, you can alert all sellers on eBay about the exact type of item or items for which you are searching. Go to the Want It Now page by clicking the link on the home page under Specialty Sites:

On the Want It Now hub page, click the button Post To Want It Now.

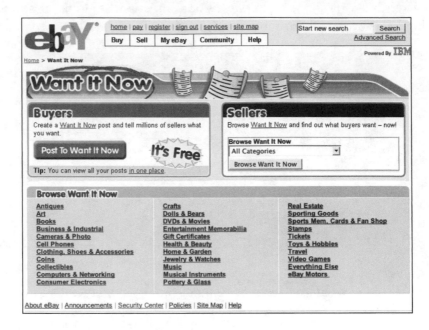

Enter in a title and description for the item you want.

Click the Post To Want It Now button and your Want It Now post is confirmed with an actual number!

Click View Your Post to view it.

The post will remain on the site for thirty days. Others can see your location, feedback score, and your "Member since" status. If a seller has an item listed on eBay that matches your want, he clicks the respond button and fills in the information:

The seller can either list his matching item right away or provide the item number of a matching item from his current eBay listings.

Sellers can view lists of Want It Now items by category from the same Want It Now hub page.

Your wanted post is now available for all sellers to view, and if they list a matching item, they can send you an e-mail alerting you of the listing. One note: The seller never sees your e-mail address or User ID. You, of course, can view the item and the seller's User ID (but not her e-mail address). This provides a solid wall of security to help avoid spam and unsolicited offers to purchase outside of eBay.

Using these search tips, you can hunt for eBay treasure with the precision of a shark! Pam Withers, an avid eBay buyer, sent me the following story about finding a long-lost item on eBay:

When I was about five, I received a wooden apple as a gift. No big deal . . . but the apple contained a little wooden tea set. It was adorable . . . and I lost it! I had looked for many years (I am now fifty-four) to find one like it, to no avail. Then, one day, I asked about this little wooden apple tea set on eBay and was amazed to get a response. The funny part of this story is that my last name is Withers and so was the seller's. However, the seller thought that I was his daughter, who lived in the same town, and was just trying to play games! Imagine his (and MY) surprise after returning e-mails a couple times when we got to the bottom of the whole thing! I still laugh when I think about his response to my first e-mail to him after learning that he had what I wanted. Thinking I was his daughter, he simply mailed back an e-mail that said, "Why don't you come over and look at it?" After he received my response to that e-mail, he e-mailed me again, explaining how he had been thinking I was his daughter. He was VERY embarrassed! . . . Call it luck or coincidence . . . he had the wooden apple tea set and I bought it. By the way, even though we have the same last name, we are not related. Ain't life amazing?

Now that you know, like Pam, how to browse and search for your heart's desire, it's time to learn how, once you have found it, to bid for or buy it!

4

Shopping on eBay—
Buy It!

Now that you know how to search and browse eBay like an expert, you are ready to start shopping!

Most hard-core Internet users will agree—online shopping, and in particular, shopping at eBay, is the most fun anyone can have on a computer. The exquisite thrill of hunting for, bidding on, and winning your first eBay purchase never really fades, even after many years of eBaying! I started buying at eBay back in 1996 and I have never stopped enjoying it, and I have a house overflowing with eBay-bought treasure to prove it.

You discovered a priceless treasure you cannot live without. Your bidding finger is sweaty with anticipation. You gotta have it. You just can't wait to get a bid in.

Stop right there! You should never just rush in and bid or buy. To assure that your eBay buying experience is safe and satisfying, you must always do a quick bit of homework before you bid or buy.

eBay shopper Sharon Maracci had a bit of shock when she learned her eBay purchase was thousands of miles away.

I wanted to buy a discontinued Fisher Price toddler bed for my niece. I had bid on several on eBay but was always outbid at the last minute. I couldn't afford to bid too much because I knew shipping would be very high.

Finally I was the high bidder for the bed by going over what I could afford, only to find out that the bed was all the way in New York. When I wrote the seller about my concern over shipping, she wrote back, "I actually am selling the bed because

*I'm moving. I just got a job offer from Cisco in Silicon Valley. If that's anywhere near you, I'll throw the bed in the moving van and you can get it when I arrive."
I said sure.*

Two weeks later, I got a call. The seller had been given temporary housing by Cisco in an apartment complex less than a mile from my house in Campbell. Now my niece is sleeping in that bed that came to her all the way from New York shipped courtesy of Cisco.

(And I have a REALLY cute picture of my niece in the bed!)

Sharon lucked out this time, as the seller of the bed was more than happy to help resolve her shipping problem (eBay sellers can be very accommodating), but the lesson of the story is to always ask a seller about shipping details before you submit a bid or commit to an outright purchase. This is just one of the important items on our eBay Safe Trading Checklist, which we will outline in detail later in this chapter.

First, let's shop for something specific. My friend's birthday is coming up and I would like to buy him a new, brand-name 4.0 megapixel digital camera in a fixed-price, Buy It Now format. I want to pay for it with PayPal. My budget cap is $400. I start on the eBay home page in the Cameras & Photo category.

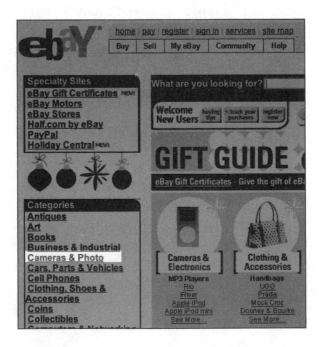

Then, I click the link Digital Cameras.

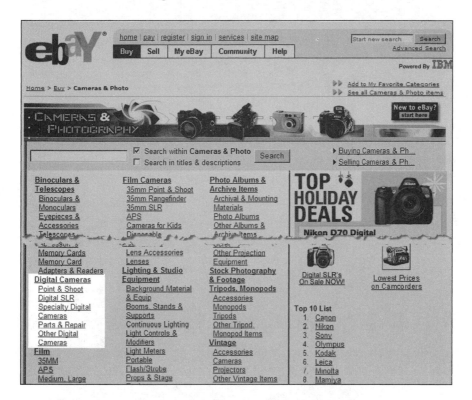

This gives us all 26,846 items currently listed in that category.

Let's reduce it to a number practical for browsing. Click Buy It Now . . .

. . . reducing the number by half. Let's continue to filter the results using our search criteria with the Digital Cameras Finder. I don't really have a camera type in mind so I'll leave that set to the default, "any." Same with "brand" and "optical zoom," but I do know that the camera should be at least 4.0 megapixels and I only want to view "new" cameras, so I select those options and click Show Items.

This leaves 1,607 items to browse but . . . we are not done yet. Scroll down to the Search Options box and check "Items listed with PayPal" and enter our price range, $0 to $400. Then click the Show Items button.

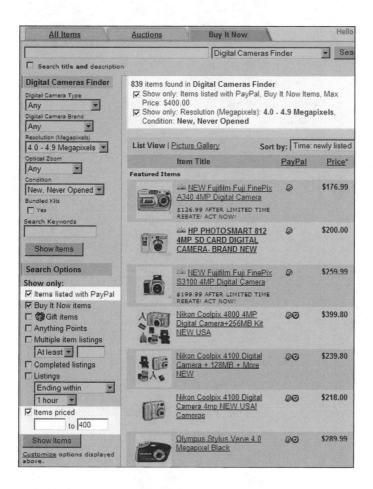

Now we are down to 839 items. That is five pages of cameras; an easy number to browse. Still, there is one more step before we set out. Click the link for Customize Display . . .

839 items found in **Digital Cameras Finder**
☑ Show only: Items listed with PayPal, Buy It Now Items, Max Price: $400.00
☑ Show only: Resolution (Megapixels): **4.0 - 4.9 Megapixels**, Condition: **New, Never Opened**
· Add to Favorite Searches

List View | Picture Gallery	Sort by: Time: newly listed ▾		Customize Display
Item Title	**PayPal**	**Price***	**Time Listed ▾**
Featured Items			
☀ NEW Fujifilm Fuji FinePix A340 4MP Digital Camera	🅿	$176.99	⫫Buy It Now Nov-27 13:25

. . . and select the option "Show comparison check boxes," then click Save.

Now you see a row of check boxes to the left of each item's Gallery image.

These check boxes allow us to mark and save items in which we are interested so that we can line them up and compare them.

I browse through the five pages of items and select nine cameras by checking their boxes. Each one may be a good candidate for consideration. Then I scroll down to the bottom of the page and click the button Compare.

This lines up all my selected listings so that I can more easily compare for item features, prices, shipping options, and individual sellers (based on their feedback numbers and percentage of positive comments).

Compare Items

| Watch All | Remove All | | Sort by: | Order Selected: recent first ▼ |

Item	Remove Item	Remove Item	Remove Item	Remove Item
	Nikon Coolpix 4300 Digital Camera Cameras+Warranty NEW	SONY CYBERSHOT DSC-P73 DIGITAL CAMERA + $430 IN EXTRAS	OLYMPUS C-765 C765 4MP DIGITAL CAMERA + EXTRAS! NEW!	NEW CANON ELPH SD10 IUXS I 4MP 288MB 5 Y WTY FREE SHIP
	[Buy It Now] Email to a friend | Watch this Item	[Bid Now!] [Buy It Now] Email to a friend | Watch this Item	[Buy It Now] Email to a friend | Watch this Item	[Bid Now!] [Buy It Now] Email to a friend | Watch this Item
Time Left	8 days 5 hours	5 days 5 hours	3 days 5 hours	2 days 19 hours
Bids		0 bids	Purchases	0 bids
Seller	ebizlinks (108 ★) 100% Positive	panwebi-auctions (15869 ✈) 99.0% Positive me ⚡Power Seller	myvbuy (4359 ★) 95.5% Positive me	electronet (4940 ★) 98.9% Positive ⚡Power Seller
Price	US $249.00 ⇌Buy It Now	US $319.99 US $329.99 ⇌Buy It Now	US $314.99 ⇌Buy It Now	US $289.99 US $299.99 ⇌Buy It Now
Shipping	US $16.00 (within United States) (Including insurance)	US $29.99 (within United States) (Plus optional insurance)	US $29.99 (within United States) (Including insurance)	US $9.00 (within United States)
Ships From	United States	United States	United States	United States
Payment Methods		Money order/Cashiers check	Money order/Cashiers check, Credit card (Visa/MasterCard, American Express, Discover), See item description for payment methods accepted	

Digital Cameras

Digital Camera Type	Point & Shoot	Point & Shoot	Point & Shoot	Point & Shoot
Digital Camera Brand	Nikon	Sony	Olympus	Canon
Product Line	Nikon Coolpix	--	Olympus CAMEDIA C	--
Model	4300	--	765 Ultra Zoom	--
Resolution	4 megapixels	4.1 megapixels	4 megapixels	4 megapixels
Manufacturer Part Number	4300	--	C-765	
Bundled Kits	--	Camera Bag, Extra Memory, Lens Cleaning Kit, Memory Reader, Tripod	Tripod, Lens Cleaning Kit, Camera Bag	
Optical Zoom	3x	3x	10x	--
Digital Zoom	4x	--	4x	--
Manufacturer Warranty	--	Yes	Yes	--
Flash Type	Built-in flash	--	Pop-up flash	--
Memory Card Format	CompactFlash Card	--	XD-Picture Card	--
Battery Type	1 x camera battery - rechargeable - lithium ion - 650 mAh	--	1 x camera battery - rechargeable - lithium ion	--
Condition	New, Never Opened	New, Never Opened	New, Never Opened	New, Never Opened
	Remove Item	Remove Item	Remove Item	Remove Item

| Watch All | Remove All |

I can also whittle down the list by removing items. After comparing prices, shipping, packages, and sellers, I decide on this camera:

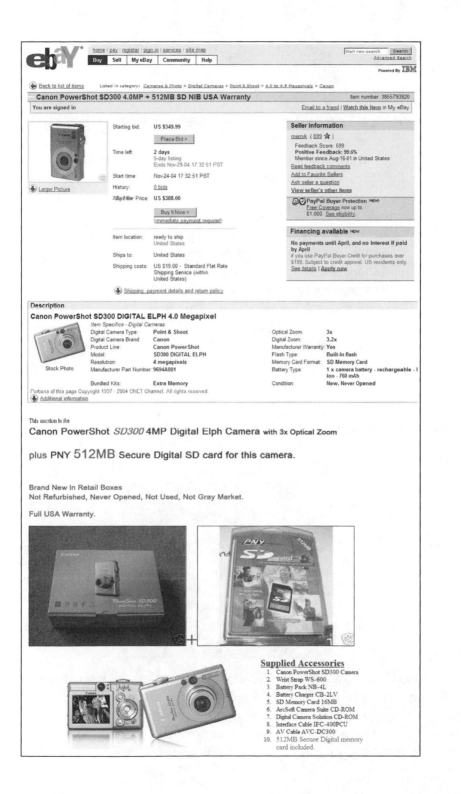

I like that the shipping cost is less than $20 and that the seller is including a 512MB SD memory card.

Before You Bid or Buy—a Safe Trading Checklist

We still need to learn a few things about the listing and the seller before we actually commit to bidding on or buying this camera. Enter the Safe Trading Checklist:

Check the seller's Feedback.
Read the Item Description page thoroughly.
Examine the photos.
Read and understand the seller's TOS (Terms of Service).
Questions? Ask the seller *before* bidding or buying.

Eventually, this simple checklist should become second nature, but till then, keep it handy whenever you are shopping on eBay. Let's apply the checklist to our digital camera listing.

CHECK THE SELLER'S FEEDBACK

Start off by scanning the box "Seller information":

Seller information

memvk (699 ☆)

Feedback Score: 699
Positive Feedback: 99.6%
Member since Aug-16-01 in United States

Read feedback comments
Add to Favorite Sellers
Ask seller a question
View seller's other items

PayPal Buyer Protection NEW!
Free Coverage now up to
$1,000. See eligibility.

This box tells us a lot about the seller. He has a feedback score of 699. That's 699 unique positive comments received from other eBay members since he started on eBay, *minus* any and all unique negative comments (more on feedback scoring later). His positive feedback rating is 99.6 percent, which is extremely good. He registered on eBay in August 2001, a long time in eBay terms. All together, these feedback statistics are reassuring, but we can (and should) go deeper by reading the seller's complete Feedback Profile.

To read a seller's Feedback Profile, click either the number in parentheses next to the seller's User ID or the link "Read feedback comments."

Make this a habit. Before you do anything, before you read through the item description or start figuring how much you are willing to spend, and for heaven's sake, *before* you bid or buy, always check the seller's Feedback Profile first.

This seller has excellent feedback. NOTE! Most high-volume sellers receive the occasional negative feedback. It's important to take the negatives in context and as a percentage of the seller's total. This seller has less than one percent negative to positive—an excellent ratio indeed!

The purple star next to the feedback number indicates that this seller has a feedback score between 500 and 1,000. There are different colors and types of stars for different levels of feedback. A change of star status is a major milestone for every eBay member, buyer and seller alike.

Yellow star = 10 to 49 points
Blue star = 50 to 99 points
Turquoise star = 100 to 499 points
Purple star = 500 to 999 points
Red star = 1,000 to 4,999 points
Green star = 5,000 to 9,999 points
Yellow shooting star = 10,000 to 24,999 points
Turquoise shooting star = 25,000 to 49,999 points
Purple shooting star = 50,000 to 99,999 points
Red shooting star = 100,000 or higher

In addition to feedback, you should view the seller's About Me page, if he has created one. Many (but sadly, not all) sellers have an About Me page. (All sellers should!) If a member has created an About Me page, a little "me" icon will appear to the right of his feedback number:

Just click the Me icon to view that seller's About Me page.

You can learn a lot about sellers by what they tell you on their About Me page. Some sellers use their About Me page to advertise their standard payment, shipping, packing, and return policies.

READ THE ITEM DESCRIPTION PAGE THOROUGHLY

Start at the top. For auction format listings, look for the amount shown as the value for Starting or "Current bid." The starting bid shows the amount needed to start the bidding. The first bidder must enter this amount or more to start the auction. Once a bid has been submitted, the indication changes to "Current bid."

152

It changes each time a bidder submits a bid (with only one exception: A bidder cannot raise his own bid by rebidding). Any bid amount you are considering as your bid—for an item that has already received one or more bids—must be greater than the amount shown for "Current bid."

More about bidding later.

Is There a Reserve?

Our seller is not specifying a reserve for our item of interest, but many sellers will place a reserve price on their item. The optional reserve price is the amount below which the item will not be sold. The reserve price is always private—only the seller knows the reserve price for his or her listing.

You can always tell if a listing has a reserve price by the indication next to the "Current bid" amount, which will state either "Reserve not met" or "Reserve met." Here is one from a different listing:

This item's reserve has not yet been met. If the item were to close at this point, there would be "no sale"—that is, the seller is not obliged to sell the item and the high bidder has no claim on the item.

This reserve has been met. The item will end with a high bidder. The seller is obliged to sell to the high bidder at the end of this listing.

Two Important Features of Reserve Price Listings!

1. If, in a reserve listing, the bidder bids an amount lower than the reserve, the amount for "Current bid" will increase accordingly, but the reserve indication will remain "Reserve not met."
2. If a bidder should bid an amount equal to or greater than the reserve amount, the amount for "Current bid" will rise, and the indication next to the amount will change to "Reserve met."

Q. Griff, why would a seller use a reserve? Why doesn't the seller just start the bidding at the reserve amount?

A. Because in most cases where the first bid amount is equal to or near the market value of the item, few people will actually bid.

It's all about psychology.

For example, a seller has a recognizable collectible that she will not consider selling for less than $100, and the item has a high-end book or market value of $125. The seller offers the collectible for bid at eBay without a reserve, but with a starting bid of $100. Potential buyers for the item will be lukewarm at best about bidding on the item since there is so little room for "play." Sure, the item is $25 lower than high market, but the smaller the margin for a possible bargain, the less likely any bidder is to jump in and bid.

If, however, the same seller offers the collectible item with a starting bid of $1 and a reserve of $100, potential buyers are more likely to bid because the possibility of a bargain is much greater; that is, at least the *appearance* of a possible bargain is greater. Remember, no one but the seller knows the reserve amount. At a starting bid of $1, someone is more inclined to start the bidding.

Eventually, a second bidder will enter the fray, and then something very interesting happens that I call "ownership delusion." Once a person has the high bid on an item, emotionally they immediately begin to consider the item "theirs"—which is truly a delusion since the seller is the actual owner of the item until the auction ends.

The strength of this "ownership delusion" is directly proportional to the bidder's desire to own the item, and this desire increases dramatically once a new bidder outbids a current bidder. The previous high bidder irrationally feels as though he or she has been robbed. The first and strongest instinct of those who believe they have been robbed is to retrieve the item, in this case, by rebidding until they are once again the high bidder.

This often starts a back-and-forth of "It's mine!" . . . "No . . . it's *mine*!" "Excuse me, I believe this is *my* item you are attempting to win." "Yours? *Au contraire,* the item is most definitely *mine*!" "What? Who do you think you are?" With both parties bidding and rebidding, in the heat of battle the reserve price is met and is even surpassed, with one person happily winning the item—sometimes for much more than she would have dreamed of paying if the same item were offered to her for direct sale.

The auction becomes much more than just a fun shopping format. It becomes a life-and-death struggle between the champion and the vanquished, and nobody wants to be the vanquished.

Actually, the real champion in a case like this is the seller, who is more than pleased to watch two bidders fight for the honor of overpaying for an item.

Let's get back to the checklist.

Is There a Buy It Now Option?

Some listings will have two ways for a bidder to win the item. The old standard way is to bid for it and hope for the best. A second format was introduced in 1999 that allows a potential bidder to skip the bidding and purchase the item directly for a price specified by the seller. This format at eBay is called Buy It Now.

If the seller has provided potential buyers with the Buy It Now option, a Buy It Now icon and button will appear under History. Next to the icon will be the price:

In this example, the seller has provided a Buy It Now price of $388. (See page 191 for how to purchase an item using Buy It Now.)

The Buy It Now option will immediately disappear if a buyer places any bid less than the stated Buy It Now price, in this example, $388. (A bid of $388 or higher will close the auction with a final price of $388.)

If a buyer opts to pay a Buy It Now price, the listing will immediately close and show the following:

If a seller has opted to have a Buy It Now price and a Reserve Price for the listing, the text will state:

In this instance, the Buy It Now option will remain in place, even if bidding starts, as long as the bidding is below the seller's reserve price.

In some cases, the Buy It Now price might be equal to or lower than the maximum bid amount you are willing to pay for the item. In that case, it might be smart to simply Buy It Now!

How Many Items Is the Seller Offering in This Listing?

If the seller is offering more than one of the item, a Quantity field will show the number of items available. If there is no indication of quantity, then the seller is offering only one lot. Note that "one lot" can mean one piece or a lot of two or more pieces all sold together.

If a quantity is displayed, the format is no longer the standard eBay proxy auction format but is instead either a Multiple Item Listing (aka Dutch Auction) or a straight, no-auction-format-at-all Fixed Price Listing.

The procedures for each auction format are different. We discuss them in detail later in this chapter.

How Much Time Is Left?

You can determine when the item closes by looking for the "Time left" field. Under "Time left" one finds the duration of the listing and the actual closing date and time (displayed as Ends).

The time and date in the "Start time" field show the exact date and time (PST) the listing went "live."

The History field shows the actual number of bids placed on this item. It does not necessarily show the actual number of bidders, since a bidder may bid more than once. If there has been at least one bid, the number will display as a link. Click the link to view the item's bid history page.

300 4.0MP + 512MB SD NIB USA W:	
Starting bid:	US $349.99
	Place Bid >
Time left:	**1 day 19 hours** 5-day listing Ends Nov-29-04 17:32:51 PST
Start time:	Nov-24-04 17:32:51 PST
History:	0 bids
=Buy It Now Price:	US $388.00
	Buy It Now > (immediate payment required)

The "High bidder" field displays the User ID of the current high bidder.

Current bid:	US $2,025.00
	Place Bid >
Time left:	**5 days 12 hours** 7-day listing Ends Dec-03-04 11:00:00 PST
Start time:	Nov-26-04 11:00:00 PST
History:	3 bids (US $1,999.00 starting bid)
High bidder:	softoutlet355 (48 ☆)
Item location:	New York United States
Featured Plus! Listing	
Ships to:	United States, Canada
Shipping costs:	US $40.00 - Standard Flat Rate Shipping Service (within United States)
⬇ Shipping, payment details and return policy	

The "Item location" field for the seller can be found directly under the High bidder field.

Current bid:	**US $2,025.00**
	Place Bid >
Time left:	**5 days 12 hours** 7-day listing Ends Dec-03-04 11:00:00 PST
Start time:	Nov-26-04 11:00:00 PST
History:	3 bids (US $1,999.00 starting bid)
High bidder:	softoutlet355 (48 ☆)
Item location:	New York United States
Featured Plus! Listing	
Ships to:	United States, Canada
Shipping costs:	US $40.00 - Standard Flat Rate Shipping Service (within United States)
	⬇ Shipping, payment details and return policy

The next field will show if the seller has added an upgrade—Featured Plus! or Home Page Featured—for the item. These upgrades place a copy of the item title in highly visible locations on the site.

Current bid:	**US $2,025.00**
	Place Bid >
Time left:	**5 days 12 hours** 7-day listing Ends Dec-03-04 11:00:00 PST
Start time:	Nov-26-04 11:00:00 PST
History:	3 bids (US $1,999.00 starting bid)
High bidder:	softoutlet355 (48 ☆)
Item location:	New York United States
Featured Plus! Listing	
Ships to:	United States, Canada
Shipping costs:	US $40.00 - Standard Flat Rate Shipping Service (within United States)
	⬇ Shipping, payment details and return policy

The "Ships to" field lets buyers know the countries to which the seller will ship.

Current bid:	US $2,025.00
	Place Bid >
Time left:	**5 days 12 hours**
	7-day listing
	Ends Dec-03-04 11:00:00 PST
Start time:	Nov-26-04 11:00:00 PST
History:	3 bids (US $1,999.00 starting bid)
High bidder:	softoutlet355 (48 ☆)
Item location:	New York
	United States
Featured Plus! Listing	
Ships to:	United States, Canada
Shipping costs:	US $40.00 - Standard Flat Rate
	Shipping Service (within
	United States)
	⊕ Shipping, payment details and return policy

The "Shipping costs" field displays the seller's choice for carrier and shipping price if the price is based on a flat rate for all buyers.

Current bid:	US $2,025.00
	Place Bid >
Time left:	**5 days 12 hours**
	7-day listing
	Ends Dec-03-04 11:00:00 PST
Start time:	Nov-26-04 11:00:00 PST
History:	3 bids (US $1,999.00 starting bid)
High bidder:	softoutlet355 (48 ☆)
Item location:	New York
	United States
Featured Plus! Listing	
Ships to:	United States, Canada
Shipping costs:	US $40.00 - Standard Flat Rate
	Shipping Service (within
	United States)
	⊕ Shipping, payment details and return policy

If the seller is using the eBay Shipping Calculator, the text will indicate that the buyer should utilize the zip code field on the Item Description page for an exact shipping price to the buyer's location.

The "Seller information" box provides critical seller statistics such as User ID, seller status, and feedback (score and percentage). Besides feedback, the box will indicate whether the seller accepts PayPal and if she provides PayPal Buyer Protection.

Directly under the seller's User ID are three links. The most important of the three is "Ask seller a question." Click this link to open a Web e-mail form.

You can use this form to communicate directly with the seller.

That covers the top section of the Item Description page. Let's read the actual (seller supplied) description.

Reading an Item Description

While I was with eBay Customer Support, I learned the two biggest mistakes a bidder can make:

1. Not reading a seller's feedback profile before bidding
2. Not reading carefully the seller's item description before bidding

We showed you how to avoid mistake number 1 in the section before this one. Let's dive into how to avoid mistake number 2.

The seller supplies all of the text found between the Description bar and the Payment Options/Payment Instructions bars. You simply *must* make a habit of carefully and thoroughly reading everything the seller has provided in the way of a description, payment options, shipping and handling charges, return policies, any bidder restrictions, etc.

If you have questions or concerns about the item or the seller's policies, you must e-mail the seller for a clarification before you bid. Hold off bidding on or buying an item until the seller has answered your questions to your satisfaction. You can always place the item in your "My eBay" Watch list for access later once the seller has answered your questions and concerns to your satisfaction.

Here is the seller's description for the item on which we plan on submitting a bid.

Description

Canon PowerShot SD300 DIGITAL ELPH 4.0 Megapixel

Item Specifics - Digital Cameras

Digital Camera Type:	**Point & Shoot**	Optical Zoom:	**3x**
Digital Camera Brand:	**Canon**	Digital Zoom:	**3.2x**
Product Line:	**Canon PowerShot**	Manufacturer Warranty:	**Yes**
Model:	**SD300 DIGITAL ELPH**	Flash Type:	**Built-in flash**
Resolution:	**4 megapixels**	Memory Card Format:	**SD Memory Card**
Manufacturer Part Number: 9694A001		Battery Type:	**1 x camera battery - rechargeable - ion - 760 mAh**
Bundled Kits:	**Extra Memory**	Condition:	**New, Never Opened**

Stock Photo

Portions of this page Copyright 1997 - 2004 CNET Channel. All rights reserved.

Additional information

This auction is for

Canon PowerShot *SD300* 4MP Digital Elph Camera with 3x Optical Zoom

plus PNY 512MB Secure Digital SD card for this camera.

Brand New In Retail Boxes
Not Refurbished, Never Opened, Not Used, Not Gray Market.

Full USA Warranty.

Supplied Accessories
1. Canon PowerShot SD300 Camera
2. Wrist Strap WS-600
3. Battery Pack NB-4L
4. Battery Charger CB-2LV
5. SD Memory Card 16MB
6. ArcSoft Camera Suite CD-ROM
7. Digital Camera Solution CD-ROM
8. Interface Cable IFC-400PCU
9. AV Cable AVC-DC300
10. 512MB Secure Digital memory card included.

UPC on the box was carefully removed for rebate purpose.

4.0 Mega Pixels   3.0x Optical Zoom   3.6x Digital Zoom   11x Combined Zoom

Exif Print   DIRECT PRINT   PictBridge   UA Lens   2.0 in LCD

PowerShot SD300
DIGITAL ELPH

4.0 MEGA PIXELS   DiGIC II   3x ZOOM LENS

164

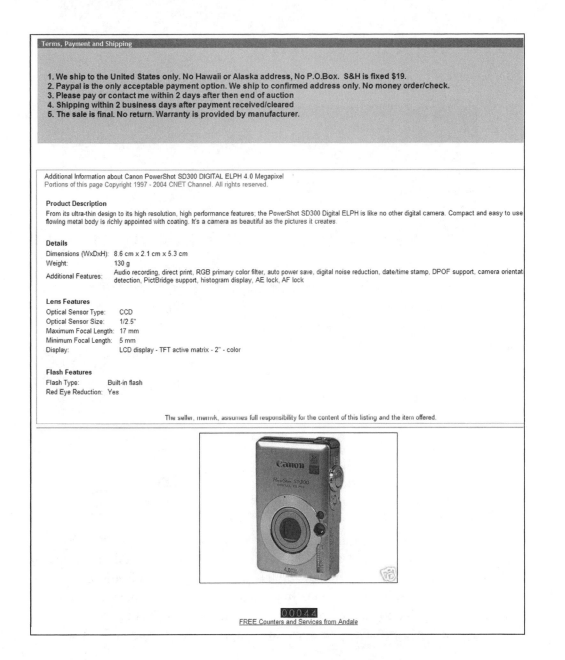

Terms, Payment and Shipping

1. We ship to the United States only. No Hawaii or Alaska address, No P.O.Box. S&H is fixed $19.
2. Paypal is the only acceptable payment option. We ship to confirmed address only. No money order/check.
3. Please pay or contact me within 2 days after then end of auction
4. Shipping within 2 business days after payment received/cleared
5. The sale is final. No return. Warranty is provided by manufacturer.

Additional Information about Canon PowerShot SD300 DIGITAL ELPH 4.0 Megapixel

Product Description

From its ultra-thin design to its high resolution, high performance features; the PowerShot SD300 Digital ELPH is like no other digital camera. Compact and easy to use
flowing metal body is richly appointed with coating. It's a camera as beautiful as the pictures it creates.

Details

Dimensions (WxDxH):	8.6 cm x 2.1 cm x 5.3 cm
Weight:	130 g
Additional Features:	Audio recording, direct print, RGB primary color filter, auto power save, digital noise reduction, date/time stamp, DPOF support, camera orientat detection, PictBridge support, histogram display, AE lock, AF lock

Lens Features

Optical Sensor Type:	CCD
Optical Sensor Size:	1/2.5"
Maximum Focal Length:	17 mm
Minimum Focal Length:	5 mm
Display:	LCD display - TFT active matrix - 2" - color

Flash Features

Flash Type:	Built-in flash
Red Eye Reduction:	Yes

The seller, memvk, assumes full responsibility for the content of this listing and the item offered.

00044
FREE Counters and Services from Andale

The description of the actual item accurately describes the item and, along with the picture the seller provided, provides a sufficient accounting of the item's condition.

✔ EXAMINE THE ITEM PICTURES

This seller has provided several good photos of both the item and the extras:

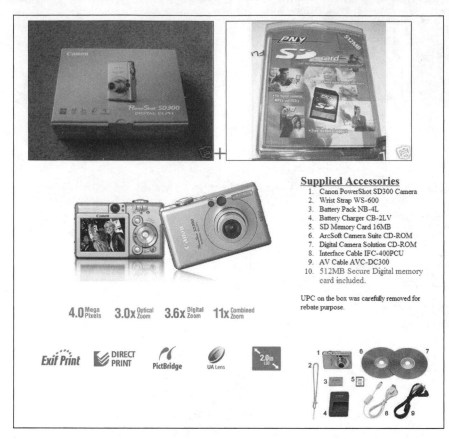

Are the pictures of the item an adequate representation?

Most sellers understand the importance of clear, sharp, well-lit photos of their items. If the item you are viewing has less-than-perfect photos, e-mail the seller and ask him or her for some better shots (and please do mention this book as an excellent guide for taking perfect eBay item pictures. Thank you).

This seller's pictures are clear, focused, and show the item in various aspects.

✔ ARE THERE VIEWS OF THE ITEM THAT YOU WOULD LIKE TO SEE?

Most sellers will provide photos of all aspects of an item. Sometimes they don't. For example, I might like to see a top view of this camera.

If there is a view that you need to see before you make your bid, again, e-mail the seller and ask for a photo of that particular view. I once found a beautiful chest of drawers on eBay. The seller provided excellent pictures of the chest including the back, underside, top, and bottom. However, I needed to see a photo of the drawer sides, specifically the method used to join the sides of the drawer to the drawer front, to determine if the chest was handmade or machine-made. I e-mailed the seller asking if he could send a photo of the drawer sides, and he happily agreed. The photos proved that the chest was indeed handmade, and I bid accordingly. In the end, I didn't win the chest. I was sniped! (Outbid in the final minutes.)

✔ **CHECK THE SELLER'S PAYMENT AND SHIPPING OPTIONS AND POLICIES (TOS—TERMS OF SERVICE)**

This seller has provided a comprehensive set of shipping and handling terms.

> **Terms, Payment and Shipping**
>
> 1. We ship to the United States only. No Hawaii or Alaska address, No P.O.Box. S&H is fixed $19.
> 2. Paypal is the only acceptable payment option. We ship to confirmed address only. No money order/check.
> 3. Please pay or contact me within 2 days after then end of auction
> 4. Shipping within 2 business days after payment received/cleared
> 5. The sale is final. No return. Warranty is provided by manufacturer.

What Type of Payment Does the Seller Accept?

There are several popular ways to pay for an eBay item:

> PayPal
> Credit cards
> Wire transfer/electronic check
> Money orders (domestic and international)
> Checks (personal and cashier or bank)
> Cash

Our seller only accepts PayPal, a practice that more and more sellers are now adopting. Sellers are usually clear about which of the above they accept. The first place to look for a seller's payment options is in the top section of the listing page as shown above. But there should also be some indication inside the item description.

If the seller has not provided details about accepted payment methods, remember to ask for details, *before you bid!* (Use the "ask the seller a question" e-mail feature as described above.)

Credit Cards

Most eBay sellers accept credit cards for payment through PayPal (more on Pay-Pal in the next chapter). They may also provide credit card payment options through their own, non-PayPal merchant account.

Using PayPal is the quickest and safest way to pay for an eBay item. If the seller is not offering the PayPal option but does offer to accept credit cards through their own merchant account, check with your credit card issuer before you bid and obtain details regarding the buyer protection your card issuer provides.

Electronic Check

Most online payment services like PayPal will provide secure electronic bank transfer as a buyer payment option. Online payment services also will back up wire transfers and electronic checks for their full amount.

Money Orders

Most (but not all) eBay sellers will accept a money order for payment. Again, don't assume. If the seller doesn't state his terms, ask first before bidding.

Paying with a money order is not as quick as with a credit card, nor does a money order offer the buyer the same protection as a credit card.

Checks

Besides money orders, many (but not all!) sellers will also accept a check as payment for an eBay item. Sellers who accept checks usually specify a "waiting period" of three or more days in their item description before they will ship the item. This is to allow ample time for the check to clear their account.

Cash

Some sellers will accept cash for payment.

Never send cash through the mail.

eBay doesn't prevent sellers from stating "cash" as a payment option since in some situations cash might be acceptable (for example, if you arrange with the seller to pay for an item in person). However, whenever you pay cash for an item in person, make sure the seller hands you a detailed and signed receipt at the time of the transfer of goods and money. If you are purchasing a vehicle, demand the seller provide a legal and clear title along with the receipt and ask for a license or passport (to check the face with the name on the title).

Does the Seller Offer Escrow?

Online escrow is a valuable third-party service to help protect both buyer and seller. It is a good security solution for new sellers with little or no feedback history upon which to base an assessment of that seller's honesty. In addition, many buyers of big-ticket items are more comfortable bidding or buying if the seller provides online escrow as an option.

Our seller does not indicate escrow as an option. Not surprising. The seller has extremely good feedback, a long history with eBay, and is providing the option to pay with PayPal, which provides the buyer with up to $1,000 in coverage should something go awry with the transaction.

If a seller offers escrow, you will find the indication at the top of the item page as well as sometimes within the seller's item description.

eBay recommends only one online escrow service: *www.escrow.com.*

First, the buyer and seller agree to the terms of the escrow transaction. This may include a number of days for the buyer to inspect the item, shipping information, and who pays the escrow fee.

Then the buyer sends payment to escrow.com, which verifies and processes the payment. Once the payment has been verified (cleared), escrow.com authorizes the seller to ship the merchandise to the buyer.

Once the buyer receives the item, he has the previously agreed-upon number of days to inspect and accept the item. Once he informs escrow.com that he accepts the item, escrow.com pays the seller.

Online escrow can offer great peace of mind for certain types of eBay transactions. If you are looking at possibly buying a big-ticket item such as an expensive car, piece of jewelry, or work of art, and the seller for the item has little or no feedback, then you may want to ask her if she would consider using online escrow should you be the high bidder or buyer when the listing closes. Always ask the seller about using escrow *before* you bid!

Of course, many newer eBay sellers, realizing that their lack of a feedback history at eBay may give pause to otherwise eager potential bidders or buyers, will offer the escrow option in their listing description, but note: eBay sellers are not required to accept escrow! It is a seller choice. If a seller does not offer it explicitly, contact the seller to inquire about possible escrow as a payment option *before you bid.*

Sellers who offer escrow services will have various terms for sharing or not sharing the costs of using an online escrow service. Again, make sure you understand who is bearing what costs for using escrow *before you bid!*

Does the Seller Provide a Return or Refund Policy?

Most anyone who sells online realizes that a buyer cannot know if she is truly happy with an item until that item is actually in her hands. No one wants to be stuck with an item she doesn't like.

Most, but not all, sellers understand this and will offer a reasonable return and refund policy. Make sure to check for a seller's return policy *before you bid*. If the seller has not provided a return policy, send him an e-mail inquiry.

The best return policy is one that offers you your full money back for any reason whatsoever, no questions asked, no return fees. The worst return policy is none at all. A seller will usually indicate "no returns" by stating that the item is sold "as is." Bid if you must on such an item, but always remember "Caveat emptor!" (Latin for "Buyer beware!") You bid at your own risk!

The majority of sellers offer something in between. Some sellers will accept returns but will charge you a fee for doing so. Others restrict returns to a specific time, such as three days upon receipt. Make sure you fully understand the seller's return policy before you submit your bid.

Our seller indicates that all sales are final. I am usually not comfortable with such a policy. However, I have done ample research about the camera, the seller, and the current price and feel confident that the camera is brand-new. In addition, the seller indicates that the manufacturer provides a warranty. I double-checked with the manufacturer, and indeed this is true.

Does the Seller Ship Internationally?

Although the eBay community of buyers and sellers extends around the globe, some eBay sellers (mostly based on the U.S. site) will not ship items outside of the United States. These sellers will usually state this fact clearly within their terms. Our seller states right off that he will only ship to the continental United States and will not ship to P.O. boxes.

If you are an eBay buyer based outside of the United States, make sure that the item's seller is agreeable to shipping internationally *before you bid*.

Another option for non-U.S. buyers is to establish a contact within the United States (a friend or family member) who will accept delivery of eBay items on your behalf.

Other Seller Terms of Service

Does the Seller Have Special Requirements for Buyers?

For example, some sellers prohibit bidding by eBay members who have a certain number of negative comments in their feedback profile or hidden feedback. (Users can opt to hide all their feedback comments. Their feedback number will still display. Not recommended.)

Sellers are free to employ this type of restriction based on feedback.

Does the Seller Have Specific Time Limits for Contact and for Receiving Payments?

eBay sellers are usually quite specific about how long they will wait for contact and payment from you, the buyer. Read these specifications *before you bid!*

STILL HAVE QUESTIONS? ASK THE SELLER!

If you go through the checklist and you still have questions about the item or the seller's terms, ask the seller *before you bid*.

ONLINE PAYMENTS—THE SAFEST WAY TO BUY ON EBAY

The best way to ensure your security as an eBay buyer is to give preference to items for which the seller accepts online payments through PayPal or some other similar payment service.

During the first few years of Internet commerce, many folks had reservations about using their credit cards online. They feared that enterprising thieves would break into an online transmission to hijack the credit card information for their own use.

Today, most e-commerce Web sites employ a special form of data transmission for sensitive data such as credit card numbers. This special form is called Secure Socket Layer or SSL. SSL uses an extremely secure type of data encryption that makes it virtually impossible for anyone to break into an SSL transmission of data.

Without getting extremely technical about how SSL works, all you need to know about any e-commerce Web site's security is that they provide SSL for you. How do you tell if a Web site is using SSL?

First, check the Web site's own text, especially on the page or pages where you are asked to enter your credit card information. If they are using SSL, they will state the fact clearly on this page for your peace of mind.

Second, check your Web browser's status bar (the little bar along the bottom of the Web browser) and Address window (where the current Web page's URL or address is displayed). If the page you are viewing is employing SSL technology, a little yellow padlock will show on the far-right-hand side of the browser status bar.

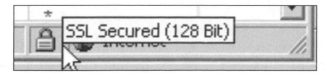

Another way to determine if the page you are viewing is using SSL technology is to look at the URL or address for the page. The URL for the page can be found in the little window on the top of your Web browser marked Address or Location. URLs usually start with "http://www . . ." The URL for a SSL page will start with "https:// . . ."

We've Found It . . . We've Checked It Out . . . Let's Buy it!

We've gone through our Safe Trading Checklist and are now ready to commit. We have two options. We can bid for the camera or buy it outright with Buy It Now.

Let's cover basic bidding first.

BIDDING

Two auction formats are in use at eBay: the Proxy format and the Multiple Item Listing (formerly known as the Dutch Auction). First, Proxy Bidding.

eBay's Proxy Bidding System

The majority of items listed on eBay in an auction format (as opposed to those listed exclusively with the fixed price Buy It Now format) are using the default eBay Proxy Bidding system.

The Proxy Bidding system is not at all complicated. To begin, let's use a real-life auction example to illustrate the concept of proxy bidding in the off-line world.

What Are Friends For? (If Not to Act as Proxies?)

You and I are old friends who have met at an off-line auction. Some dear old richer-than-King-Tut grandma has passed away, and her loving family, unable to agree on how to split up her worldly goods, have decided to call in a local auctioneer to sell it all—money being easier to split than worldly goods. (Too bad none of the heirs uses eBay or bought this book—they could have sold it all online!)

There's a wonderful old Oriental rug at the auction that you desperately want for your living room, but the auctioneer isn't putting it up for bid until noon, and you have to leave at 11:45 A.M. to meet a client, fifteen minutes away. (By the way, you're a real estate agent.)

Oh, what to do! You can't leave your client hanging, but you simply *must* have this rug!

Thinking quickly, you lean over and ask in a whisper if I might be willing to bid for you in your absence.

"Why, dear old friend, of course I would! How much are you willing to spend?" I whisper back.

You look around quickly to see if anyone is listening. People are. You think fast.

"I will write it down so no one hears it."

You rummage in your bag for a slip of paper and pen, find them, and, using your thigh as a desk, scribble a figure. You then hand the slip of paper to me. I read, *Bid $1,000 and not a single penny more. Destroy this immediately!*

I silently mouth, "No problem. Consider it done!"

I have just agreed to act as your "proxy"; that is, I will bid for you in your absence.

At noon, the auctioneer puts up the rug as promised. He asks for an opening bid of $100. Someone else starts the bidding. The auctioneer accepts the bid of $100 and asks for a bid of $125—$25 being his choice of increment. Your best friend and proxy, me, springs into action. I raise my hand and enter the fray with a bid of $125.

Thus it begins. The auctioneer calls out for a bid of $150, and sure enough, another bidder bids. I rebid $175. The bidder bids again, $200. I rebid $250. And so on it goes back and forth between us as we battle it out to see who will pay the most. Suddenly, the bidding stalls out at $550. The other bidder has reached her limit! The auctioneer roars, "I have five hundred fifty. Do I hear six hundred? Six hundred? Going, going . . . gone! Sold to the handsome man in the back row for five hundred fifty dollars!"

You, my dear old friend, arrive back at the auction at twelve thirty, and I rush up to meet you to share the good news.

"I got it for five hundred fifty dollars!"

You are deliriously happy. You have sold a house and your dear old friend, me, has successfully acted as your proxy and nabbed you the prize you sought.

You bear-hug me with joy. You were willing to pay $1,000 but your plucky proxy, me, got it for you for only $550. (I don't charge a percentage. After all, we *are* dear old friends.)

Bidding at eBay is nearly identical to our example above, except instead of me acting as your proxy, eBay does.

Let's use a real eBay listing to illustrate the process, step by step. Here is an interesting Oriental rug I found on eBay. The starting bid is $.99. There are no bids.

Rare Vegetable Dye Afghan Chobi Rug 5x4		Item number: 3765774404
You are signed in		Email to a friend | **Watch this item** in My eBay

				Seller information
		Starting bid:	US $0.99	pakobelrugs (6764 ☆)
			Place Bid >	**Power Seller**
		Time left:	**4 days 23 hours** 5-day listing Ends Dec-03-04 16:42:00 PST	Feedback Score: 6764 **Positive Feedback: 99.4%** Member since Jun-04-02 in United States
⬇ Go to larger picture		Start time:	Nov-28-04 16:42:00 PST	Read feedback comments Add to Favorite Sellers
		History:	0 bids	Ask seller a question View seller's other items
		Item location:	Rugs At Lowest Prices United States	**PayPal Buyer Protection** NEW!
		Ships to:	Worldwide	Free Coverage now up to $1,000. See eligibility.
		Shipping costs:	US $25.00 - Standard Flat Rate Shipping Service (within United States)	

We've read the Title and Description sections, viewed the pictures, and made sure we read the seller's terms of service. Now we have to settle on the maximum price we are willing to pay.

After due consideration, I decide we are willing to pay up to $25 *and not a penny more.*

I could bid the $.99 starting bid amount and then check every few minutes to see if a new bidder has joined the auction so I can outbid them, or I could simply submit a proxy bid, much like you did at the real live estate auction, but instead of me acting as your proxy, the eBay system will do so. You only need to decide on a maximum amount you will pay for the item (just like in the live auction), and once you have, you then submit it as a bid. The eBay system will act as I did for you at the live auction by rebidding every time some one outbids you up to the exact amount you submit as your bid (your "proxy" bid). If no one bids over the amount of your proxy, you win the item for the current high bid. If someone bids more than your proxy, you lose, or better put, don't have to shell out any dough.

I scroll down to the bottom of the Item Description page to the section "Ready to bid?" I type my absolute maximum bid amount, $25, in the box "Your maximum bid."

Ready to bid?

Rare Vegetable Dye Afghan Chobi Rug 5x4

Starting bid: US $0.99

Your maximum bid: US $ [25]   (Enter US $0.99 **or more**)

[Place Bid >]   You will confirm in the next step.

eBay automatically bids on your behalf **up to** your maximum bid.
Learn about bidding.

Then I click the Place Bid button to go to the "Review and Confirm Bid" page.

Review and Confirm Bid

Hello uncle_griff! (Not you?)

Item title: Rare Vegetable Dye Afghan Chobi Rug 5x4
Your maximum bid: **US $25.00**
Sales tax: 7.000% (only in FL)

Shipping and handling: US $25.00 - Standard Flat Rate Shipping Service (within United States)
Shipping insurance: US $5.00 (Optional)
Payment methods: PayPal, Personal check, Money order/Cashiers check,
                      Visa/MasterCard, American Express, Other - See Payment Instructions

By clicking on the button below, you commit to buy this item from the seller if you're the winning bidder.

[Confirm Bid]

You are agreeing to a contract -- You will enter into a legally binding contract to purchase the item from the seller if you're the winning bidder. You are responsible for reading the full item listing, including the seller's instructions and accepted payment methods. Seller assumes all responsibility for listing this item.

Reviewing this information, we see not only my maximum bid but also shipping and handling (if provided by the seller), as well as sales tax of seven percent for all buyers located in Florida (the seller's home state).

Since there are no previous bidders, we know what the current bid will be once I submit my bid of $25. It will be $.99. And indeed, the next screen shows my Bid Confirmation:

Bid Confirmation   Item number: 3765774404

Hello uncle_griff! (Not you?)   Email to a friend | This item is being tracked in My eBay

✔ **You are the current high bidder**

Important: Another user may still outbid you, so check this item again before it ends. eBay will send you an email if you're outbid.

How do you keep track of this item? Use My eBay.

How does bidding work? See example.

Title: Rare Vegetable Dye Afghan Chobi Rug 5x4

Time left:	4 days 23 hours
Current bid:	US $0.99
Your maximum bid:	US $25.00

The current bid shows as $.99. Why not my maximum of $25? Since I am the first bidder, there are no bids beneath my bid to boost it up toward or to the maximum amount, $25. In addition, I cannot bid against myself and raise the current bid, thus even though I submit a bid of $25, the current bid will show me as the high bidder with a current bid of $.99.

What if there had been bids made previous to mine? If that had been the case, the current bid shows what the current high bid will be; once I actually submit my bid and *if the current high bid for the item ($x) is the maximum proxy amount of the current high bidder.* This point is important. The actual outcome of your bid is not known in the "Review and Confirm Bid" page—it can only be known once you have committed to your bid by actually submitting it. Let's look at another example using another rug from the same seller—one that already has two bids and the current bid is $1.29.

Rare Vegetable Dye Afghan Chobi Rug 7x6   Item number: 3764919455

You are signed in   Email to a friend | This item is being watched in My eBay (48 items)

Go to larger picture

Current bid:	US $1.29
	Place Bid >
Time left:	**3 days 3 hours** 7-day listing Ends Dec-01-04 20:37:00 PST
Start time:	Nov-24-04 20:37:00 PST
History:	2 bids (US $0.99 starting bid)
High bidder:	50oasis (30 ☆)

Seller information

pakobelrugs (6764 ☆)

🏆 Power Seller

Feedback Score: 6764
Positive Feedback: 99.4%
Member since Jun-04-02 in United States

Read feedback comments
Add to Favorite Sellers
Ask seller a question
View seller's other items

PayPal Buyer Protection NEW!
Free Coverage now up to $1,000. See eligibility.

I am willing to pay $103. I submit that as my bid:

Ready to bid?

Rare Vegetable Dye Afghan Chobi Rug 7x6

Current bid: US $1.29

Your maximum bid: US $ [103]   (Enter US $1.54 **or more**)

[Place Bid >]   You will confirm in the next step.

eBay automatically bids on your behalf **up to** your maximum bid.
Learn about bidding.

The "Review and Confirm Bid" screen:

Review and Confirm Bid

Hello uncle_griff! (Not you?)

Item title:	Rare Vegetable Dye Afghan Chobi Rug 7x6
Your maximum bid:	**US $103.00**
Sales tax:	7.000% (only in FL)

Shipping and handling:	US $35.00 - Standard Flat Rate Shipping Service (within United States)
Shipping insurance:	US $5.00 (Optional)
Payment methods:	PayPal, Personal check, Money order/Cashiers check, Visa/MasterCard, American Express, Other - See Payment Instructions

By clicking on the button below, you commit to buy this item from the seller if you're the winning bidder.

[Confirm Bid]

And the final Bid Confirmation:

Bid Confirmation   Item number: 3764919455

Hello uncle_griff! (Not you?)   Email to a friend | This item is being tracked in My eBay

✓ **You are the current high bidder**

Important: Another user may still outbid you, so check this item again before it ends. eBay will send you an email if you're outbid.

How do you keep track of this item?
Use My eBay.

How does bidding work? See example.

Title: Rare Vegetable Dye Afghan Chobi Rug 7x6

Time left:	3 days 3 hours
History:	3 bids
Current bid:	US $48.00
Your maximum bid:	US $103.00

Congratulations to me. I am the current high bidder at $48. What does this tell me about the previous high bidder? Her actual maximum bid, held by proxy on eBay, was one increment below the current bid of $48. The increment at play between $25 and $99 is $1. Therefore, the previous bidder's maximum bid was $47. What do you want to bet she rebids and outbids my maximum bid of $103? We will check back later.

Here are some additional important facts about proxy bidding:

BID INCREMENTS

The following bid increments are used by the eBay Proxy Bidding:

Current Price	Bid Increment
$ 0.01 - $ 0.99	$ 0.05
$ 1.00 - $ 4.99	$ 0.25
$ 5.00 - $ 24.99	$ 0.50
$ 25.00 - $ 99.99	$ 1.00
$ 100.00 - $ 249.99	$ 2.50
$ 250.00 - $ 499.99	$ 5.00
$ 500.00 - $ 999.99	$ 10.00
$ 1000.00 - $ 2499.99	$ 25.00
$ 2500.00 - $ 4999.99	$ 50.00
$ 5000.00 and up	$ 100.00

NOTE: A bidder may be outbid by less than a full increment. This would happen if the winning bidder's maximum bid beats the second-highest maximum by an amount less than the full increment.

A bid increment will go higher than the standard increment in two situations:

- To meet the reserve amount
- To beat a competing bidder's high bid

If you were bidding against another bidder's maximum bid, your bid had to meet the other bidder's maximum bid plus one cent to become the current high bidder on the item.

Sometimes the auction page for an item will show that there are two bids, yet there is only one bidder. This happens when a member places more then one bid to increase their maximum bid amount. For example, if you are the first bidder on an item and you place a second bid to increase your maximum bid amount, the item page would show the current high bid at the opening bid amount, but would show that two bids have been placed on this item.

Tie Bids

In cases where a tie bid is submitted, the current high bid is given to the tie bidder who bid first. That is, if you submit a maximum bid equal to the current (hidden) maximum bid for an item, the current high bid will jump up to the current bidder's maximum bid amount and the earlier bidder will show as the current high bidder.

Bidding and Reserves

If one or more bidders bid amounts less than seller's hidden reserve, the bidding proceeds as any other proxy auction (with the indication next to the current price stating "reserve not met").

Once a bidder submits a bid equal to or greater than the seller's hidden reserve, the current high bid "jumps" to the reserve amount. From there, the bidding again proceeds as a regular proxy bidding auction (with the indication next to the current price changing to "reserve met").

PROXY BIDDING STRATEGIES

Always give serious consideration to the absolute maximum you are willing to pay for an item. In this case, you decide that you would not pay a penny more than $1,000. This means that should you be outbid for $1,000.01 (rare but possible), you will not whine at losing out for a penny. If you can picture yourself at the auction's closing and you are spitting and kicking at being outbid for one cent, and you can also picture yourself saying, "Darn it! I would have paid $1,000.02!" then you are telling yourself a big fat lie when you say your maximum is $1,000, because your real maximum is $1000.02.

The solution? Settle on an absolute maximum and stick to it. Think, "If someone outbids my maximum by even a penny, then I will breathe a sigh of relief at not having to shell out more than my maximum." So much for deciding exactly how much to bid; now, you need to decide *when* to bid it.

Bid Early—Bid High

As a bidding strategy and tool, the eBay Proxy Bidding system works like a charm. You simply determine a maximum amount you are willing to pay for an item, bid that amount, and walk away. The Proxy Bidding system will execute your bid and will protect your high-bidder position by outbidding all new bids using the lowest increment possible until and if someone bids an amount higher than your proxy bid. This offers you the convenience of submitting your absolute maximum bid early in a listing's run rather than having to revisit the listing over and over to rebid every time you are outbid. Early proxy bidding provides not only convenience but also, more important, peace of mind. eBay will act as your trusty proxy, freeing up your time to hunt for other eBay treasure.

Sniping

There is, however, another popular bidding strategy known in eBay parlance as sniping; that is, waiting until the last moments of an auction-format listing and then submitting a maximum bid mere minutes or even seconds before the listing closes. It's a heart-pounding, sweat-inducing roller-coaster ride and definitely not for the faint of heart or weak of wallet.

Does sniping work? Sometimes, but all potential snipers should consider the possible risks. If you tend to get caught up in the frenzy of last-minute bidding to the extent that you suffer a momentary lapse of common sense and end up insanely bidding much more than you would have under more relaxed circumstances, then sniping may not be for you. Remember, regardless of when you bid, the rules of the auction format still apply—he who bids highest, wins. Someone equally as caught up as you might snipe an insane bid amount just a few pennies short of your insane bid amount, in which case you will be the proud winning—albeit overpaying—bidder.

Also, your success at sniping depends to some extent on the speed of your Internet connection: the slower your Internet connection, the less likely your chances of success.

What about these sniping software and sniping services I see advertised? What are they? Do they provide an advantage? Sniping software or a sniping service snipes your bids for you. You enter the item number, the time you want your bid submitted, and the amount of your bid. The software or service supposedly does the rest. The only possible advantages that sniping software or sniping services provide are that they allow a sniper to be somewhere else at the end of the auction (like in bed asleep), and if it is a service, it may have a high-speed Internet connection faster than yours.

NOTE: As of this writing, eBay neither prohibits nor condones the use of sniping software or services. Use them at your own risk.

A Popular Manual Sniping Method

Determine a safe but effective snipe time. If your Internet connection is superfast, you can usually get away with waiting until the last few seconds to snipe. If instead your connection is slow, you may have to snipe sooner rather than later. To make a more accurate determination of the time it might take over your connection, visit any listing set to close in the next hour. Note the time on "Time Left."

Current bid:	**US $20.00**
	[Place Bid >]
Time left:	**29 mins 6 secs** 7-day listing Ends Nov-28-04 19:38:55 PST
Start time:	Nov-21-04 19:38:55 PST
History:	1 bid (US $20.00 starting bid)
High bidder:	mscolvin- (80 ★)

Refresh the window and note the new time left.

Current bid:	**US $20.00**
	[Place Bid >]
Time left:	**29 mins 8 secs** 7-day listing Ends Nov-28-04 19:38:55 PST
Start time:	Nov-21-04 19:38:55 PST
History:	1 bid (US $20.00 starting bid)
High bidder:	mscolvin- (80 ★)

The difference in seconds is the minimum amount of time you should wait before the auction closes to submit your snipe bid. In the example above, this would be two seconds. Thus, my snipe bid should be submitted no later than "Time left—2 secs," and to be safe, I might want to leave myself three or four seconds.

Determine a snipe bid amount. Snipers tend to use high snipe bid amounts as an offensive move against other snipers. Although chances are good that you, as a sniper, won't actually have to pay your high snipe amount should you win the item, it is possible you might get stuck if someone snipes you with a bid just under yours.

Open a Web browser window and navigate to the item you wish to snipe. Do this five minutes or more before a listing is set to close.

← Back to list of items	Listed in category: <u>Health & Beauty</u> > <u>Fragrances</u> > <u>Men</u> > <u>Other Brands</u>	

PENHALIGON'S BLENHEIM BOUQUET 1.7OZ. EDT SPRAY -- NIB   Item number: 5537621209

You are signed in   <u>Email to a friend</u> | <u>Watch this item</u> in My eBay

	Current bid:	**US $20.00**
		Place Bid >
	Time left:	**29 mins 6 secs** 7-day listing Ends Nov-28-04 19:38:55 PST
	Start time:	Nov-21-04 19:38:55 PST
↓ <u>Larger Picture</u>	**History:**	<u>1 bid</u> (US $20.00 starting bid)
	High bidder:	<u>mscolvin</u> (80 ★)
	Item location:	New York, NY United States
	Ships to:	Americas

Seller information

<u>mtonyc</u> (452 ★) ☆ Power Seller

Feedback Score: 452
Positive Feedback: 100%
Member since Jul-25-01 in United States

<u>Read feedback comments</u>
<u>Add to Favorite Sellers</u>
<u>Ask seller a question</u>
<u>View seller's other items</u>

PayPal Buyer Protection NEW!
<u>Free</u>
Coverage now up to $1,000.
See eligibility.

Once the item is displayed, open another copy of the window with the item by simultaneously pressing the Ctrl and N keys on your Windows computer keyboard.

Substitute the Apple or Command key for the Ctrl key if you use a Mac. (You can also open a copy of the window by clicking "File, New, Window" or "File, New Window" on the Web browser's menu command bar.)

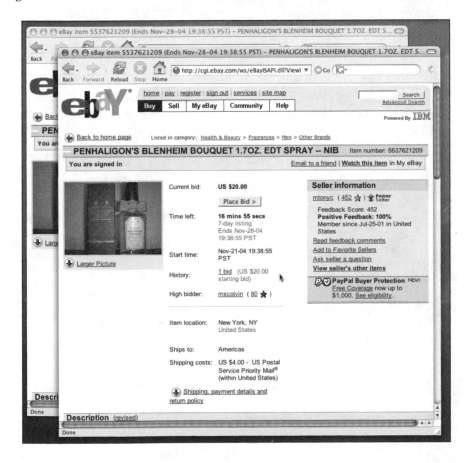

Now you have two windows open, preferably to the same item page. If not, navigate to the item so that the two windows look like this:

Click the Place Bid button.

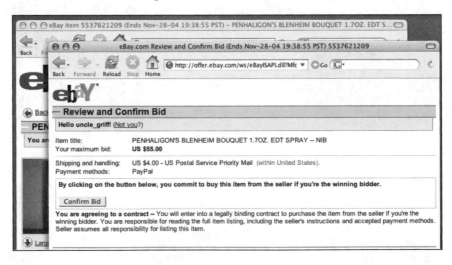

In this copy of the window, enter a bid amount in the "Your maximum bid" text box.

Leave this window open on the "Review and Confirm Bid" page with the Confirm Bid button showing.

Arrange the two Web browser windows side by side. You can drag the windows and resize them with your mouse. Another quick way to do this if your operating system is any version of Windows is to open both windows. (Make sure any and all other programs or applications are closed or else they will tile as well.) Then, right click anywhere on the Windows task bar. Select Tile Windows Vertically.

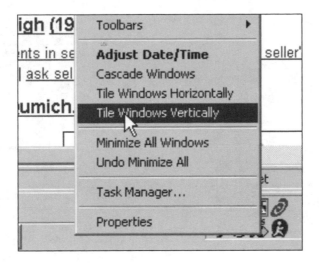

This will display the two open browser windows side by side like so:

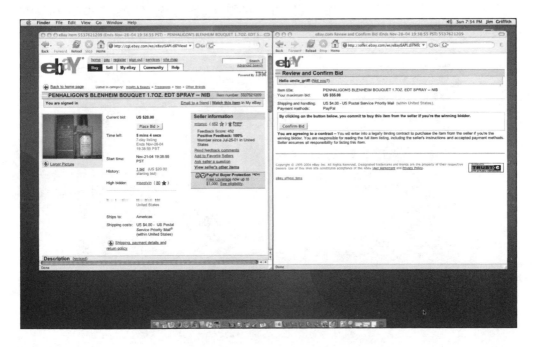

Make sure the second window is opened to the "Review and Confirm Bid" page and that it shows the Confirm Bid button clearly.

Use the first window to watch the time wind down by refreshing the page at regular intervals. Click the browser's Refresh or Reload button to refresh the page:

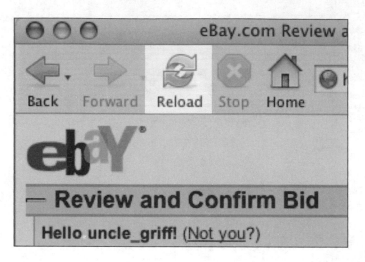

When the time left shown in the first window is close to or at your predetermined snipe time, quickly move your mouse to the second window and click the Confirm Bid button.

Window one shows 3 seconds or less left! Time to snipe!

— Review and Confirm Bid

Hello uncle_griff! (Not you?)

Item title: PENHALIGON'S BLENHEIM BOUQUET 1.7OZ. EDT SPRAY

Your maximum bid: **US $55.00**

Shipping and handling: US $4.00 - US Postal Service Priority Mail (within United Sta

Payment methods: PayPal

By clicking on the button below, you commit to buy this item from the seller if yo

[Confirm Bid]

You are agreeing to a contract -- You will enter into a legally binding contract to purcha winning bidder. You are responsible for reading the full item listing, including the seller's Seller assumes all responsibility for listing this item.

Copyright © 1995-2004 eBay Inc. All Rights Reserved. Designated trademarks and brands are the pro owners. Use of this Web site constitutes acceptance of the eBay User Agreement and Privacy Policy.

Click that Confirm Bid button!

Congratulations, sniper! Now, cross your fingers and hope you've won. (I did not actually snipe the example item.)

eBay member Bill Cawlfield told me an amazing tale of sniping from a most unusual location . . .

Well, I had to have this one radio, about three years ago. The item was going to end while I was flying. This was long before sniper programs. So, not thinking about having someone else snipe for me, I decided to snipe from a plane on the way from Denver to L.A. The connection was just awful in those days, maybe 7,600 baud. I finally loaded the item page, turned off all graphics, and counted down the seconds, not daring to hit refresh because that would tie up the reload too long.

I hit bid and then refreshed, which took another couple of minutes . . . I won!!

It proves that speed does not count, only the size. Sniping from thirty-five thousand feet. A new meaning of the mile-high club.

Multiple Item Bidding—How It Works

Whereas the Proxy Bidding format is used for listings with one single lot up for sale, the Multiple Item Listing format is used for selling multiple identical items in one listing.

Multiple Item bidding does not work like Proxy Bidding. When you bid in a Multiple Item Listing, you specify the number of items you're interested in and the price you're willing to pay. All winning bidders will pay the same price: the lowest successful bid.

For Multiple Item Listings, you cannot enter a maximum bid. The amount of your bid is the price you pay (if yours is the winning bid). For example, if there are ten items available and the opening bid is $4, and there is one bidder who bids $20 for ten items, that bidder pays $20 for each item.

Much of the time, all buyers pay the starting price in Multiple Item Listings. However, if there are more bids than items, the items will go to the earliest successful bids.

To beat another bid, yours must have a higher total bid per item than other bids, regardless of how many items you are bidding on. Reducing this total bid value in subsequent bids is not permitted.

For example, for a listing with ten available items and two bidders:

- Bidder A bid for three items at $5 each.
- Bidder B bid for eight items at $6 each.

In this case, the lowest successful bid is $5. So the outcome of this listing is:

- Bidder B wins eight items at $5 each.
- Bidder A wins two items at $5 each.

Winning bidders have the right to refuse partial quantities. This means that if you win some, but not all, of the quantity you bid for, you don't have to buy any of them. In the above example, Bidder A bid on three items but won only two of them. Bidder A can refuse to complete the purchase, as she didn't win the quantity she bid on.

Successful bids are displayed when you click on the link "see winning bidders list" link. The complete bidding history (including any unsuccessful bids) is displayed when you click on "Bidders list."

Most Multiple Item Listings are for vast quantities of a single item, for example, mounted insects. In the example shown below, the seller is offering one hundred giant blue butterflies in a Multiple Item Listing with a starting bid of $24.95.

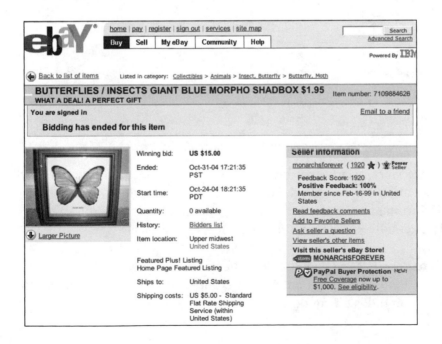

Based on this seller's past listings, odds are good that most if not all of these butterflies will be purchased in this auction. For example, if we visit a previously completed Multiple Item Listing by the same seller:

We can see how many of these sold by clicking "Bidders list."

ebaY® home | pay | register | sign out | services | site map   Search / Advanced Search

Buy | Sell | My eBay | Community | Help

Powered By IBM

← Back to item description

Bid History   Item number: 7109884626

Hello uncle_griff! (Not you?)   Email to a friend | Watch this item in My eBay

Item title:	BUTTERFLIES / INSECTS GIANT BLUE MORPHO SHADBOX $1.95
Quantity:	10
Currently:	US $15.00
Time left:	Auction has ended.

Only actual bids (not automatic bids generated up to a bidder's maximum) are shown. Automatic bids may be placed days or hours before a listing ends. Learn more about bidding.

User ID	Bid Amount	Quantity wanted	Quantity winning	Date of bid
jojomayday (45 ☆)	US $15.00	1	1	Oct-29-04 02:23:10 PDT
dayooper71 (1)	US $15.00	1	1	Oct-26-04 02:20:56 PDT
ancientarsenal (111 ☆)	US $15.00	2	2	Oct-31-04 16:26:40 PST
danmower (44 ☆)	US $15.00	1	1	Oct-29-04 08:28:44 PDT
aquatintman (6)	US $15.00	2	2	Oct-31-04 17:20:09 PST
anicia123 (1)	US $15.00	1	1	Oct-27-04 09:33:04 PDT
petprice (74 ★)	US $15.00	1	1	Oct-29-04 16:13:58 PDT
jerseylily76 (0)	US $15.00	1	1	Oct-31-04 14:35:25 PST
dinhelga (528 ☆)	US $15.00	1	0	Oct-31-04 16:12:53 PST
howsthatsound (13 ☆)	US $15.00	1	0	Oct-31-04 16:37:55 PST
sugarcookie71 (8)	US $13.00	1	0	Oct-26-04 11:50:17 PDT
edje4him (574 ☆) me	US $12.51	2	0	Oct-31-04 14:55:07 PST
jscottyrocket2 (9)	US $12.00	1	0	Oct-31-04 12:44:47 PST
scrally (26 ☆)	US $10.00	2	0	Oct-27-04 19:25:04 PDT
alaskafinds (212 ☆)	US $8.97	1	0	Oct-30-04 20:01:39 PDT
inletcampus (115 ☆)	US $6.77	1	0	Oct-29-04 17:19:12 PDT
teresa22000 (1)	US $6.00	1	0	Oct-27-04 20:06:28 PDT
mvia722 (12 ☆)	US $5.65	1	0	Oct-27-04 20:02:05 PDT
milai1964 (29 ☆)	US $5.50	1	0	Oct-26-04 16:05:33 PDT
3199918918 (18 ☆)	US $5.00	1	0	Oct-25-04 01:45:56 PDT
thankyoustan (16353 ☆) ⊕	US $5.00	5	0	Oct-25-04 02:28:23 PDT
phillipsp4009 (70 ★)	US $1.95	1	0	Oct-24-04 19:02:03 PDT

There were twenty-two individual eBay bidders chasing ten butterflies—an ideal situation for the seller! They started at $1.95 and all ten ended up selling for $15 to the bidders shown in the highlighted box at the top of the list. Some bidders actually purchased more than one.

Points to Keep in Mind about Multiple Item Listing Bidding

Multiple Item Listing bid amounts are not kept secret during the auction. The amount you bid is the amount that shows in the bidding history immediately after you bid.

Your Bid Value is calculated as the amount of your bid times the quantity of items for which you have bid. For example, the Bid Value for a listing in which you bid $30 for two items is $60. A rebid by a Multiple Item Listing bidder must have a Bid Value greater than his or her previous bid. Thus, if I bid for two items at $30 apiece, my bid value is $60. If I rebid in this auction, my Bid Value cannot be equal to or lower than $60. Thus, I could not bid $31 for one item. This automatic restriction is intended to prevent one bidder from tying up all the items in a Multiple Item Listing and then rebidding for a lower quantity at the last moment of the auction.

The Bid History for a Multiple Item Listing shows everyone who has bid, successful or not. The Winning Bidders List shows the current successful bidders for the item.

Regardless of their actual bid amounts, the winning bidder(s) in a Multiple Item Listing all pay the same final price (known as *the lowest successful bid*) times the quantity they each bid for. The lowest successful bid is the amount bid by the last bidder on the Winning Bidders List. In our example above, everyone shown on the list of winning Multiple Item Listing bidders would pay the lowest successful bid, in this case, $15.

BUY IT NOW—HOW IT WORKS

For all their fun and excitement, auctions are not for everyone or for every buying situation. Sometimes, a seller wants to move an item fast. He or she may not want to wait three or more days for the item to sell. Sometimes, a buyer may want to purchase an item immediately and not wait for three or more days for an auction to close.

To meet both needs, eBay instituted a fixed-price format called Buy It Now.

Buy It Now is fairly simple. All items that offer the option will have a Buy It Now icon next to their title in both category and Title Search list results.

There are two types of Buy It Now listings: those with an auction-format option and those without (otherwise known as Fixed Price). When you open a Buy It Now item's description page, you will find either type. Those that are straight fixed-price with no auction component will look something like this:

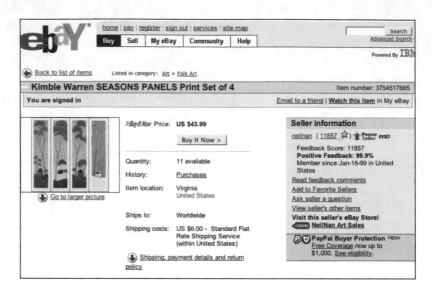

Those with an auction component look like this listing:

I can always use a new bottle of cologne. I don't want to bid on this, though. I am willing to simply buy it outright for the seller's Buy It Now price of $15 (plus $6.99 for shipping—a great deal!).

To Buy It Now, I scroll to the bottom of the page and look for the Buy It Now section next to the "Place a Bid" section.

Ready to bid or buy?   help

* PS * PAUL SEBASTIAN COLOGNE MEN 4.0 OZ EDT New In Box

Place a Bid   (or)   **Buy It Now**

Starting bid: US $14.00   ⏅BuyItNow price: US $15.00

Your maximum bid: US $ [_____] (Enter US $14.00 **or more**)

        [Place Bid >] You will confirm in the next   [Buy It Now >] You will confirm in
        step.   the next step.

eBay automatically bids on your behalf **up to** your maximum bid.   Purchase this item now without bidding.
Learn about bidding.   Learn about Buy It Now.

Click the button, review the details, and click the Commit to Buy button . . .

— Review and Commit to Buy

Hello uncle_griff! (Not you?)

Item title: * PS * PAUL SEBASTIAN COLOGNE MEN 4.0 OZ EDT New In Box
Buy It Now price: **US $15.00**

Shipping and handling: US $6.99 - Standard Flat Rate Shipping Service (within United States).
Payment methods: PayPal, Personal check, Money order/Cashiers check, Other - See Payment Instructions.

By clicking on the button below, you commit to buy this item from the seller.

[Commit to Buy]

You are agreeing to a contract -- You will enter into a legally binding contract to purchase the item from the seller. You are responsible for reading the full item listing, including the seller's instructions and accepted payment methods. Seller assumes all responsibility for listing this item.

. . . and it's yours. No bidding, no wondering if you will win it.

Buy It Now Confirmation   Item number: 5539519891

Hello uncle_griff! (Not you?)   Email to a friend

✓ **You committed to buy (Click 'Pay Now' to complete your purchase)**

[Pay Now >]   **How much should you pay?** You can view shipping and
                                         payment details or request total from the seller.

Payment methods accepted: **Have you already received this item?** If so, please leave
💬 This seller, perfumeinc, **prefers PayPal.**   feedback for the seller.

• **PayPal** (MasterCard VISA DISCOVER AMEX eCHECK) **What is PayPal?** With PayPal, it's **free** to pay for items online
• Personal check   with a credit card or bank account. It's fast, easy and secure.
• Money order/Cashiers check
• Other - See Payment Instructions for payment methods   Protect your eBay account and reputation by creating a unique
  accepted   eBay password.

To complete the transaction, click the Pay Now button.

Buy It Now—Immediate Payment

Sellers may opt to include a special component to their Buy It Now listings, called "immediate payment required." Our seller has, in fact, included this option.

To actually win a Buy It Now when the "immediate payment required" option is displayed, you must pay for the item using PayPal as soon as possible! The item will not "close" until you do so, which means that until you complete the transaction through PayPal, someone else can come along and Buy It Now right from under you.

Why this feature? Some sellers have been inconvenienced by the new or confused buyer who clicks the Buy It Now button without understanding how Buy It Now works. When the buyer discovers that clicking the button effectively ends the listing and obliges him to purchase, he backs out.

The "immediate payment" option prevents this type of confusion from ending a Buy It Now listing until the buyer pays for the item.

Whether you bid on the item and won it or bought it outright using Buy It Now (with or without the "immediate payment" option), the next step is to pay for it. We cover how to pay for an item in the next chapter. For now, it's time to go purchase our camera.

Except, an interesting thing has happened. While I was writing this chapter, bids were placed on the camera!

Once a bid is submitted on a nonreserve, Buy It Now/Auction combo format listing, the Buy It Now option disappears. The lesson, of course, is that if you find an item that you want to purchase with Buy it Now, you have to do so *before* someone else decides to put in a bid. Now, if I want to purchase the camera, I will have to submit a bid and hope I can win it.

Darn.

After three bids, the current bid is now $371—lower than the original Buy It Now price of $388, but it could go higher once I put in my bid. I was willing to pay $388. Perhaps I would pay a little more? I will submit a bid of $393 and keep my fingers crossed. I have only ninety seconds to place a bid. Fingers crossed . . .

I won! And I paid less than I would have using Buy It Now. The previous bidder must have had a maximum bid of $375 (the bid increment at this level is $5).

Now that we've won the camera, we can immediately pay for it . . . in the next chapter . . . after we pay for our bottle of cologne.

5

Shopping at eBay—Pay for It!

Congratulations! You've bought your first item on eBay. Get out your pocketbook—it's time to complete the transaction. But first, I want to share a story sent to me that illustrates the generosity and kindness typical of eBay members.

eBay seller Terry Wagner (sheop) lives in New Jersey with her husband and three little girls. Terry lost her Internet-based job a few years ago. At the same time, she learned that she had a rare blood disorder that makes her feel constantly fatigued, with daily dizzy spells, leg and hand cramps, and pounding headaches.

By 2001, Terry was in a constant pain. Her disability was cut off. Her dad was fighting bladder cancer and her mom was recovering from heart surgery. Then came the terrible events of September 11. Terry had previously worked at the World Trade Center, and she lost many old friends in the attacks.

"I knew people who never came home. I cried for days and days and still cry when I think about it."

Christmas, 2001, looked bleak at best. She was hunting for affordable gifts at eBay when she came across a beautiful but expensive quilt—a perfect gift for her mother. Terry e-mailed the seller to ask if she had less expensive quilts. The seller wrote back and told Terry that she did indeed and would be happy to hold one for her.

"After a few weeks, I had to write her back and explain that I still couldn't afford the quilt and was so sorry for leaving her hanging."

Two days later, Terry received an e-mail with the subject line "Ho, ho, ho! We want to send you the quilt!" The seller had told her husband about Terry and, as the seller explained to Terry, "He took money out of his pocket and said, 'Send her the quilt!'"

The seller insisted Terry send her address so she could send the quilt to her in time to give to her mom for Christmas.

"She sent not only the quilt for my mom, but a small gift for me and a small gift for my thirteen-year-old daughter, who had written her to thank her for making us all so happy!"

Terry and the generous seller correspond regularly and have exchanged family photos as well.

"I just can't get over the kindness. This is not the first person that I have met via eBay who has turned out to show what true human spirit is all about! Life continues to be a struggle. I'm in pain every day, but my friends on eBay keep me smiling."

Completing the Transaction

Many sellers offer detailed instructions on how to complete a transaction for their item by including payment options and shipping and handling amounts in their item descriptions. In fact, some sellers will actually provide a link to an auction management service—or even better, a Pay Now button right on the closed listing page—where you can immediately view an invoice for the item and select a payment method. Let's go back and pay for the two items we won in the previous chapter. Here's that closed item page for the cologne. First step is to click the Pay Now button:

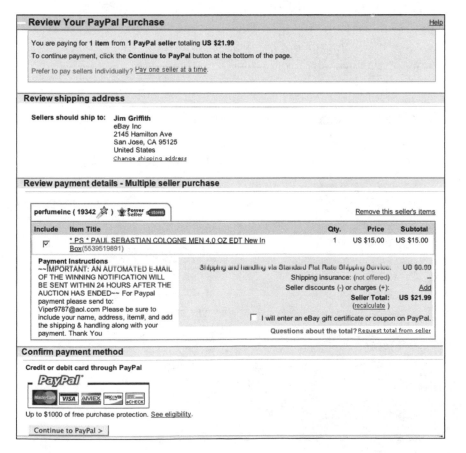

Review the details and click "Continue to PayPal."

On the next screen, you have two choices.

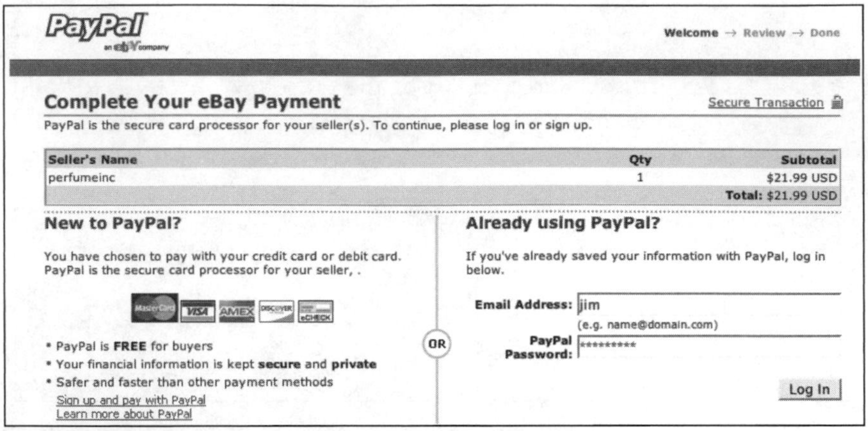

If you are already signed up for PayPal, simply type in your PayPal log-in (your e-mail address) and password and click "Log In."

If you haven't yet opened up a PayPal account, well, what are you waiting for? Click the link "Sign up and pay with PayPal."

Review the payment details:

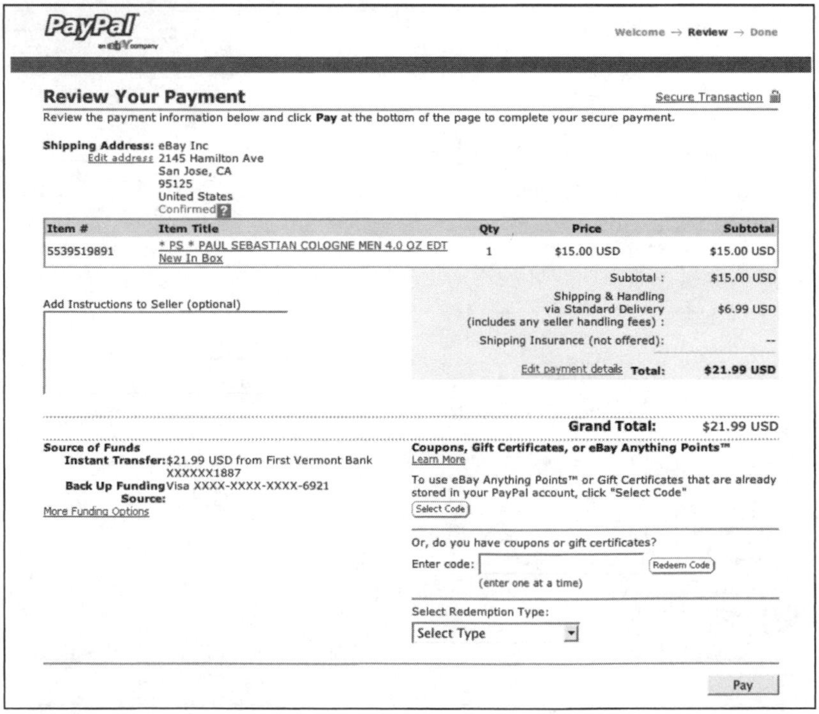

Click Pay . . .

. . . and you are done! You can also print out a receipt by clicking the link button on this page. Now, let's pay for the camera. We'll start in our All Buying > Won section of "My eBay":

Read through the Purchase details.

Review Your Purchase From memvk

You are paying for **1 item** totaling **US $399.00** from **memvk**.

To continue payment for memvk, click the **Continue** button at the bottom of the page.

Review shipping address

Seller should ship to: **Jim Griffith**
eBay Inc
2145 Hamilton Ave
San Jose. CA 95125
United States
Change shipping address

Review payment details

memvk (756 ☆)

Item Title	Qty.	Price	Subtotal
Canon PowerShot SD300 4.0MP + 512MB SD NIB USA Warranty	1	US $380.00	US $380.00

Payment Instructions
please make paypal
payment through the auction
page. Money order/check is
NOT accepted. I will ship the
order in 1 business day of
payment. thanks

Shipping and handling via Standard Flat Rate Shipping Service: US $19.00
Shipping insurance: (not offered) --
Seller discounts (-) or charges (+): Add
Seller Total: US $399.00
(recalculate)

I will enter an eBay gift certificate or coupon on PayPal.

Questions about the total? Request total from seller

Confirm payment method

Credit or debit card through PayPal

PayPal

VISA AMEX DISC_VER eCHECK

Up to $1000 of free purchase protection. See
eligibility.

Continue >

Log in to PayPal or create a PayPal account if you haven't done so already
(and exactly why haven't you?).

Click the Pay button . . .

. . . and this payment is complete! Now I will wait in eager anticipation for the camera.

These two sellers offered incredibly easy payment processes that took literally less than a minute to complete. If you follow the suggestions for shopping on eBay provided in previous chapters, you will limit your searches to only those sellers that offer the most convenient and safest of options for payment. However, you will also come across items that you really want but the sellers of said items may provide little or no information on how to complete the transaction.

If you did your homework by either reading the item description carefully or e-mailing the seller before you bid on or bought the item, you should at least have a good idea of the following:

The amount due for shipping/handling
The types of payment the seller accepts

Here are four examples of eBay sellers' shipping and payment terms taken from actual eBay listings:

HIGH BIDDER pays $29.99 UPS shipping cost within the continental USA.
Alaska & Hawaii $10.00 more. No International orders, please. No APO/FPO Addresses.
Cashier's Checks, Money Order, or use your credit card with either PayPal, BidPay.Com.
NY State Residents must add 8.25% Sales Tax to final total.

- **Preferred form of payment is EBAY PAYMENTS. We also accept PAYPAL ONLY from VERIFIED members. Over the phone we accept U.S. BANK ISSUED VISA, MASTER CARD, AMEX and DISCOVER. A toll free number will be provided to the winning bidder that chooses this option (e-mail us with a request). Electronic Checks (Via Ebay Payments or PayPal only). We DO NOT accept personal checks. Money Order is okay, as long as we get it within 7 days of auction ending date.**
- **We ship items within 24-48 hours of payment being received. We use UPS in the continental US and Canada.**
- **INTERNATIONAL BIDDERS WILL AGREE TO PAY VIA EBAY PAYMENTS, PAYPAL or BIDPAY and shipping is via USPS-EMS (Express Mail Service) only. (Except Canada). Custom Fees are BUYERS responsibility. We also ship to APO via USPS Priority Mail Insured. Shipments via USPS (United States Postal Service) are issued Monday and Thursday.**
- **Winning bidders, when the auction has ended please confirm the destination address no later than 3 days, so that we may bill you accordingly for shipping and handling. DO NOT SEND PAYMENT WITHOUT SHIPPING BEING QUOTED, PLEASE!**

SHIPPING INFO: All of our prints are professionally packed and double wrapped for safe delivery. Shipping/packing charges are $6.50 for Insured UPS (Priority Mail for Box holders, APO/FPO addresses or upon request). I will ship ANY NUMBER of Gallery quality prints together for that price!

(International orders are sent via DHL Worldwide. International shipping costs are: Canada - $16.00, all other International - $24.00).
(Please allow 2-4 days for order processing).

I'm always happy to combine multiple items to save on shipping!
Buyer to pay actual shipping charges. I never charge a handling fee!

BY BIDDING ON THIS AUCTION, YOU AGREE TO THE TERMS AND CONDITIONS LISTED BELOW:

Buyer agrees to contact us within 3 days with your complete billing address and contact information. Buyer also agrees to make payment within 10 days of auction end. If buyer does not abide by these conditions, negative feedback will be reported to Ebay.

Buyer understands that purchase price for the item described is AS IS, WHERE IS. We will hold you item for up to 30 days if you would like to pick it up.

SHIPPING:
Buyer pays all shipping charges. You may use the shipper of your choice or we can arrange shipping for you via a delivery company. We have very good rates and offer inside delivery. Placement, setup and cleanup of packing materials can be arranged for an additional charge.

RETURNS:
Returns must be made within 10 days of receipt of item. Refunds will be issued after item has been received in its original condition minus a 20% standard restocking fee. Please allow at least 2-4 weeks to process returns after item has been received. Delivery fees are non-refundable.

PAYMENT:
I accept Visa, Mastercard, American Express, Paypal, Personal Checks and Money Orders

By contrast, here is an example of a listing where the seller hasn't included any shipping or payment terms, only that he accepts credit cards.

Description
The catalogue is from a comprehensive exhibition held at Craftsman Farms in Parsippany, New Jersey from November 15, 1992 to January 31, 1993. Extensive photos of exceptoṕnal pieces of furniture with emphasis on rare, early material & signatures. Production and text by A. Patricia Bartinque including commentary and essays from other knowledgeable people. This is an unused, new copy published by Turn of the Century Editions.

If you were interested in purchasing this item, you would have to e-mail the seller for more information. This seller would do his potential customers a great service by putting some shipping and payment information into the description.

CONTACT THE SELLER

Usually, once an eBay listing has closed, the seller will send an e-mail to the winning bidder or buyer with exact payment instructions. However, there is no set protocol or rule stating who should e-mail whom first. As a bidder, instead of waiting for the seller to contact you, you should always e-mail the seller immediately after the listing has closed. If the seller hasn't included an actual price for shipping or hasn't provided the eBay Shipping Calculator in his item description, provide your shipping address in the e-mail and your preferred method of payment so the seller can calculate shipping and respond with an amount.

ASK SELLER A QUESTION

As we mentioned in the previous chapter, whenever you have a question or doubt about an item, e-mail the seller. Use the "Ask seller a question" link on the Item Description page.

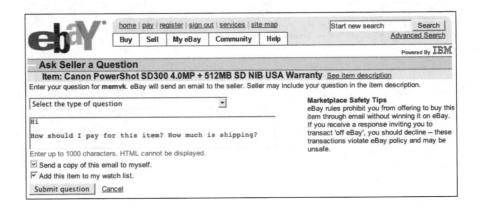

The "Ask Seller a question" form looks like this:

Fill in your message and click the "Submit question" button. Your message will be e-mailed to the seller with a blind carbon copy sent to your own e-mail address for your records.

Regular E-mail

You can also e-mail the seller from your own e-mail application.

eBay member e-mail addresses are not displayed on the site. However, once a listing has closed, the high bidder and seller for that listing can see each other's e-mail address. To view the seller's e-mail address, go to the Sign In preferences page in your "My eBay" My Account > eBay Preferences, and click "change" for eBay Sign In Preferences:

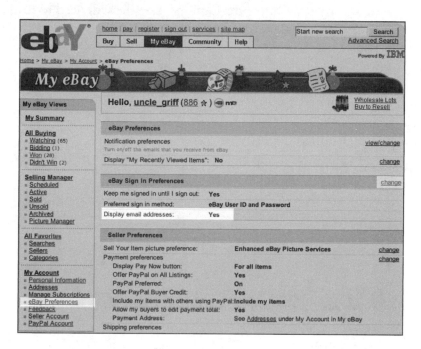

Under Display Settings, check the box "See e-mail addresses when viewing User IDs—if you are involved in a transaction."

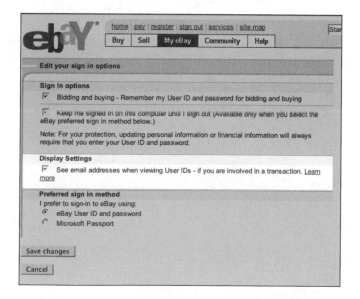

Regardless of which method you use for contacting the seller, you can never be too conscientious or detailed in your message.

Provide the seller with all the information he or she will need to formulate a total amount due that includes shipping. To this end make sure you provide the following in your e-mail:

The item number and title
Your eBay User ID
The item price
Your shipping address
Your preferred method of payment (from the options provided by the seller)

PAYMENT OPTIONS

All eBay sellers offer at least one of the following five possible payment methods:

PayPal
Credit cards (through the seller's own merchant account)
Electronic (wire) transfers
Money orders
Checks

PayPal

Before 1998, any eBay seller who wished to accept credit card payments had to apply and pay for a special merchant account. Now, with online payment services like PayPal, anyone can accept credit cards without the expense or hassle of setting up a merchant account at a bank.

Opening a PayPal account is easy. Just go to *www.paypal.com* and click the link Sign Up.

Follow the easy instructions from there.

Make it a habit in your search for treasure at eBay to give preference to those items where the seller accepts PayPal for payment. Using PayPal to buy on eBay affords you the highest possible level of security. It's also the quickest way to pay for an item. That means it's not only the safest way to pay for the item, but it's also the fastest way to get your item shipped to you, since most sellers will ship an item the same day payment is received.

Credit Cards

Many sellers have established their own merchant accounts for accepting credit cards. Although paying with a credit card through such an account is usually safe and secure, always ask the seller if they can provide you with a secure method of transmitting your credit details to them (a secure server link).

Electronic (Wire) Transfers

Along with credit cards, online payment services like PayPal provide a second option for payment: electronic check.

Electronic checks are an alternative for those buyers who have a checking account but do not use credit or debit cards. PayPal electronic checks are protected for up to the full amount transferred, making it as safe a payment method as a credit card.

Money Orders

Although paying with money orders is very old-fashioned, many sellers accept them either as one of a selection of payment options or, in some cases, as the only payment method!

When paying with a money order, make it a habit to write the item number and the seller's eBay User ID in the memo section of the money order, and make sure to keep your money order receipt in a safe place in case you need it later.

For a fee, the online money-order service BidPay (*www.bidpay.com*) allows you to use your credit card to purchase a money order. BidPay then mails the money order directly to the seller. The seller does not have to have an account with BidPay to receive payment through their service. All you need is the seller's mailing address, the total due, the item number, and the seller's e-mail address.

Checks

As a payment method, checks are less popular than they were in the early days of eBay. It's easy to see why as more and more eBay sellers are accepting PayPal. Still, some sellers will only accept checks or money orders.

If you pay using a check, make sure to keep a record of the check in your checking account register. Although not as secure or fast as paying with a credit card, a canceled check could be sufficient evidence of your having paid for an item.

As with a money order, make sure you put the item number and seller's User ID in the check's memo field.

Cash?

Never send cash through the mail. Should something go wrong (the seller doesn't receive the cash or you don't receive your item), you will have no record of payment and, consequently, no avenue of redress.

Cash as payment is only appropriate if you plan to pay for and pick up the item yourself; for example, if you bought something at eBay from a seller in your area. When paying with cash, make sure you obtain a detailed and signed receipt. If the item is a vehicle, don't hand over the cash until the seller has provided adequate proof of identity and a legal, clear title.

The Pay Now Button

As we have seen above with our two purchases, many eBay sellers will provide their buyers with the ease and speed of the Pay Now button. The Pay Now button facilitates the last steps of an eBay transaction by collecting all of the payment and shipping information and options into one central place.

Not all sellers take advantage of the Pay Now feature. If the seller has set her preferences correctly, look for the Pay Now button on the closed listing page as well as in any end-of-listing e-mails you receive.

GRIFF TIP! Since each seller will have different payment options, shipping totals, etc., always follow the individual seller's instructions contained within any of the above windows to request a total or to pay for the item.

Bid and Purchases Management with "My eBay"

The "My eBay" All Buying page—there is simply no better tool for tracking your current bids and completed auctions within the last thirty days.

You can read more about My eBay in Section One, chapter 2.

COMPILING AND ARCHIVING LISTINGS IN WHICH YOU ARE THE WINNER

It's smart to save a copy of all your winning bids at eBay. You never know when you might need the copy. For example, if you sell the item later, you may need some documentation to show how much you paid for it. A copy of your payment receipt plus a printout of the Item Description page should prove more than adequate proof of price and date of sale.

This simplest archive consists of copies of each Item Description page in which you were the buyer. To make a print record, navigate to an Item Description page, let it load completely (look for "done" on the status bar on the bottom of the browser window), then print out the listing page by selecting "File, Print . . ." on your Web browser's command bar.

It helps to have a color printer.

You can save a soft copy of any item page by clicking the "File, Save As . . ." command on your Web browser's menu command bar.

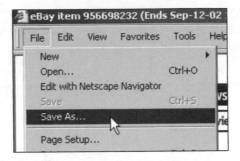

If you are using a Windows machine, when you save the file, in the "Save as type" box choose "Web Page, complete (*htm,*html)" and note where you save it. (We are saving ours on our Desktop.)

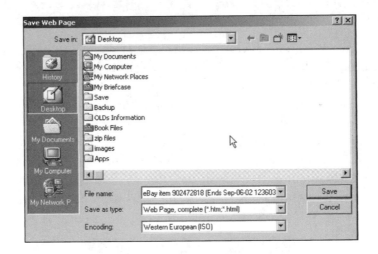

If you are using a Mac computer, depending on which Web browser you are using, choose File and then "Save As . . ." and select Web Archive as Format (Internet Explorer) . . .

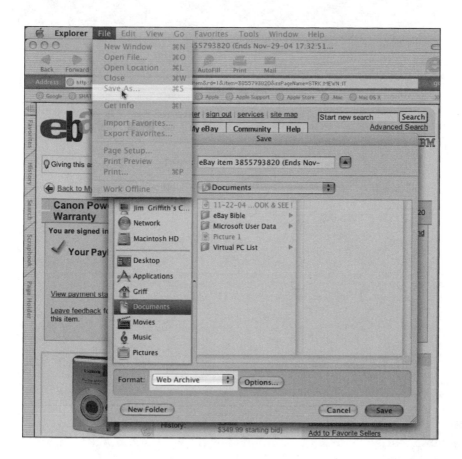

. . . or "Save Page As . . ." and then "Web Page, complete" for Firefox.

In either case, with Windows or Mac, you may also want to give the saved file a name that will make it easier to locate in the future. You can type in a new name in the Save As box.

GRIFF TIP! Some sellers have limited Web server space for their pictures. Once one of their listings ends, they tend soon after to delete the picture files from their Web server to free up space for pictures of new listings. Consequently, it is not uncommon to visit a completed listing and find the images are all missing and in their place are little boxes with red *x*'s. Therefore, if you wish to archive a closed listing as hard or soft copy and you want to include the pictures of that item, you should do so as soon as possible after the item closes, before the seller has deleted the picture files.

If there is an eBay Picture Services image that you want to save as a file and only the thumbnail for that image is showing on the item page, you need to do the following.

Save the entire page per the previous instructions.

Click on the selected thumbnail to open the bigger copy of that image.

Hover your mouse cursor over the image. A small box with four icons will pop up on the upper left-hand corner of the picture. Click on the icon for "Save this image."

In the Save Picture dialog box, navigate to the same folder created by the "Save as type: Web Page, complete" when you saved a complete copy of the page. Ours is on our Desktop, and the folder uses the item title within its folder name.

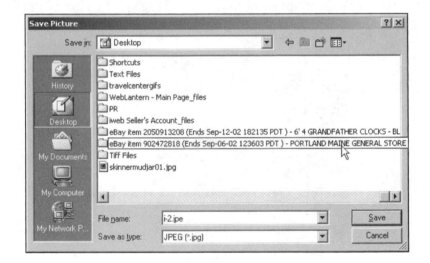

Click on the folder to open it.
Click the Save button (don't change the name of the file).

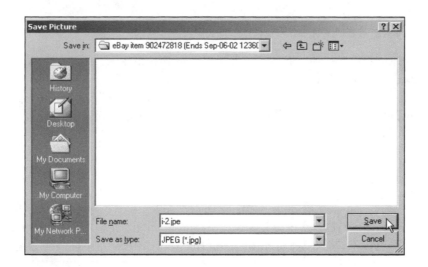

Repeat the above steps for each image you want to save for future use.

Unpacking Your Item

You've contacted the seller and paid for the item. The seller has shipped the item to you.

Finally, the package arrives and you are giddy with delight. In fact, no small part of the appeal of regularly shopping on eBay is waiting for the UPS, FedEx, or USPS deliveryman to drop off your treasure. Your first impulse is to rip the package open.

But wait. If the item is fragile or expensive, you may want to go get your camera and maybe a friend or family member before you open the package, especially if the item inside the package is breakable.

As you open the package, have your friend or family member photograph the process with a minimum of three shots. One shot of the package before you open it; one shot of the package as you are just finished opening it; and finally, one shot of you lifting the item out of the package.

Even better, use your video camera if you have one. Either way—photos or video—you want to create a record of your opening the package and inspecting the item.

Why the record? Why, for insurance of course! If, for whatever reason, the item was damaged, either before or during transit, the photos or video could prove invaluable when submitting a claim with the delivery service.

E-MAIL THE SELLER . . . AGAIN!

As a common courtesy, let the seller know that the package arrived and that you are pleased with the item.

If you are not pleased, or if the item arrived damaged or never arrived, let him know. Any good eBay seller will usually bend over backward to assist with insurance claims or missing packages.

LEAVE FEEDBACK

Based on how your experience went with the seller, leave appropriate feedback to let the rest of the eBay world know. You can leave feedback from the Feedback link in "My eBay" > My Account or from the appropriate link on the closed-item page.

6

Special Bidding and Buying Considerations

In the previous chapters, we've covered almost every aspect of bidding, buying, and paying for goods offered by eBay sellers. Almost everything.

Some specialty eBay items and categories bear closer scrutiny.

Buying Big Stuff at eBay

When most folks think of eBay, they tend to think of things that can fit in a cardboard box: toys, collectibles, clothing, pottery, small pieces of furniture, etc. Although many of the items for sale on eBay are indeed small enough to ship through the post, more and more eBay sellers are putting up big items for bid and sale.

EBAY MOTORS CARS, TRUCKS, BOATS, ETC

eBay is the perfect place to buy a car. Car sellers range from the individual owner to used, new, and classic car dealerships.

All things "automotive" have their own special area on eBay, called eBay Motors. This includes cars, trucks, motorcycles, boats, ATVs, campers, snowmobiles, buses, and aircraft. Also for sale on the eBay Motors site are accessories for all of the above as well as manuals, collectibles, tools, parts, and apparel.

You can get to eBay Motors from the home page:

Although the eBay Motors site is slightly different in design, the basic layout of the site is identical to the rest of eBay. Categories are on the left-hand side of the page and include every aspect of all things automotive, nautical, and aeronautical.

Searching, bidding, and paying for items at eBay Motors is just like for the rest of eBay, with a few special considerations.

Some eBay Motors sellers have special payment terms, such as a percentage deposit immediately at the end of the listing. As always, make sure you read the seller terms carefully and that you fully understand and accept them before you bid. When in doubt, contact the seller for information and clarification.

If you are buying a car, boat, or any other similarly heavy item at eBay Motors, you will probably be more involved in the shipping aspect of the item than you might be for nonautomotive items. Unless the big item is near your location, you will have to arrange and pay for shipping. If the item you are interested in will need to be shipped, you should determine a close estimate of the shipping costs before you bid.

Most eBay Motors sellers provide, within the item descriptions, links to various third-party auto shippers who can help you, prebid, to figure shipping costs from the car's current location to your location.

Under the section Services Center, eBay also provides some suggestions for shippers, as well as for insurance, warranties, and registration options.

Finally, check out the "How To" Center. All of the information you need for effective car shopping on eBay Motors can be found under one of the links in this box.

REAL ESTATE

eBay might not jump to mind when you are hunting for a new home or property, but as of this writing there are thousands of listings in the eBay Real Estate category, ranging from residential homes to businesses.

Also as of this writing, all items in the eBay Real Estate category are "nonbinding." The real estate listings look and feel just like other eBay listings in the auction format, and anyone may submit a bid, but the owner is not obliged to sell to the high bidder.

However, this is changing. As eBay obtains the proper licenses for each state, real estate listings for those states will become binding. Check the eBay site for more information and updates as they are announced.

When considering buying or bidding on real estate at eBay . . .

More so than with non-real-estate listings, always get as much information as possible before you bid. If the house or property is listed by an individual, e-mail her for more pictures, etc.

Whenever possible, arrange to view the property before bidding.

For more information, visit the Real Estate Rules page. From the eBay home page, look for and click the links for Real Estate:

Categories
Antiques
Art
Books
Business & Industrial
Cameras & Photo
Cars, Parts & Vehicles
Cell Phones
Clothing, Shoes & Accessories
Coins
Collectibles
Computers & Networking
Consumer Electronics
Crafts
Dolls & Bears
DVDs & Movies
Entertainment Memorabilia
Gift Certificates
Health & Beauty
Home & Garden
Jewelry & Watches
Music
Musical Instruments
Pottery & Glass
Real Estate
Sporting Goods
Sports Mem, Cards & Fan Shop
Stamps
Tickets
Toys & Hobbies

This will take you to the Real Estate home page.

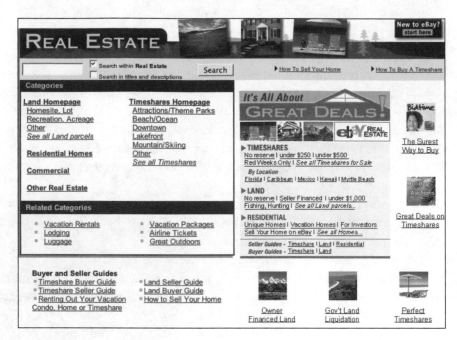

From here you can view homes, land, commercial property, and time-shares. Give special attention to the Buyer and Seller Guides:

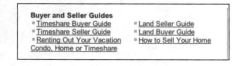

International Buying

eBay may have started out as a small hobby site in San Jose, California, in 1995, but in just ten short years, it has expanded to cover the globe!

As of this writing, over fifty countries are represented on eBay on twenty-three separate eBay International sites. You can navigate directly to any of the eBay International sites from any of the links on the bottom left corner of the eBay home page.

Although instantly recognizable by the eBay logo and colors, each international eBay site has its own distinct look and feel and language.

Although *www.ebay.com* may have been the first and, for a while, the most popular of all the eBay sites, eBay's international sites are growing at an astounding clip. As eBay continues to expand around the world, folks from other countries are searching both their own eBay sites and the U.S. eBay site.

Any registered eBay member can search for and bid on items listed on any of the eBay International sites. The only requirement is some ability to read and understand the description and terms for the item. For example, loads of fabulous items are listed on the eBay Italia site:

If you have some grasp of Italian and the seller is not averse to shipping the item to your location, then by all means, bid away!

Searching International eBay Sites

In addition to shopping on various international eBay sites, you can also include selected international sites in your eBay keyword searches by selecting the appropriate option under the Location area on the fully expanded Search page. Click the Advanced Search link on the top of any eBay page, then scroll down to the section for Location:

There are three options. The default is to search all items listed on the U.S. site (eBay.com) only.

The second option will limit the returned results to only one selected eBay site. Click on the "Items located in" button and pick the appropriate country from the drop-down list. **NOTE:** Even though you have limited your search to a specific country, make sure to read a seller's descriptions carefully to make sure they will ship to your country.

The third option will show all items that are available to you. Check the button "Items available to," then select your country location from the drop-down list. This will limit the search results to all listings where the sellers are willing to ship to your country. This search will limit the results to only those where the seller will ship to the United States.

Finally, you can also search for items listed in a specific currency by selecting a currency from the drop-down list.

MORE ON CURRENCY

When you are shopping on an eBay International site, the items listed will show bid amounts in the currency of that country. If you are going to shop on the eBay global sites (and I encourage you to do so), it helps to have a basic understanding of the conversion rate between various currencies.

On eBay, you can see the current bid price of an international item in your currency by looking on the top of the Item Description page next to the seller-specified currency:

This seller is located in the United Kingdom. He has made his items available to U.S. shoppers. The price shown will be in the seller's currency first, with a conversion to the shopper's currency in parentheses.

NOTE: This feature only displays the price in both your currency and the seller's currency when you have accessed the item through the eBay U.S. Advanced Search box.

You can also get a more accurate conversion amount by using one of the several online currency-conversion sites, such as *http://www.xe.com/*.

Keep in mind that should you win an item listed on an international site, you are obligated to pay the seller the final bid amount in the currency of the seller's country. The closest estimate of the final bid price is shown in red in parentheses next to the high bid. Use this figure when writing a check, making a wire transfer, or using your credit card.

PayPal will make the conversion for you automatically with no extra input on your end.

Credit card issuers will convert currency automatically from dollars into the foreign currency of the international eBay seller. You only need to know the correct amount in dollars for the final bid price.

For wire transfers handled directly by your bank, your bank will convert the currencies for you. Again, you need only let them know the amount in dollars.

As for international money orders or checks, you will have to find out from the seller how to make out the amounts so they are properly converted.

PAYMENT OPTIONS

If the seller accepts online credit card payments, pay using your credit card. Most international sellers now have access to some type of online payment service. PayPal, for example, is now available to sellers in many countries around the world.

If you have a preferred method of paying and the seller doesn't offer that method in their item description, suggest it via e-mail to the seller, *before you bid!* Otherwise, understand that you are obligated to use one of the payment methods specified by the seller in his auction description.

An international money order is a workable alternative for those listings where the seller doesn't or cannot offer an online credit card payment option. Note that in a limited number of foreign countries, USPS international money orders are accepted. Check with the USPS site for more information *(www.usps.com)*.

Remember to include any and all shipping costs and any additional fees/taxes with your payment.

SHIPPING COSTS AND METHODS

International shipping costs are dependent on one or more of the following factors:

- The weight and dimensions of the packaged item
- The method of shipment (Ground, Next Day Air, etc.) and the carrier (UPS, International Post, FedEx, etc.)
- Seller location
- Buyer location

In addition to shipping costs, buyers are usually responsible for any additional costs such as duties, taxes, and customs clearance fees.

To calculate costs for UPS shipped items, visit the UPS Quick Cost Calculator at *http://www.servicecenter.ups.com/ebay/ebay.html#qcost*.

FedEx also has a rate calculator page, at: *http://www.fedex.com/us/*

TAXES

In most instances, as a U.S. buyer purchasing from an international seller, you will not be liable for taxes. If you are unsure, e-mail the seller and ask about taxes before you bid.

OTHER LANGUAGES

It's overstating the obvious, but if you are interested in bidding on or buying an item from a French-speaking seller on the eBay France site, it would probably be a good idea to have some fluency in French.

If you don't, you may want to e-mail the seller first, in English, asking politely for a description in English.

There are Web sites that can help you translate text or an entire Web page from one language to another. My favorite is BabelFish, at *http://babelfish. altavista.com/.*

GRIFF TIP! Translation Web sites can be helpful in getting the gist of information from an item description, but they tend to translate word for word with no regard for idioms and colloquialisms. This can result in translated sentences that do not make sense or, worse, mean something other than what they appear to mean.

CUSTOMS

The duty rate for many items typically bought online is zero; however, you should never assume this is the case.

All goods brought into another country must clear that country's customs. In some cases, a customs duty may apply. If so, the recipient of the item is liable for the duty.

The sender is responsible for filling out a customs form for the item before the item is shipped. Again, not all items incur a customs duty. It can depend on the country, the value of the item, the type of the item, and the type of delivery. For example, it is much less complicated to send an item via international post as opposed to a courier service (private shipping company). There is no duty for most items valued at less than $200 sent via international post. In any case, make sure that the seller provides you with a receipt on his letterhead for customs, indicating the age and the value of the item. The value can usually be the price the buyer pays the seller. Depending on the item, you may need to make an export declaration or acquire an export license.

The U.S. Customs Web site has a page devoted to Internet transactions: *http://www.customs.ustreas.gov/impoexpo/impoexpo.htm.*

Buying Locally

Another way to buy big things is to do so locally. eBay provides a simple search tool that lists only items by sellers in your metropolitan area. The tool is based on zip code. You enter your zip code and select a distance radius from that zip code. You can find the option on the Advanced Search page:

Regional trading comes in handy for such items as:

- Hard-to-ship items like cars, appliances, and furniture
- Fragile or breakable items like glassware, computers, and chandeliers
- Items of local interest like tickets and real estate

There's one more important eBay buyer-related chapter in this book: eBay Guidelines, Rules, and Help for Buyers.

eBay Guidelines, Rules, and Help for Buyers

eBay Buyer Guidelines and Rules

All members of the eBay Community have a responsibility to ensure that their buying, selling, and chatting on the site is conducted within all eBay rules and guidelines. During my time with eBay Customer Support, the lion's share of the buyer mistakes and subsequent difficulties I witnessed were due primarily to ignorance of these rules and guidelines.

You can avoid difficulties of this sort by reading through the eBay rules and guidelines. Included in this chapter are the most basic topics regarding bidding and buying rules and guidelines. Everything in this chapter can also be found on the eBay site Help.

You can reach these pages from the eBay Navigation Bar via the box Help. Then click Help Topics and scroll down to eBay Policies.

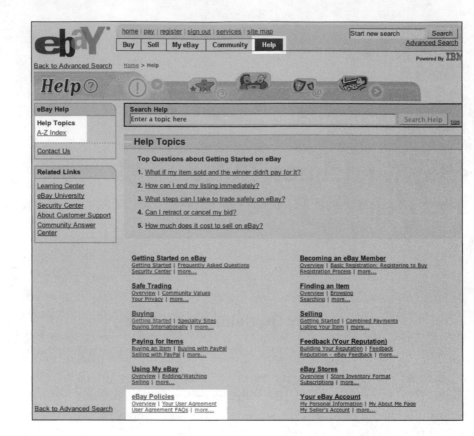

Click the link "Rules for Buyers."

From there, follow the various links for each buyer rule or policy:

The rules are fairly simple and straightforward. The most important rules for any buyer to keep in mind:

- Every winning bid or purchase is binding.
- Buyers should pay for their eBay purchases quickly.

We provided a Buyer Search and Purchase Checklist in an earlier chapter. Here's a Buyer Trust and Safety Checklist.

GRIFF TIP! You can never have too many checklists!

A BUYER TRUST AND SAFETY CHECKLIST

Much of the grief and frustration in the world is traceable to someone, somewhere, who makes a few innocent assumptions and then forges ahead, only to find himself unexpectedly enmeshed in chaos and confusion—realizing too late that his initial assumptions were, in fact, false.

This holds true for eBay members as well. Whenever shopping on eBay, never assume! A fully informed eBay shopper is a happy eBay buyer. This means asking questions, doing research, and informing yourself of the eBay rules regarding bidding and buying.

Here is a basic checklist for the responsible eBay Buyer.

Ask First

If a seller isn't clear in her listing about the condition of an item or her payment and shipping terms, ask her before you bid.

Research

If you are unsure about an item's value, condition, or authenticity, ask or research before you bid. For the actual condition or authenticity of an item, always ask the seller first. For value, use the eBay chat boards or search the Internet to do some price comparison. Browse the various eBay topic-specific chat boards to seek out experts in a field and ask them about a particular item.

Check Feedback and Leave Feedback

Although I have mentioned it many times throughout the preceding chapters, it bears repeating—always check a seller's feedback, even before you read his item description or look at the item pictures! And don't just rely on the feedback number. Page through the list of comments left for that seller to best determine what type of seller he is.

No rule states that you must leave feedback for sellers. However, the giving and receiving of feedback is a lot like the sport of logrolling; both parties must cooperate for it to work.

To establish your own sterling feedback history, you will often have to take the initiative and leave positive feedback first.

Keep Your eBay Password to Yourself!

Never grant access to your eBay account to anyone except maybe your spouse, and only if you trust him or her implicitly. Avoid granting password access to your children. No matter what the circumstances may be in your defense, you are responsible for any and all activity conducted using your eBay User ID, and you, as the account holder, will be held responsible if your account is employed for nefarious or illegal activity on eBay.

Use a Secure Method of Payment

Look for those listings in which the seller accepts payment with a credit or debit card or provides a wire-transfer or electronic-check option through PayPal. Give these listings preference. Yes, many good, honest sellers do not accept credit cards. If you simply must have their item, make sure their feedback is acceptable to you and read up on their return policy. If a seller doesn't have a refund policy on her item page, "Ask First" before you bid.

Avoid Questionable Activity

Some specific bidding activities are prohibited on eBay. It is your responsibility to know what these prohibited activities are and to avoid employing them. You can find a comprehensive list of questionable and prohibited activity by clicking on the Help link on the eBay Navigation Bar and clicking the links "eBay Policies" and "Rules for Buyers" (as described earlier).

eBay Rules for Buyers

The following describe the more common buyer infractions and how to avoid them.

- **Transaction interference.** Defined as e-mailing buyers in an open or ended transaction to warn them away from a seller or item. If you have had an unsatisfactory experience with a seller, you can let the rest of the eBay Community know by leaving appropriate feedback.
- **Contacting a seller and offering to purchase the listed item outside of eBay.** Although not a major offense in the scheme of things, it is definitely not in keeping with the spirit of eBay.
- **Bid retraction.** You can, as a bidder, retract your bid for any eBay auction that has not yet ended. The link for retracting a bid can be found on the bottom of the "My eBay" page for All Buying.

It's OK to retract a bid if . . .

- You accidentally enter a wrong bid amount. For instance, you bid $99.50 instead of $9.95. (If this occurs, you will need to quickly reenter the correct bid amount.)
- The description of an item you have bid on has changed significantly.
- You cannot reach the seller. This means that you have tried calling the seller and his or her phone number doesn't work, or you have tried e-mailing a message to the seller and it comes back undeliverable.

It's NOT OK to retract a bid if . . .

- You change your mind about the item.
- You decide you can't really afford it.
- You bid a little higher than you promised yourself you'd go.
- You only bid to uncover the seller's reserve amount or the current high bidder's maximum bid. (This is a serious offense that could result in the suspension of your eBay registration.)

Special Retraction Rules
If you place a bid before the last twelve-hour period of the auction:

- *You can retract the bid* with more than twelve hours left before the listing ends. When you do this, all your previous bids will also be eliminated. You will have to bid again if you canceled the previous bid due to an incorrect bid amount.
- *You cannot retract the bid* during the last 12 hours of the listing unless the seller agrees. You will have to contact the seller via e-mail and request she cancel your bid.

If you place a bid during the last twelve-hour period of the auction:
- You may retract the bid only within one hour after placing the bid.
- When you retract a bid within the last twelve hours of the listing, you will eliminate only the most recent bid you placed. Bids you placed prior to the last twelve hours will not be retracted.

Your total number of bid retractions in the past six months is displayed in your Feedback Profile on the top of the page in the ID Card section:

eBay will thoroughly investigate bid retractions, and abuse of this feature may result in the suspension of your eBay account.

Unwelcome Buyer

Defined as bidding or buying in violation of the terms set forth by the seller in the listing description. Some examples:

- Seller states he ships to "home country" only and the buyer is outside the stated shipping area.
- Seller states she will not accept bids from members who have negative feedback.
- Bidder rebids after the seller has canceled his bid and requested he not bid on or purchase her items. (Sellers have every right to reject bids from certain bidders for whatever reason they choose. A bidder who has been asked not to bid must comply with that seller's wishes.)
- Bidder uses a second eBay registration to bid on an item after his first registration has been blocked by a seller.

Bid Shielding

Defined as the deliberate use of secondary User IDs or other eBay members to temporarily raise the level of bidding and/or price of an item to extremely high levels to protect the low bid level of another bidder.

Shill Bidding

Using secondary User IDs or other eBay members to artificially raise the level of bidding and/or price of an item is called shill bidding and is strictly prohibited. Additionally, to avoid the appearance of being involved in this activity, family members and individuals living together, working together, or sharing a computer may not bid on each other's items.

Feedback Offenses

If you are not happy with the item, contact the seller and let him know *before you leave negative feedback!* It's always best to try to work out a solution with the seller first. If you and the seller are unable to reach a solution agreeable to both parties, then consider dispute resolution through a third party like Square-Trade *(www.squaretrade.com).*

Leave negative feedback only as a last resort.

Never use profanity or vulgar language in your feedback comments or responses to others.

Never include any part of another user's contact information in a feedback comment or response. This includes names!

Never post a Web or e-mail link in a feedback comment or response.

Unpaid Items (UPI)

When a buyer bids on and wins or buys an item at eBay and subsequently does not pay the seller for that item, the transaction becomes what is known in eBay parlance as an UnPaid Item, or UPI for short. (We used to call them nonpaying buyers. Before that, they were called deadbeat bidders. Some sellers still use that term.)

A bid is binding at eBay. Winning the bid and then not following through with the transaction is against eBay rules.

When a buyer does not pay for his item, the seller can file a report with eBay requesting a credit for the Final Value Fee for that item. In filing, the seller will be prompted to select a reason for the request. If the reason selected is "buyer backed out," an Unpaid Item alert will be made against your account.

Buyers with one or more UPIs run the risk of scathing negative feedback. In addition, upon receipt of a third UPI alert, that bidder is suspended from eBay.

AVOID BIDDING ON QUESTIONABLE ITEMS

During your quest for treasure at eBay, you may stumble upon an item whose legitimacy or legality may be questionable, and indeed, sellers may not offer many categories of items and specific items at eBay. Some of these prohibited items are no-brainers—controlled substances, nuclear weapons—but others are not so obvious.

Did you know that the sale of bear parts is not allowed at eBay? Bear rugs, paws, heads, organs, etc., are legal to sell everywhere in the United States save for one state, California. The black bear is the California state animal. It is illegal in California to trade in bear parts. eBay is headquartered in California, thus is subject to the state prohibition against the sale of bear parts.

There is a list of prohibited items on the eBay Web site at *http://pages.ebay.com/help/community/png-items.html*.

Navigate to this page by clicking the Help link on the eBay Navigation Bar, then click the Selling topic, and finally the link for "What items may not be sold on eBay?"

REPORTING QUESTIONABLE ACTIVITY OR ITEMS

eBay members can report questionable activity or items directly to eBay Trust & Safety (a special department of eBay Customer Support).

To do so:

1. Click the Help link on the eBay Navigation Bar.
2. Click the link Contact Us.
3. Select the appropriate topics.

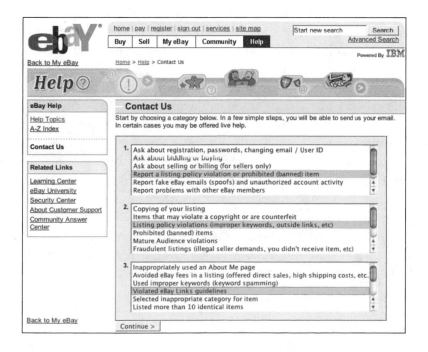

Within a matter of minutes of sending your report, you will receive an auto-acknowledgment e-mail from Customer Support to confirm the receipt of your e-mail report. **NOTE:** eBay Customer Support investigates each and every report sent in. However, it does not issue outcome reports back to the reporting member.

DISPUTE RESOLUTION

Most eBay sellers, especially the more successful sellers, know how important it is to put the needs of the customer first. Buying from these sellers is a dream. You can tell if a seller is a customer-first seller by checking her feedback and her item description.

Even so, you may someday find yourself in a dispute with a seller, and fault or blame may be impossible to assign. Don't get angry. Keep your mind focused on your goal: resolving the dispute as soon as possible and putting the transaction behind you. *No other goal is worth pursuing!* Any warlike behavior like "getting even," "one-upmanship," "tit for tat" . . . all are pointless and only contribute to the world's already vast pool of ill will. They certainly won't get you a resolution.

In the event of a dispute with a seller, stay calm and civil.

Even though you and I know that the customer is always right, some sellers are not convinced. It doesn't mean that they are bad sellers—just that they haven't quite gotten the picture yet. Help them. Never lose your temper. Keep your e-mails polite and nonprovocative. If you resist the temptation to start screaming in an e-mail, the seller will be more likely to listen to your complaint and your suggestions for resolution.

Offer to work out the dispute with the seller. If the seller is agreeable, third-party dispute services like SquareTrade can help.

www.squaretrade.com

SquareTrade is a third-party fee-based service that will assign a professional, qualified arbitrator to listen to both sides of the dispute before issuing a best remedy. In most instances, the SquareTrade arbitrator can assist in reaching a solution that is agreeable to both parties.

Many sellers sign up with SquareTrade as a matter of good business, thus agreeing to a certain standard of conduct on eBay. Sellers who sign up will display the SquareTrade icon in their item descriptions:

Resolving a Transaction

If you have paid for an item but didn't receive it or if you paid for an item and received it but it is significantly different from the item description, follow these nine steps.

1. Check the item listing (within 10 days after the listing ends). Review the seller's terms of sale (if available), item description, and shipping and payment terms. Have you allowed enough time for the seller to receive and confirm payment? Have you read the seller's shipping terms? There are many reasons why delivery may take longer than you expect. For example, shipping and customs for international transactions can take time. Additionally, international bank transfers can take up to 14 days to complete.

Media mail shipments (containing items such as books, videotapes, DVDs, etc.) may take significantly longer than other shipping methods.

Some items may be custom-made or assembled before shipping, which may cause delays.

2. E-mail the seller (within 10 days after the listing ends).

If you are still concerned, e-mail the seller with your questions. If you don't have the seller's e-mail address, you can request it from eBay or use the "Ask seller a question" link on the item listing page.

3. Check your e-mail spam filters for messages from the seller (within 10 days after the listing ends).

It's possible that the seller is trying to e-mail you but your spam filters are blocking their messages.

4. Check your own contact information (within 10 days after the listing ends).

It's possible that the seller is trying to e-mail you but your contact information is incorrect. Go to "My Account" in My eBay and click on "Personal Information." Make sure your e-mail address is correct.

5. Call your seller (anytime after completing the first four steps).

Request the seller's contact information and give her a phone call. Many issues are just simple misunderstandings that can be resolved with a single phone call.

✔ Click the Advanced Search link on the top of any eBay page
✔ Click the option for Find Contact Information under the Members section in the Search box on the left hand side of the page
✔ Enter in the User ID of the seller and the item number of your transaction

eBay will send you the phone number of the seller.

6. Use eBay's Item Not Received or Significantly Not as Described process (10 to 60 days after the listing ends).

The majority of all transactions on eBay complete successfully but sometimes a problem can occur. The Item Not Received process is designed to help facilitate buyer and seller communication. To begin the process, click the Security Center link found at the bottom of every eBay page. Check the option for Item Not Received, click the Report Problem button, and follow the instructions from there.

If the Item Not Received process does not result in a satisfactory resolution to the transaction, the buyer can employ PayPal Buyer Protection or eBay's Standard Purchase Protection programs.

7. Go to PayPal (First 45 days after the listing ends).

If you paid with PayPal, please visit the PayPal Resolution Center to file a complaint. Your item may have enhanced protection through PayPal Buyer Protection if the item description page shows the PayPal Buyer Protection shield under the Seller Information box. To start the process, click the Security Center link on the bottom of the PayPal home page (*www.paypal.com*) and follow the instructions from there for PayPal Buyer Protection.

8. Contact your credit card company (First 45 days after the listing ends). Credit card companies typically provide some level of identity and purchase protection whether you paid with your credit card through PayPal or directly to the seller. Contact your credit card company to learn more.

9. File an eBay Standard Protection claim (After completing the Item Not Received or Significantly Not as Described process, but within 90 days after the listing ends).

Once you have completed the Item Not Received or Significantly Not as Described process, you may be eligible to file a claim under eBay's Standard Purchase Protection Program. Note: You must file a claim with your credit card company prior to filing a claim with eBay (if applicable).

The eBay standard purchase protection program provides partial reimbursement for losses resulting from non-delivery or misrepresentation of most items up to $200 (minus $25 processing cost).

Filing a fraud alert is the **initial step** toward potential reimbursement through the program.

✔ Click on the Help link on the top of any eBay page
✔ Type the words "fraud alert" into the Search Help box and click the Search Help button
✔ Click the link for Filing a Fraud Alert and follow the instructions from there

Once the fraud alert you have filed is processed, you'll be given instructions to file a protection claim.

Spoof e-mail

Also known as "phishing e-mail." Nearly everyone with an e-mail account has received at least one. A spoof e-mail appears to be from a trusted company like PayPal or eBay. They are usually formatted as an alert or warning that either your information needs updating or your registration or account has been flagged for some reason. A spoof e-mail often contains official company logos, text, links, and formatting. The "from" address and links appear to be from eBay. Overall, spoof e-mails often *look* official and legitimate. They aren't.

A Spoof Example

ebaY®

Update Your Account Information Within 24 Hours

Valued eBay Member,

You (or someone else) entered three times wrong the password to log in with your eBay ID.

According to our site policy you will have to confirm that you are the real owner of the eBay account by completing the following form or else your account will be suspended within 24 hours for investigations.

Never share your eBay password to anyone!

Establish your proof of identity with ID Verify (free of charge) - an easy way to help others trust you as their trading partner. The process takes about 5 minutes to complete and involves updating your eBay information. When you're successfully verified, you will receive an ID Verify icon ✪ in your feedback profile. Currently, the service is only available to residents of the United States and U.S. territories (Puerto Rico, US Virgin Islands and Guam.)

Please double check before you click Submit button.

ebaY®

| **Sign In** | | ⑦ Need Help? |
| Verify your e-bay account now! | or | Already an eBay user? |

Enter Your Registration Information

User ID [   ]

Password [   ]

Account type ☐ Seller ☐ Buyer

Name [   ] [   ] [   ]
First Name   M.I.   Last Name

email [   ]

City [   ]

State [Select State   ▼]

Postal Code (Zip) [   ]

Country [USA   ▼]

Primary phone # [   ]
for example, (415) 555-0304

Secondary phone # (optional) [   ]

Fax # (optional) [   ]

Gender (optional) [Unspecified ▼]

[Update registration information]

ebaY®
The World's Online Marketplace®

Announcements | Register | Safe Trading Tips | Policies |
Feedback Forum | About eBay

eBay or PayPal would never ask you to enter your User ID and password in an e-mail nor would they ask you to click a link to a Web page containing entry fields for this information or other information like your ATM PIN, security code, or social security number.

What do you do when you receive an e-mail that you suspect might be a spoof? First, never provide personal information (passwords, Social Security numbers, ATM PINs, etc.) when requested to so by instructions within an e-mail, no matter how convincing that e-mail might be. If you suspect that there may indeed be an issue or problem related to your registration or account, you should go directly to the site. Start by typing the site's address into a Web browser's Address box. Then navigate to your account or registration page. On eBay, go to "My eBay." On PayPal, go to My Account.

Learn more about protecting yourself from the potential danger of spoof e-mails by visiting the eBay Security Center. The link for the Security Center is displayed on the bottom of all eBay Web pages—even the eBay Sign In page:

On the Security & Resolution Center page, follow the links "Spoof (fake) e-mail" and eBay Marketplace Safety.

Protecting yourself from spoof e-mail is easy. Simply do not respond to the request. Do not click any links contained inside the e-mail. Provide no information. Report the e-mail to eBay by forwarding it to *spoof@bay.com* per the instructions on the eBay Security Center. Then delete the original e-mail.

In addition, you should download a free copy of the eBay Toolbar with Account Guard. The eBay Toolbar is a Web browser plug-in that not only helps alert you when you are about to visit a Web site that claims to be an eBay page but is not; the eBay Toolbar also makes shopping on eBay a lot simpler.

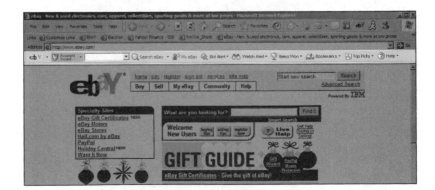

Download the eBay Toolbar by clicking the Services link on the top of any eBay page.

Then click the link for Buyer Tools (eBay Toolbar).

How to Get Help on eBay

Although I have tried to make this book as comprehensive as possible—covering every imaginable aspect of eBay and more—it would be impossible to anticipate everything that could possibly happen on eBay. You may find yourself with an issue or question that this book does not address (heaven forfend!). The following pathways to eBay Help should address these rare instances.

EBAY HELP

As discussed in chapter 2, "The eBay Web Site," a mountain of information about all things eBay, is on the eBay site itself. Most of it is pretty easy to find.

Click the Help link on the top of any eBay page. This will take you to the Help Hub:

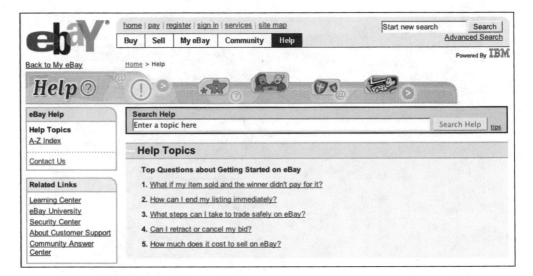

From here, you can search Help in two ways:

- Navigating through Help topics
- Searching Help using keywords

If you need to send an e-mail to eBay Customer Support, click the link Contact Us and follow the instructions from there.

LIVE HELP

In addition to the e-mail channel to Customer Support, you can also reach a support rep via our Live Help feature. Live Help lets you talk to a real, live support rep in a real-time "instant message" chat session.

Click the link for Live Help on the eBay home page.

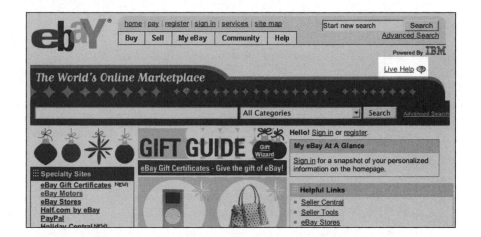

This will open a chat window. Enter your e-mail address or eBay User ID and select a topic from the drop-down list.

Wait while the window loads, and a rep will be with you shortly. eBay Help and eBay Live Help can provide answers to questions from the most basic to the most complex. However, eBay Help doesn't stop there. eBay provides other channels for learning, both on- and off-site. All of these channels are grouped together under the eBay Learning Center, the hub page for eBay Education.

EBAY EDUCATION

eBay is dedicated to helping new and experienced eBay members alike learn how to use the eBay site more effectively. To this end, many on- and off-line eBay educational initiatives are available to all eBay members.

You can reach the Learning Center at *http://pages.ebay.com/education/*.

The Learning Center is your one-stop hub page for all things related to eBay Education, including on-site tours, tutorials, workshops, and seminars.

eBay On-Site Tours and Tutorials

For those eBay members who desire a detailed explanation of how to bid, how to sell, etc., excellent real-time basic tutorials are available at the eBay Learning Center.

In addition to the links to tours and tutorials, the left-hand sidebar has a link for eBay University.

eBay University

In June of 2000, eBay started a program called eBay University. An eBay U seminar consists of a daylong series of one-hour classes or workshops on all aspects of buying and selling on eBay. The seminars are held in a different city approximately every two weeks throughout the year. Attendance at a single eBay U varies from about five hundred to fifteen hundred eager new and experienced eBay members.

The eBay University instructor roster is made up of eBay selling experts. Each instructor leads a specific workshop. Currently, I instruct most of "Basic Selling."

eBay University seminars are incredible learning experiences for both the brand-new as well as the seasoned eBay member.

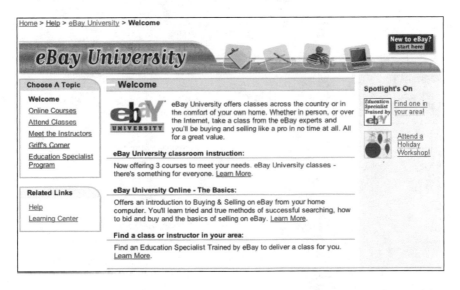

eBay University seminars provide an excellent opportunity for picking up a few tips, passing on your suggestions to eBay staff face-to-face, and meeting other eBay members (who are, without a doubt, the most enthusiastic and fun group of people I've ever had the pleasure of meeting).

If you are looking for eBay instruction and classes in a more traditional setting, check the eBay University schedule for a list of upcoming events at *www.ebay. com/university*.

If the eBay University schedule doesn't include your town, don't despair! In 2003, eBay University was expanded to include online seminars as well as on-site events. You can download the entire eBay U curriculum in streaming video or order the courses on CD-ROM. But wait! There's more!

In 2004, eBay launched the eBay Education Specialist program to help support the hundreds of individual instructors who either lead their own workshops or provide instruction to eager new eBay members across the country. If you are looking for a more immediate eBay class or if you require one-on-one coaching to help you get started selling on eBay, locate a specialist in your area through the eBay Education Specialist Directory. If you are currently teaching others how to use eBay, you might want to sign up to become an eBay Education Specialist.

The eBay Education Specialist Program page is reached by the sidebar link on the eBay University page.

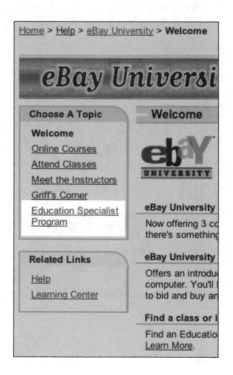

eBay Workshops

eBay hosts a series of regularly scheduled eBay Workshops on specific eBay topics, such as "International Trading" or "Repairing Antique Reed Organs." These workshops are presented in a moderated chat-board format with a guest "speaker" answering real-time questions from eBay members.

You can see the current schedule of chat workshops by visiting the Workshop section of the Community page:

See the About Me page for workshop events at *http://members.ebay.com/ aboutme/workshopevents/*.

If you have questions related to specific aspects of selling, you should check the Workshop schedule regularly.

If you are interested in hosting a workshop in your particular field, send an e-mail to *workshopevents@ebay.com*.

COMMUNITY DISCUSSION BOARDS

Chat boards played an important role in the formation and growth of eBay, and they continue to do so today. In fact, if there is one thing not lacking in the eBay Community, it's chat!

eBay started out with one chat board, called the AuctionWeb Bulletin Board. There, a new eBay member could learn from other eBay members, among many topics, how to list an item for sale, how to create and host digital pictures, how to pack an item correctly, and how to find the best deals on packing materials.

There, folks could meet and chat about almost anything.

Over time, this one board grew into two, then three, and then four. Today, there are over a hundred separate chat areas on eBay. Each is dedicated to a special topic or aspect of buying, selling, or collecting, and most contain hundreds of threaded discussions.

These discussion boards are often a source of excellent help and information provided by other expert eBay members themselves. I urge you to visit them by clicking on the Community link on the eBay Navigation Bar and selecting the link for either Chat or Discussion Boards.

Talk... Boards

Discussion Boards | Chat | **Answer Center**

Community Help Boards

Auction Listings
Bidding
Checkout
eBay Sales Reports NEW!
eBay Stores
Escrow/Insurance
Feedback
International Trading
Miscellaneous
My eBay
Packaging & Shipping
PayPal
Photos/HTML
Policies/User Agreement
Registration
Search
Seller Central NEW!
Technical Issues
Tools - SA Basic
Tools - SA Pro
Tools - Selling Manager
Tools - Selling Manager Pro NEW!
Tools - Turbo Lister
Trading Assistant
Trust & Safety (SafeHarbor)

Category-Specific Discussion Boards

Animals
Antiques
Art & Artists
Bears
Book Readers
Booksellers
Business & Industrial
Children's Clothing Boutique
Clothing, Shoes & Accessories
Coins & Paper Money
Collectibles
Comics
Computers, Networking & I.T
Cooks Nook
Decorative & Holiday
Disneyana NEW!
Dolls
eBay Motors
Health & Beauty
Historical Memorabilia
Hobbies & Crafts
Home & Garden
Jewelry
Motorcycle Boulevard
Movies & Memorabilia
Music & Musicians
Needle Arts & Vintage Textiles
Outdoor Sports
Photography
Pottery, Glass, & Porcelain
Real Estate & Timeshares
Science & Mystery
Speciality Services NEW!
Sports Cards, Memorabilia & Fan Shop
Toys & Hobbies
Travel, Vacation & Adventure
Vintage Clothing & Accessories

General Discussion Boards

New to eBay Board
  Are you new to eBay? Welcome. Come on in and join the fun.
The Front Porch
  Sit down and relax with eBay friends!
The Homestead
  Talk with other members about home-related subjects.
The Park
  Visit with other members, discuss pleasant recreational topics or hobbies, play games and find out about

The discussions can become pretty raucous at times, but it's all in good fun. Find a topic that interests you and either lurk (read the posts without participating) or get involved and ask a question, introduce yourself, or help answer questions.

You will find instructions on how to use the chat forums—how to post, how to search, the rules of conduct, etc.—by clicking any of the links on the various chat pages.

eBay member Deanna Rittel has this to say about the eBay chat forums:

I truly enjoy the chat boards on eBay. I usually "hang out" at the Town Square but have been known to wander over to the others occasionally. I've learned more on them than I ever thought I would, and sometimes more than I ever needed to! In three days I had three different items that I needed to identify. In each case I literally had the item identified in less than five minutes. There are very knowledgeable and helpful people willing to help at the drop of a pin.

Just last week, I posted on the Town Square that I was looking for a couple of specific "state" quarters for my two children who are collecting them. Everyone went through their change and located the ones I needed within minutes. We had been looking for them for weeks—a couple of months at least! One specific poster e-mailed me directly—he offered to send my children "mint uncirculated" coins every time they come out. He collects them also and told me he would love to make my children happy and complete their collection for them. These quarters only come out every few months and only five are issued each year. So these will take quite a few more years to complete. He said it was worth the money to make them happy. We have already received the quarters I had originally been looking for from some wonderful individuals on Town Square, and we also received the first "shipment" from the poster who is completing their collections. No one wanted to be reimbursed—I TRIED! My children are just absolutely thrilled, and to quote my six-year-old daughter, "Mom, have you ever met such a nice people? They aren't like those people who call you at work!" I work at an insurance company, if that tells you anything—I guess she really listens to my horror stories—LOL!

Finally—I would like to say that the eBay community is truly that—a community. There is always someone around on the boards to answer a question when you have one, make you laugh when you need to, offer a shoulder to cry on, and, of course, there is always a good dose of controversy when you need a good argument!

EBAY LIVE

In June of 2001, eBay hosted its first user conference in Anaheim, California. "eBay Live" was attended by over five thousand eBay members of all ages and occupations from across the continental United States.

The three days of peace, love, and trading—featuring parties, workshops, seminars, roundtable discussions with eBay employees, vendor booths, guest speakers, special events, and panel discussions with eBay executive staff—was such a hit that we've made eBay Live an annual event.

Check the eBay Calendar of Events for more information about future eBay Live and other special eBay events. Go to the Community link on the eBay Navigation Bar, which takes you to the Overview page. Click the link for Calendar.

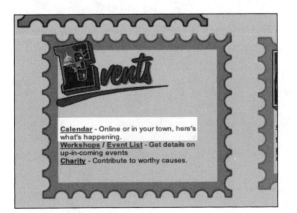

That will take you to the current calendar of eBay events.

In addition, a special page is devoted to eBay Live at *http://pages.ebay.com/ ebaylive/*.

You've reached the end of Section One. Take a deep breath. Section Two deals with the fine (and simple!) art of eBay selling.

Selling
the eBay Way!

"How do I get started selling on eBay?" This is definitely the question I hear most frequently. Selling on eBay is actually quite easy to grasp . . . once you have listed your first item. It's the first item that can overwhelm the new eBay seller into total paralysis. Don't panic. Listing your first item on eBay will be a snap now that Griff is here to help guide you through the entire process, step-by-step. Not everyone was so lucky. Take Dave for example.

In January of 1996, business owner Dave Rayner suffered a serious back injury, costing him his business and livelihood. By March of that year, he and his wife were barely surviving off a combination of their diminishing savings and the meager wages she earned working at a grocery store twenty miles away from their home.

The night that Dave discovered eBay, he stumbled upon the eBay chat board and found eBay founder Pierre Omidyar chatting with others. Pierre personally welcomed Dave to eBay. Dave noted Pierre's e-mail address.

Dave needed to replace a malfunctioning computer mouse. He turned to eBay to find a quick replacement.

"I found an auction featuring PS 2 Mice with a starting bid of $1. Wow, that's a bargain, and it was a Dutch Auction to boot, so I bid for two mice at a top bid of a buck."

Dave watched the auction for a full day until the final seconds passed and the auction ended with him as a high bidder for 2 brand-new mice for $2. Or so he thought.

"I got an e-mail from the seller stating, 'CONGRATULATIONS! YOU'VE WON 2 LOTS of Mice for 400 DOLLARS!!'"

Dave was dumbfounded. He discovered that he had misread the item description and was indeed the proud owner of two lots of two hundred mice at one dollar apiece for a total of $400!

Dave went into a panic. His wife and he had only $600 left in their savings account.

"I knew my wife would go through the roof when I told her what I'd done. I e-mailed Pierre for help."

Within a day, Dave received a reply back from Pierre suggesting that Dave contact the seller to see if they might work out a solution. In the meantime, Dave had noticed an advertisement in a computer magazine for a company in Maine that was selling the very same type of computer mice that Dave had purchased at eBay.

"I called the company and asked if they'd be interested in buying four hundred mice. The guy on the other end said he would take them off my hands."

The gentleman offered Dave $8 apiece for the mice for a total of $3,200, which, after subtracting the initial $400 cost to the eBay seller, left Dave with a profit of $2,800!

Elated and relieved, Dave e-mailed Pierre to inform him of the tale's happy ending.

"Pierre told me if I could turn deals like that, I'd never have a problem selling on eBay. I started selling a week later after winning another mouse . . . you see, I sold ALL of that two-lot batch and forgot to keep one out for myself!"

Dave continued buying and selling at eBay for another year. In 1997, he started an image-hosting service called AuctionPix, which is today a profitable and popular image-hosting solution for thousands of other eBay sellers.

Dave has never looked back.

"I will always remember that day I opened the box to see four hundred mice staring back at me, knowing that not only had I turned a disaster into a profit but also had a chance to meet one of the nicest people in the online world—Pierre, founder of eBay!"

Selling Setup, Step-by-Step

You have one thing you want to sell, you want to sell it quickly, and you don't have time to take a three-day course in eBay Selling 101. This section is for you.

FOLLOWING THE STEPS

Selling your first item on eBay can be broken down into ten steps:

Preparation
Step 1. Set Up an eBay Seller's Account (Onetime Step)
Step 2. Research Your Item
Step 3. Photograph the Item
Step 4. Describe the Item
Step 5. Pack and Weigh the Item

List the Item
Step 6. The Sell Your Item Process

After the Sale
Step 7. Contact the Buyer
Step 8. Accept Payment
Step 9. Ship the Item
Step 10. Leave Feedback

But first, here are the three most common questions asked by brand-new sellers:

How long will it take to list my first item?

If you use a digital camera to take a picture of your item for Step 3, and if you follow the next chapters carefully, the five "Preparation" steps for listing your very first eBay item can take as little as forty-five minutes to one hour. Using a print-film camera will add from one to several hours to this time, depending on how quickly your local film developer does his job.

Listing moves much faster once you have listed a few items.

How long will it take to sell my first item?

Your first eBay item could sell on the first day you list it, if you provide the Buy It Now format as an option, or if you use the standard auction format and select the "one day" duration. Otherwise, your item could take three, five, seven, or ten days to sell, depending on the duration you select.

How long will it take me to receive payment for my first item?

Receiving payment for your item after the sale can take as little as a few minutes if you use PayPal to accept credit card payments from your buyer, or it can take as long as a week or more for mailed checks or money orders.

In this chapter, we will start you on your way to eBay selling by first walking you through Step 1, "Setting Up an eBay Seller's Account."

Selling on eBay, Step 1— Setting Up an eBay Seller's Account

To sell something on eBay, you need to be a registered eBay user. If you are not yet registered, follow the instructions in Section One, chapter 1, "Let's Get Started." Once you are registered, you are ready to set up an eBay Seller's Account. The process is fairly simple and quick.

To set up an eBay Seller's Account, you must provide eBay with credit-card and bank-account information, or you can utilize the ID Verify feature (provided to eBay by Verisign).

SETTING UP A SELLER'S ACCOUNT WITH A CREDIT CARD AND BANK-ACCOUNT INFORMATION

As always, start at the top of any eBay page:

Click on the Sell link. This will bring you to the Sell hub page.

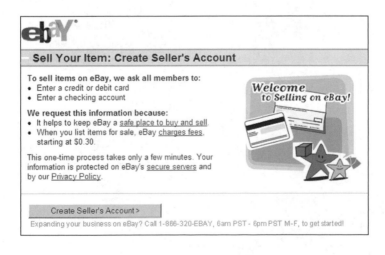

Click on "Sell Your Item." If you haven't signed in for this session, you will be prompted to do so. After signing in, you will see the following:

As the screen says, have a credit or debit card and bank-account check on hand. Then click Create Seller's Account. The first screen looks like this:

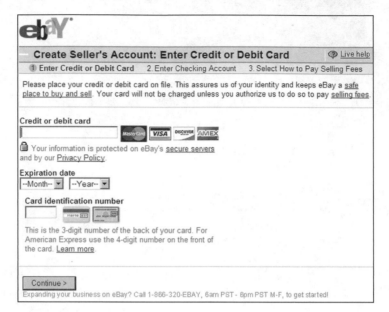

Enter a valid credit or debit card and details. Click Continue.

Now enter the requested bank-account details. The location on the check for the information needed is shown on the page. Click Continue. On the next screen, you select an option for paying your eBay seller fees.

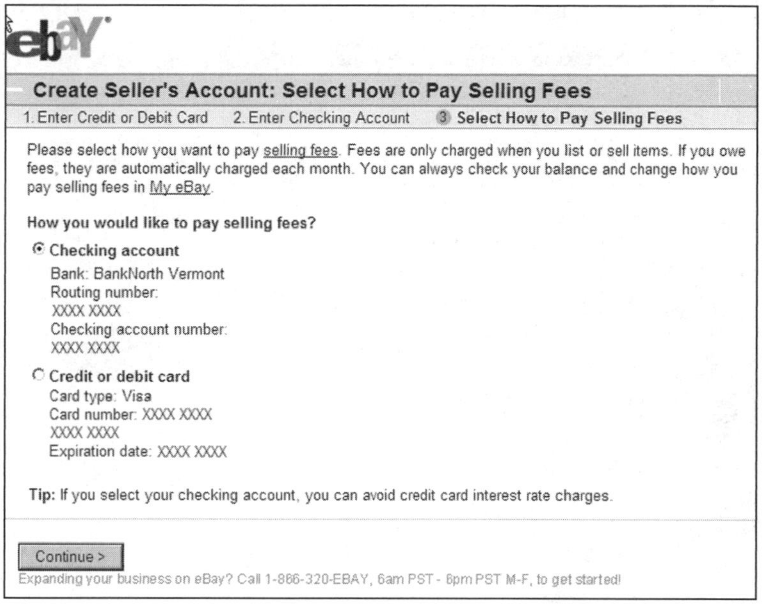

Depending on your selection, you then must authorize eBay to make deductions from your account or card.

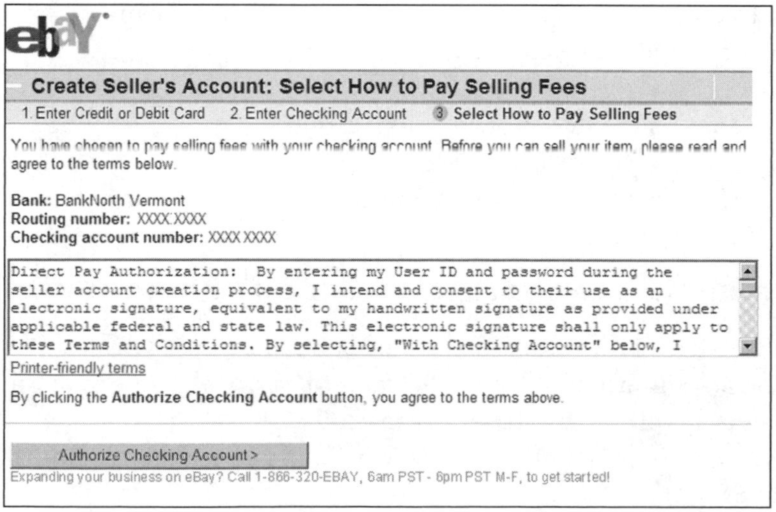

Click Authorize . . .

. . . and you are ready to start listing items on eBay.

TROUBLESHOOTING

If eBay is unable to verify the bank or credit card information you provided, it will most likely be that eBay is unable to connect to your bank or credit card issuer for verification. The solutions are to:

1. Try another credit card and bank account.
2. Try again later (my least favorite).
3. Use ID Verify to verify your eBay Seller's Account information.

SETTING UP AN EBAY SELLER'S ACCOUNT USING ID VERIFY

If your bank-account information cannot be verified or if you would prefer not to provide a bank account or credit card to verify the information for your seller's account, you can use ID Verify instead.

ID Verify is a service provided by Verisign. The process is quick, easy, and only costs $5.

GRIFF TIP! ID Verify requires you to enter financial and personal information that only you should know. This information is *not* kept on file and is only checked once for accuracy. You should have on hand all of your bank loan, car loan, mortgage, and credit card numbers so you don't have to go a-hunting for them in the middle of the process.

To verify your Seller's Account information using ID Verify, click the Services link on the top of any eBay page. The link for ID Verify is located under General Services, Trust and Safety section:

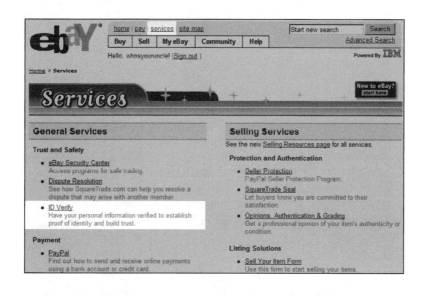

Click the ID Verify link to go directly to the ID Verify start screen.

Click Sign Up Now to begin.
This will take you to the first step: Accept Terms.

Read the terms, and if you agree, click I Agree. Next, sign in and click Sign In Securely.

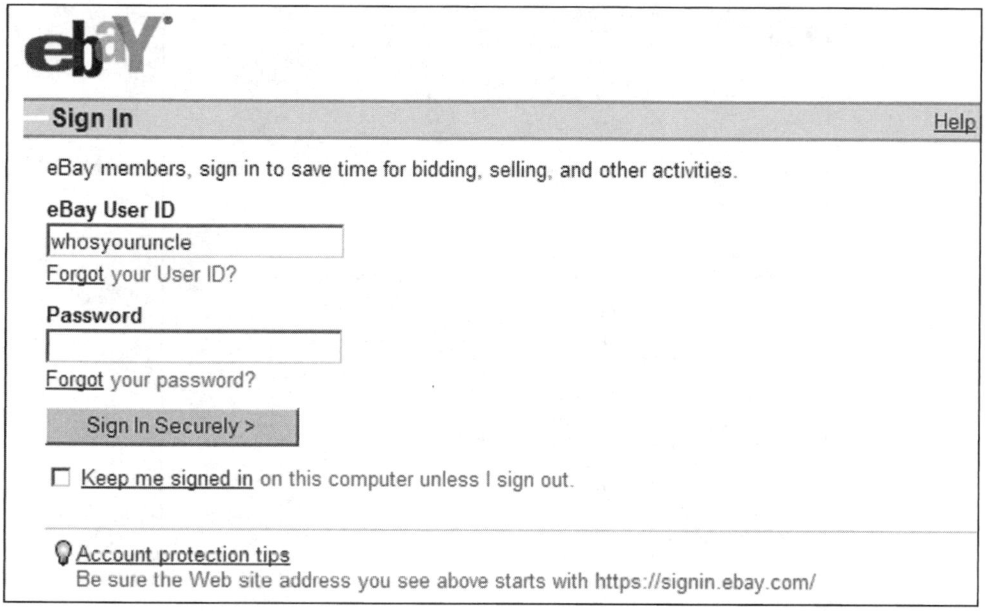

eb**Y**

Sign In   Help

eBay members, sign in to save time for bidding, selling, and other activities.

eBay User ID

whosyouruncle

Forgot your User ID?

Password

Forgot your password?

Sign In Securely >

☐ Keep me signed in on this computer unless I sign out.

💡 Account protection tips
Be sure the Web site address you see above starts with https://signin.ebay.com/

Next, enter the requested information. Again, this information is not stored on eBay. It is only used one time for verification.

ID Verify: Verify Account Information

① Verify Account Information   2 Verification Questions   3 Confirm

Providing the information below helps us confirm who you are and
ensures that no one can use your information to sell on eBay.

?Questions about
Additional Verification?

- Your information is secure! Protecting your information and privacy
  is important to us.
- Transfer of your information is protected by secure 128-bit
  encrypted SSL.

Contact Information

Please verify your Information below. Accurate information is required to
maintain your eBay account. Changing any of the contact information
below will also update your eBay account.

* = Required

Full Name*   James   J   Griffith
e.g., John H. Doe   First name   M.I.   Last name

Company Name

Address *

City *   San Jose

State *   California

Postal Code (Zip) *

Primary telephone * (408)   -   ext.:

Secondary telephone (408)   -   ext.:
(optional)

Identification Information

Please complete your information below. It's a secure process and your
personal information is safe. Transfer of your information is protected by
secure 128-bit encrypted SSL.

Date of Birth *   19

Social Security
Number *   -   -

Driver's License   California
Number *   e.g. A189764530

You understand that by clicking on the Continue button below, you are
providing "written instructions" to eBay under the Fair Credit Reporting
Act authorizing eBay and its service partners to obtain information from
your personal credit profile from a credit bureau on eBay's behalf. You
authorize eBay and its service partners to obtain such information solely
to confirm your identity to avoid fraudulent transactions in your name. If
you wish to "opt out" of sharing your personal information with eBay and
its service partners, DO NOT click on the Continue button.

Continue >

Once you have filled out all the fields, click Continue. This will display the
information. Check for accuracy. Otherwise ID Verify will not proceed.

On the next page, you will be asked to provide bits of personal information (such as your previous address) and financial information connected to some of your financial accounts (loans, mortgages, or credit cards).

Once you have completed the page, click Continue. If the information you provided is accurate (i.e., matches what is on file at Verisign), you will see the following:

eBay®
home | pay | services | site map   Start new search   Search
Buy   Sell   My eBay   Community   Help   Advanced Search
Hello, whosyouruncle! (Sign out)   Powered By IBM

ID Verify: Successful

You have successfully completed the ID Verify process.   ② Questions about ID Verify?

Check your ID Verify icon 🔵 in your feedback profile.

About eBay | Announcements | Security Center | Policies | Site Map | Help

Copyright © 1995-2005 eBay Inc. All Rights Reserved. Designated trademarks and brands are the property of their respective owners. Use of this Web site constitutes acceptance of the eBay User Agreement and Privacy Policy.

eBay official time

You are now ID Verified, a Seller's Account has been added to your eBay registration, and you are ready to list items on eBay!

GRIFF TIP! ID Verify not only works as an alternative to setting up a Seller's Account with a credit card and a bank account; it also removes bidding and listing restrictions based on feedback scores. For example, using the Fixed Price format requires a seller to have a feedback score of 30 or higher. With ID Verify, this restriction is removed. It also allows the seller with a 0–29 feedback score to set up an eBay Store. My advice? Set up your Seller's Account with both a credit card and a bank account as well as with ID Verify. You'll bypass pesky low-feedback restrictions and provide a greater sense of security for your potential buyers.

Congratulations! You have set up an eBay Seller's Account. Before we move on to the next step, I want to share another incredible eBay story sent to me by eBay member Heather Luce:

Several years ago I was working at a countywide newspaper as the editor. It was a fun job, but it wasn't anything I was terribly passionate about. On the side, I was doing my artwork and creating costumes for people to pose in as reference for my paintings. The costumes were primarily Renaissance in design, and my closets started to fill up. I began giving the costumes to friends and family, and after a while they told me, "NO MORE!" Apparently THEIR closets were starting to fill up too.

At that time, I had been to eBay a few times and had bought some small items. My experiences had all been pleasant, and on a whim I decided to try my hand at selling. I pulled out two of the costumes I had made but had never used for any of my paintings and listed them at $75 each, for seven-day listings. I still remember them: a milkmaid gown, "The Artiste," and a gold Italian Renaissance gown. Each gown sold for over $100 and I was instantly addicted. For four weeks I made new gowns and listed them while working full-time at the newspaper. (I was also a full-time nontraditional college student as well.) At the end of four weeks, I had made more money from the gowns I had sold on eBay than from my regular full-time job. I knew that I had found my passion, and two weeks later I quit my job and plunged full-time into the world of Renaissance Costuming.

That was almost two years ago and my business has grown by leaps and bounds. I now have a wonderful Web site and a customer base from all around the world. In fact, just today I sent a gown to Australia, and last week I was contacted by a woman from Germany who wants a new Renaissance gown as well. I've costumed actors from Renaissance faires—even "Queen Elizabeth" (aka Ms. Flores)! I get e-mails all summer long from people claiming, "I saw one of your gowns at my Renaissance faire last weekend!"

It's been a huge struggle. During this time I was still going to college full-time and was also going through a divorce. There were times when I was worried that eBay wouldn't be enough and I would have to give up my "dream" job as a costume designer. But eBay has never failed me. My business has grown from a hobby to a full-time professional career and shows no signs of slowing down.

None of it would have been possible without eBay.

eBay allows average, everyday folks like me the opportunity to realize dreams. It puts us in touch with people from around the world for mere pennies. Nowhere else can you get as much advertising for your dollar—and be extremely successful in the process. eBay is a forum that allows people of ALL interests to shop in one convenient place. It allows for competitive pricing, and most important to me, it allows sellers a chance to really get to know their customers.

I have made some of the most wonderful friendships through eBay. (I swear, I have the nicest customers in the WORLD!)

I heard that eBay was going to open storefronts a few weeks before they made them open to the public. The week before they opened, I took pictures and wrote up all the listings for my anticipated storefront. The morning they were made available to the public, I rose at 6:00 A.M. and got to work opening mine. It was terribly exciting and within weeks the orders started pouring in.

Everything I have done has all been due to eBay. Without eBay I would still be working at a job that was not my "passion." Now I wake up every morning eager to get to work (which I can now do in my pj's!) and I spend all day and well into the night creating magnificent gowns—something I have always loved doing. The rewards come in the form of ecstatic e-mails (and sometimes boxes of chocolate through regular mail) from my customers. (Have I mentioned that I have the BEST customers in the WORLD?)

Because of eBay I now work with a group of Renaissance-gown eBay sellers and we work to promote eBay as a whole and we share tips and tricks to provide our customers with the best service and quality garments possible. They are absolutely delightful to work with and we have all become good friends. . . .

2

Research Your Item

Many sellers skip this step. Don't! To ensure the best possible chances for your listing's success, you must first determine the current market value for the item on eBay, as well as determine and adopt the best possible listing practices of those who are already successfully selling on eBay.

First consideration: what to list?

Of course, it helps if you already know what you plan on selling. If so, then you are ready to start searching for similar items on eBay so you can compare and learn what works for that type of item and, more important, what doesn't.

Maybe you have no idea what to sell. In that case, select from your possessions something of little or no value to you. Perhaps some thoughtful but unfortunate item gifted to you by a dear friend or relative. Don't let that treasure continue gathering dust in the back of the closet. Recycle it! eBay is the perfect "regifting" destination.

Whatever you select as your first eBay listing, try to make it something that is not too valuable, fragile, large, or heavy. Small, durable, and easy-to-pack items are best for a first-time listing. And except for choice collectibles or antiques, your first eBay item for sale should be something new, preferably in its original box.

Once you have settled on the your first item, it's time to research similar items . . . on eBay of course!

Completed Listings Search

eBay is not only an active and dynamic marketplace, it's also transparent; that is, anyone can view the market for any item or category. This transparency provides you with an excellent research tool called Completed Listings Search.

Using Completed Listings Search, any registered eBay member can, by keyword or category, search for any item that has closed in the last two weeks. Completed Listings Search lets you locate closed items that match yours so you can compare them by title, description, photos, starting and ending price, shipping and handling costs, payment options, number of bids, number of page hits, etc. You can then adopt and tailor for your own use those listing practices that work (i.e., result in high final-bid amounts) and avoid like the plague those that don't (i.e., result in low or no bids).

NOTE: Use the best listing descriptions as examples to emulate in your own words and formatting, but never lift another seller's description and formatting to paste into yours!

At a local yard sale, I found a small, colorful pottery pitcher for only a quarter! The bottom is marked Honiton. It's small and easy to pack and ship. This little pitcher will make the perfect first listing on eBay.

SEARCHING COMPLETED LISTINGS

Start by clicking the Advanced Search link on the top right-hand corner of any eBay page.

In the box provided, enter the keyword or words that best describe your item. Then check the box "Completed listings only" and click Search.

Sign in (if prompted).

Sort the results if appropriate. In this case, I am only interested in looking through pottery items, so I'll click the "Pottery & Glass" link on the left under Matching Categories.

This reduces the number of results from 109 to 70. Scroll through the list of completed listings.

Pick a few listings and compare them using this handy checklist:

Completed Listings Checklist

Title
Starting price
Description
Photos
Selling format
Number of bids
Payment options
Shipping/handling fees
Return/refund policy
Category
Hit counter

Title

Titles are composed of keywords. Keywords are what eBay shoppers use to find items. A good listing title should contain as many appropriate keywords as possible and few or no unsearchable words (such as *rare, beautiful, L@@K,* etc.). Compare these two titles and the amount of bids received.

HONITON VASE

GBP 14.99   Not specified   0   Jan-03 07:26

* View similar active items
* List an item like this

Two Honiton Devon Handpainted Egg Cups and Saucers

GBP 12.50   GBP 4.78   19   Dec-29 09:44

* View similar active items
* List an item like this

GRIFF TIP! If you are unfamiliar with the category or type of item you plan on listing—for example, a collectible like a Honiton pitcher—the list of similar completed listings on eBay can provide clues. For example, my research has already taught me that my pitcher may be from the 1950s, might be called a Manaton vase, and was made in England! eBay isn't just a fun place to buy and sell; it's a veritable gold mine of information.

Starting Price

The starting price is the amount at which the bidding will begin. Check any listing on eBay that closes without a bid. Although other factors may be involved, the most common reason for an unsuccessful listing (i.e., no bids received) is a too high starting price.

Check the starting prices for those listings that have sold to determine what your starting price should be.

NOTE: A low starting price in conjunction with a reasonable reserve can provide the optimal solution: a starting price to entice bidders and a reserve to prevent your item from selling for lower than your lowest acceptable price.

Description

A good description will always include all item details (size, color, make, model, serial number, condition, age, etc.), as well as detailed shipping and handling costs and accepted payment methods (PayPal, checks, money orders). Also, the best descriptions on eBay always contain a detailed return and refund policy.

Then there are the one- or two-sentence descriptions like "Item in good condition. e-mail me with questions."

Which description do you imagine encourages the most bids and, consequently, the highest sales-to-listing ratio? Your research of completed-item descriptions may provide an answer.

Photos

Some listings include several sharp, well-lit, professional digital photos. Other listings display one image, often poorly lit and focused. There are even listings with no photos. Study examples of photos for completed items. Think about how you can provide even better, more professional-looking photos.

Another important photo factor: Listings that have a Gallery image (the little thumbnail next to the item title) tend to receive more attention than those that don't. For example:

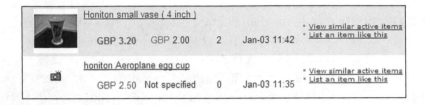

Selling Format

Although there is no hard-and-fast rule, some items are better served by the auction format (rare or valuable items), while others are usually best listed with a fixed-price format. By checking the successful listings that match your item, you can better determine which format might work best for you.

Number of Bids

The number of bids is a good indication of item desirability: the higher the bid number, the more this item was of interest to buyers. Low bid numbers? Check the other factors like starting price, photo, and description.

Payment Options

Most sellers provide more than one way for a buyer to pay for their item. The most popular online payment option is PayPal, and many buyers will only shop for items they can purchase with PayPal. Other sellers state "money orders or checks only." Providing as many payment options as possible (and including PayPal) is definitely a "best listing practice," but check matching completed items for yourself to see if this holds true for your item. If you discover that many sellers of your type of item are not offering PayPal, maybe offering it will give you a competitive edge.

Shipping/Handling Fees

Your research will often show that, all other factors being equal, the seller that offers the clearest shipping and handling terms, the most reasonable shipping and handling fees, and more than one shipping option will usually win the most bidders (which often results in the highest final-bid amounts). Later, we will see tools that you can provide your buyers so they can calculate accurate shipping costs before they bid or buy.

Return/Refund Policy

A reasonable and clear return and refund policy will go a long way toward instilling buyer confidence. Notice how listings with good return and refund policies often have a higher number of bids compared to those that don't. Find examples of return and refund polices that will work for you and adopt them.

Category

Although most eBay buyers find their items through a keyword search of titles (or titles and descriptions), many sellers limit their keyword descriptions to specific categories. Improperly categorizing an item often results in fewer buyers finding the item.

Also, some sellers can actually increase the potential of their listing by listing in two categories. Check your seller competition and see if they are listing their items in two categories.

Hit Counter

Sellers can add a free hit counter to the bottom of their listing description. The counter indicates the number of times the page has been viewed. An item with a high counter number and low or no bids indicates that something is amiss with one of the other checklist items.

In summary, research is crucial. You cannot expect to succeed in a marketplace unless you fully understand the workings of that marketplace, and that includes all possible listing practices, both good and bad. Adopt and emulate the good listing practices and avoid the bad. It's as simple as that! Finally, markets are not static. Make a habit of conducting regular searches of eBay completed listings.

GRIFF TIP! Never stop researching. Even if you should become an experienced and successful eBay seller, you will find the key to maintaining success is to stay on top of your competition, and the only way to do so is to check their listings, both current and completed.

Let's move on to our photos.

3

Creating and Editing Digital Pictures of Your eBay Item

Chris and Kim Hecker (theblueox) joined eBay in 1996, only nine months after Pierre launched the original site.

"It was a moment of inspiration when we stumbled upon eBay, thanks to my brother," Chris said. "My wife and I looked at each other, our mouths dropped, and we knew we had to give it a try. We were both looking for a way out of corporate America."

At first Chris and Kim listed a few collectibles they had purchased at local auctions. To their delight, all of the items sold. Thus began the Heckers' long and successful careers as eBay sellers.

They converted their Chicago basement into "the blue ox" headquarters, from which they now run a global operation selling vintage toys exclusively on eBay. Today, the Heckers are official eBay Power Sellers with an average of fourteen hundred or so available listings on any given day for everything from rare Hot Wheels cars to Pink Panther dolls.

Both Chris and Kim quit their "real" jobs to sell on eBay full-time. It could not have been an easy decision. No matter how much we might hate our current job, it takes real determination and, yes, courage to toss aside the security of a steady paycheck for the uncertain and scary world of self-employment. Not everyone who strikes out on the entrepreneurial road discovers instant riches—being your own boss has its own set of perils and trials—but nearly everyone I have ever met who has taken the plunge and started his or her own business on eBay admits that the experience has changed her life, sometimes in profound, sometimes in unexpected ways, but always for the better.

Having completed more than twenty-eight thousand unique transactions in the last eight years, with over fifty-one thousand positive feedbacks left, the Heckers have helped people around the world complete their toy collections, now and then ending searches that have lasted for twenty or even thirty years. They have learned, firsthand and on their own, the ins and outs of running a business, and though they are the first to admit that selling full-time on eBay takes a lot of work and time, Chris and Kim obviously love what they do.

They are the masters of their own destinies. They are eBay sellers!

What Are "Digital Pictures"?

To define and explain what makes up a digital picture, we first need to define a film picture.

A *film picture* is a mechanical and chemical recording of visual information. It is created by focusing reflected light from an object or view onto a piece of film. The light changes the chemical layers that make up the film. When the exposed film is chemically developed, a reaction in the layers of chemicals on the film re-creates the initial visual information, but only as a negative of the original image. The negative is then converted into a print by a sort of reverse process of what happened in the camera. The image on the print picture is made up of microscopic bits of color, so fine the eye cannot see them as separate dots but instead sees them as bands and areas of different color.

A *digital picture* is an electronic recording of light reflected off an object or scene that has been converted to, or created as, a digital computer file. In a digital image, the light from the camera lens (or from a scanned print) strikes a special recording device, which converts the light information into binary information (ones and zeros) and stores this information as a digital file either within the camera or on your computer.

Do I Need Digital Pictures of My eBay Item?

Do you want to sell your item? Then you *will* need a picture of your item. Items without pictures usually end up closing out with no bidders or buyers—a waste of time and insertion fees.

eBay buyers are a funny lot. They like to see what they are buying. Imagine that! As a seller, you must provide the best possible pictures of your wares if you want to generate any buyer interest. Your item pictures should be clear, focused, uncluttered, and as close a representation of your item as possible. In addition, they should be big enough to show all important details, but, since they will be digital files, small enough to download through the Internet and onto the item page as quickly as possible.

To the newbie, the whole concept of digital images can seem overwhelming. In reality, creating, editing, and uploading digital images is a snap *if* you approach the subject methodically, step-by-step. After you have finished your first digital picture, creating more will be a piece of cake, I promise.

There are three parts to "Quick and Painless eBay Picture Mastery":

1. Taking the picture
2. Editing the picture
3. Uploading the picture to your listing

Parts 1 and 2 are described in great detail in this chapter. Part 3 is covered later in the book.

Read through this chapter carefully and you'll have a good image of your item ready for your first eBay listing in no time!

Taking the Picture—Selecting a Method

Before we start setting up the item for photographing, we first need to consider which of the three basic options for creating digital pictures we will use. Depending on what equipment you have at your disposal, you could:

1. Take a picture of the item with a regular camera and have a local *film developer* convert your prints or negatives directly into digital files on a CD-ROM.
2. Take a picture of the item with a regular camera, have the film developed, and scan the prints into your computer using a *flatbed scanner*.
3. Take a picture of the item with a *digital camera*.

Which of the three options is right for you? Let's discuss their pros and cons.

FILM DEVELOPERS

If you don't have a digital camera or a flatbed scanner, use a regular film camera to take pictures of your item and take the exposed film to your local film developer—one that can create digital files of your images either on floppy disk or CD-ROM. Most local film and camera stores, national chain pharmacies, and even some supermarkets now offer this service.

PRO: Film developers are ideal for the first-time or occasional seller. No shelling out for or mussing or fussing with a digital camera or scanner. If time and budget are concerns, and you don't have access to a digital camera, go with the film-developer option.

CON: As a long-term option, buying and developing film will prove counterproductive. The money spent in just a few months on film and processing will pay for a good digital camera. Also, as part of developing—whether by machine or person—irreversible decisions will be made regarding the tone, brightness, etc., of your image files. Usually, this is not an issue, but occasionally the resulting digital pictures may not be entirely to your liking.

FLATBED SCANNERS

Flatbed scanners create digital images of flat or nearly flat items. You can skip the camera steps altogether if you are selling flat items (comic books, trading cards, coins, stamps, ephemera, autographs, etc.). For flat stuff, scanning as opposed to photographing will provide you with the highest-quality image file possible.

Simply place your flat item directly on the flatbed scanner. No cameras or developers. Of course, you can also scan print photographs of your item.

PRO: The perfect tool for flat things. Otherwise . . .

CON: Same as for film developers if you are scanning photos of your items. You will still be paying for film and developing.

DIGITAL CAMERAS

Digital cameras work almost exactly like film cameras. They have a lens and a shutter and usually a flash, but instead of recording an image on film, the digital camera focuses the light from the item onto a small chip containing millions of receptors. The chip and other hardware and software inside the camera then transform the received light of an image into the 1's and 0's that make up a digital file. The camera then stores the digital image file on a small removable chip or disk inside the camera. The digital image can then be transferred to your computer by removing the chip or disk from the camera and then inserting it directly into your computer or by connecting special cables from your digital camera to your computer. (Each make and model of digital camera has a slightly different way of transferring digital image files. Consult your camera's user manual or guide for more details.)

PRO: Easy to use. If you can shoot pics with a film camera, you can shoot pics with a digital camera. Most good digital cameras are "point and shoot." There's no waiting for film to develop. You have total control over the quality of your pictures. A digital camera can pay for itself in only a few months of regular eBay selling.

CON: Initial cost might be a burden to some new sellers. Still, good new and used digital cameras suitable for your eBay pictures are available starting as low as $50. Of course, check eBay first before you buy.

What to Look For in a Digital Camera

So many different brands, models, prices, and levels of quality are available in digital cameras that choosing one can be tough. What follows is my smart-shopping checklist for digital cameras.

Buy the Best You Can Afford

Although you don't need to buy the top-of-the line digital camera to take excellent images for eBay, it never pays to scrimp when purchasing an electronic gadget of any type. Buy the best your budget will allow.

2.0 Megapixels or Higher

Digital camera resolution is measured in "megapixels." A pixel is the basic unit of programmable color on a computer display or in a computer image or in a digital camera—the higher the megapixels, the higher the quality of the image. Today, most brand-name digital cameras start at a resolution of 2.0. For creating images that are meant to be displayed on a Web page (such as an eBay item page), 2.0 is sufficient resolution.

Look for Brand Names

For example, Sony, Nikon, Olympus, Kodak, Canon, Fuji, HP, Leica, Epson, etc. If you've found a great deal and it's for a brand name you have never heard of before, it's probably best to avoid it.

Macro Is a Must

Look for cameras with "macro" capability (the ability to get your camera an inch away from an item without losing focus). Most new digital cameras have macro built in, but since macro is *the* digital camera feature that you will need when selling at eBay, ask before purchasing.

Zoom, Autofocus, and Autoexposure Come in Handy

Although not absolutely necessary, zoom, autofocus, and autoexposure can make your photography tasks easier. Luckily for you, nearly every recent make and model digital camera has all three features built in.

Used Is OK

Buy new if possible, but don't rule out a used digital camera. You can find both new and used digital cameras at, oh, let's see . . . where might one find digital cameras . . . ?

Look for the "Complete Package"

If buying a used digital camera, look for those deals where the seller provides the complete contents of the original package, including software, cables, and accessories. Owners who preserve all the original contents and packaging for a device like a digital camera are usually the type of people who take excellent care of their belongings, including their digital cameras.

For more detailed information about digital camera features, price, and picture quality, try the Digital Photography Review Web site: *http://www.dpreview.com/.*

This excellent site contains hundreds of detailed professional and user reviews of all the most popular digital cameras. They can help you decide which model is right for your needs and budget.

For the record, I am currently using an older but trusty Sony DSC-F707 for all my eBay pictures and other fine photography projects.

Once you have selected which option works best for you, the next step is to set up the item and photograph it.

Taking the Picture—Setting Up the Item

SELECTING A SPACE

For onetime eBay sellers, any well-lit spot in your home or apartment will do just fine. Under certain conditions, you can also set up your shots outdoors.

The table for photographing your item should be about two feet deep by four feet wide by forty-two inches high. If you plan on selling only small items, you can scale these dimensions down accordingly except for the table height, which, to save you from bending over for long periods, should be no lower than thirty-six inches.

For our setup example, we will be photographing a small pottery pitcher. I have set up a table, some halogen work lights, and a digital camera on a tripod.

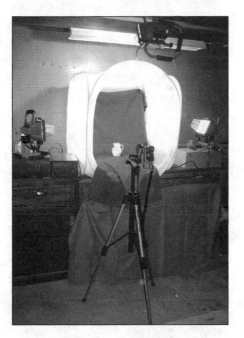

On the table, I placed a box to bring the height up to about 40 inches, then I draped a backdrop of dark blue cotton cloth over a piece of thin plywood, over the box, and down over the front of the table. (More on backdrops and lighting later.)

SETTING UP THE CAMERA

Film camera or digital camera: The rules of picture taking are the same for both. If you have a tripod, use it. If not, find a sturdy, flat surface upon which you can rest the camera. In a pinch, try holding the camera steady and hope for the best.

Regular eBay sellers: Invest in a tripod. You can buy one new for about $20–$40 and you can find excellent new and used tripods . . . on eBay!

BACKDROPS

Many eBay sellers do not use backdrops for their item pictures. They instead simply plop the item on the nearest table or, in some cases, even the baby's crib! This can often lead to interesting pictures.

It's hard to tell just what is for sale in the following picture. Is it the dinette set or that thing on the table? The seller at least took the time to show the newspaper he plans to use for packing the "thing."

You can avoid these sorts of embarrassing and unprofessional picture mistakes by using a solid-color backdrop to isolate and focus attention on your item.

A backdrop can be a wide piece of solid-colored paper, board, or cloth placed behind and under the item. As a rule, the backdrop's color should contrast with the color(s) and brightness of the item. For example, a pale item usually looks best on a dark background. A dark item usually looks best on a pale background.

Don't spend a fortune on backdrops. You can purchase fabric suitable for backdrops from any fabric store. Check the remnants bins for good deals. Look for matte-finished cotton or linen yardage in solid colors (no patterns!), and purchase a selection of muted colors. For most purposes, you can get by with two to three yards of forty-five-inch-wide cloth.

You can also find incredible bargains for remnants . . . on eBay, of course! Search eBay using *cotton fabric*. Also search in eBay's Cameras & Photo category using *backdrop* to find good deals on professional backdrop cloth and paper rolls.

If you are photographing your item on the table against the wall, use pushpins to fasten the fabric or paper into place on the wall itself, or place a piece of poster board or thin plywood on the table against the wall and drape the backdrop over it (as in our example above). Make sure your backdrop covers both behind and underneath the item.

You may need to shoot large items in situ, or in place. If so, try to isolate the object as best you can from its surroundings. If the item isn't too large, place a large sheet of paper or cloth behind the item and follow the same rules below for lighting the object to its best advantage. Large bolts of scenic muslin work well. Again, try searching eBay's photography category.

If the item is too large to isolate, place the item in the least conspicuous location (against a wall of a house or a tall hedge), and try to fill the camera viewfinder frame with as much of the item as possible.

LIGHTING YOUR ITEM

Inadequate lighting is a common digital picture mistake. How do you determine if your item is inadequately lit? A good rule of thumb is to rely on your camera. Aim the camera at the item. If the camera's built-in light meter or flash indicator shows that a flash is needed, then add more lighting, either artificial or natural.

Indoor—direct lighting: For most situations, your item should be lit from two or more directions. Three or more clip-on lamps with hundred-watt halogen floodlights will usually provide adequate illumination. Position the lights above and to the sides of the item. Make sure they are slightly in front of the item (avoid lighting from behind). Experiment with lighting positions. Move the lamps around to get the best positions and the right blending of light and shadows. Shadows are not always bad. For items with complex surfaces (carving, embroidery, etc.) a prominent shadow in one direction can help emphasize the surface texture. Still, for most items, you will want to "wash" the item to be photographed with light sources crossing each other from opposite directions.

Indoor—indirect lighting: Some items may suffer from direct lighting. Examples might be glossy pottery or porcelain, glassware, shiny jewelry, or harsh white objects. In these cases, you may need to light the item indirectly with diffused or bounced light. There are a number of ways to accomplish this type of lighting. A quick and cheap way is to point the light sources away from the item and onto white or metallic sheets of poster board. You can even "bounce" strong light off a white ceiling. A more professional (and expensive) way is to use professional photography studio light boxes or reflective screens. These devices bounce and diffuse light off white or metallic material. The resulting diffused light illuminates the item without glare or harsh shadows.

NOTE: Reflected lighting usually takes more wattage to achieve the same level of illumination as using direct lighting. Translation: Double or triple the number of lamps and hundred-watt bulbs. Without using a light meter, you can always take a test shot to see if your lighting is adequate.

GRIFF TIP! Check eBay for good lighting deals: I found two halogen work-light trees for $35 each. Each tree has two 150-watt halogen lamps bolted to a solid, tripod-based, extendable pole. The combination of four 150-watt halogen lamps is more than adequate for most of my eBay photography needs. They provide excellent direct or diffused light when bounced off my studio's white ceiling or used with a translucent cloth "light box."

ANOTHER GRIFF TIP! The light from halogen or tungsten incandescent lamps tends to be more hot (yellow or red) than cool (blue). This may distort the colors of your item.

You can adjust for this by using your digital camera's white-balance feature if it has it. (Check your camera's manual.) Otherwise, you may need to use blue gels over your light sources or slightly blue reflective surfaces to counter the strong yellow light. Some sellers like to use natural-spectrum lightbulbs since they produce roughly the same neutral white light of sunlight. Verilux makes a good natural-spectrum lightbulb.

Outdoor—direct and indirect lighting: Your indoor photography space should suffice for nearly all your eBay pictures, but in some instances you may find it necessary to take your item pictures outdoors.

When shooting outdoors, avoid placing the item in direct sunlight. Bright, harsh sunlight can wash out or distort colors and can also cast unwanted dark shadows. The north side of a house is usually a good spot for photographing your item outside, as north light tends to be more even and less harsh, especially on a bright, sunny day. A lightly overcast day offers the ideal outdoor light for taking item pictures.

ANOTHER GRIFF TIP! When shooting your item outdoors, you should isolate the background with something solid. Of course you can and should experiment and try all types of compositions in your shots. If you are selling antique lawn furniture, it might look smashing against a hedge of privet but not so smashing against the family minivan. The only way to know for sure is to experiment. For those who are unsure of their design talents, a solid background will always do the trick as a first or last resort.

CAMERA SETTINGS

Resolution (digital cameras only): Set or configure your digital camera to take medium- to high-quality resolution pictures. Resolution is usually described in pixels. The lowest resolution you should use is 640 x 480 pixels. For eBay pictures, you should not need anything higher than 1,024 x 768 pixels. At that resolution, the resulting image file will be large, but we will be reducing the size of the file in editing.

Some digital cameras come with "e-mail" resolution. This setting is for taking small pictures suitable for sending as attachments to e-mail. Don't use this setting if it is lower than 640 x 480 pixels. As we will see in editing, you can always reduce the size of a digital picture, but you cannot increase the size without noticeable degradation of the image.

Autoexposure, autofocus: Why make extra work for yourself? If your film or digital camera has autoexposure and/or autofocus, by all means, use them.

Flash: Most cameras have a "flash off" setting. Make sure your digital camera flash is set to "off." The intense light from a camera flash can wash out the colors of your item and can also obliterate details. If your film or digital camera indicates you need to use the camera's built-in flash to light the item properly, you need to add more lamps and watts to your lighting scheme as we discussed in the lighting section.

Macro: If you need to place your digital camera a few inches or less away from the item, make sure the camera's macro feature is enabled. Consult your digital camera's user manual for more information on changing your camera settings for resolution, autofocus, autoexposure, flash, and macro.

FRAMING THE ITEM IN THE CAMERA VIEWFINDER

We've draped a backdrop cloth down the wall and over the table. We have also set the lights, and the camera is set securely on its tripod. Finally, we have positioned the item on the table.

Time to frame the shot and take the picture.

First, this item is taller than it is wide, so I will shoot it in portrait mode. I do this by turning my camera ninety degrees clockwise as shown here:

If your camera has a variable lens, set it to the widest angle. Position the camera and tripod in front of the item, usually no more than twenty-four inches away. (This varies with the size of the item you are photographing.) Adjust the height of the camera, using the tripod. Some items photograph best when shot straight on; others look better shot slightly from above. Try different angles and use the one that works best for your item. Our little pitcher looks best shot from slightly above, so I have raised the camera about a foot higher than the pitcher. While looking into the camera's viewfinder, move the camera away from or toward the item or, if your camera has zoom, zoom in or out until you have the item framed within the view window so that it nearly fills the frame.

SNAP THE SHOT

Everything is in place. Lighting looks good. The item fills the frame. It's time to take the picture. Here is what this first shot looks like.

Not bad. Remember, the pitcher is taller than it is wide, so I repositioned my camera to take the shot in *portrait* format. When the digital image is displayed, it shows in the default *landscape* format. That's why it appears on its side now. Later in editing, we will *rotate* the image clockwise ninety degrees.

Also, my digital camera's autoexposure was set so that the dark blue background actually appears almost black. I like it. We'll keep it.

GRIFF TIP! It's always best to get all your photography done in one session, so if you have two or more items to list at eBay, photograph them in succession.

I took two other shots of this pitcher; one of the other side and one of the underside to show the maker's mark. It always pays to show all aspects of your item, including flaws and imperfections!

We will use these pictures in our listing in the next chapter.

A LIST OF QUICK PICTURE-TAKING TIPS

Whether you use a digital camera or film camera to take the picture, you should always follow a few simple picture-taking rules:

- If possible, avoid holding the camera to take the shot. Use a tripod or place the camera on a sturdy, flat surface. This will help guarantee the image is in focus. You can find good deals on inexpensive tripods on eBay, of course.
- Don't take a picture of the item sitting on your kitchen table where the rest of your fabulous 1970s-era kitchen will be in the picture (unless of course you are selling the kitchen). Isolate the item you are photographing by placing a solid-color cloth or paper backdrop behind it. As a general rule, if the item is light in color, use a darker background color. If the item is dark, use a lighter-colored background.
- Lighting—outdoors: Avoid photographing an item in direct sunlight. Bright sunlight can distort colors and cast dark shadows. If you must shoot outdoors on a sunny day, shoot the picture out of direct sunlight. A good spot is often the north side of a wall or building. An ideal time to shoot outdoors would be on a lightly overcast day.
- Lighting—indoors: Avoid using a flash to take a picture of your item. Just like direct sunlight, it can distort colors and cause white spots on shiny objects. Instead, light your item from three or more angles using any common household light sources such as table lamps with translucent shades, clip-on floodlights, halogen work lights, etc. (You can correct the yellow cast caused by incandescent lights by using your digital camera's "white balance" feature or later on during editing. Consult your digital camera manual for information on "white balance.")
- If you are using a digital camera, make sure it is set at a pixel resolution of 640 x 480 or higher. (Again, your digital camera's manual will explain how to change your camera's resolution.)
- Whenever possible, aim your camera at the center of the item. Using zoom or by moving the camera closer or farther away, position the item image in the viewfinder so that it fills the frame with as little background showing as possible.
- In some instances, you may find it best to shoot the item from an angle above the item, but generally, you should position the item and the camera so that the camera is level with the item (the item and camera are roughly the same distance from the ground).

Although one image may suffice for your listing, take two or more photos to show a variety of aspects of the item: close-ups, the back of the item, etc. If the item has a flaw, make sure to take a picture of it!

Once you have taken the pictures and have copies of them as digital image files, you will need to get them into your computer for editing and uploading. Transferring digital pictures from the digital camera to the computer depends on the make and model of the camera.

Most digital cameras store their images on a memory chip or card that can be popped out of the camera and into a chip or card reader or, in some cases, right into your computer if it has the appropriate slot.

Nearly all digital cameras also provide an option for transferring digital picture files from the camera to a computer via a specially provided USB cable. Consult the user's manual that came with your digital camera for the methods for transferring your pictures.

SAVING YOUR DIGITAL IMAGE FILES

Before you move or copy your digital image files onto your computer, you should create a special folder on your computer where you can safely store them so they will be easy to find later.

Some cameras come with special software that will automatically set up special folders on your computer, into which it will transfer copies of the images on your camera. This feature can be useful in keeping your image files organized.

You can also create a special folder for your eBay images. For information on how to create a new folder on your computer, consult your computer's operating system's Help section. For Windows, click Start, Help. For Macs, click the Help link on the top of the desktop window.

Editing the Picture (Using Software)

Now that you've created digital images of your item and have moved them to your computer, you are no doubt itching to get them up on an eBay listing so you can start the sale of your item. Hold on, we aren't finished. We need to edit the image files first.

Many eBay sellers skip editing. Big mistake. It is highly unlikely that your image files are perfect right out of the camera. Many will need to be rotated. Some will need cropping. Almost all will need resizing. To rotate, crop, or resize an image file, you will need image editing software. You have options. You can pay for top-of-the-line image-editing software like:

Adobe Photoshop
Adobe Photo Elements
Jasc Paint Shop Pro
Corel Photo-Paint

GRIFF TIP! Make it easier to find Photo Editor next time! If your Windows computer has a copy of Photo Editor, the file icon for it will display as a search result in the pane on the left. If you see the icon for PHOTOED.EXE, hover your cursor over the icon, click the mouse's right-hand button, and select Send To and then "Desktop (create shortcut)."

Now you have a copy of the Photo Editor icon on your Windows desktop for easy access later.

Or you can look for software that comes with your computer operating system or applications, for example:

iPhoto (Mac OS X)
Microsoft Photo Editor
Microsoft Picture Manager

If you have recently purchased a new digital camera or scanner, it will have come packaged with a CD-ROM containing, among other things, a simple, bare-bones image-editing application. Slip the CD into your computer and look for the option for loading free software. Follow the instructions from there.

Finally, if all else fails, there is always the Internet. My favorite free image-editing software download is Irfanview, available for download at *http://www.irfanview.com/*.

We'll use Microsoft Photo Editor for our image-editing software examples in this chapter. If you don't have Photo Editor, don't panic. The basic editing commands used by Photo Editor are common to *all* versions of image-editing software.

Many, but not all, Windows users will have a copy of Photo Editor on their computer as part of either the Windows operating system or Office XP.

Microsoft Picture Manager, which comes with Office 2003, replaces Photo Editor. Mac OS X users are in luck. OS X comes with a built-in image application called iPhoto. Look in the Applications folder or on the Dock.

Not sure if your Windows computer has a copy of Photo Editor? Here's how to check:

For Windows, click on Start, Search and select "For Files or Folders . . ."

This will display the Search Results window. In the text-entry box "Search for files or folders named:" type in *photoed.exe*.

Then click Search Now.

If you don't have a copy of Photo Editor, or if you are a Mac 9 (Classic) or earlier user, don't despair! The basic editing commands (Crop, Rotate, Resize) are available with any good image-editing software and can usually be found in roughly the same places on each application's menu command bar.

And remember, if you've purchased a new digital camera, it will have come with image-editing software that should work on a PC or a Mac. Load the CD-ROM that came with your device, and install and use it.

OPENING A DIGITAL PICTURE FILE

First, we need to find our digital picture files. I moved copies of the three digital picture files for my small pitcher from my camera to a folder I created on my computer hard drive called "eBay Digital Pictures."

Once you know where the files are located on your computer, you can open them for editing.

There are several ways to open these files for viewing or editing. One way in Windows is to click Start, Accessories, and Windows Explorer.

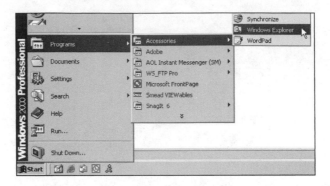

In the Windows Explorer window, navigate to your picture files, then select the file you wish to edit first by hovering your cursor over the file's name and clicking the right-hand mouse button. Select Open With from the pop-up menu and then Choose Program to select the appropriate application from the list of choices presented.

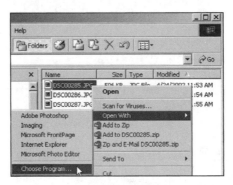

The list of applications on your computer will show in the Open With box.

> **GRIFF TIP!** Check this list carefully. You may discover an image-editing application on your computer that you didn't know was there!

Another way to open files for editing would be to start Photo Editor or any other image-editing application (by clicking on its shortcut either on your desktop or on the Start, Programs menu) and use the "File, Open . . ." command on the application's toolbar to bring up an Open dialog box.

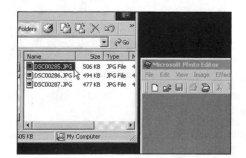

Still another way would be to open both Photo Editor and a Windows Explorer window and drag and drop each file from Windows Explorer to the Photo Editor window.

Drag and Drop

This is an excellent time to illustrate a helpful computer feature that many people never use: drag and drop.

For Windows, start by placing the image-editing application window and the window containing the file you want to open next to each other on your computer screen in such a way that you can see the file you wish to open and the blank space inside the application window (in this example, Photo Editor).

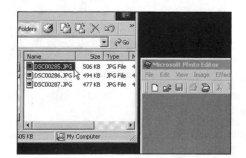

Place your cursor over the file name. Hold down the left-hand mouse button. While still holding down the left-hand mouse button, move your cursor over to the application window. You will notice that you are now "dragging" the file name along with the cursor. Don't release the mouse button . . .

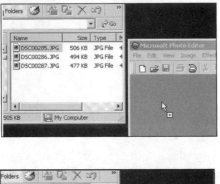

. . . until your cursor is completely over the application window. To "drop" the file, release the mouse button.

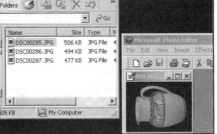

When you do release the mouse button, the file will "drop" into the application window and open.

For Mac OS X users, it's even easier! Simply drag and drop the file on top of the application icon on the Dock or in the Application folder.

Regardless of the method you use to open the file, the result is the same: We open our digital picture file in an image-editing application in order to perfect the picture for use on eBay.

Now that we've opened the digital picture file in Photo Editor, let's start editing!

Editing Digital Pictures

ROTATE (AKA FLIP, SPIN, OR TRANSFORM)

Our jug picture was taken in portrait mode; that is, with the camera held at a right angle. The resulting picture shows the item on its side. For the picture to make sense when viewed on eBay, we need to rotate it ninety degrees clockwise.

All image-editing software has a command for rotating a digital picture. In Photo Editor, the "Rotate . . ." command is found on the submenu under Image.

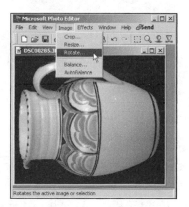

Clicking the "Rotate . . ." command will display the Rotate dialog box. This is where you can select exactly how the picture will be rotated: left or right, degrees, etc.

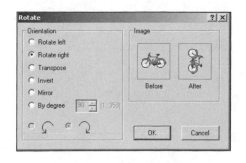

Our digital picture needs to rotate ninety degrees clockwise, which just so happens to be the default setting in Photo Editor. Click OK.

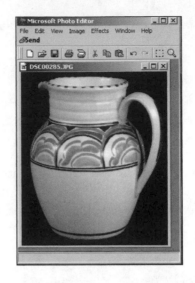

Our digital picture is now right side up. The next step is to crop all extraneous visual information from around the jug.

CROP

Just before we snapped this picture, we framed the picture of the jug so that it nearly filled the frame of the digital viewfinder. Thus there is little to crop. Still, nearly all digital pictures can benefit from cropping. In our picture, there is just enough extra black border around the jug itself for us to crop.

We start by clicking on the Select tool located on the Photo Editor toolbar.

The Select tool lets you use your mouse to "select" an area on the digital picture by creating a box. To start, position your mouse cursor somewhere on the upper left-hand corner of the picture.

While holding down the mouse button, drag the cursor diagonally down toward the right-hand side of the picture.

Once you have reached the other corner, release the mouse button. You will see something like the following:

The dotted line has little square nodes in the corners and on the sides of the box. You can change the dimensions and position of the box by dragging these nodes with your mouse cursor. **NOTE:** Not all image-editing software allows for repositioning of the crop lines. For those applications, you will have to press the Cancel key and redraw the box till it's perfect.

When you have arranged the sides of the box to your liking, click on Image on the menu command bar and select "Crop . . ."

In Photo Editor, this will display a Crop dialog box. Not all image-editing applications have a Crop dialog box. If your application displays a Crop dialog box, leave the settings as they are and click OK.

The cropped digital picture!

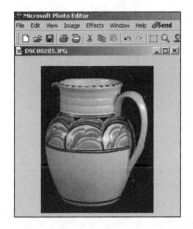

The next step in editing is to resize the digital picture.

RESIZE

If the picture doesn't look too big, why are we resizing?

Notice the little box on the menu bar that shows a percentage. This is the current zoomed view. Photo Editor has automatically "zoomed out" on the view so that we can see the entire image within the application window without scrolling back and forth. At the moment, we are viewing the digital picture at twenty-five percent of its actual size.

Remember, millions of items are for sale at eBay. If your digital picture files are so big that they take forever to download onto an eBay shopper's computer, that shopper might just give up waiting and browse away from your listing in search of other similar items. Also, we are going to use a feature called eBay Picture Services. For our pictures to work with this service, they have to be within a certain range of height/width pixel dimension, and that is only accomplished by resizing.

Let's select 100% from the drop-down list of percentages so that we can see just how big the digital picture actually is.

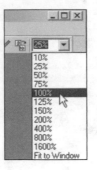

I've reduced the window, but you can clearly see that this digital picture is enormous.

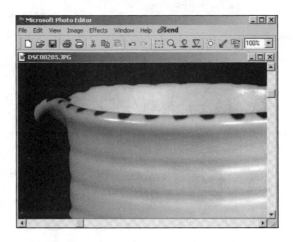

In full screen, only the very top of the jug is viewable. Remember, the larger the image size, the longer it will take to appear on a bidder's screen. If you were to load this digital picture on your eBay listing, it would take forever to download over a dial-up connection. In addition, a viewer would have to scroll back and forth and up and down to view the item (and never in its entirety).

Let's resize the picture.

Click on Image and then "Resize . . ." on the menu command bar.

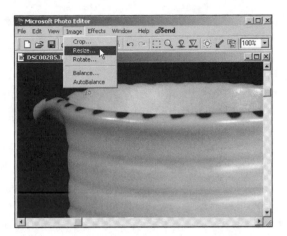

Any command that is followed by ellipses will bring up a dialog box, as does clicking on "Resize . . ."

If the Units box is not showing Pixels, please select it now. When creating digital pictures for viewing over the Web, the standard measurement is always pixels.

Our jug picture is 865 pixels by 1,085 pixels. Remember, you should think of a pixel as that dot of light on your computer monitor. Pixel density varies from monitor to monitor, so pixels do not relate in any absolute way to inches or centimeters. However, the number of pixels for height and width of a digital picture is extremely important.

GRIFF'S *NEW* PIXEL GUIDELINE

After much experimentation, and with the changes to eBay Picture Services since the first edition of *The Official eBay Bible,* I have adjusted the old pixel guidelines to the following:

If you keep your digital pictures within a range of a minimum of 330 pixels high and 440 pixels wide, and a maximum of 600 pixels high by 800 pixels wide, your digital pictures will always be large enough to show the complete item in detail (provided you have followed all of the previous steps for digital pictures), yet small enough to download quickly for those bidders with slow dial-up connections. In addition, they will be the optimum size for eBay Picture Services.

NOTE: If you plan on using the SuperSize option for eBay Picture Services, your images should be close to, but no bigger than, 800 pixels wide by 600 pixels tall. We'll learn more about eBay Picture Services later when we list the item.

When faced with higher-than-acceptable pixel dimensions for height and width, always select the larger of the two and reduce it to within the range suggested above. The largest dimension of our image is the height, 1,085 pixels. Let's reduce it to 600.

Notice that you don't have to change the other dimension; it changes automatically, and in ratio, to 478 pixels. All good image-editing software is configured to keep the ratio between height and width constant. When you change one dimension, the other will change to keep the correct proportion.

Changing the height from 1,085 pixels to 600 pixels automatically reduces the width to 478. This is well within the parameters of Griff's Pixel Guidelines. Click OK to accept this new size.

Here is the resized digital picture of our jug.

It's a perfectly proportioned picture, if I do say so myself. Let's save a copy of this priceless work of art.

Saving and Archiving Your eBay Digital Pictures

Once we have edited our digital picture to perfection, we must save it to our computer.

I'm a digital pack rat. Pictures, e-mails, text files . . . I archive most everything sent to me or created on my computer. Unless an image is unusable, I archive *all* of my pictures. Why? Given the low cost of storage on CD-ROM or extra hard drive, it seems foolish to delete perfectly good pictures. Besides, as the mantra of all pack rats goes, "You never know when you might need them!"

You may not be as obsessively concerned about saving your images as I am, but you should keep copies of your eBay item pictures for at least three months after your eBay listing ends. And, if you are going to save copies of your picture files, you might as well start out right, with a *system*!

First things first. We need to save our magnificently edited digital picture. With the edited digital picture open in your image-editing application, choose File and "Save As . . ."

In the resulting Save As dialog box, select a folder on your hard drive for your edited eBay picture. Since we have already created a main folder called eBay Digital Pictures, I will create a subfolder within this folder for our eBay listing.

To create a folder, click the Create New Folder icon.

Now we must name the folder. If I don't name it, the computer will simply call it "New Folder." Here's the folder-naming convention I use:

My picture folders all begin with the date (yy-dd-mm) followed by a hyphen and a name descriptive enough so that days or weeks or years from now, it will be clear to me what the folder might contain. This folder is going to contain our jug picture and eventually many other pieces of Honiton pottery. Therefore, I will name it "04-25-02-honiton":

Once I have named the folder, I double-click it to open it.

Remember, we initially set out to save the edited digital picture of our jug, and that is what we do next. To save a new file, I have to give it a name. I will rename the file from the name my Sony CyberShot gave it, "DSC00285.JPG," to something more memorable and descriptive, "honiton-pitcher01.jpg."

Before we click the Save button, let's click the button More (only applicable to Photo Editor, but many image applications have a similar dialog feature. If yours does, follow along).

Nearly every good image-editing application will prompt you, before saving a jpg file, to select a JPEG quality factor. For example, in Photoshop, you are automatically asked to select a quality level between 1 and 10 when you click the Save button. In Photo Editor, if you wish to change the default setting from "high" to something lower, you need to do so before you click Save. Clicking the More button on the Photo Editor Save As dialog box displays a slider that you can move left to right to change the JPEG quality factor.

Why would you want to change from high quality to lower quality? The higher the quality value for a JPEG digital file, the bigger the file is in kilobytes, the longer it takes to download. You want pictures that snap as quickly as possible into your item description.

When creating digital images for eBay items, lowering the image-quality factor will have little or no discernible effect on the final digital picture. As a rule, I usually reduce the image quality factor to at least a point midway between the lowest and highest qualities (which I have done for this picture). Let's save it to view the change, if any.

honiton-pitcher01.jpg

There is virtually no change at all in our image. It looks better than ever. But what if there had been a noticeable and consequently unacceptable change in the image's quality? Would we be stuck with it? Not at all! You still have the original image on your hard drive. (Remember, we saved the edited version as a brand-new file.) You would simply start the editing process again with the original digital file.

Examples of the Crop, Rotate, and Resize Commands in Other Software

Photoshop

Crop
In Photoshop, the Crop tool is found on the floating tool bar.

With the Crop tool selected, drag a box around the area to save using the mouse.

Once the box is set, click Image on the Photoshop tool bar and select Crop from the menu list.

Rotate

To rotate an image in Photoshop, click Image on the toolbar, select Rotate Canvas, and select one of the options.

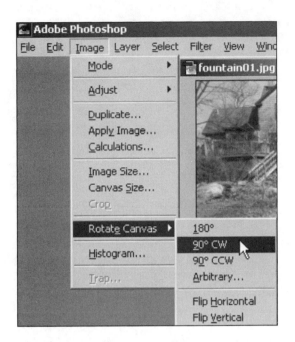

Resize

To resize an image in Photoshop, click Image on the toolbar and select "Image Size . . ."

Change the pixel dimensions for either Width or Height.

Image Size

Pixel Dimensions: 2.74M

Width: 1180 pixels

Height: 809 pixels

OK

Cancel

Auto...

Print Size:

Width: 5.9 inches

Height: 4.045 inches

Resolution: 200 pixels/inch

☑ Constrain Proportions

☑ Resample Image: Bicubic

Irfanview

Crop

To select an area of an image to save using Irfanview, simply hold down the cursor and start drawing a box.

Irfanview's Crop command is located under Edit on the toolbar.

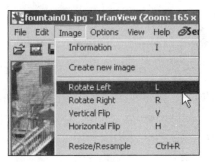

Rotate

To rotate an image in Irfanview, click on Image, then select one of the Rotate options.

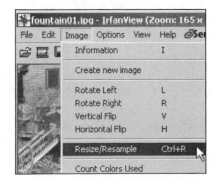

Resize/Resample

To resize an image in Irfanview, click on Image, and Resize/Resample.

Change the pixel dimension numbers for Width or Height.

Resize/Resample image

Set new size:

Current size: 413 x 994 pixels

⦿ New size:

Width: 413   Height: 994

○ Percentage of original:

Width: 100 %   Height: 100 %

☑ Preserve aspect ratio

Some standard dimensions:

○ 640 x 480 Pixels
○ 800 x 600 Pixels   [Half]
○ 1024 x 768 Pixels   [Double]
○ Best fit to desktop

Filters for Resample (enlarging only):

○ Hermite filter (fastest)
○ Triangle filter
○ Mitchell filter
○ Bell filter
⦿ B-Spline filter
○ Lanczos filter (slowest)

⦿ Use Resample routine (better quality)
○ Use Resize routine (faster)

[OK]   [Cancel]

Taking good pictures is a skill that anyone with an eye can acquire. Hundreds of good books on basic photography are available on- and off-line. I urge you to explore the basics of photography. The knowledge and skill will help you create better and better eBay images.

You've now got your perfect pictures captured, edited, named, and saved—ready to go on your eBay listing. Our next task is to compose a good item description worthy of our excellent photo and to put the two together in our first eBay listing.

4

Writing a Description and Packing the Item

Our eBay Seller's Account is activated; we've located an item to sell and we have researched similar items using the Completed Listings page; we've taken and edited digital pictures of the item.

Before listing our item on eBay, we still have two more steps to complete:

- Writing an item description
- Packing (and weighing) the item

But first, let's hear from an artist who "self-represented" herself to success on eBay.

Traditionally, only those artists lucky enough to have a great agent, gallery owner, or patron could count on any semblance of a sustainable career as an artist. An artist's success was limited by the twin evil realities of geography and the unavoidable curse of obscurity.

Starving is never romantic. Artists usually pick up a second line of work—"a day gig"—to make ends meet. Trouble is, balancing a day gig and one's art often takes so much energy that both suffer.

However, as artist Keri Lyn Shosted discovered, starving as an artist is not inevitable. eBay can offer an artist instant access to a vast potential customer base from around the globe.

"I went from begging galleries to give my work a shot, to selling full-time—for over three years now on eBay, with a large following of customers and about fifteen shops around the country carrying my line of dog art prints. Not to mention over a hundred commission paintings, all brought to me through the magic of eBay. I even now have a greeting-card company in Canada publishing my work. . . . How did they find me? eBay!"

Hundreds of artists and craftsmen and -women have leveraged eBay as a platform for finding eager customers for their work.

"I know that eBay has made what was once impossible a true reality for many other eBay members as well, especially artists. By cutting out the middleman hundred-percent-mark-up gallery, buyers are now able to search thousands of artists and buy direct."

With dedication and planning, anyone can make a go at eBay selling, even artists!

The next step is to create the text for our item description.

A Simple and Thorough Description

Every item for sale at eBay should have a clear, concise, and comprehensive item description. We could simply type in our description extemporaneously in the box on the Sell Your Item form, but I want you to get into the habit of always typing your description into a text editor before you start the listing. For Windows computers, use Notepad. For Mac, use Simple Text or TextEdit.

NOTE TO MAC USERS: We will use Windows to illustrate our examples. Macintosh users should follow the instructions step by step. The only difference for Mac users will be the name of the text editor and the steps necessary to open the text editor and Web browser. Everything else in this chapter is identical for Windows and for Mac users.

OPENING A TEXT EDITOR

PC users: To start, we open a blank Notepad file. Notepad can be started from the Windows Start menu at Programs > Accessories > Notepad:

(MAC users: Look in your Applications folder for a program called Simple Text or TextEdit. Either will work and will pretty much resemble Notepad.)

This will open an Untitled Notepad (or TextEdit or Simple Text) window.

For the remainder of this chapter, you will type everything into your Notepad (or for Mac, Simple Text or TextEdit) window. (Please do *not* use Word, Word-Pad, or some other word-processing application. This exercise will only work perfectly if you use a plain text editor.)

Now, let's start writing our description.

Every good item description should contain the following:

1. A detailed description of the item
2. Your terms of service for payment, shipping, and returns
3. Your pictures

We are going to use eBay Picture Services for our pictures, so we don't need to include them in our item description. (We cover other image-hosting options in Section Two, chapter 8, "Advanced Image Hosting Solutions.")

A DETAILED DESCRIPTION

Your item description should include the following item attributes, as appropriate:

> Name of the item
> Age
> Dimensions
> Place of origin or manufacture
> Condition (including flaws and imperfections)

Here's what I wrote about our pottery pitcher:

```
🗒 Untitled - Notepad                                          _ □ X
File  Edit  Format  View  Help  efax
Honiton Exton Small Pitcher

I was culling treasure from the china closet and found this
Honiton pitcher, 4 1/2 inches tall, circa 1950's. White clay.
Exton shape. Pitcher is in excellent condition; no cracks,
breaks, chips or stains. Embossed mark on bottom: "Honiton
Potteries Exton England" with a black hand painted "t."

A Brief History of Honiton Pottery: Hontiton pottery was (and
is) located in the town of Honiton in Devon, England. The
pottery was started by Foster and Hunt at the turn of the
19th/210th century. It was purchased by Charles Collard
shortly after WWI. In 1947, Collard sold the pottery to Norman
Hull and Harry Barratt who ran it until 1961 when it was sold
to Paul Redvers. All production ceased in 1997 and the pottery
was shuttered. The premises were recently reopended as pottery
and craft shop.

Payment:

PayPal (preferred)

Money Orders

Checks

Shipping: I will ship this item anywhere to anyone.
International bidders and buyers welcome. Please enter your
zip code in the box provided below this description. This will
provide you up to three shipping options and costs from which
you may select one.

Return Policy: If you win or purchase this item from me
through this listing and upon receiving it, are not 100%
satisfied, you may return it to me within 14 days from the
close of the listing, for a full refund of the winning bid
plus shipping. |
```

Honiton Exton Small Pitcher

I was culling treasure from the china closet and found this Honiton pitcher, $4\frac{1}{2}$ inches tall, circa 1950's. White clay. Exton shape. Pitcher is in excellent condition; no cracks, breaks, chips or stains. Embossed mark on bottom: "Honiton Potteries Exton England" with a black hand painted "t."

In a short paragraph, I included the history of the pottery. This type of information can help spark interest in new collectors:

A Brief History of Honiton Pottery: Honiton pottery was (and is) located in the town of Honiton in Devon, England. The pottery was started by Foster and Hunt at the turn of the 19th/20th century. It was purchased by Charles Collard shortly after WWI. In 1947, Collard sold the pottery to Norman Hull and Harry Barratt who ran it until 1961 when it was sold to Paul Redvers. All production ceased in 1997 and the pottery was shuttered. The premises were recently re-opened as pottery and craft shop.

Next I typed in my payment, shipping, and return policies and fees:

Payment:

PayPal (preferred)

Money Orders

Checks

Shipping: I will ship this item anywhere to anyone. International bidders and buyers welcome. Please enter your zip code in the box provided below this description. This will provide you up to three shipping options and costs from which you may select one.

Return Policy: If you win or purchase this item from me through this listing and upon receiving it, are not 100% satisfied, you may return it to me within 14 days from the close of the listing, for a full refund of the winning bid plus shipping.

It pays to be as detailed as possible regarding a buyer's obligations. Buyers don't like surprises. Make sure you provide as clear a picture as possible regarding acceptable payment options, shipping fees, and any other special "terms of service" (TOS).

Later, we will copy and paste this description into the Item Description text entry box on the eBay Sell Your Item form.

NOTE: Windows users can format their description text using a simple and elegant eBay tool called the HTML Editor, which is built around the Item Description text entry box on the eBay Sell Your Item form. Alas, if you are a Mac user, the HTML Editor tool will not display. Fret not. You can easily format your item description manually using basic HTML commands. Advanced HTML tips can be found in chapter 7, "HTML for eBay Sellers."

It's always wise to save your finished item description text as a file on your computer's hard drive. That way, you always have a copy ready to edit and copy and paste into the eBay Sell Your Item Web form.

Select "File, Save As . . ." from the Notepad toolbar:

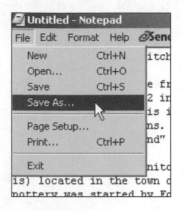

1. In the "Save in" box, choose a location on your hard drive for the new file. We will use the Desktop.
2. In the box "File name," type in a name (we'll type "itemtext.txt").
3. Click Save.

We have set up our eBay Seller's Account, created a digital picture of our item, composed our item description, and saved it to our hard drive for later access when we actually list the item on eBay.

The next step is to pack the item. Why pack the item now? Shouldn't we pack it after the item sells?

During the Sell Your Item process, we will have the opportunity to add the eBay Shipping Calculator so our potential buyers can view the shipping fee to their zip or postal code before they bid or buy. We will need to enter the weight and maybe the dimensions of the package into the Calculated Shipping box. To obtain the exact weight for shipping, we need the weight of item *and* the box and packing materials. Besides, it is much safer to store a listed item in a properly packed box as opposed to on an open shelf or tabletop where it could be damaged.

Packing—Do It Right!

You could be the most accommodating, customer-oriented seller in the world. It's all for naught if you pack the item inadequately. No one wants to receive an item damaged in transit. If you take pains to pack your items properly, you will avoid the hassles of having to fill out insurance forms and, more important, placating an unhappy buyer with a refund. Besides, it takes just about as much work to pack an item properly as it does to pack it poorly, so you might as well do it right.

eBay seller Melissa Hornyak provided a great tip on shipping clothing:

EBAY MEMBER TIP: When shipping articles of clothing (mostly what I sell), put the item in a plastic bag and tape it before placing it into the box/envelope/whatever. This protects the item from rain, in case the package ends up sitting on someone's front porch for a while. This saves many a ruined item and shows the buyer that you are willing to do a little bit extra to make sure that their purchase arrives in the promised condition.

PICTURE IT WHILE PACKING IT

If the item you are packing is extremely fragile or valuable, you may want to take digital or film pictures of the item as you pack it. Whenever I have sold a rare or breakable item, I take two digital pictures of it; one sitting just outside the box into which I am about to pack it, and one showing the item sitting in the box before sealing.

Documenting the packing of the item with pictures could prove to be wise insurance. On the remote chance that the item is damaged in transit, you will have a record of the item's condition just prior to your sealing the package. Plus, even under the best of circumstances, it can be extremely difficult to win a claim of damage in transit from any of the major carriers. Armed with evidence of a properly wrapped and packed parcel, you stand a slightly better chance of collecting an insurance claim for any item damaged in transit by a carrier.

I did hear from a seller who actually videotapes the packing of extremely valuable or breakable items from start to final sealing.

Again, although this precaution is not necessary, especially for sturdy or less expensive items, you can never overdo documenting the item and its packing. Better safe than sorry.

MATERIALS—OVERDO IT

When packing, you should always err on the side of caution. Give the item more protection than it may actually need for making the trip safe and sound. For breakables like pottery and glass, *always* double box (see below). For all items, use a box that is at least twenty-five percent bigger in all dimensions than the item you are packing. For items that could be damaged by moisture, seal them in plastic before sending. Bendable items such as old LPs, photographs, autographs, ephemera, etc., should always be packed sandwiched between stiff boards.

PACKING MATERIALS

Styrofoam packing peanuts are probably the most commonly used packing material for eBay items. They are extremely lightweight so they don't noticeably increase the weight of the package. They are reusable. They work for any size box.

Biodegradable Packing Peanuts are growing in popularity among eBay sellers. They are usually made of air-puffed corn or potato starch. When wet, they disintegrate harmlessly into the environment.

Shredded paper is an inexpensive and abundant source of biodegradable packing material, but not recommended as a primary packing material. By volume, paper weighs more than Styrofoam and is prone to compression. However, for those items that are not superfragile, shredded paper can be a cost-effective secondary packing material if used correctly. (By the way, we are talking about thin strips of shredded newspaper. Never use balled-up or scrunched-up sheets of newspaper.) If you plan on doing a lot of packing and you have access to enough paper (newspaper, old printouts, etc.), you may want to invest in a small paper shredder to make your own shredded paper.

Bubble wrap should be used to protect all individual items before placing them in their packing box. Even when packing in peanuts, the extra layer of bubble wrap helps protect the item from damage. The combination of peanuts or shredded paper and sufficient bubble wrap will help guarantee your item arrives at its destination safe and sound.

Use the right-size bubble for the right job. The rule of thumb for size of bubble: the more fragile the item, the bigger the size of the bubble. Wrap the item with the bubbles facing in against the item. If you are using the proper-size bubble wrap for the item, wrapping around the item twice will suffice. Finally, use just enough tape to hold the bubble wrap together; one or two small tabs of tape should be enough. Don't bind the bubble-wrapped item like a mummy! Pulling, tearing, and unwrapping excessively taped items can be extremely painful and frustrating for those of us with arthritis. Thank you.

eBay seller Leah has some good points about packing in general and is happy to share them with you:

> "Don't be stingy with bubble wrap.
>
> "When packing a box, shake it. If you hear things moving around, you need to add more packing materials.
>
> "Make sure the box is folded properly (i.e., the two small ends of the box go in the INSIDE, not the outside) and taped securely.
>
> "Don't write the 'to' address on top of the packing tape. The party the package is being sent to will be lucky to actually receive the package. (The tape could separate and only a small portion of the address will be left.)"

I have to admit—I never thought of that last one. Thanks, Leah!

BOXES AND CONTAINERS

The lion's share of all eBay item shipping is done in plain corrugated boxes. You can buy these from a packaging supplier, from your local post office, from moving companies, and from eBay sellers! You can also pick them up for free from many supermarkets. (For obvious hygiene concerns, avoid picking boxes from Dumpsters or that were initially used to store perishables. Thank you.)

Regardless of the source, the primary concerns when selecting a box for shipping are condition, size, and strength. The golden rule of packing is to avoid having any part of your item touching the sides of the packing container. This means that the box you select for your item should be about twenty-five percent bigger in all three dimensions than the item you are packing—height, width, and length (including the bubble wrap, if used). A twenty-five percent difference in size will usually leave adequate room for packing material to fill around the sides, top, and bottom of the item.

WHERE TO GET PACKING SUPPLIES

Here's a suggestion from eBay seller Michael Ford (heritageharborcollectibles) about where to get free shipping supplies from the USPS Web site (to be used only if you are using a USPS Priority Service).

EBAY MEMBER TIP! Sellers can order any size box, from video size to large boxes designed to hold tons of books . . . sturdy and reliable, delivered fast, and absolutely free. This also includes tape, tons of tape, mailing labels, various customs forms, protective mailers, envelopes— nearly anything and everything you need to ship an item using USPS Priority or Express Mail can be obtained at the www.usps.com Web site. It's so easy! Everything you desire will be mailed directly to you for free!

You'll never have to worry again about asking people for boxes *or* running to the store to grab a package of labels or that always-in-demand tape! It's all free. Usually these are free so you will use the service they are designed for, in most cases Priority Mail, which is first-class.

You will save time and money by always looking for ways to reduce shipping costs. There is no need to spend $3 on a pack of labels or $5 on a roll of tape that'll be gone after you wrap up a few boxes. Be smart. You're selling items on eBay to make money; don't let your bottom line get swallowed up by the costs of mailing supplies.

Also, if you do need tape or other various mailing/office supplies, don't pay full price for them. Take advantage of any low-price or dollar stores in your area.

Excellent advice, Mike. Thanks!

eBay is an excellent source of great deals for all types of packing materials. In fact, a handful of eBay sellers have made a full-time business of selling packing materials exclusively. Check out the Shipping and Packing Supplies categories under the main category Everything Else.

DOUBLE BOXING

You should double-box extremely fragile items like glass, pottery, thin metal, or items constructed of delicate materials like paper or papier-mâché. In fact, some sellers double-box everything they ship. It helps provide maximum protection against damage or breakage in transit.

Wrap the item in a layer of bubble wrap.

Select a first (inner) box that is at least twenty-five percent bigger than the item and a second (outer) box that is at least twenty-five percent bigger than the first box.

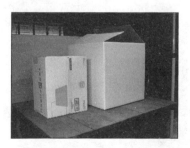

Add a layer of packing material (foam or peanuts) to the bottom of the first box. Place the item inside the box.

Fill the spaces between the wrapped item and the box walls with packing material. The item should not touch the box walls at any point. Here is my first box filled to the top:

Lightly seal the first box with a single strip of packing tape. You may need to reopen the box before shipping.

Add a layer of packing material to the bottom of the second box and place the first box inside the second box.

Use packing material to fill in the space between the boxes. Note that there should be at least three inches of space between the two boxes.

Add a layer of packing material to cover the top of the inner box.

Seal the outer box with a small piece of tape (in case you need to open the box before shipping the item to the buyer). Write the name or a description of the item on a sticky note and stick it on the box (for easy identification later). Now it's time to weigh the box.

Place the box on a postal scale. On the sticky note, jot down the weight in pounds and ounces. You will need the weight when you list the item. Our item weighs 2.25 pounds.

For now, store the boxed item in a safe place. Later, after the item has sold, you'll place a shipping invoice or receipt in the box, seal the box more securely, print out and slap on a prepaid shipping label, and ship the box to the buyer.

PACKING IN A SMOKING HOUSEHOLD

And I don't mean a household that's on fire. Nothing is quite as nasty as opening a box and having your nose assaulted with the smell of stale cigarette smoke. Second-hand tobacco smoke permeates everything it contacts. The smoker is usually unable to smell this residual odor, but it is painfully apparent to the nonsmoker. Once an item has been "smoked," it is almost impossible to eliminate the smell unless the item is safely washable. For most art and antiques, this is usually not the case.

If you or someone else in your household smokes, store your items and packing materials in either a sealed smoke-free room or in a separate building.

Or maybe it's finally time for the patch!

USED PACKING MATERIALS

Saving and reusing packing materials is not only a thrifty habit, it's a "green" duty. By reusing materials, you help extend their usefulness. This is extremely important for materials that may not be easily reclaimable, such as Styrofoam peanuts.

Keep your packing materials clean. If you save packing materials for reuse, store them in a dry, smokeless environment.

Boxes can usually be used at least twice, if not three or four times, depending on how well they have weathered previous shipping. Always check used corrugated cardboard boxes for fold fatigue before reusing. If the sides of the used box feel soft or floppy, it may be at the end of its safe usefulness. Cover up any old shipping labels. Don't tear them off. Doing so usually results in some of the outer skin of the box coming off as well, which can weaken the structural integrity of the container.

As long as they are kept clean and dry, packing peanuts have an indefinite shelf life. Use your judgment. If the peanuts are starting to look funky to you, then they will probably look funky to your buyers. When a batch of peanuts reach the end of their usefulness, you should take them to your local recycling center for proper disposal.

Shredded paper is best used once (if at all) and then discarded. Paper excelsior is biodegradable and can always be sent to your local recycling center or placed in your compost pile.

Bubble wrap is endlessly reusable as long as it's clean and *as long as the bubbles are intact.* Do not use bubble wrap if even just a few of its bubbles have been "popped." It will be just your luck that the place where the bubbles are popped is where your item will be damaged in transit. It happens.

Let's summarize: We've photographed the item, typed and saved a description, packed the item, and weighed it in its box. We have noted the weight for inclusion in our description and for use with the eBay Shipping Calculator.

Fine-Tuning Your Web Browser for eBay

We are just about ready to go to eBay and start listing our item, but let's first double-check our Web browser Java, ActiveX, and Cookie settings to make sure that they are properly set for the eBay Sell Your Item form.

The eBay site is rich with new features and enhancements meant to make navigating and using the site easier. Many of these new features incorporate and rely on Java, JavaScript, ActiveX controls, or "cookies." Some older Web browsers or Web browsers that have their Java settings disabled may prevent access to certain key features in the Sell Your Item form such as the category selector, eBay Picture Services, or the Sign In page. To take full advantage of eBay features like the enhanced category selector, your Web browser must be configured properly.

Two popular Web browsers are in use today: Internet Explorer versions and Netscape versions. (A third Web browser, Opera, though excellent, is not yet popular enough for me to include it in this section.)

Note to Mac users: The Web browsers Safari and the Mac version of Internet Explorer are adequate for listing items on eBay. Use the instructions below as a reference for checking the settings for your particular Mac-flavored Web browser.

CHANGING SETTINGS FOR INTERNET EXPLORER (VERSION 6.0 AND HIGHER)

1. With an Internet Explorer window open, click on Tools on the menu bar, then select "Internet Options . . ."

2. In the "Internet Options . . ." window, select the Security tab on the top of the page, then click the "Custom Level . . ." button.

3. In the Security Settings box, you'll find a scrollable window. This window contains options for various settings.

4. Make sure you have selected the options for each section as noted below.

ACTIVEX CONTROLS AND PLUG-INS

Download signed ActiveX controls: Prompt
Download unsigned ActiveX controls: Disable
Initialize and script ActiveX controls not marked as safe: Disable
Run ActiveX controls and plug-ins: Enable
Script ActiveX controls marked safe for scripting: Enable

Downloads

File download: Enable

All of the other settings you may leave as they are. Click OK to return to the Internet Options window, then select the Privacy tab.

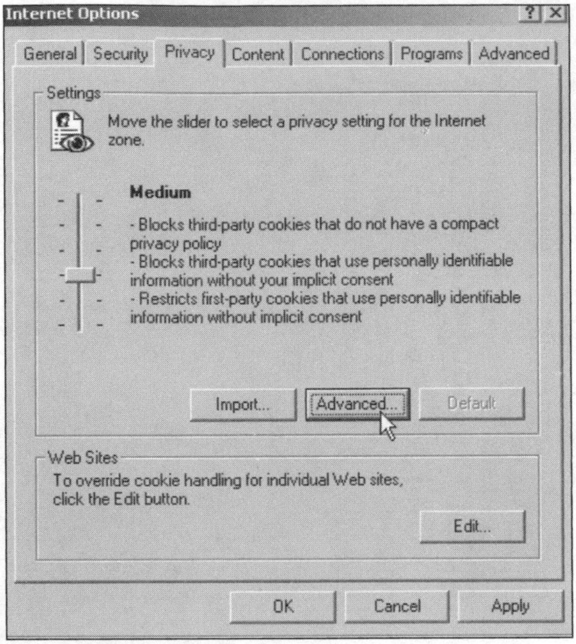

Click the "Advanced . . ." button. (Note: Your Privacy tab window may look different from the figure shown. Ignore the difference and click "Advanced . . .") Make sure the setting options for Advanced Privacy Settings are as follows:

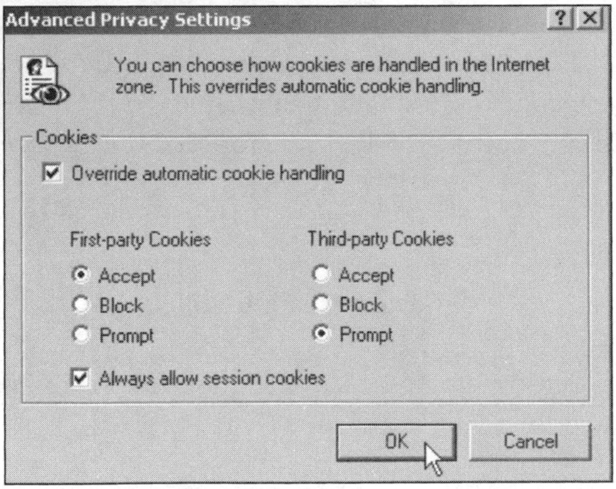

Click OK to return to the Internet Options window. (You may set "Third-party Cookies" to Block if you so desire. You will not need third-party cookies to use eBay effectively.)

Select the Advanced tab at the top of the Internet Options window to open the Advanced tab view.

There are many options here—we are concerned with only a few, and most of these will properly have been set by default. Begin by scrolling down the window and checking each section as noted below:

- Under Browsing, make sure that the option "Always send URLs as UTF-8" is checked.
- Under Microsoft VM, make sure that the options "Java console enabled" and "JIT compiler for virtual machine enabled" are both checked.
- Under Multimedia, make sure that the option "Show pictures" is checked. (Although not crucial, I also like to make sure that the option "Enable automatic image resizing" is *not* checked.)
- Under Security, make sure that the options "Use SSL 2.0" and "Use SSL 3.0" are both checked.

Click Apply, then click OK. Your browser's settings are configured for optimal eBay use.

Now we can go to eBay and start the Sell Your Item process!

The eBay Sell Your Item Form

NOTE: The Sell Your Item form, like all features on eBay, is subject to changes in layout and design. Although what I show here for screen-shot examples may look slightly different when you list your item, the core functionality of the five steps will remain the same. They are:

> Select a category
> Title and description
> Pictures and details
> Payment and shipping
> Review and submit

First, sign in.

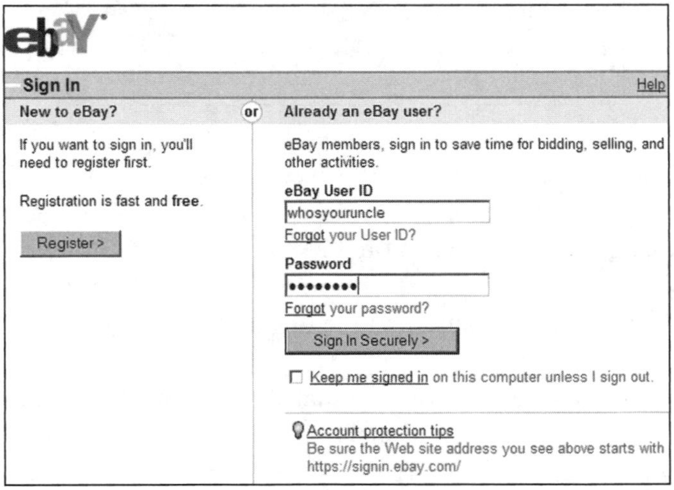

Click the Sell link on the eBay Navigation Bar to reach the Sell hub page.

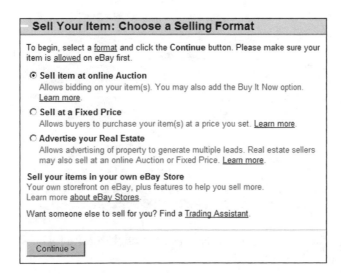

Click Sell Your Item. This will take you to the "Choose a Selling Format" section.

There are four possible choices for a format:

> Sell item at online Auction
> Sell at a Fixed Price
> Advertise your Real Estate
> Sell your items in your own eBay Store

Note that you may only see two of these formats. You need a feedback score of 30+ (or you need to have completed the ID Verify process) for the Fixed Price format to be available to you. The eBay Store format option will only appear if you have set up an eBay Store (more on eBay Stores). We will select "Sell item at online Auction" and click the Continue button.

This takes us to Step 1 of the Sell Your Item process.

STEP 1. SELECT A CATEGORY

We need to select an appropriate category for our item. If you are a brand-new seller, you will have two choices: Select a category from the list, or enter keywords into the box provided and let eBay suggest a category (based on which categories contain the most matching items).

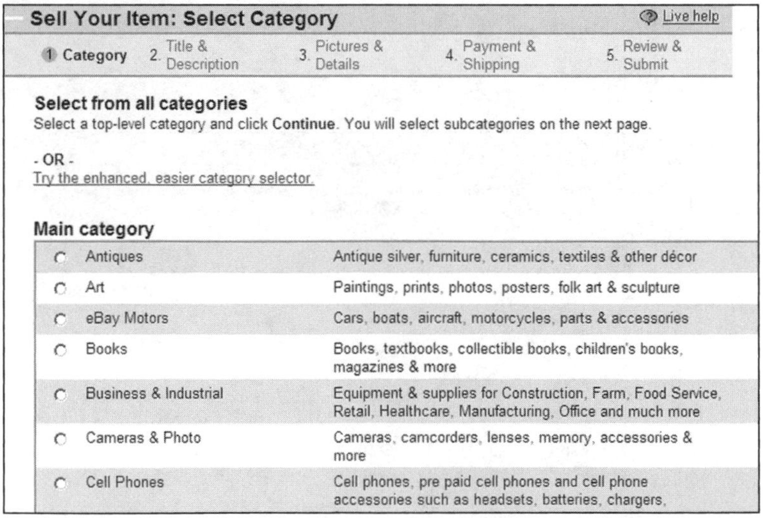

If you see the above list of categories, try clicking the link "Try the enhanced, easier category selector."

This will load the "film strip" category selector:

If you know into which category your item should fit, select it from the windows under "Browse categories." Let's start by selecting Pottery & Glass from the first window.

Now, we must continue selecting subcategories until we reach a lowest-level category (indicated by a gray window). In the second window, let's select Pottery & China, then we select Art Pottery in the third window.

Next, select an entry from the list in the next box. Since Honiton is not found in the list of art pottery manufactures in the fourth window, we select Other.

When you have reached the end of a category hierarchy, the remaining windows will gray out with text stating "Main category selected. Continue below."

GRIFF TIP! On the top of the category selector windows, you'll find a box containing the category number you have selected.

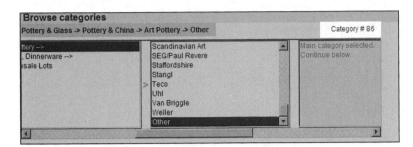

If you plan on regularly listing in this category, you should jot this number down. The next time you list an item in this category, simply enter the number in the box presented and the matching category will automatically fill in. You can also use this category number to quickly fill in a category tree in many of eBay's listings tools.

Also note, at the bottom of this page, the option for listing the item in a second category. Some items might benefit by exposure in two categories. In fact, eBay's data show an eighteen percent increase in the number of bids and a seventeen percent rise in final sale price for those listings that use a second category, so it is a feature worth considering.

Two notes: Selecting a second category will result in a doubling of the listing fees for the item, and the second category must be appropriate for the item.

We are listing this item in one category.

If you are not sure what category would be best suited to your item, let eBay suggest one for you. In the box provided in this section, enter one or more keywords that best describe your item. Let's enter one keyword, *honiton*.

Click Search. eBay will search every current listing for those containing the keyword we provided. It then ranks the returned items by category with the highest percentage on top.

Find a Main Category

Top 10 categories found for **honiton**

You can select a suggested main category below and click **Sell In This Category**, or use different keywords to refine your search.

Enter item keywords to find a category

| honiton | Search | Tips |

For example, "gold bracelet" not "jewelry"

Category

⦿ Pottery & Glass : Pottery & China : Art Pottery : British Art	(43%)
○ Pottery & Glass : Pottery & China : Art Pottery : Other	(20%)
○ Antiques : Textiles, Linens : Lace, Crochet, Doilies : Other	(10%)
○ Dolls & Bears : Bears : Other Bears	(7%)
○ Pottery & Glass : Pottery & China : China, Dinnerware : Other	(7%)
○ Collectibles : Animals : Dog : Corgi	(3%)
○ Collectibles : Cultures, Ethnicities : British	(3%)
○ Collectibles : Housewares & Kitchenware : Kitchenware : Cookware : Other Cookware	(3%)
○ Collectibles : Transportation : Railroadiana, Trains : Other Railroadiana	(3%)
○ Pottery & Glass : Pottery & China : Art Pottery : Poole	(3%)

| Cancel | Sell In This Category | 💡**Tip:** Add a second category to increase your item's exposure. You can do this at the bottom of the main category page. |

Interesting. It appears there is a better category for our item than the one we initially selected. Instead of "Pottery & Glass : Pottery & China : Art Pottery : Other," let's try the one eBay suggests, "Pottery & Glass : Pottery & China : Art Pottery : British Art." Accept the suggested category or select one from the list. Then click the Sell In This Category button.

○ Collectibles : Transportation : Railroadiana, Trains : O	
○ Pottery & Glass : Pottery & China : Art Pottery : Pool	

| Cancel | Sell In This Category | 💡**Tip:** Ad exposure. category p |

This will take you back to the Select Category section of the Sell Your Item form. Note that you can also select a second category. Why would you list in a second category? To quote the text on the page, "Adding a second category enables more buyers to see your listing. Boost bids by 18% and final sale price by 17% on average when you list in a second category."

Once you have selected your category or categories, click Continue to move on to Step 2 in the Sell Your Item process, "Describe Your Item."

STEP 2. DESCRIBE YOUR ITEM (TITLE AND DESCRIPTION)

Two tasks must be completed in this section: typing a title and pasting and formatting the description. There are also two possible views of this section. If you have a PC, you will see this:

If you have a Mac, you will see something like this:

Sell Your Item: Describe Your Item   Live help

1. Category ② **Title & Description**   3. Pictures & Details   4. Payment & Shipping   5. Review & Submit

Item title *Required

55 characters left; no HTML, asterisks, or quotes.
Include specific details about your item. Get tips on writing a good title. Learn More.

Subtitle ($0.50)

55 characters left.
Add a subtitle (searchable by item description only) to give buyers more information. See example.

Item description *

Describe your items features, benefits, and condition. Be sure to include in your **British Art** description: brand, condition (new, mint, near mint -- describe chips and cracks), and original or reproduction. Also consider including a brief history of how you acquired it. See more tips for British Art.

Enter <p> to start a new paragraph. Get more HTML tips.

< Back   Continue >

Unfortunately, the Standard tab and its nifty Description Editor tool will only appear on a Windows (PC) computer. It will not appear on a Mac. (Mac owners can format their descriptions using either HTML—see Section Two, chapter 7—or by using a stand-alone Web editor.)

Type a title in the "Item title" box. Your title should be composed entirely of keywords that relate directly to your item. Here's our title:

Item title *Required

Honiton Collard Poole Devon Pitcher Jug Creamer Exton

2 characters left; no HTML, asterisks, or quotes.
Include specific details about your item. Get tips on writing a g

Subtitle ($0.50)

55 characters left.
Add a subtitle (searchable by item description only) to give buy

"Honiton Collard Poole Devon Pitcher Jug Creamer Exton" may not sound elegant, but elegant syntax is not our goal when it comes to creating an item title. Remember that most shoppers on eBay use keywords to search titles for those items in which they are interested. I did some research in Completed Listings and discovered that past items similar to mine did best when they contained words like *jug, creamer, pitcher,* and all words relating to the place of manufacture, such as *Devon, Collard,* and *Poole. Exton* is the design of the piece.

Some Item Title Tips

1. Avoid using punctuation or symbols in your titles. They will not help buyers find your item, and they take up valuable character space.

2. In cases where a noun in your title could be plural or singular, type the singular and plural forms if there is enough room.

3. Avoid editorial adjectives like *rare, wonderful, stupendous, gorgeous,* etc. No one wakes up in the morning thinking, "Say, I think I will search eBay for all the *rare* items up for bid or sale." Don't believe me? Go search on the word *rare.* I did and found over 310,000 items:

That being the case, the Subtitle feature might be a better place for using such words. In fact, in your optional subtitle, you can expound about your wondrous and rare item to help market it.

4. Usually, articles or prepositions are superfluous in an eBay item title. Use them only if they are absolutely necessary or if there is enough space after you have exhausted all the possible keywords relating directly to your item.

Subtitle

Subtitle provides the opportunity to offer preview information about your item to prospective buyers. Describe interesting details and facts about your item such as age, origin, or previous ownership. Promote the extras you offer, such as free accessories or money-back guarantee. I will opt for the Subtitle feature. Here is the text of my subtitle:

Item title *Required

Honiton Collard Poole Devon Pitcher Jug Creamer Exton

2 characters left; no HTML, asterisks, or quotes.
Include specific details about your item. Get tips on writing a g

Subtitle ($0.50)

Free Shipping with Buy It Now - Flawless Example

7 characters left.
Add a subtitle (searchable by item description only) to give buy

Subtitle is a perfect tool for special promotions like mine. It could be the extra enticement needed to compel a shopper into clicking my item title. Think of it as getting the customer into the door of your shop. (Later, I will add a Buy It Now price, which will include my initial cost, plus shipping and ten percent.)

One other subtitle plus: The text of a subtitle is included in any search that included title and description.

Next we have to supply an item description. We've already created ours in a text file. To add it to our description, we must "copy" and "paste" it into the box on the Describe Your Item page. We do this by using the Copy and Paste features that come built into Windows or Mac operating systems.

Cut, Copy, and Paste

I'm always amazed to find out just how many otherwise computer-savvy folks have no idea how to use the three basic text editing commands:

> Cut
> Copy
> Paste

Cut, Copy, and Paste are the ultimate time-saver tools for moving text from one place to another or creating copies of long pages of text. If you sell on eBay, make no mistake: You *will* need them. If they are new to you, you will wonder how you lived without them.

The three commands Cut, Copy, and Paste can be executed in three ways. The first and most common place to find the commands is under the menu bar Edit command for any Windows (or Mac) application. Here is an example of where the commands are usually found in any application using Notepad's Edit menu command.

Let's say we want to copy some text from Notepad and paste it into the "Item description" box on the eBay Sell Your Item page. First, we highlight some or all of the text in Notepad by clicking the cursor on either side of the text and, while holding down the mouse button, dragging the mouse across the text.

You can also easily select all the text in the file by clicking Edit, Select All. Let's select all of the text with our mouse. Then we click Edit on the Notepad menu bar, then select Copy from the drop-down menu.

What this does is copy all of the selected text into a built-in Windows applet called Clipboard. Anything copied to the Windows Clipboard can be pasted into the same or another application. Until some new text is copied to the Clipboard, this text will be available for pasting into any other application any number of times. Now we can paste the contents of the Clipboard (the entire text of the

Notepad file) into another application, namely, the Sell Your Item page's text entry box "Item description."

In the example below, I clicked my cursor so it is blinking inside the box. I then clicked the right-hand button on my mouse and selected Paste from the resulting pop-up menu box.

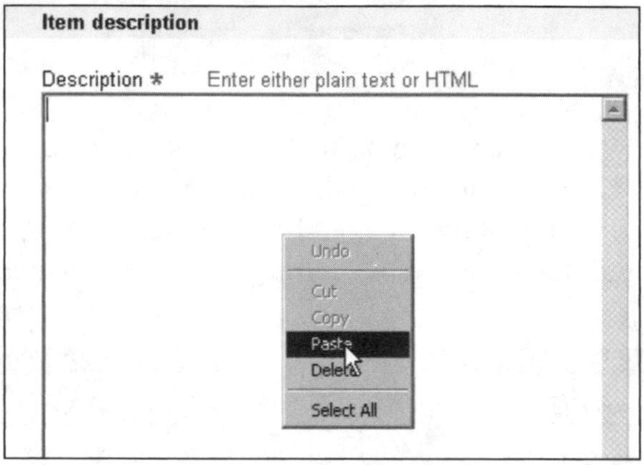

Item description

Description *   Enter either plain text or HTML

> Undo
> Cut
> Copy
> **Paste**
> Delete
> Select All

This will cause the text you copied from Notepad to be pasted into the "Item description" box.

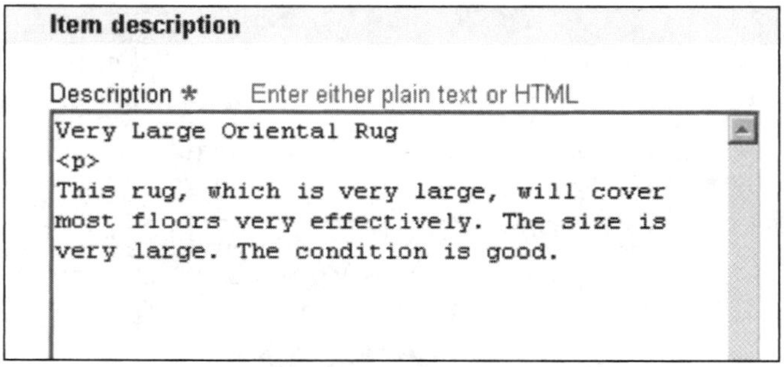

Item description

Description *   Enter either plain text or HTML

```
Very Large Oriental Rug
<p>
This rug, which is very large, will cover
most floors very effectively. The size is
very large. The condition is good.
```

The Cut command is similar to the Copy command with one difference—the Copy command leaves the original text untouched and copies it to the Windows Clipboard. The Cut command "cuts" or removes the original text and copies it to the Windows Clipboard. The Cut command comes in handy when you want to actually move text from one place to another.

As I mentioned earlier, there are three ways to call up the Cut, Copy, and Paste commands. We have explored one of them—using pop-up menus—but there are two others, one of which is better than the other two. Here are all three ways to reach the editing commands:

1. From the main menu bar
2. From the pop-up menu (reached by clicking the right mouse button)
3. Using keystrokes

Keystrokes are the most efficient way of accessing the basic text-editing commands. In the old, old, old days of DOS (before Windows—yes, there was a time before Windows), way before everyone used a pointer device like a mouse, anyone who did a lot of text editing or word processing relied upon these keystroke combinations to do all their basic text editing. There were no other options!

It takes a little practice getting used to them, but once you are comfortable using keystrokes for text editing, you won't ever want to use anything else! Any tip or trick that keeps you from moving your hand over to the mouse and back a hundred times a day not only saves time but also will help prevent repetitive-motion pain or injury.

To Copy using keystrokes, first select the text you want to copy by placing your mouse cursor to the left of the text. Next, hold down the right mouse button and drag the cursor to the right (and down if you need to copy more than one line of text) as in previous illustrations.

Once your selected text is highlighted, press and hold down the Ctrl key on your keyboard. (Use your little finger on your left hand. *Do not* get in the bad habit of using two hands for keystroke combinations—it will defeat the whole purpose!)

Keep the Ctrl key down, and using your index finger, click the C key once.

This will Copy the text to the Windows Clipboard.

Next, select the application and location where you wish the text to be copied. (Usually, this means clicking the mouse cursor into a box or blank page so that it is blinking in just the place you want the text to appear.) Now, using the keyboard, once again hold down the Ctrl key, and this time, click the V key once.

This keystroke combination (Ctrl + V) Pastes the text into the application where the mouse cursor is currently active.

A third common text-editing keystroke combination is:

Ctrl + X for Cut

The following combinations work for *most* Windows applications but not all!

Ctrl + A for Select All
Ctrl + N for New Window
Ctrl + S for Save

Try them all and see how much more efficient and quick they are when compared to selecting commands from a menu!

Now we're ready to go back to the Notepad file (or Mac TextEdit/Simple Text file) containing our item description. Click on the Edit and Select All commands on the text file's menu command bar:

This will highlight all of the text in the file. Once it is highlighted, click on Edit and Copy on the text file's menu command bar as we did in the above exercise.

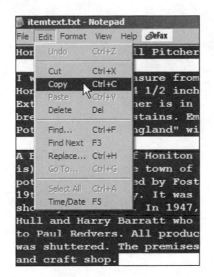

Go back to the Internet Explorer window showing the eBay Sell Your Item form. Click your mouse cursor anywhere inside the box marked "Item description." With the mouse cursor blinking in the "Item description" box, click your mouse's right-hand button and select Paste.

This will paste a copy of the entire item description text into the "Item description" box.

Use the Description Editor toolbar to format your text with different colors and sizes of fonts, alignments, font typefaces, bulleted lists, and other standard formatting.

For example, to change the size of some text, highlight the selected text with your mouse.

Then select the new text size from the Size drop-down box. We'll select 18.

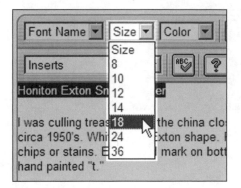

The new, larger text appears in the window.

Another Description Editor feature lets you create bulleted lists. First, make sure that the items you wish to bullet are separated by double line breaks. Then highlight them and click one of the two bullet option buttons. One will create a numbered list. The other will create a bulleted list. Let's try the numbered list.

You can preview your description by clicking the link labeled Preview Your Description. I have added some simple underlining and bold to the description. Now, let's preview it.

It's plain but it is readable, and readability is the single most important aspect of an item text description layout. Later, in Section Two, chapter 7, "HTML for eBay Sellers," we will learn how to dress up the description with other HTML tags.

NOTE: You could type your item description directly into the "Item description" box on the Sell Your Item form. However, I suggest that you always type your description in a separate file before you begin the listing. It is easier to "proof" your description in the bigger Notepad window, and should the text in the "Item description" box erase for some reason (it does happen), you won't have to type it over—you would only need to copy and paste it from the Notepad file.

Click the Continue button to move on to the next step in the listing process.

STEP 3. ENTER PICTURES AND ITEM DETAILS

In this section of Sell Your Item, we set our price, listing duration, add photos, and choose optional item upgrades.

NOTE: If your computer has never been on this page before, you may see a Security Warning asking if you want to "Install this software? Name: EPUWAL Control . . ." Click the Install button.

You will not be able to use eBay Picture Services properly if you do not allow the ActiveX Control to download and install on your computer. You have my assurance that this file is safe to download. Let's get back to our listing.

Starting Price

A starting price is mandatory. It is the amount needed to start the bidding. What should your starting price be? It depends on the market value for the item of course. Keep in mind the two basic tenets of any auction format:

1. Low starting prices tend to attract potential bidders.
2. High starting prices tend to discourage bidding.

It's that simple. In my experience at eBay, the most common reason for no bids is a too high starting price. Many sellers enter a starting price that is approximately equal to the current market value of the item. This is a mistake.

Bidders in an auction-format marketplace expect to set the final price. If a seller doesn't allow enough room to "play," they simply will not enter the bidding.

Your research prior to listing should have provided some indication of the current market value for your item on eBay. Of course, your starting price should take this market research into consideration, but regardless of the market value, always remember that the lower your starting price, the better the chances that two or more buyers will submit a bid.

The amount of your starting price will determine the insertion fee charged to your Seller's Account. Here is the schedule of insertion fees:

INSERTION FEES

Starting or Reserve Price	Insertion Fee
$0.01–$0.99	$0.30
$1.00–$9.99	$0.35
$10.00–$24.99	$0.60
$25.00–$49.99	$1.20
$50.00–$199.99	$2.40
$200.00–$499.99	$3.60
$500.00 or more	$4.80

I am entering a starting price of ninety-nine cents, which will incur an insertion fee of thirty cents.

Pricing and duration

Price your item competitively to increase your chance of a successful sale.

New! Get ideas about pricing by searching completed items

Starting price *Required
$ .99
A lower starting price can encourage more bids.

Reserve price (fee varies)
$ Remove
The lowest price at which you're willing to sell your item is the reserve price.

Buy It Now price ($0.05)
$
Sell to the first buyer who meets your Buy It Now price.

If I need some insurance that my item won't sell for less than a certain amount, I could always opt for a reserve price.

Reserve Price

The reserve price is an optional tool you as the seller can use to "protect" your investment. Your reserve amount can be any amount above the starting price. The reserve will be hidden from the public. Buyers will know that you have added a reserve by the text indication of Reserve Not Met next to the Current Price. If someone bids an amount equal to or greater than your reserve, the indication next to the Current Price will change to Reserve Met.

If you add a reserve to your listing, you will be charged a fee. If your item sells—that is, if someone bids an amount equal to or greater than the reserve—the fee will be refunded. Here is the reserve fee schedule:

RESERVE FEES (FULLY REFUNDED IF ITEM SELLS)

Reserve Price	Fee
$0.01–$49.99	$1.00
$50.00–$199.99	$2.00
$200.00 and up	1% of reserve price (up to $100 maximum)

I almost never use a reserve price, and this example will be no exception. I click the "remove" link to hide the reserve amount box.

Pricing and duration

Price your item competitively to increase your chance of a

NEW! Get ideas about pricing by searching completed items

Starting price *Required

$ [.99]

A lower starting price can encourage more bids.

Buy It Now price ($0.05)

$ [   ]

Sell to the first buyer who meets your Buy It Now price.

Re
No

Buy It Now

The Buy It Now feature is also optional. If you opt for a Buy It Now price, set it at the lowest amount you are willing to take for the item. The first buyer who's willing to pay your price gets your item. To set a Buy It Now price, you need to meet at least one of these requirements:

- Achieve a feedback score of at least 10.
- Verify your contact information (using ID Verify).
- If you have a PayPal account, achieve a feedback score of 5 and accept Pay-Pal as a payment method.

If a buyer is willing to meet your Buy It Now price before the first bid comes in, your item will sell immediately to that buyer, and your item listing will be considered complete.

Or

If a bid comes in first, the Buy It Now option disappears. In that case, the item listing will proceed normally. If you have also set a minimum price, or reserve price, the Buy It Now feature will disappear after the first bid is at least as high as the reserve price.

I am setting a Buy It Now price of $20.

Duration

The choices are 1, 3, 5, 7, and 10 days. I have selected 10 days. (The 10-day duration costs extra. All others are free.)

I've been asked thousands of times in the last nine years what the best duration is for insuring a successful sale.

There is no one answer. In fact, there are as many strategies for durations (and for ending times and days of the week) as there are sellers on eBay. First, your market research may yield some clues. Check the listings that received the most bids and sold for the highest amounts and determine if they share some pattern in their times, days, and durations. Second, experiment with as many as you can to see what works best for your items.

Start Time

The default start time is when the listing is submitted. A listing posted using this default will immediately go "live to site" and will end one, three, five, seven, or ten days later on the hour, minute, and second indicated as the start time.

If you have a credit card on file, you will have an additional option called Scheduled Start Time.

This feature allows you to schedule a listing by date and time up to three weeks into the future. To schedule a time for your listing, click the Date and Time boxes and select a start date and time for your listing. After you have finished and submitted the listing, it will appear in the Pending Items section of "My eBay," All Selling.

- You can schedule a maximum of three thousand listings, up to three weeks in advance of the time you wish them to start.
- A fee will apply for each listing you schedule to start at a later time.
- Fees charged are applicable at the actual start time, not when the listings are submitted using the Sell Your Item form, so you will incur no fees if you delete a pending listing from your pending queue.

Quantity

I have a quantity of one item so a type "1" in the appropriate box.

Quantity *	Minimize

Individual Items | **NEW! Lots**

Number of items *
1

Learn more about <u>multiple item</u> listings.

Selling similar or identical items together in a "lot"?
Help buyers find your listing - just enter the number of items you have in the <u>Lots tab</u> above.

NOTE: Typing any other number will default your listing to a Multiple Item Listing. The quantity number should reflect the lot. If you have six wineglasses to sell as a set, then the quantity should be 1, not 6.

Item Location

Check the information showing for Item Location. It should reflect the information for your address on file at eBay. If not, or if you wish to change it for any reason, click Change and follow the instructions.

Item location

ZIP Code: 95116
Location display: San Jose, CA, United States
<u>Change</u>

Add Pictures

We have two options: eBay Picture Services or Your Own Web Hosting.

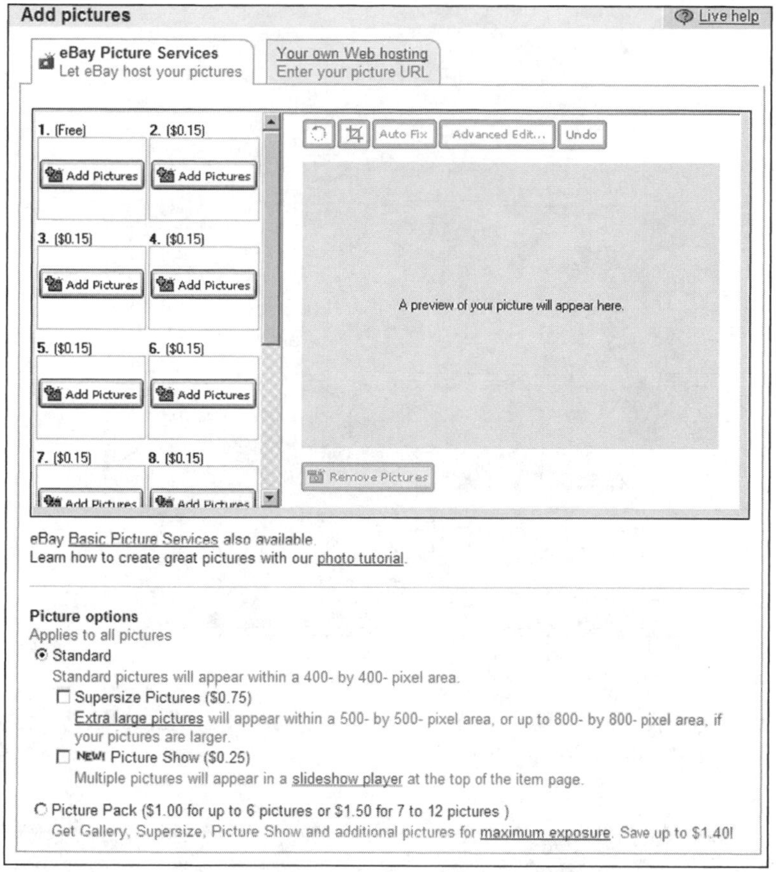

Add pictures   ⦵ Live help

eBay Picture Services
Let eBay host your pictures | **Your own Web hosting**
Enter your picture URL

1. [Free]   2. ($0.15)
🎦 Add Pictures   🎦 Add Pictures

3. ($0.15)   4. ($0.15)
🎦 Add Pictures   🎦 Add Pictures

5. ($0.15)   6. ($0.15)
🎦 Add Pictures   🎦 Add Pictures

7. ($0.15)   8. ($0.15)
🎦 Add Pictures   🎦 Add Pictures

Auto Fix   Advanced Edit...   Undo

A preview of your picture will appear here.

🗑 Remove Pictures

eBay Basic Picture Services also available.
Learn how to create great pictures with our photo tutorial.

Picture options
Applies to all pictures
⊙ Standard
    Standard pictures will appear within a 400- by 400- pixel area.
☐ Supersize Pictures ($0.75)
    Extra large pictures will appear within a 500- by 500- pixel area, or up to 800- by 800- pixel area, if your pictures are larger.
☐ NEW! Picture Show ($0.25)
    Multiple pictures will appear in a slideshow player at the top of the item page.
○ Picture Pack ($1.00 for up to 6 pictures or $1.50 for 7 to 12 pictures)
    Get Gallery, Supersize, Picture Show and additional pictures for maximum exposure. Save up to $1.40!

We'll use eBay Picture Services for our first listing. Later, in chapter 8, "Advanced Image Hosting Solutions," we will go over the finer points of hosting your own images.

NOTE: If the eBay Picture Services tab does not display the six square boxes but instead shows six narrow text boxes, you may need to reconfigure your Web browser's settings. Go to the section "Fine-Tuning Your Web Browser for eBay," earlier in this chapter.

Remember, we have copies of our edited digital pictures ready to go on our computer's hard drive. To begin, make sure the eBay Picture Services tab is selected in the Add Pictures section. Click on the first (free!) picture box.

This will bring up an Open box. Navigate to the image files for the item. Mine are in a subfolder called "04-25-02-honiton."

Highlight the first image and click Open. This will add that picture to the first eBay Picture Services box.

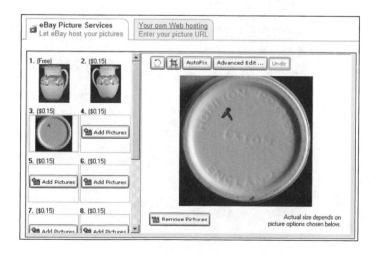

GRIFF TIP! Does it matter which image is first? It sure does. The first image you select will appear as your Gallery image should you opt for Gallery. The Gallery image is the thumbnail that appears next to your item's title in the category and search result lists. Consequently, make sure your first image is one that will look enticing when resized down to a small thumbnail.

Following the same steps, add the other two photos.

Note that you can add up to twelve images using eBay Picture Services. The first image is always free. Subsequent images are fifteen cents each.

In the chapter on digital photography, we learned how to edit an image for eBay using third-party software. eBay Picture Services includes a simple editing feature as well. I'll add a fourth, unedited image of our pitcher to better show how the edit feature works.

eBay Picture Services Edit Features

Once the image we wish to edit is displayed in the main eBay Picture Services window, we can edit it using the command buttons displayed for "rotate," "crop," and "autofix." (Autofix adjusts the contrast and brightness of the image based on what eBay Picture Services thinks works best.)

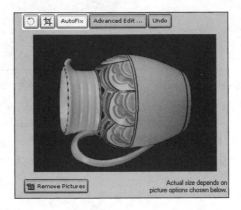

Click on Advanced Edit for more control over the editing features. The Advanced Edit window has four command buttons. Rotate:

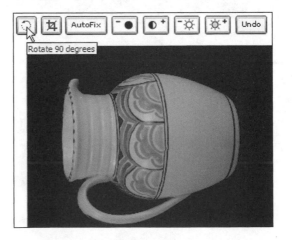

Crop (move the corner nodes to adjust a "keep" area):

Decrease/increase contrast:

Let's click the "increase contrast" button three times. And finally, the decrease/increase brightness button:

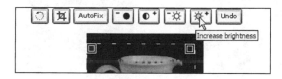

Let's click the "increase brightness" button three times as well. Once you have finished editing, click Save.

"But, Griff," I hear you say. "If eBay Picture Services lets me rotate and crop, why did we spend time learning how to edit using separate software?"

Good question. Notice that eBay Picture Services does not supply the resize command. That's one good reason. There's another. I want all eBay sellers to be as educated as possible about *all* areas of listing. An educated seller is usually a more effective, more successful seller. Thus, the other reason: I did it for you.

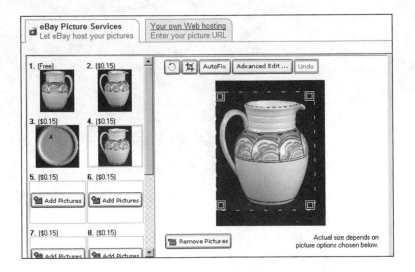

NOTE: These digital pictures haven't yet been uploaded to eBay! They have only been selected. Once we click Continue on the bottom of this page, uploading will begin. But first, we have more information to fill in on this page.

Picture Options

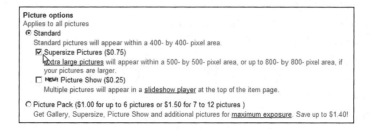

There are two main options for how your pictures are displayed:

1. Standard (with two optional features)
   - SuperSize
   - Picture Show
2. Picture Pack

SuperSize

My favorite option is SuperSize. This option allows you to upload images of about 600 pixels tall by 800 pixels wide (Griff's *New* Pixel Guideline!). The images will initially be displayed as thumbnails with a viewer window of about 500 x 500 pixels. The viewer (your potential buyer) has the option of enlarging the image to their original size, that is, the size to which you edited them.

NOTE: SuperSize will *not* stretch an image to pixel dimensions greater than those of the original image as uploaded. If you upload an image that is 330 x 440 pixels, SuperSize will not display the image any larger than that.

Picture Show

This option can be added to SuperSize or used alone. It adds a slide-show viewer window at the top of your listing page. Viewers can watch the show progress automatically, or they can use the buttons below the images to stop the show on any slide of their choice or move manually back and forth through the images.

GRIFF TIP! If you only have one image to show, don't opt for Picture Show.

Picture Pack

Picture Pack is a discounted bundled-feature option that provides free images, Gallery thumbnails, plus SuperSize and Picture Show. The discounted price for up to six images is $1. From seven up to twelve images, the fee is $1.50, for a savings of up to $1.40.

Listing Designer

Although our listing description layout and formatting looks good as is, we can also add a professional-looking graphic border around the entire image by selecting one from the over one hundred precreated designs available through the Listing Designer feature.

You can preview any of these designs by highlighting it, then selecting the Preview Listing link. I am partial to the template named Blue Bricks.

The feature costs a dime. I believe it's a great deal for adding color and interest to your item description, and it's definitely cheaper than trying to design and use one of your own or paying a Web designer to make one for you.

Increase Your Item's Visibility

In the next section, you can select from several features to promote your item more effectively.

Increase your item's visibility

☐ Remember my selections in the section below.
Selections will be saved for the next time I list.

Gallery options
This will be displayed as your first picture
◉ No Gallery picture

◯ Gallery ($0.25)
Add a small version of your first pictures to search and listings. See example.

◯ Gallery Featured ($19.95)
Add a small version of your first pictures to search and listings and showcase your picture in the Featured area of the Gallery View. See example.

Make your listing stand out
☐ Bold ($1.00)
Attract buyers' attention and set your listing apart in search results - use **bold**. See example.

☐ Border ($3.00)
Get noticed -- outline your listing with an eye-catching frame. See example.

☐ Highlight ($5.00)
Make your listing stand out with a colored band in search results. See example.

Promote your listing on eBay
Featured Plus! ($19.95)
Requires a feedback rating of 10+. Learn more.

Home Page Featured ($39.95 for 1 item, $79.95 for 2 or more items)
Requires a feedback rating of 10+. Learn more.

Gift Services
Increase exposure for your gift, promote services, and get an icon.
☐ Show as a gift 🎁 ($0.25)
Provide cost and details in item description for services offered.
☐ Gift wrap/gift card   ☐ Express shipping   ☐ Ship to gift recipient

In the first section—Gallery options—we can select to have a Gallery thumbnail appear next to our item title. A Gallery image will cost twenty-five cents. eBay statistics show that listings with Gallery pictures get more traffic and more bids. In fact, Gallery listings are shown to increase final price by an average of eleven percent.* That's two bits well spent.

If you are unsure of the value of a Gallery thumbnail, put on your buyer's hat and visit any category list or title keyword search-result list. Which items tend to catch your eye first? Which items do you tend to overlook?

I thought so.

Bold

Draw additional attention to your listing by bolding the text of your item's title as it appears in category or search result lists. Bold listings are shown to increase final price by an average of twenty-five percent.*

Border

The Border option showcases your listing by surrounding it with a colored band.

---

*The statistical averages cited here come from the Parthenon Group's study and do not constitute a warranty that individual eBay businesses will achieve the same results.

Highlight

Highlight employs a colored band behind your item title to emphasize the listing in the search results and category lists.

Featured Plus and Home Page Featured

With Featured Plus, a copy of your listing title is placed within the Featured Items located in the top section of the listing and search results pages that buyers see first. Your item also appears in the general listings and search results, for double the exposure. Featured Plus listings are twenty-eight percent more likely to sell!

Home Page Featured places a copy of your item's title in the eBay Featured Listings section, available from the eBay home page. With Home Page Featured, your listing has a chance to rotate into a special display on eBay's home page. The Home Page Featured fee is charged per listing and is in addition to other fees, such as insertion fees and Final Value Fees.

NOTE: You need a feedback score of at least 10 to use Home Page Featured.

Gift Services

If you have an item that would make a great gift or if you are willing to promote your item with special services like gift wrapping or express shipping, you can opt for this feature. For a quarter, this feature places a blue Gift Services icon next to your item title in category and search result lists. In addition, your item is searchable using the gift icon filter from the Advanced Search page:

The last feature on the page is for a Hit Counter (free). Adding a counter to your item page lets everyone see how many unique visitors have visited your listing. Once you have selected your options (if any), click Continue.

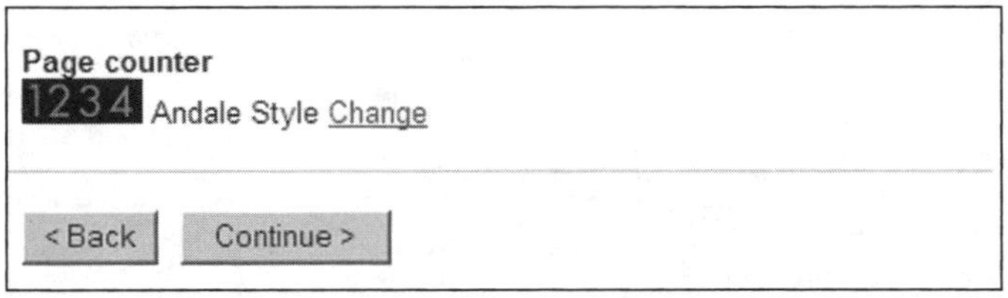

Page counter
1234 Andale Style Change

`< Back` `Continue >`

eBay Picture Services will now start sending copies of our digital pictures through our Internet connection to the eBay Picture Services Web server at eBay. You should see a pop-up box indicating that the pictures are being sent.

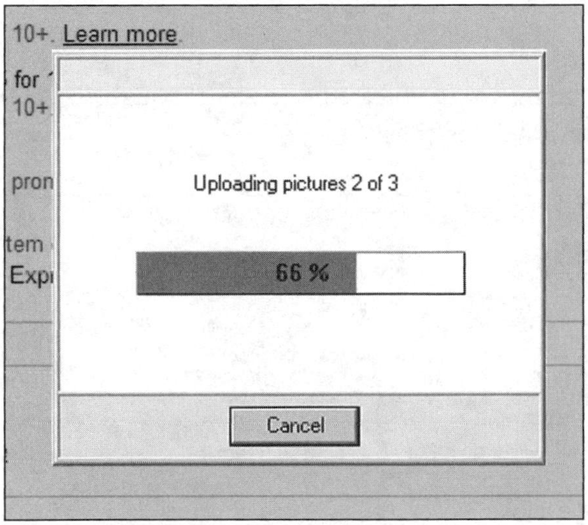

10+ Learn more

for
10+

pron

tem
Expi

Uploading pictures 2 of 3

66 %

`Cancel`

Depending on the speed of your Internet connection, the upload can take from a few seconds to a few minutes.

The eBay Picture Services Web server does the rest of the work for you. You don't have to type in URLs for the pictures. You don't have to worry about where the pictures are actually located. Once you are finished with listing, your images will automatically display under your item description.

The next displayed page will provide payment and shipping options for you to select for your item.

STEP 4. PAYMENT AND SHIPPING

Here's where we set our payment and shipping terms as well as decide which features to provide to our buyers.

First, we are going to accept credit cards (through Paypal), so I make sure that the option for PayPal is checked.

If the Payment Methods section on your Sell Your Item page doesn't show the above options, or if you haven't previously set your eBay PayPal preferences, you should to do so now. Click the link for Edit Preferences.

Make sure the following options are checked:

This will help guarantee that your buyers can pay you quickly and easily using PayPal. Scroll down and click Submit.

Because I have included a Buy It Now option for this listing, I have two choices for payment methods: Immediate Payment or Other payment methods (check, money order, other). However, if we select the option for Immediate Payment, the Other payment methods will disappear. Here's why: If a buyer opts for Immediate Payment for a Buy It Now listing, she can only pay with PayPal.

NOTE: If a buyer wins a Buy It Now item by submitting a bid as opposed to using Buy It Now, the seller can still accept a check or money order from her.

I am a big fan of Immediate Payment. Let's select it:

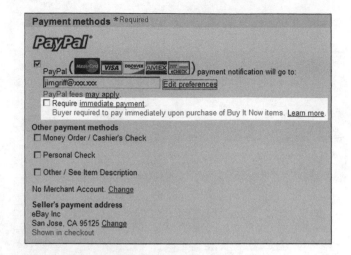

The other options disappear.

Payment methods *Required

PayPal

✓ PayPal (MasterCard VISA DISCOVER AMEX eCHECK) payment notification will go to:

jimgriff@xxx.xxx   Edit preferences

PayPal fees may apply.
☑ Require immediate payment
   Buyer required to pay immediately upon purchase of Buy It Now items. Learn more

Seller's payment address
eBay Inc
San Jose, CA 95125 Change
Shown in checkout

Ship-to Locations

What you select here not only shows up in your listing description, it also determines who can find and bid on or purchase your item.

GRIFF TIP! eBay is a global marketplace. To sell successfully in this marketplace, an eBay seller should be willing to sell to anyone, anywhere on the planet, and not limit his potential customer base to only those living within the United States. There are eager, honest eBay buyers around the world for your item. Don't cut them off! Selling and shipping to international eBay buyers is not difficult or complicated. In fact, it's easy. (More on international shipping in chapter 5.)

I've opted for Worldwide.

Ship-to locations *

☉ Will ship to the United States and the following (check all that apply):
- ☑ Worldwide
- ☐ Americas ☐ Europe ☐ Asia
- ☐ Canada ☐ United Kingdom ☐ Australia
- ☐ Mexico ☐ Germany ☐ Japan

○ Will not ship - local pickup only
Specify pickup arrangements in the Payment Instructions box below.

Shipping Costs

Remember earlier when we packed and then weighed our item and you wondered to yourself, "Griff, why are we packing the item now? We haven't even listed it yet!"

Well, here's why, the eBay Shipping Calculator!

Shipping costs *   ⌧ Minimize   ⍰ Live help

Specify a flat cost for each shipping service you offer, or have costs calculated automatically based on your package and the buyer's address. Learn more about specifying shipping costs.

Flat: same cost to all buyers	Calculated: based on buyer's address

Estimated Weight   **Package Size**   📦 Preview rates that will be shown to
1 lb. or less ▾   Package (or thick envelope) ▾   buyers.
Weight and size   ☐ Irregular or unusual package
help

Domestic Shipping (offer up to 3 services)
Select a shipping service ▾

Add service   Remove service   and have buyers contact me later

International Shipping (offer up to 3 services)

Add service

Packaging & Handling Fee   **Shipping Insurance**
Change   Not offered. Change

Seller ZIP Code   **Sales Tax**
95116 Change   I don't charge tax. Change

Now that we have the weight of the package, we can enter the weight (and dimensions if necessary) into the eBay Shipping Calculator. We can also provide our buyers with up to three domestic and three international shipping services from which they can select the one that works best for them.

In addition to the calculated method, there is also an option for flat costs.

Shipping costs * ⏳ Minimize 👁 Live help

Specify a flat cost for each shipping service you offer, or have costs calculated automatically based on your package and the buyer's address. Learn more about specifying shipping costs.

Flat: same cost to all buyers	Calculated: based on buyer's address

Domestic Shipping (offer up to 3 services)

Standard Flat Rate Shipping Service ▾ $ [_____]   📃 Research rates and services

Add service   Remove service   and have buyers contact me later

International Shipping (offer up to 3 services)

Add service

Shipping Insurance   **Sales Tax**
Not offered. Change   I don't charge tax. Change

Consider using the flat option for items that weigh less than a pound, for example, CDs or DVDs. With flat-cost shipping, you still have the option of adding up to three domestic and three international services. Enter the information in the Shipping costs section.

Let's fill in the Calculated option with the accurate package information.

Shipping costs * ⏳ Minimize 👁 Live help

Specify a flat cost for each shipping service you offer, or have costs calculated automatically based on your package and the buyer's address. Learn more about specifying shipping costs.

Flat: same cost to all buyers	Calculated: based on buyer's address

Estimated Weight   **Package Size**

2+ to 3 lbs. ▾   Large Package (Oversize 1) ▾   📃 Preview rates that will be shown to buyers.
Weight and size   ☐ Irregular or unusual package
help

Domestic Shipping (offer up to 3 services)

Select a shipping service ▾

Add service   Remove service   and have buyers contact me later

International Shipping (offer up to 3 services)

Add service

Packaging & Handling Fee   **Shipping Insurance**
Change   Not offered. Change

Seller ZIP Code   **Sales Tax**
95116 Change   I don't charge tax. Change

Select a service from the drop-down list:

Click the Add Service link to add more options.

Continue selecting services as needed.

Shipping costs ∗   ⊼ Minimize   ⊕ Live help

Specify a flat cost for each shipping service you offer, or have costs calculated automatically based on your package and the buyer's address. Learn more about specifying shipping costs.

| Flat: same cost to all buyers | Calculated: based on buyer's address |

Estimated Weight
2+ to 3 lbs.
Weight and size help

Package Size
Large Package (Oversize 1)
☐ Irregular or unusual package

🖼 Preview rates that will be shown to buyers.

Domestic Shipping (offer up to 3 services)
US Postal Service First Class Mail

Dimensions
___ in. X ___ in. X ___ in.
Only required for UPS Air Services.

US Postal Service Priority Mail

US Postal Service Parcel Post

Remove service

International Shipping (offer up to 3 services)
USPS Economy Parcel Post

To: ☑ Worldwide   ☐ Americas   ☐ Europe   ☐ Asia
   ☐ Canada   ☐ United Kingdom   ☐ Australia
   ☐ Mexico   ☐ Germany   ☐ Japan

USPS Airmail Parcel Post

To: ☑ Worldwide   ☐ Americas   ☐ Europe   ☐ Asia
   ☐ Canada   ☐ United Kingdom   ☐ Australia
   ☐ Mexico   ☐ Germany   ☐ Japan

UPS Standard To Canada

To: ☐ Worldwide   ☐ Americas   ☐ Europe   ☐ Asia
   ☑ Canada   ☐ United Kingdom   ☐ Australia
   ☐ Mexico   ☐ Germany   ☐ Japan

Remove service

Next, we can add or change information for Packaging & Handling fees, Seller Zip Code, Shipping Insurance, and Sales Tax (if applicable).

Packaging & Handling Fee
Change

Shipping Insurance
Not offered. Change

Seller ZIP Code
95116 Change

Sales Tax
I don't charge tax. Change

Let's display the boxes for each option by clicking its "change" link and enter the information as requested.

Packaging & Handling Fee
$ 2
This will not be shown to buyers, but will be included in your shipping total.

Shipping Insurance
Required
Calculated based on the final item price.
UPS and US Postal Service Express Mail include free insurance up to $100.

Seller ZIP Code
95116
US Only

Sales Tax
California   8.25   %
☐ Apply sales tax to the total which includes shipping & handling.

Sales tax? Your state may require you to collect a sales tax from any buyer who resides in your state. If so, you can select your state from the drop-down box and enter the appropriate percentage for your state. This amount will be added to the total of any bidder who is located in your state. There's more on sales tax and other business-related questions in chapter 6.

Now, on our listing page there will be a box where buyers can enter their zip code to view shipping and handling costs *before* they bid or buy. In addition, the winning bidder or buyer's invoice will automatically include shipping, handling, insurance, and sales tax (if the buyer is registered on eBay in the same state that we are—in this case, California).

Return Policy

In the Return Policy section, you can provide detailed criteria on accepting returns or issuing refunds. I selected the "within 14 days" and "Money back" options. I typed the following into the box:

If you are not happy with your purchase, for whatever reason, please alert me with an e-mail. Once I receive the item back from you, I will refund your money plus shipping back to you via PayPal. This policy is good for up to 14 days after the close of the listing.

Payment Instructions

Although I have included this information within the body of my item description, it doesn't hurt to repeat it:

I prefer PayPal but will accept money orders and checks. Payment should be received within five days of purchase or listing close. If you pay with PayPal, you can pay immediately after the listing closes by clicking the Pay Now button on the closed item page. I will then ship immediately! If you don't have a PayPal account, it's easy! Go to www.paypal.com today and open yours!

Checks must clear before item will be shipped. (They are SO "last century"!)

This text will remain as the default text for all my future listings until I change it.

Buyer Requirements

Sellers can restrict their items to certain bidders based on specific criteria. Click Edit Preferences to set buyer requirements for your listings.

This takes us to the "My eBay" Buyer Requirements page. We can:

- Block buyers from countries to which we don't ship. Since we will ship to any country, we leave this one unselected.
- Block buyers with a -1, -2, or -3 feedback score. We will select this one.
- Block buyers who have received two Unpaid Item strikes in the last thirty days. We will select this one as well.
- Block buyers without a PayPal account. For now, I will leave this one unselected, but I may employ this restriction in the future.

Buyer Requirements

Buyer requirements can help you reduce your exposure to buyers who might make transactions more difficult or expensive.

To allow specific eBay members to bid on or purchase your items regardless of any requirement(s) you select, add them to your buyer requirements exemption list.

Select requirements

⚐ **Important:** Select buyer requirements carefully - they may reduce your selling success. The requirement(s) you select will be applied to your current and future listings, except as noted. eBay encourages you to learn more by visiting the Buyer Requirements Help page.

Buyers in countries to which I don't ship
☐ Block buyers who are registered in countries to which I don't ship.
This requirement can help you avoid buyers who agree to purchase your items without realizing you don't ship to their location.

Buyers with a negative feedback score
☑ Block buyers who have a feedback score of ⌐-1 ▼⌐ or lower.
This requirement can help you avoid buyers who have received more negative than positive feedback from other eBay members.

Buyers with Unpaid Item strikes
☑ Block buyers who have received 2 Unpaid Item strikes in the last 30 days.
This requirement can help you avoid buyers with a history of not paying for items they have agreed to purchase.

Buyers without a PayPal account
☐ Block buyers who don't have a PayPal account. (Note: This block **only** applies to future listings and can be disabled per item on the Sell Your Item form.)
This requirement can help you avoid Unpaid Items, as PayPal account holders have up to an 80% lower Unpaid Item rate.

[Submit]

STEP 5. REVIEW AND SUBMIT LISTING

Before our listing goes "live," we have the chance to review and change the information and features for each section. This is an important step! Please don't rush through it. Check each section to make sure that the information is correct.

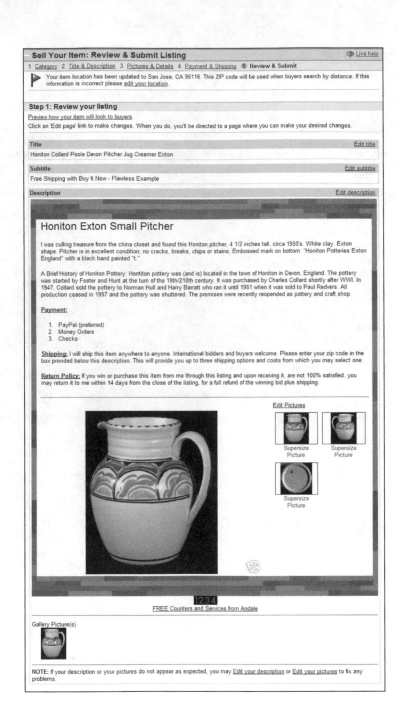

Main Category	Edit Main Category
Pottery & Glass:Pottery & China:Art Pottery:British Art (#1043)	

Second Category	Add second Category

Title & Description	Edit title & description
See above for preview of title, subtitle, Item Specifics and description.	

Pictures & Details	Edit pictures & details
Pictures:	3 picture(s) added to your listing. See above for preview of pictures
Duration:	10 days (a $0.20 surcharge)
Quantity:	1
Price:	$0.99
Buy It Now:	$20.00
Item Location:	San Jose, CA, United States
Listing Designer:	Theme: Blue Bricks Layout: Standard
Listing Upgrades:	Gallery
Free page counter:	Andale style See above for preview of counter

Payment & Shipping	Edit payment & shipping
Seller-accepted payment methods:	I accept PayPal. Payment will go to jimgriff@mail.com;
Ship-to locations:	Will ship to Worldwide.
Shipping costs	Charge shipping cost based on where the buyer is located

Services Available	Available to
US Postal Service Priority Mail®	United States Only
US Postal Service Parcel Post®	United States Only
US Postal Service Express Mail®	United States Only
USPS Economy Parcel Post	Worldwide
USPS Airmail Parcel Post	Worldwide
UPS Standard To Canada	Canada

Shipping insurance required
CA sales tax: 8.25%

Calculated Shipping Details (not shown to buyers):
Package weight: 2+ to 3 lbs.
Package size: Large Package (Oversize 1)
Dimensions: 24 in x 24 in x 18 in
Packaging & Handling Fee: $2.00
Seller ZIP Code: 95116

Buyer requirements:	Block buyers who: Have a feedback score of -1 or lower Have received 2 Unpaid Item strikes in the last 30 days
Item must be returned within:	14 Days
Refund will be given as:	Money Back
Return Policy Details:	If you are not happy with your purchase, for whatever reason, please alert me with an email. Once I receive the item back from you, I will refund your money plus shipping back to me via PayPal. This policy is good for up to 14 days after the close of the listing.
Payment instructions:	I prefer PayPal but will accept money orders and checks. Payment should be received within five days of purchase or listing close. If you pay with PayPal, you can pay immediately after the listing closes by clicking the Pay Now button on the closed item page. I will then ship immediately! If you don't have a PayPal account, it's easy! Go to www.paypal.com today and open yours! Checks must clear before item will be shipped. (They are SO "last century!"

Step 2: Review the fees and submit your listing

Listing fees	
Insertion fee:	$ 0.30
Subtitle:	0.50
10 day duration fee:	0.20
Additional pictures:	0.30
Supersize pictures:	0.75
Gallery:	0.25
Buy It Now Fee:	0.05
Listing Designer:	0.10
Total listing fee:	$ 2.45

If your item sells, you will be charged a Final Value Fee. This fee is based on a percentage of the final sale price.

Current account balance before adding this item: **$5.00**

Attention Sellers:

Add Bold!
BOLD Go for the **bold**! Item titles with **bold** (see example) sell for 39% more, on average. A wise investment for $1.00.

[Add It Now!]

[< Back] [Submit Listing]
Your item will be listed on eBay and the above fees will be charged.

Make it a habit to carefully review the information in each section. If you find something that needs correction or change, look for and click its "change" link. For example, I have decided to reschedule this listing to go live in three days instead of instantly upon submission. The schedule option is located in the Picture & Details section of the Sell Your Item form. Click the "Edit picture & details" link:

Pictures & Details		Edit pictures & details
Pictures:	3 picture(s) added to your listing. See above for preview of pictures	
Duration:	10 days (a $0.20 surcharge)	
Quantity:	1	
Price:	$0.99	
Buy It Now:	$20.00	
Item Location:	San Jose, CA, United States	
Listing Designer:	Theme: Blue Bricks	

To schedule the listing to start at a later date and time, I simply click the option "Schedule start time" under the Duration section.

Sell Your Item: Enter Pictures & Item Details

1. Category 2. Title & Description ③ Pictures & Details 4. Payment & Shipping 5. Review & Submit

Title
Honiton Collard Poole Devon Pitcher Jug Creamer Exton

Subtitle
Free Shipping with Buy It Now - Flawless Example

Pricing and duration

Price your item competitively to increase your chance of a successful sale.

NEW! Get ideas about pricing by searching completed items...

Starting price *Required
$ 0.99
A lower starting price can encourage more bids.

Reserve price (fee varies)
No reserve price. Add

Buy It Now price ($0.05)
$ 20.00
Sell to the first buyer who meets your Buy It Now price.

Duration *
10 days ($0.20 fee) ▼
When to use a 1-day duration.

Private auction
No private auction. Add

Start time
○ Start listing when submitted
● Schedule start time ($0.10) Tuesday, Feb 01 ▼ 7:30 PM ▼ PST
Learn more about scheduled listings.

Make sure to scroll down to the bottom of the page and click Save Changes.

Page counter
1234 Andale Style Change

Cancel Changes   Save Changes

This takes us back to the Review & Submit section. Once you have made any necessary changes or edits, scroll down to the bottom of this page to review the "Listing fees" for this item listing:

Click Submit Listing, and congratulations! Our listing is now queued on eBay as a "pending" listing. It will go live on the date and at the time we specified (February 1, 2005, 7:30 P.M. Pacific).

Only the seller can view a scheduled listing. Click the linked title to view the pending listing:

Here it is!

You can also manage this pending listing from "My eBay," all Selling, Scheduled:

NOTE: We can reschedule the listing to a later or earlier date or time, or we can schedule it to go live immediately, or we can simply delete it. If we delete it before it goes live, we will not incur any insertion fees.

Finally, let's check out the "Calculate shipping" feature, located directly under the item description text. I've entered the following zip code:

Click Calculate to display the shipping costs to this zip code:

Shipping Calculator Rates
This seller is using the shipping calculator to provide shipping rates based on your location. To see your rates, select your country and press **Calculate.**

Postal Code (optional)   Country
05777   United States

[Calculate]

Shipping services and rates available for shipping to United States.
All prices include any packaging and handling fees charged by the seller.

US Postal Service Priority Mail®
Estimated delivery time: 2-3 days.
Learn more about US Postal Service shipping.
Shipping & Handling: $27.39
Insurance (required): --

US Postal Service Parcel Post®
Estimated delivery time: 2-9 days.
Learn more about US Postal Service shipping.
Shipping & Handling: $19.85
Insurance (required): --

US Postal Service Express Mail®
Delivery: Overnight to most areas.
Includes insurance up to $100.
Learn more about US Postal Service shipping.
Shipping & Handling: $29.80
Insurance (included): --

Important : Insurance price will be calculated based on the final values of the item(s).

▶ Insurance price will be calculated based on the final value of the item(s).

Note: Delivery times are dependent upon the day and time the seller actually ships the item.

United States Postal Service, the Eagle logo, and their combined form, as well as US Postal Service, Parcel Post, and Priority Mail, are registered trademarks, and Media Mail is a trademark, owned by the United States Postal Service.

This invaluable tool helps inform buyers of all after-sale costs *before* they bid.

Congratulations! If you have followed along with the instructions and steps of this chapter, you should have listed your first item on eBay. There's nothing quite like the thrill of satisfaction you feel when you have completed your first eBay listing. Take a moment to relax and savor the accomplishment.

But don't get too relaxed. Your eBay selling tasks are not over. You still have to be available for buyer e-mails, and if the item sells, you will have to accept payment and ship the item. In the meantime, here are some seller troubleshooting tips.

Selling Troubleshooting

MY EBAY PICTURE SERVICES IMAGES ARE NOT SHOWING ON THE REVIEW LISTING PAGE!

This is a rare problem—but it does happen. Usually, this is due to a faulty connection between your computer and eBay. If your images are not showing up on the "review" page, go back and start your listing again from the beginning.

OOPS! I NEED TO CHANGE SOMETHING IN MY LIVE LISTING!

You can make major changes to your listing after it has gone "live" to the site, but only before it actually receives a bid. Since items do not usually receive bids for at least thirty minutes after they are listed, this gives you some time to revise your item.

To make revisions to a live item where no bids have been placed, go to the Item Description page. Click the link "Revise your item" on the top section of the item page:

Honiton Collard Poole Devon Pitcher Jug Creamer Exton	Item number: 3776657451
Free Shipping with Buy It Now - Flawless Example	
You are signed in	Email to a friend | This item is being tracked in My eBay
Revise your item	Want to sell more quickly and efficiently? Learn about
Promote your item	how Turbo Lister can help you save time.
Sell a similar item	

The next page will show the item number for the listing you wish to revise.

Revise Your Item

Revise your listing or add features to attract more buyers
If you want to add more information or features to your listing, just enter your item number and click the Revise Item button below.

If your item has received NO bids or sales and does not end within 12 hours

Revise anything in your listing except the selling format (for example, you can't change your auction item to an eBay Stores item).

If your item has already received a bid/purchase or ends within 12 hours, you can *only*:

- Add to the item description
  (Exception: If your listing already has a bid/purchase AND ends within 12 hours, you can't add to your description or add a second category)
- Add optional seller features to increase your item's visibility.

Enter the Item Number: 3776657451

Continue >

You can also change your cross-promotions.

Click Continue to go back to the Review & Submit page, where you can change almost anything about your listing.

REVISING AN ITEM AFTER BIDS ARE RECEIVED— ADD TO AN ITEM DESCRIPTION

In cases where bids have been received and you need to correct an error but the error is not so serious as to warrant ending the auction early, you can always add to the listing's description. To add to your item's description, go to the "My eBay," All Selling page. There's the column Related Links. Click "more . . ." on the bottom of that column:

This will open the page Selling-Related Links. Look for the link "Add to Item Description":

Follow the instructions from there. (You will need the item number.) This feature is handy for adding information about the item.

I NEED TO END MY LISTING EARLY!

A seller may, at any time and entirely at her discretion, end her auction listing early. This might occur if the item was damaged or stolen after the item was listed, or if the seller inadvertently described the item incorrectly.

The link End My Listing Early is found on the Selling-Related Links page we referenced in the previous troubleshooting tip.

Follow the instructions from there. Again, you will need the item number of the listing you need to end. If there are active bids on the listing you wish to end early, the system will cancel them before you end the listing. You should also, as a courtesy, e-mail all bidders whose bids were canceled to inform them of the reason.

I WANT TO RELIST MY ITEM—USING THE RELIST FEATURE

Once a listing has ended, there are two ways to relist the item quickly and easily: from "My eBay" or from the Closed Item page. To relist from "My eBay," go to the "My eBay," Selling, Unsold or Sold page. Find the listing, click Action, then select Relist.

You can also relist an item by clicking Relist on the closed-listing page. It's located under the Seller Services section on the top section of the item page.

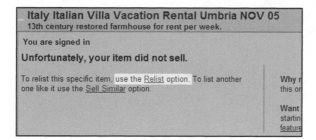

If you are using the Relist feature, the fee for the relisting may be waived if the item sells on the second attempt. When you relist, if your previous item had a reserve, you will have to lower the reserve price for your listing to be eligible for the listing-fee credit. If your item did not have a reserve, you will need to lower the opening bid amount to qualify for the listing credit.

You can also use the Relist feature to list a new, similar item and save yourself a lot of typing. If you use the Relist feature to sell a similar item, make sure you change the appropriate information (pictures, text, title, etc.) before submitting the listing.

MY BIDDER RETRACTED HER BID! IS THIS ALLOWED?

Yes, it is, but only under certain circumstances. If a bidder has made an error in her bid amount, she may retract her bid and reenter the bid correctly. A bidder may also retract due to extraordinary circumstances that place an unreasonable burden on the bidder should he or she win the item.

A bidder may not employ the bid-retraction privilege for frivolous reasons, for example, a change of heart or finding the item someplace else for less.

All bid retractions are tracked on a user's Feedback Profile card.

Member Profile: uncle_griff (904 ☆)				
		Recent Ratings:		
			Past Month	Past 6 Months	Past 12 Months
Feedback Score:	904				
Positive Feedback:	99.9%	⊕ positive	22	127	193
Members who left a positive:	904	◉ neutral	0	0	0
Members who left a negative:	1	⊖ negative	0	0	0
All positive feedback received:	1098				
Learn about what these numbers mean.		Bid Retractions (Past 6 months): 0			

Chronic bid retractions are routinely investigated by eBay and can result in suspension of the retracting bidder's eBay registration.

The ability to retract a bid is limited by the time left in an auction and the time between your first bid and the next. Bid retraction rules are explained in detail in Section One, chapter 7.

MY BIDDER IS NOT RESPONDING TO E-MAIL

How to Contact a Bidder

First, don't panic! Sometimes bidders find themselves unexpectedly pulled away from their computers for a time. Bidders can experience crises. Always give your bidder a few days before moving to the next step.

If your buyer hasn't responded to your e-mail within three to five days, then you should attempt to contact him by phone. You can obtain the phone number of any high bidder on your listings by clicking on Advanced Search and then "Find a Member." Then click on Find Contact Information.

Enter the buyer's User ID and the item number in the box provided for Contact Information. (Note: Only the high bidder(s) and the seller in a specific eBay transaction can obtain each other's phone number.)

REPORTING AN UNREACHABLE BIDDER

If a bidder's phone number is not valid or if a e-mail sent to a bidder is bounced back to you as undeliverable, you should report the bidder to eBay.

Click on the Security Link found on the bottom of any eBay Web page. It will take you to the Security & Resolution Center page.

Select the option for "Report another problem" and follow the instructions from there.

MY BIDDER BACKED OUT!

Sometimes a winning bidder may back out of a sale. If a bidder contacts you with extenuating circumstances and asks to be relieved of their bidder obligation, you may allow them to do so. Or, if the "back out" is for reasons you consider frivolous or if the bidder does not respond to repeated e-mails or phone calls, you may want to report the sale as an Unpaid Item.

In either case, if the transaction is not completed, you can and should file for a Final Value Fee credit by filing an Unpaid Item claim.

FILING AN UNPAID ITEM CLAIM

To start, go to the "My eBay" page, click on the All Selling view, find the Related Links column, click "more . . ." and then click Unpaid Item Process.

SECOND CHANCE OFFER

Sometimes, a buyer may back out leaving you with an unsold item—one for which you have paid insertion and other fees. Instead of relisting the item (and incurring more fees) you might want to try the Second Chance Offer feature.

Second Chance offers can be sent to any of the nonwinning bidders if the high bidder does not buy the item, if a seller has duplicate items, or if the reserve price is not met in a reserve-price auction. Second Chance offers can be created immediately after a listing ends and for up to sixty days. Please note that Second Chance offers will not be sent to bidders who have opted not to receive them.

Before sending a Second Chance Offer because of an Unpaid Item (see above), a seller should be sure that everything has been done to resolve the issue with the original buyer. Also, the number of offers you send can't be more than the number of items you have for sale.

There are no insertion fees for using the Second Chance Offer feature on an unsold item. In addition, all the regular eBay features such as Feedback and Buyer Protection are available to both the buyer and the seller in a Second Chance Offer transaction.

To learn more about the Second Chance Offer feature, click on the All Selling on the "My eBay" page, scroll down to Related Links, and expand the list if necessary by clicking "more . . ." Then click "Send a Second Chance Offer." Follow the instructions from there.

GRIFF TIP! Do you notice a pattern here? Almost everything you may need to accomplish as a seller, be it filing an Unpaid Item script, ending a listing, or relisting an item, can be done through "My eBay." If you ever have a question about your items, your Seller's Account, or your eBay preferences or information, go to "My eBay" first!

Now that you have your first item listed, you'll find the rest are a snap. Who knows? This may be the start of *your* business on eBay! Before we move on to the next chapter, eBay seller Robert Sachs has a great selling tip to share. He employs it around the holiday sales season, but any eBay seller could use it anytime:

I found a neat little trick to help boost my holiday sales enormously: free shipping!

I combined Buy It Now with free shipping and came up with a killer offer. If the buyer used Buy It Now, I would zero out the shipping charge. I changed the heading for my auctions to be sure to include "FREE SHIP" in each one. My auctions, normally set for five days, would close within twenty-four hours! This allowed me to post more without flooding a particular item. And posting more meant more sales!

My normal closing rate for the year 2001 averaged around forty-five percent. My closing rate during November and early December pushed closer to eighty percent, with the vast majority being Buy It Now sales!

5

After the Sale

In 1998, Mike Driscoll was selling restaurant equipment and antiques out of an old 1880 home he had recently purchased. On weekends, he would move most of his inventory outside to attract roadside attention, and he was lucky if he sold $500 in two days—not nearly enough to survive and certainly not worth the strain of moving furniture in and out of his home shop every weekend.

Then, in 1999, Mike found eBay, started selling, and, in his own words, "fell in love with eBay."

"I now own three computers. I never sat at one until thirteen months ago. I no longer open my front door to my antiques store, as I sell all my antiques, and even some restaurant equipment stuff that has sat downstairs in my basement for three years, on eBay."

Today, Mike has an average of 200 items up for sale or bid on eBay. His feedback stands at 4,450 and climbing. He is also a member of the eBay Power Seller team. eBay has indeed changed his life, but not only in a business sense.

"I sold an item that was not as I described. It was an ice cream syrup pump that I sold as a catsup, mustard, and relish pump."

The buyer contacted Mike to alert him to his error, and he immediately obtained the buyer's contact information so that he could quickly refund the buyer's money without even waiting for the item to be returned.

"She surprised me by showing up at my doorstep one day. The rest is history.

"I thank you, eBay, for changing my life! I have been richer in money, romance, and confidence since finding eBay."

Your item sold! Congratulations! Now, the after-sale tasks begin:

> Invoicing the Buyer
> Leaving Feedback
> Shipping

Invoicing the Buyer

When one of your items has sold on eBay, the next step is to send the lucky winning buyer an e-mail invoice or notice. You can send an invoice manually, or if you set up your eBay selling preferences appropriately, eBay will automatically send out an invoice with an item total that includes shipping, handling, sales tax (if applicable), and your payment instructions. In addition, if you integrated PayPal fully into your listings (per the instructions previously), the automatic invoice will contain a clickable Pay Now button that will take the buyer directly to his PayPal account.

SENDING AN INVOICE—"MY EBAY"

"My eBay" provides the quickest and easiest method for manually sending an invoice to a buyer. Navigate to the page view for "My eBay," All Selling, Sold:

Click Send Invoice to the right of the item for which you need to send an invoice. This will display the invoice for this item.

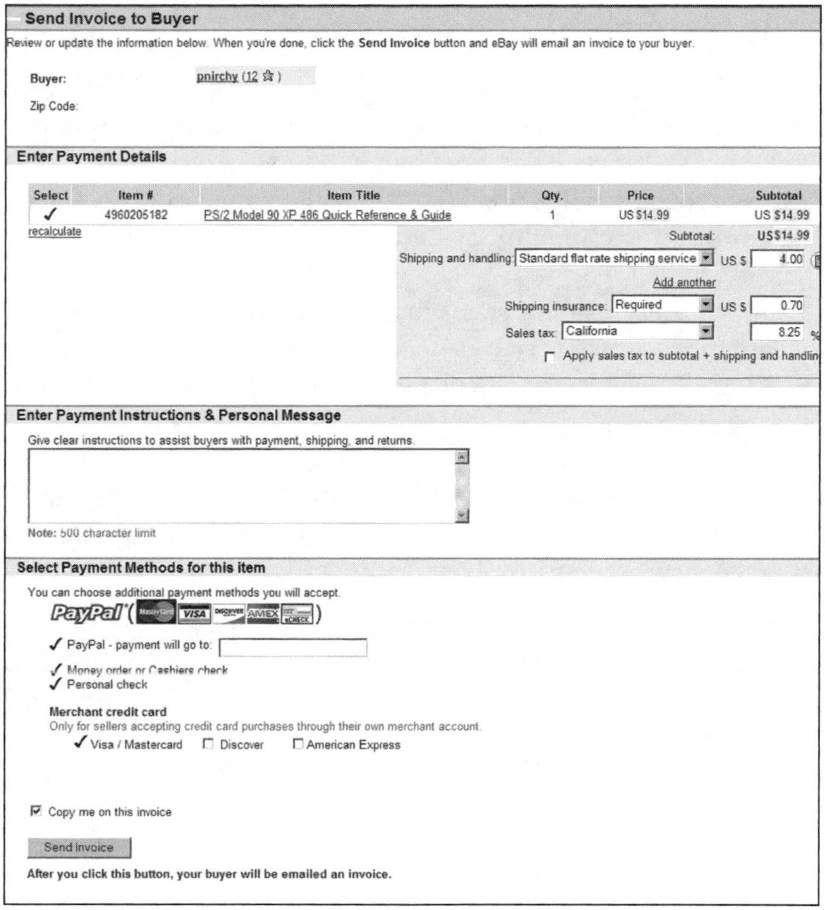

Send Invoice to Buyer

Review or update the information below. When you're done, click the **Send Invoice** button and eBay will email an invoice to your buyer.

Buyer: pnirchy (12 ☆)

Zip Code:

Enter Payment Details

Select	Item #	Item Title	Qty.	Price	Subtotal
✓	4960205182	PS/2 Model 90 XP 486 Quick Reference & Guide	1	US $14.99	US $14.99

recalculate

Subtotal: US$14.99

Shipping and handling: Standard flat rate shipping service ▾ US $ 4.00

Add another

Shipping insurance: Required ▾ US $ 0.70

Sales tax: California ▾ 8.25 %

☐ Apply sales tax to subtotal + shipping and handling

Enter Payment Instructions & Personal Message

Give clear instructions to assist buyers with payment, shipping, and returns.

Note: 500 character limit

Select Payment Methods for this item

You can choose additional payment methods you will accept.

PayPal (MasterCard VISA DISCOVER AMEX eCHECK)

✓ PayPal - payment will go to:

✓ Money order or Cashiers check
✓ Personal check

Merchant credit card
Only for sellers accepting credit card purchases through their own merchant account.

✓ Visa / Mastercard   ☐ Discover   ☐ American Express

☑ Copy me on this invoice

Send Invoice

After you click this button, your buyer will be emailed an invoice.

Make additions or changes as needed and click Send Invoice.

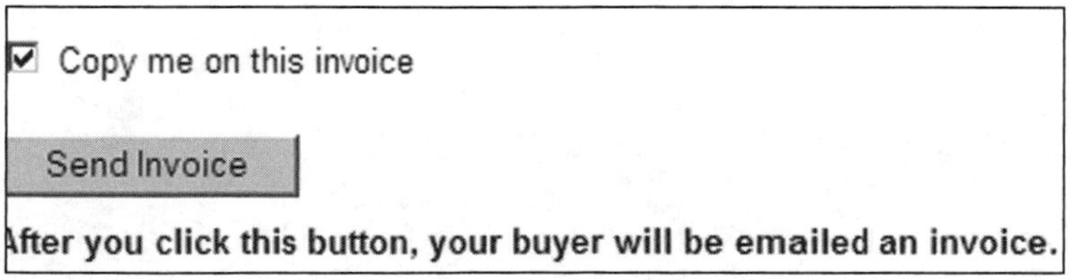

☑ Copy me on this invoice

Send Invoice

After you click this button, your buyer will be emailed an invoice.

(I've blocked out any personal information out of respect for my buyer's privacy.)

SENDING AN INVOICE—MANUALLY

You can also send an e-mail invoice of your own creation directly to your buyer through your e-mail program. Although this is not the most efficient method for invoicing, some sellers still employ it.

First, set your eBay Preferences so that the e-mail address for buyers (and sellers) in your transaction displays automatically on the listing page.

NOTE: eBay's privacy policy states that eBay will only show e-mail addresses in specific situations. A seller can view all the e-mail addresses of his bidders and buyers. A buyer can view the e-mail address of any seller from which she has purchased or won an item.

Click the eBay Preferences link under the My Account section in the left-hand column on your "My eBay" page. Check the box "See seller e-mail addresses when viewing items you've won":

Now, the e-mail addresses of all winning buyers in listings where you are the seller will display automatically next to their User IDs. In addition, the e-mail addresses of all sellers of items you have won will display automatically.

NOTES ON INVOICING A BUYER

As a professional eBay seller, you should always take the initiative and send any e-mails or invoices to your buyer immediately after the listing closes.

Nothing is less professional or more annoying to a buyer than receiving an e-mail invoice from a seller containing little or no information or instructions on what to do next. Even if you have stated all terms and instructions explicitly in your listing description, *repeat them in your invoice e-mails to bidders and buyers.* Some eBay members have bids out on ten, twenty, or more items and may not recall your payment options, instructions, or general terms. There is nothing to lose and everything to gain by repeating your complete list of terms and options for your buyer. Believe me, we eBay buyers *really* appreciate those sellers who do.

To this end, your e-mail invoice should contain all the information the buyer needs to complete his transaction obligations. This should include:

- Payment options with detailed instructions for each
- Links to payment services wherever possible
- Shipping options and costs
- Your full name, address, and phone number
- Any reminders regarding your terms of sale

Here are some examples:

This is the e-mail that Paypal sends automatically to a winning bidder:

Payments by PayPal. You won an item from fragranceexpress

Dear uncle_griff,

Thank you for purchasing my item!

Pay Now! WITH PAYPAL

I accept the following payment methods:

VISA   MasterCard   DISCOVER   AMEX   eCheck

Note: If you have already sent payment for this item via PayPal or other means, please disregard this notice.

Paying for Your Item

I prefer payment through PayPal, which lets me receive your payment instantly and ship your item sooner.

With over 35 million members, PayPal is the #1 payment service on eBay! If you pay using PayPal, this purchase is eligible for up to $1,000.00 USD of coverage at no additional cost.

Payment Details

Amount: $17.90 USD   **Pay Now With PayPal**

Shipping & Handling: Determined by Shipping Calculator

Insurance: Determined by Shipping Calculator

FL Sales Tax: 6.00%

Note: Shipping & Handling and Insurance will be automatically calculated when you click Pay Now.

Item Details

Seller: fragranceexpress

End Date: Nov. 25, 2004

Item Number: 5538535270

Item Title: Homme de Cafe' 100ml (3.4oz) EDT New/Retail Box

Message from fragranceexpress

For more information on my shipping, insurance, and other policies, or if you would like to pay for this item with a method other than PayPal, please see the item listing for details.

Thank you,

Fragrance Express

P.S. To view this item (for up to 90 days), click here.

This is an e-mail sent by an eBay seller:

```
Congratulations!

You have won the bid on this item. The total is:

Bid:  $616.01
S&H:   $60.00
==================
        $676.01 Total


Please read the following notes about payment carefully:

+++++++++++++++++++++++++++++++++++++++++++++++++++
We do not accept personal or business checks.
+++++++++++++++++++++++++++++++++++++++++++++++++++

If you are a resident of state of Georgia please add 7% tax to Bid
amount.
If you have already made your payment just reply that you  have.

Thank you.

persianmasterpiece.com

=================================================
```

The seller omitted any payment instructions, which could hamper the buyer from completing the transaction. Note that the previous PayPal invoice contains a Pay Now button.

A responsible bidder should and will respond to your e-mail invoice as quickly as she can. In fact, if you accept PayPal and have it fully integrated into your listing page, and if you have used set shipping rates with the Flat or Calculated shipping feature, you will find that many of your buyers will not wait for an invoice, but will instead simply complete the transaction immediately without further input from you.

However, in those cases where buyers are slow in responding, *do not,* I repeat, do not berate, lecture, or criticize them in an e-mail. Always, always, always maintain your professional poise and courtesy whenever corresponding with a customer.

If you need to send them, your payment reminders should be informative and polite, even if you are informing a customer that you are about to file an Unpaid Item alert.

Your nonresponsive, nonpaying buyer may eventually respond with either an apology or a diatribe. If you receive an apology, accept it and move on either with the transaction or, if necessary, with the Unpaid Item process. If you receive a diatribe, avoid responding with a diatribe of your own.

Buyers can find themselves in the most unexpected of circumstances. eBay seller Barry Lamb sent me this amusing tale:

> In well over five thousand transactions on eBay, there's one that I'll always remember.
>
> I had a buyer purchase a set of car speakers from me. The first e-mail, where she replied to my congratulations e-mail, she wrote, "I can't pay you now, I have to go to the hospital." In her second e-mail, she wrote, "I'm having a baby, my boyfriend will send you the money." Her third e-mail: "My boyfriend is an idiot, He didn't send you no money." Then nothing for about four days and then "I have a 6½ pound baby boy, I'm sending it to you."
>
> Boy, was I glad when the payment showed up and NOT the baby.

The rule in brief: There is never a reason or excuse for any seller to behave unprofessionally. You never know what the situation might be on the buyer's end!

Leaving Feedback

Chances are, if you are an eBay seller, you will previously have received feedback as an eBay buyer. You know how important leaving feedback can be. As an eBay seller, you may find many of your buyers are relatively new to eBay and do not quite understand how to leave feedback or, if they do, are not familiar with the protocol of leaving feedback.

Your eBay duty is to help educate your buyers on how eBay feedback works. eBay user Carolyn Lanzkron has an unusual but effective method of reminding her buyers about the importance of leaving feedback . . .

> "I'm a new seller, and I'm hungry for feedback. I'm hoping my gimmick will help. In the package with the item I put a candy bar, with a wrapper that says, 'Thank you for making this eBay transaction such a sweet experience,' with my eBay ID. On the back of the candy bar, I put the following: 'Ulterior motive disclaimer: Now that I've fed you, I'm hoping that you'll feedback! (Pretty please?)'
>
> "I'm not sure how successful this will be, but the idea is to demonstrate that I'm willing to deliver more than was in the original bargain."

Carolyn is going to be a very successful eBay seller. Not only is she giving a little extra gift to her buyers, she is showing by example how feedback works at eBay.

FEEDBACK—WHO LEAVES IT FIRST?

In the early days of eBay, the accepted protocol was for the seller to leave feedback immediately upon receiving payment. This has, unfortunately I believe, changed. Many sellers wait until the buyer has left feedback before they will leave feedback in kind. I've been told by some of these sellers that this is a defensive strategy they employ to protect themselves in cases where a buyer leaves them a negative feedback. By waiting, they are then in a position to leave a negative in kind for the buyer. It is not against any eBay rules to practice this strategy, but I believe it is an unfortunate and misguided practice.

Consider: A buyer's transaction obligations to the seller end when they send payment for the item. A buyer is not obliged to alert a seller that the item has arrived or that she is happy with the item (though it is definitely good eBay etiquette to do so). Thus, once the seller receives payment (check has cleared, or PayPal payment has been transferred to the seller's PayPal account, etc.) he should really leave appropriate feedback for the buyer . . . first. Interestingly, I have found that most sellers who do not receive feedback from their buyers also, as a rule, do not leave feedback first.

As for the buyer leaving the seller feedback . . . the seller's transaction obligations are not complete until the buyer has received the item and is satisfied with it. Only then should the bidder be expected to leave feedback.

FEEDBACK—WHAT SHOULD IT SAY?

You have eighty-five character spaces in which you may type a comment. If the bidder has paid for the item and sent payment quickly, make sure to mention this. Nothing makes bidders happier than to have an eBay seller tell the world that he or she, the bidder, is quick to send payment.

Here are some samples:

"Excellent transaction. Buyer sent payment immediately."
"A reputable eBay buyer. Always pays fast and is cordial in e-mails. A+"
"Great to do business with! A definite asset to eBay! WE HIGHLY
    RECOMMEND!!!"
"Outstanding eBay buyer, sets the ultimate standard. Amazing!"

FEEDBACK—WHAT NOT TO SAY

As a seller, you may run into the occasional "difficult" customer. Unless the buyer has backed out of the sale, you should avoid leaving a negative feedback comment for paying customers. Instead, consider leaving an exuberant neutral or a subdued positive. The customer will get the message.

Either way, avoid using inflammatory language. Regardless of how much you believe the person deserves it, refrain in your feedback comment from calling a customer "a real jerk" or something equally pejorative. Why?

Because calling someone "a jerk" or "an idiot" or worse in his feedback ends up reflecting more on you than the other party. Coarse language is unprofessional and will put potential customers off doing business with you.

Instead, use unemotional, reasoned comments to let the rest of the community know about the transaction. You have an unpleasant customer who nonetheless sent payment immediately? Leave a positive or, if really deserved, a neutral saying something like:

"Some misunderstanding at first but it all worked out in the end. Thanks!"

or

"Very happy to have finally satisfied this customer. Thank you!"

If a bidder backs out for no reason or is unreachable via e-mail or phone, leave a neutral or negative with a comment along the lines of:

"Not a serious bidder. Recommend avoiding."

or

"Unable to contact buyer. Avoid their bids."

or

"Bidder refused to complete transaction."

Of course, in all these situations, the bidder can and just might leave you a neutral or negative in kind. Don't sweat it. Your calm and reasoned words will speak volumes about your integrity and professionalism. You can and will weather the occasional retaliatory negative comment. The only words you need to be concerned with are your own.

FUTURE CORRESPONDENCE WITH YOUR EBAY BUYERS

A good customer is an asset to an eBay seller. It's a smart strategy to keep good customers coming back to your eBay listings. A good way to do this is through a mailing list. There are, however, some important concerns about formulating mailing lists of your eBay customers.

Once another eBay member has purchased an item from you, you may, in your first e-mails to her, ask for her permission to add her to your mailing list for future eBay listings of interest.

In fact, you mustn't add your eBay customers to your mailing list without their permission. You are also only allowed to e-mail your eBay winning bidders or buyers. You must never e-mail another seller's bidders with solicitations to bid on your items or requests for their permission to place them on your mailing list. These are serious rules at eBay. Breaking them can result in the suspension of your eBay registration!

Shipping

Our listing has ended and we have a high bidder. It's time to ship the item. The last item on the list of your seller obligations is "sale fulfillment," that is, sending the item to the winning buyer.

The ultimate success of your eBay transaction depends on quick and secure fulfillment. How well you pack the item and how quickly you ship it can make all the difference in buyer satisfaction. The single most common reasons for buyer seller disputes are slow or seriously delayed shipping and items damaged in transit due to poor or inadequate packing.

WHEN TO SHIP

The standard protocol at eBay is for the seller to ship the item to the buyer once payment has been received and cleared. Most sellers wait for personal checks to clear before shipping. Nearly all sellers ship immediately upon receiving payment via PayPal, credit card, or money order.

Once you have received payment, it's your duty to get the item on its way to the happy buyer.

Speed is important. The most successful eBay sellers send the buyer's merchandise out the very day payment is received. The best sellers have the item packed before the listing has closed so that they can go into action the very second the payment is in their hands. For those bidders who pay via PayPal, this can be mere minutes after the listing has closed.

If you scan through the feedback comments for longtime eBay sellers, you will find that the most common praise is for fast or quick shipping. 'Nuff said?

PACKING SLIPS AND INVOICES

Using packing slips is one more step to assuring your item ships safely. In some instances, they are required. Regardless, providing a packing slip with the item shows that you are a true eBay professional.

As a bidder, I always appreciate those sellers who include a printout of the item page along with the item. Since I tend to buy a lot at eBay, a copy of the item page helps me to remember who sent the item, when I bought it, and how much I paid. In the case of similar items, I know to leave feedback for the correct seller.

SHIPPING LABELS

The outside of the package is the first thing your buyer is going to see. If you want to be perceived as a professional seller, make sure you use professional-looking shipping labels.

In the old days, eBay sellers had to create their own shipping labels either using a word processor or by hand. Now, any eBay seller can use the Print Label feature in "My eBay." Go to "My eBay," All Selling, Sold and check the item for which you wish to create and print a shipping label. Click "Print Shipping Labels," or click the button under Action and select Print Shipping Label.

This should take you to PayPal. Log in to continue (use the same e-mail address that is connected to your eBay Seller's Account and registration).

The fields on the next page should fill in automatically. If not, type in the address and other information as requested.

PayPal®   Log Out | Help

| My Account | Send Money | Request Money | Merchant Tools | Auction Tools |

U.S. Postal Service - Print Your Label   [See Demo]

Create, purchase and print U.S. Postal Service® shipping labels from your PayPal account. Enjoy the affordable Postal Service rates without having to leave your desk.

Shipping tools with U.S. Postal Service are currently only available for transactions where both the sender's and recipient's addresses are in the United States.

Address Information

Ship From: Jim Griffith
Edit this Address eBay Inc
2145 Hamilton
Ave
San
Jose, CA 95125
United States

Ship To: [Jim Griffith]

Address 1: [eBay Inc]

Address 2: [2145 Hamilton Ave]
(optional)

City: [San Jose]

State: [CA ▼]

ZIP Code: [95125] (5 or 9 digits)

Country: United States

Shipment Options   [?] Shipment Options FAQ

Service Type: [Parcel Post® ▼] Choose a different shipper

Package Size: [Package/Thick Envelope ▼] Learn More About Package Sizes
☐ The packaging is irregular or unusual

Mailing Date: [1/17/2005 ▼]

Weight: [1] lbs. [ ] oz.

Label Printer: Laser/Ink Jet Printer Edit Printer Settings

Delivery Confirmation: $0.13 USD

Note: Delivery Confirmation is FREE with the purchase of Signature Confirmation.

Label Processing Fee: $0.20 USD

Signature Confirmation: ⦿ Yes ($1.30 USD) ○ No
Note: Signature of receipt is available upon request for Express Mail®.

Display Postage Value on Label: ☐

Email message to Buyer: (optional)
[   ]

USPS® Insurance   USPS® Insurance FAQ

Purchase Insurance: ⦿ Yes ○ No

Insured value: [9.99] USD [?]
Provides coverage up to $200.00 USD

USPS® Insurance, available at Post Office™ locations, provides coverage up to $5,000.00 USD Insurance purchased online cannot be combined with insurance purchased at a Post Office™. When I select **Continue** to purchase insurance, I agree that my package is not perishable, flammable, or too fragile to withstand normal mail handling.
Terms and Conditions

Item(s) Being Shipped to Your Buyer

Note: If you have multiple packages for this transaction, you can print multiple labels by clicking the **Ship multiple boxes for this order** link after creating the current label.

Item #	Item Title	Qty
4351318564	PS/2 Model 90 XP 486 Quick Reference & Guide	1

[Continue] [Cancel]

Click Continue to move to the confirmation screen.

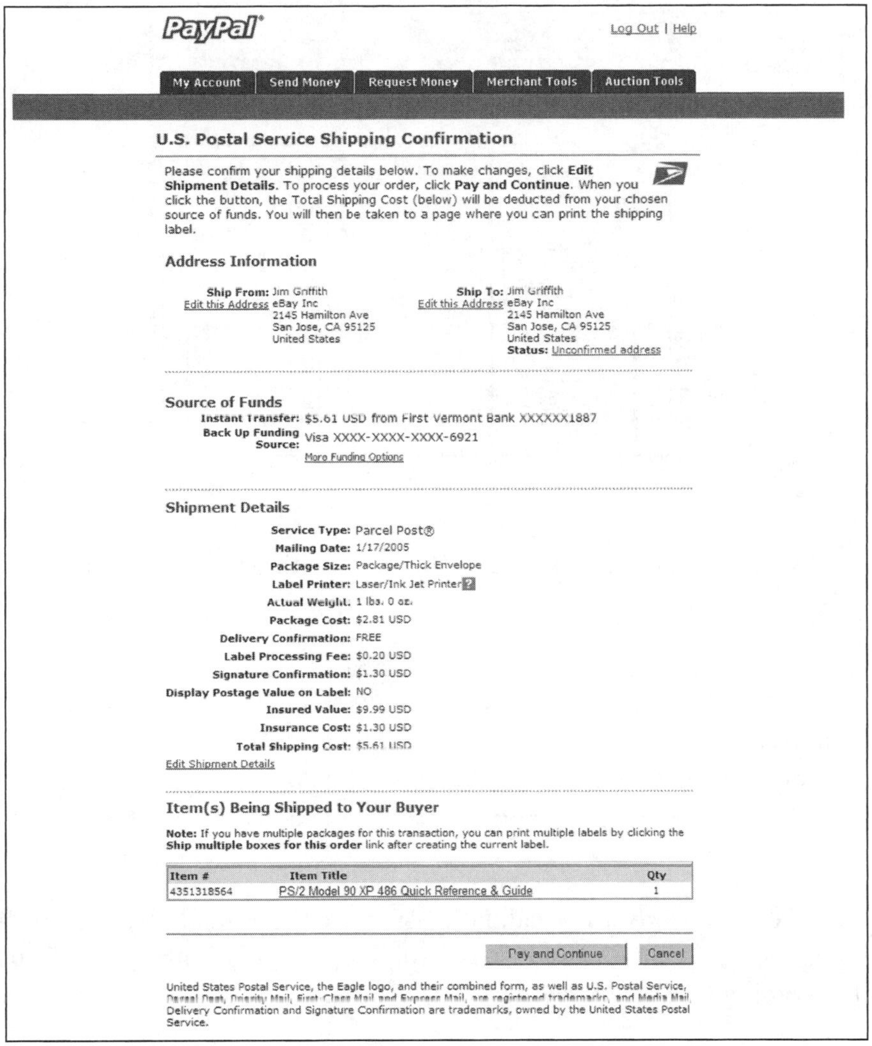

Double-check that everything is accurate. If you need to make changes, click the appropriate edit links. Do *not* navigate back one page or you will lose all the information and have to start all over from "My eBay."

Once you are satisfied everything is correct, click "Pay and Continue." The next screen is a preview of your label.

Make sure your printer is set up and loaded with paper or printing labels.

GRIFF TIP! There are self-adhesive labels that are perfect for printing out using the PayPal label feature. The USPS Click-N-Ship label is one option, but any 8-by-10 single label sheet should work.

When you are ready to print the item, click the Print Label button. Once printing is complete, the browser will display a confirmation page with instructions for voiding labels in case of error.

PayPal®   Log Out | Help

| My Account | Send Money | Request Money | Merchant Tools | Auction Tools |

U.S. Postal Service Shipping Label Completed

Shipment Details

Shipping Method: Parcel Post®

Total Shipping Cost: $5.61 USD

Your **buyer** will receive an **email receipt** with a **tracking number**, to confirm that the item is being shipped. You will also receive an email for this transaction shortly.

Items Being Shipped to Your Buyer

Item #	Item Title	Qty
4351318564	PS/2 Model 90 XP 486 Quick Reference & Guide	1

Voiding a Shipping Label

You may request a refund for the shipping label you just created within the next **48 hours**, if necessary. To request a refund, click on the Void Label link in the Transaction Details page for this transaction, or in the Shipping Confirmation Email.

What do you want to do next?
- Reprint this label
- Ship multiple boxes for this order

Take advantage of these free shipping products and services!
- Request a free carrier pickup and the U.S. Postal Service® will pick up your package, or locate a Post Office™ and drop your package off yourself
- Order free U.S. Postal Service® shipping supplies online
- Create a Packing Slip instantly that summarizes your transaction and includes a personalized message to your buyer

| Account Overview | Back to eBay |

United States Postal Service, the Eagle logo, and their combined form, as well as U.S. Postal Service, Parcel Post, Priority Mail, First-Class Mail and Express Mail, are registered trademarks, and Media Mail, Delivery Confirmation and Signature Confirmation are trademarks, owned by the United States Postal Service.

GRIFF TIP! If you use plain paper, cut the printed sheet in half and keep the right-hand side as your receipt. You can then paste or tape the left-hand side onto your package. Use clear tape to fasten the plain paper shipping label to your package, but make sure *not* to cover the bar-code area with tape. Tape can sometimes make the bar-code unreadable, which could result in shipping delays (and consequently, an unhappy buyer).

SHIPPING METHODS

Most of the items sold at eBay are small enough to pack and ship through one of the major delivery services:

> USPS (United States Postal Service)
> UPS (United Parcel Service)

FedEx
Others (Airborne Express, DLH, etc.)

If you are planning on selling regularly, schlepping boxes back and forth to pickup locations could end up taking much of your day. You will want to open an account with either UPS or FedEx for regular pickup services and invoicing.

USPS does not provide accounts but they do have a pickup service for a fee of $12.50 per visit. This covers an unlimited number of boxes. For pickup, your packages have to have postage prepaid. The USPS pickup service is available in most zip codes, but check their Web site for more information.

USPS offers two solutions for prepaid postage:

Click-N-Ship (prints out postage over the Internet)
Postage meters (prints out on a meter)

If you have a postage scale, you can purchase shipping postage over the Internet from USPS. Visit the USPS Web site for more information: *www.usps.com*.

Look for the link for Click-N-Ship and follow the instructions from there. Another postage option is to purchase or lease a postage meter. You then purchase postage by connecting the meter to a phone line, dialing a special number, and downloading postage directly to the meter.

Visit the USPS Web site for more information: *www.usps.com* and *www.usps.com/postagesolutions/*.

UPS is popular with high-volume sellers. UPS offers a regular pickup service and a wide range of shipping options. You can create an account on the UPS Web site, and just as with USPS, you can print UPS postage labels on your computer for your parcels so they are ready for pickup. UPS also has some shipping supplies.

Visit their Web site for more information: *www.ups.com*.

FedEx is also a popular shipping option with online shipping tools similar to UPS. Account creation can be done on their Web site: *www.fedex.com*.

USPS, UPS, FEDEX . . . WHICH ONE SHOULD I USE?

The three major carriers are fairly competitive when it comes to fees and shipping services. Depending on your location and the type of items you sell, one of the three may work best for you.

Investigate each of the services thoroughly before you pick one. Or, as eBay seller Peter Cini advises, offer your customers *all* of them:

Empower the customer by offering as many shipping options in your listing as is feasible for your business. Customers love options and it gives them a feeling of control over the outcome.

TOOLS AND SUPPLIES YOU WILL NEED FOR SHIPPING

You should have the following tools and supplies handy:

Printer
Postage scale adequate for parcels
Yardstick or tape measure (to weigh and measure the dimensions of each parcel accurately)
Clear packing tape
Packing tape holder/dispenser
Packing materials (bubble wrap, packing peanuts, excelsior, etc.)
Boxes (different shapes and sizes)

CALCULATING COSTS

Nothing pleases customers more than knowing exactly what shipping costs will be *before* they bid. There are many ways to help customers determine costs quickly and accurately.

One option is simply to state flat shipping costs. Here is a table with shipping costs from an actual eBay listing:

Ship To Location	Shipping (USD)
US	$5
Canada	$8
UK	$10
All Others	$15

An even better option is to utilize the free eBay Shipping Calculator for flat costs. Either way, flat shipping costs are an ideal solution for small, lightweight items. No calculations for the buyer or the seller to make, no possibility of confusion or mistakes.

GRIFF TIP! Keep your buyers happy! Provide estimated and flat-rate shipping costs as accurately as possible.

IMPORTANT: It is against eBay rules to inflate shipping costs past a reasonable amount (use common sense to determine what constitutes "reasonable"). In addition, your shipping costs cannot be based on the final price of your item; that is, you cannot employ a sliding scale or percentage of the final price to determine shipping.

For items weighing more than, say, a pound, use the free eBay Shipping Calculator to calculate rates. All you need is a scale to weigh the item and a tape measure to measure the dimensions of the package (for some shipping services).

INSURANCE

The best insurance is to overpack your item. Still, even the best-packed items can suffer damage (or worse, loss) in transit.

To safeguard the parcel, you should insure it with the carrier. In fact, you should make insurance mandatory for all your eBay sales. In your item description, state something along the lines of "All eBay item parcels will be insured for the selling price."

You can pay for the insurance yourself or state it as a buyer cost. Whatever option, always state it explicitly and clearly in your listing description!

Insurance costs should always be based on the selling price of the item, *not* its market value.

There are many ways to insure your packages. For example, USPS has several options. One is actual insurance. Others provide special services to help ensure that the intended recipient receives your package. For example, USPS offers various types of delivery and delivery-confirmation services:

> Certificate of Mailing
> Certified Mail
> Collect on Delivery (COD)
> Delivery Confirmation
> Insured Mail
> Merchandise Return Service
> Registered Mail
> Restricted Delivery
> Return Receipt
> Return Receipt for Merchandise
> Signature Confirmation
> Special Handling

You can learn more about these services at the USPS Web site.

NOTE: Collecting on a shipping insurance claim isn't always easy. Each shipper has different criteria that must be met before a claim can be granted. Meet with an authorized representative of the shipping or carrier company and ask for specifics regarding their company's insurance and claims policies.

Keep all documentation regarding the item's condition and the security of the packaging and store them with your insurance and delivery-confirmation receipts in a safe place.

CRATING AND FREIGHTING LARGE ITEMS

Furniture, machinery, appliances, farm equipment, autos, boats, Lear Jets . . . if your item is larger or heavier than the limits set by USPS, UPS, or FedEx, you will have to send it through a shipping company as freight. Don't let this discourage you! Many sellers routinely sell huge and heavy items on eBay. As long as they know the details before they bid or buy, savvy eBay buyers fully understand that they will foot the shipping and handling bill for larger items. Your duty as a seller is to fully research crating and shipping services in your location before you list a large item. Select those with the best reputations and prices, and list them in your item description. Start with the yellow pages under Shipping or Freight. Contact different freight companies and get good estimates or quotes for crating and shipping. Provide all of this information in your listing description.

Although it is not always the case, freight items usually need to be crated. Proper crating involves using wood and plywood to create a custom-built box large enough to ship the item safely. Unless you are a whiz with a power saw and don't mind hammering a crate together, you are probably better off handing this chore off to a professional crater/shipper.

NOTE: If your item is too large to ship via standard post or delivery and thus will need to be crated for freight, make certain you state this in your item description!

You can usually obtain a good estimate of crating and shipping costs from a local freight company by describing the item's size and weight. You can then pass this information along to potential buyers by including it in your item description.

Several crating and shipping companies have Web sites for calculating costs. For example, Craters and Freighters at *http://www.cratersandfreighters.com/*.

Whatever the size or weight of your item, do the research before you list, and provide as much information about cost, companies, and delivery time as possible.

You can never provide your bidders with too much information! It bears repeating: You can never provide your bidders with too much information about shipping costs and options.

INTERNATIONAL SHIPPING CONSIDERATIONS

Customs

For the most part, shipping an item overseas is only slightly more involved than shipping within the United States. Normally, shipping overseas will cost more and take longer. All other shipping and insurance considerations are the same as for the United States, except you may have to fill out a customs declaration form.

As the sender of an item to a country other than the United States, you are responsible for filling out any required U.S. Customs forms. These are available at any post office or from the carrier of your choice (UPS, FedEx, etc.).

Make sure you fill out all forms accurately and honestly.

Sometimes, an international bidder will ask you to "fudge" a customs declaration in order to save on any duty (which is paid by the package recipient).

Don't do it.

If a customs official decides to open your package for inspection and determines that your declaration is intentionally inaccurate, you could find yourself in hot water with Customs (and Customs could also confiscate the item).

These last few chapters contain eBay selling basics necessary for every seller—part-time to full-time. The next chapter will help you find ways to build and grow your eBay business.

eBay Business Tips and Tools

Owning and running your own business; what could be more exciting or more fulfilling? How many times have you dreamed of being your own boss? Who among us hasn't come just this close to marching up to that boorish supervisor to announce, "I quit"?

Many new eBay sellers begin as eBay buyers who started a small eBay selling business out of a room of their home. Still other eBay sellers are self-employed business owners who have moved a part or all of the off-line business online through eBay. Whether you already own a business or are starting a new business, using eBay for some or all of your business will help that business grow.

The Family That eBays Together

Laurie Liss (ixpensive) realized after the birth of her son that she would soon have to quit her career as a flight attendant. Still, she wasn't sure what she could do to keep income coming in. That's when a friend told her to consider selling on eBay.

Laurie's flight attendant job provided her with access to department stores across the country, where she regularly bought up discounted designer clothes at bargain prices. Laurie started off at eBay selling some of her "collection" by putting up her first fifty listings.

Everything sold!

Sensing an opportunity, Laurie made regular trips back to her old sources for more merchandise and began gradually increasing her business on eBay. When it became clear to her that eBay selling could, with work and dedication, provide her new family a steady income, she quit her flight attendant job and devoted herself full-time to selling on eBay.

"eBay has allowed me to become much closer to my family. I am able to take my son to school in the morning, come home, and work and still be home at three P.M. when he arrives home!"

The rest of Laurie's family were all intrigued by her newfound career and wanted to join in the fun. Laurie taught her mom, Darlene, and sister Hillary (guccigranny), as well as her other sisters Joey (maxxey) and Jamie (qtfashion) the finer points of online selling, and in no time they were all selling various lines of women's designer clothing, shoes, and accessories on eBay.

Even Laurie's dad, Arnie (threads4less), got into the act. While the female members of the family were specializing in women's clothing and accessories, Arnie started selling men's designer clothing, completing the Liss retail dynasty.

Recently, Laurie's sister Stefanie (beautytake-out) joined the family businesses with an eBay business of her own, selling Chinese take-out boxes filled with skin care and fun items, complete with a fortune cookie in each box. Recently, Laurie (ixpensive), Hillary (guccigranny), and Arnie (threads4less) bought houses on the same street in Arizona so they can work on eBay more closely. A true "eBay neighborhood"!

Of course, there are risks. No one can guarantee that every new business venture will be a raging success, but there are potential rewards aplenty for those who at least give it a try.

Here's a small checklist of the things you will need to take your eBay selling from an occasional pastime to a real full-time business:

- ✔ A business structure
- ✔ Something(s) to sell
- ✔ A place from which to sell it (a business location)
- ✔ Computer and office equipment (a computer, digital camera, printer, desk, shelving, lights, etc.)
- ✔ A bookkeeping system
- ✔ Office and packing supplies (tape, peanuts, boxes, printing paper, etc.)

The first step is to determine the optimum structure for your eBay business.

Business Structures for eBay Sellers

No business can grow if it cannot be managed. No business can be managed if it cannot be measured. For your eBay business to be properly measured, it will need an appropriate business structure.

The short list of possible structures:

> Sole proprietor
> Partnership
> Corporation

Each option has its advantages and disadvantages. A partnership may be perfect for some businesses, whereas a corporation may be ideal for other businesses. How do you determine which business structure is right for you? You should always get professional advice before making any decision as to how you set up your business. For a start, the Internet is a great place to get accurate and helpful information quickly (and without cost!) if you stick with trusted Web sites. For example, look for more information about business structures on the IRS Web site: *www.irs.gov.*

Hey, it's the IRS. How could they be wrong? In the search box provided on the IRS home page, try searching for *Publication 334: Tax Guide for Small Business.*

Read the introduction page for links to publications for partnerships, corporations, S corporations, direct selling, and record keeping.

In addition, check out the Small Business Administration Web site at *http://www.sbaonline.sba.gov.*

Specifically, look for the SBA Small Business Startup Kit.

For more specific information about corporations, try the National Business Incorporators Web site at *http://www.nationalbusinessinc.com/.*

"But, Griff," I hear you say. "I've only just started to figure out how to list on eBay. Isn't it a bit premature for me to start thinking of business concerns?"

No. It is never too early to plan. Too many people (and eBay sellers) on this planet seem to live their lives based on the "planning to plan" plan. That is, they continually put off taking action on matters like losing weight, building that addition to the house, taking that trip to Italy, or, for our purposes, setting up a business on eBay. Sure, figuring out how eBay works and listing your first item on eBay can seem overwhelming enough. Why else would you have bought this book? Certainly it's too early to become the CEO of your own company.

No, it isn't. In my experience, people who think "success" eventually realize success. You have to imagine your business on eBay and then start building it, from this very moment. Now. Right this minute.

Motivated? Good. Let's continue.

A FEW WORDS ABOUT TAXES

Pay them.

All kidding aside, first let me state that I am not a tax attorney and that everything I tell you in this section is from my perspective as a citizen taxpayer and does not necessarily represent the actual word of law.

**You should contact a tax accountant or tax attorney
for all your tax liability questions.**

Sorry to bring you down after giving you such a great pep talk a page ago, but "What about taxes?" is one of the top five questions I am asked by new and experienced eBay members alike. Now that we have that little disclaimer out of the way, let me dispel a popular and rather distressing myth.

There is no such thing as an exemption from tax reporting for "hobby selling," on eBay, or anywhere else for that matter.

Contrary to the beliefs of some eBay members with whom I have spoken in the past six years, big or small, successful or not, online and off-line—all businesses and individuals must report their income to the IRS (and possibly their state and even their city or county). Yes, eBay seller, that means *you*! In fact, even if you sell only one thing this year, you are by law required to report the income of that sale on your state and federal tax returns.

This doesn't mean that you will necessarily owe taxes on that sale. However, unless your relish risking the unique and exquisite instrument of torture otherwise known as an audit, and the ensuing wrath of the IRS, heavy fines and penalties, and even possible jail time, you'd better make darned sure that all of your eBay sales are reported to Uncle Sam.

Now, wipe the sweat off your brow and let's get back to our discussion on business structures.

Different business structures use different forms for reporting income from sales. Most sole proprietorships fill out a Schedule C (Profit and Loss) along with their regular Form 1040. Partnerships use IRS Form 1065. Corporations must use Form 1120. Some eBay sellers will have to pay their taxes in quarterly esti-mated installments, depending on their past tax liabilities.

Does all of this sound confusing? Don't worry. It *is* confusing. That's why I strongly suggest that any new or existing eBay business owners inform and edu-cate themselves about their tax reporting and filing responsibilities. You can get helpful information on the Web sites listed above, and of course, you should al-ways contact a tax attorney and accountant.

YOUR STATE SALES AND INCOME TAX DEPARTMENT WEB SITES

Depending on the state where your business is located, you may be responsible for charging, collecting, reporting, and sending in sales tax. In addition, some lo-cal municipalities levy business or inventory taxes or require local businesses to be licensed. How do you determine if you are responsible for collecting sales tax and possibly other taxes? What are your licensing requirements? Most state gov-ernment Web sites supply all this information along with the necessary forms and applications.

If your state charges a sales tax, you may have to apply for a State Tax Re-sale Number. You would then collect sales tax for all eBay sales made to residents of your state. Depending on your state, you may have to file sales tax returns monthly, quarterly, or yearly. You may also have to send the collected sales taxes to the state sales tax department.

What is your state's tax Web site? I found this handy URL: *http://www.taxsites.com/state.html.*

Find the site for your state sales tax department and read up. Or you can look up the phone number for your state tax department in your local yellow pages.

Finally, if your business on eBay is not new but is, in fact, established and growing and you are uncertain as to your liabilities and responsibilities, you should contact a local tax accountant for assistance immediately. It is money well spent.

What to Sell?

It's a common question. I want to start a business online at eBay but I don't know what to sell.

The possibilities are practically endless. Just about anything you can think of has a potential market on eBay. Many new sellers come to eBay knowing exactly what products they want to sell. Having a product source in place before you start on eBay certainly gives you an advantage. But, for those who don't have a product in mind, don't let this stop you. Start listing items from your possessions until you figure out exactly what your niche will be. The worst possible strategy is paralysis. So dig out stuff to list on eBay, and while you are busy photographing, describing, listing, packing, shipping, and leaving feedback, you may find yourself creating a niche or selling a product line you might otherwise never have even considered.

It pays to like, or even love, what you sell—to have a "feel" for it. Although it is possible to be successful selling a line of wares for which you have absolutely no passion, where's the fun in that? So, let's start off by asking some questions:

What type of merchandise interests you? Do you collect? If so, what do you collect? About what types of items or objects or collecting fields are you most knowledgeable?

Many of the more successful eBay sellers I meet in my travels started out as buyers or collectors at first, then started selling on eBay, either out of sheer interest or by necessity. Unless you are filthy rich, collecting as a full-time pastime tends to deplete one's resources rather quickly. To keep collecting, many collectors are compelled to sell off lesser pieces of their collection. Soon they find themselves bona fide dealer/sellers.

Many eBay sellers don't start out as collectors per se—they might just enjoy shopping at tag or garage sales, picking up items along the way because they are new and cheap or unusual.

If nothing comes to mind or if you don't collect or have a fancy for certain types of merchandise, but you are determined to be a market force on eBay, then you will need to start researching the supply-and-demand situation both on eBay and in your local area.

What types of items are readily available in your locale? For example, Vermont is home to the world's best maple syrup (sorry, Canada—Griff's a Vermont boy at heart). Maple syrup is usually cheapest and most plentiful in New England, but it can be extraordinarily difficult to find in other parts of the world. Some savvy Vermont maple syrup producers have realized this and have started offering their maple harvest on eBay with great results. Does that mean that you should start selling maple syrup on eBay? Not necessarily. A little sleuthing on eBay may show serious competition in the maple syrup business. I searched on *maple syrup*, and many more sellers are offering this product now compared with when I wrote the first edition of this book.

ENTERING AN ESTABLISHED EBAY CATEGORY

So you research eBay and find that lots of sellers are offering items similar to those that you were planning on selling on eBay. Should the threat of competition stop you? It should give you pause, of course. Competitive markets are not always easy to join. But the possibility of stiff competition in an established eBay market niche or category should not prevent you from trying to enter that market *if*:

✔ You are the type of person that enjoys and relishes competing.
✔ You fully understand and accept the risks inherent to business competition.
✔ You are ready to match and beat the competition at their own game.
✔ You are the type of person who relishes a good fight.

If you are planning to sell in a highly competitive category (jewelry, for example), you need to follow a game plan that includes (but is not limited to) the following checklist:

Watch your competitors. Visit their listings *every day*! Check their pricing strategies, their special promotions. Sometimes the tipping point for a buyer considering two similar items can be as simple as a few cents difference in shipping fees. Or better photos. Or clearer terms of service. Or even just the friendlier tone or more professional look of one seller's description. Visit your competition every day, note what they are doing, and go back to your listings and make yours better, more appealing, more successful, than theirs.

Never stop hunting for better sources of product. If your products come from a wholesaler, keep searching for other sources, even if you are happy with your current source. Business is dynamic. Sources that are good today can dry up tomorrow, leaving you in the lurch. The best insurance is to have a second or even third and fourth possible source that you can rely on if your current source grows unreliable or, heaven forfend, disappears.

Expand your product line and lines. You sell one thing on eBay that no one else sells. Let's call it a doohickey. You have established and cornered the doohickey market on eBay. You are riding high, living large, buying property. Congratulations! Now, just how long do you think you can keep top dog position in the doohickey market? Do you think other sellers aren't figuring out how successful doohickeys have been for you? Make no mistake: When it comes to business, the wolves are *always* at the door. They are watching your eBay listings *every day,* ready to pounce without warning, unleashing a torrent of doohickeys on eBay at even LOWER PRICES!!! With FREE SHIPPING!!! And QUANTITY DIS-COUNTS!!! (What? Do you think you are the only eBay seller reading this book?) The problem with a sudden torrent of doohickeys is that they tend to flood a marketplace with oversupply, which subsequently satiates demand, which subsequently lowers prices, which subsequently lowers your bottom line.

Not to panic. You can ensure your survival in case of a sudden torrent of doohickeys by two strategies:

First, expand your product line beyond doohickeys. Find a product that is related to doohickeys and start offering it on eBay. Let's look at specific examples. You sell jewelry, specifically imported jewelry from a closely guarded source. That is all you sell. No one else sells the type of jewelry that you do. The market is all yours, for now. The competition in the eBay jewelry market can be tough. Someone will eventually discover your source.

Before that happens, add to your product line. Perhaps you should start offering jewelry cleaning products or jewelry boxes or display cabinets. Maybe they are custom-made! Or maybe you add watches or some other pieces to your eBay jewelry listings. Now, when someone searches for "diamond ring cleaner," she finds your diamond cleaner, and following the links in your eBay listing, she wanders into your eBay Store, where all of your items are on full display, including a ring she is just mad for.

Or, even more drastic, you start adding new product lines that are completely unrelated to jewelry. Garden supplies! They all live in your eBay Store. Someone searching for a trowel spots one of your diamond rings, and before you know it, you've sold a trowel and a ring. (What? You don't wear your jewelry while gardening? You never know who might stop by for tea.)

Seek out market trends outside of eBay. The eBay marketplace reflects the world at large, especially when it comes to trends. Starting with Beanie Babies back in 1996, eBay sellers have been extraordinarily savvy when it comes to predicting the next hot market. Don't keep your head buried in eBay. Subscribe to trade publications and attend trade shows that relate to your product line. Search for news of upcoming new products.

In fact, search out the new products before they are released and make deals to bulk purchase them prior to public release. That's what hundreds of eBay sellers did with the first release of the Sony PlayStation 2 a few years ago. They "knew" the new PlayStation would be a hot item; that is, they bet on their intuition about the new device's appeal to gamers, and they committed to purchase as many units as they could from retailers across the country, before the actual game consoles hit the stores. I talked to several sellers who wrote checks to retail store managers for several thousand dollars, buying up the store's entire allotment of PlayStation 2 consoles before the public could get them. The result? For about three months prior to the holidays that year, the only place you could purchase a PlayStation 2—the hottest new toy on the market that year—was on eBay. Prices soared. Sellers were the beneficiaries of the craze and shortage.

GRIFF TIP! Want to know what's hot on eBay right now? Visit eBay Pulse at *http://pulse.eBay.com.*

At eBay Pulse, you can see the current top-ten most popular search terms on eBay. This list provides an excellent snapshot of what eBay buyers are looking for.

By the way, the PlayStation 2 craze didn't last. Crazes never do. That's why they call them crazes, because, just like a long night of carousing, the "craze" wears off and people come to their senses. ("Twenty-five hundred dollars for a two-hundred-dollar game console? What was I thinking?") By spring of the following year, you could find lots of PlayStation 2 consoles on eBay at no more than $250. That leads us to our next item on the checklist:

Prepare for the end of a market trend. Risks are always inherent in any marketplace strategy, and the same holds true for eBay strategies. If the trend subsides before your supply does, you could end up holding a lot of doohickeys that no one wants. Thus, timing is everything. You may ride the crest of a trend to great selling success, but you can still end up with too much product as the trend subsides.

How do you best avoid winding up with useless or devalued inventory? Easy! Just remember this rule: The best time to sell is when you have a buyer.

At the height of the trend, sell as much of your inventory on eBay as possible, even at prices lower than the going price (as long as you are still making a viable profit). Your competitors may realize greater price-per-unit profit than you, but the equation could change if they end up with units that don't sell.

Later, as the market for your items cools, keep selling, even if it means lowering your sell price to the point where you are taking a loss on some of the items. If you still have a market—that is, you have buyers—sell the items. Sell. Sell. Sell. Whatever happens, do *not* wait for the market to rise again. Sitting with devalued inventory can be deadly. The longer it sits, the more it costs you. Unless you have invested in items that are traditionally viewed as having a long-term gain in value, e.g., expensive fine art or antique furniture or rare collectibles and memorabilia, your unsold inventory can kill your business. Get what cash you can out of dying inventory so you can reinvest it in new stock; new stock that, if you plan and market properly, can realize enough profit to offset any loss you sustained in unloading the old inventory.

All this sounds risky, doesn't it? Business is, by nature, risky. If it weren't risky, everyone and her mother would be running a successful business with no worries or cares. But don't let the threat of risk paralyze you into not trying. Make your first move! Get that first listing up! Remember, first movers are not always winners, but most winners were first movers.

Begone, Inefficient Markets . . . eBay to the Rescue!

In the old days before eBay, sellers had to rely on traditionally inefficient markets to sell and liquidate inventory. Take the antiques business, for instance. My partner and I used to be in the antiques business. I remember once in the late 1970s we found ourselves needing a quick cash infusion. We had a lot of valuable stock. In fact, we were "stock poor." In the summer show season, we could have sold it all quickly to collectors for big bucks, but it was midwinter in New England—stormy, dark, and icy. With no other viable avenues of quick liquidation, we loaded up our pickup truck the next morning with choice items from our inventory and drove four hours to a well-known auction house that took consignments up to and during the day of sale. Luckily for us, a sale was scheduled for that evening. After unloading our truck, we grabbed a cup of coffee, took our seats, and watched in horror as our merchandise sold for pennies on the dollar. Normally, this auction house would have been teeming with other dealers and collectors, but the weather had kept them away. I would rather have forgotten this humiliating and depressing experience, thank you, but I dredge it up now to make a point. All this happened before the Internet and eBay. This was the time of creaking, inefficient, and unfair marketplaces where buyer and seller found each other by hit-or-miss with great expenditures of time, gasoline, money, and mental health. Sometimes you hit, sometimes you broke even, and many times you lost.

That's the beauty of eBay the marketplace. Reaching it doesn't require driving. It doesn't matter where you live, East Coast, West Coast, Ivory Coast, Amalfi coast . . . eBay is always only a few clicks of the mouse away. And it's always open, twenty-four hours a day, seven days a week, all year long. Best of all, eBay's scope is not limited to a single trading location or commodity-market bull pen. eBay is literally everywhere there is an Internet connection. In offices, homes, and hot spots across the planet, at any given moment, millions of eBay buyers are online, with cash at the ready, eager to buy, regardless of the day of the week, time of day, or even the weather. In fact, business on eBay is usually booming when the weather is at its worst. It only makes sense; where else can one go when the weather outside is too frightful for driving? Might as well hunker down with a cup of hot coffee, fire up the old PC (or Mac), and browse eBay.

FINDING PRODUCT

A few years back, I met a woman in the Midwest who lived close to a factory that made maternity clothing. Many manufacturers routinely offer their seconds at bargain prices, or worse, they toss them into the Dumpster. Most discarded seconds have fairly noticeable flaws, but many of the seconds tossed out are guilty of one or two practically imperceptible imperfections. Where the manufacturer saw throwaways, this plucky woman saw opportunity. She arranged with the manufacturer to purchase all of their seconds at mere pennies on the dollar. She then carefully sifted through the lots, culling those items whose flaws were inconsequential. She then offered the merchandise at eBay, as seconds, and soon made a viable business out of the venture.

You may not be as lucky as this woman. You may not live near an untapped source of practically free product. Even if you did, it would most definitely dry up over time. Finding good product to sell on eBay is a combination of hard work, sleuthing, experimenting . . . and luck and timing. Many eBay sellers actually travel the globe in search of good product at attractive prices. Some actually succeed. Others come up with an idea for a product, patent the idea, find a manufacturer, and start listing the items on eBay, all the while doing what they can to market and promote their new item on eBay.

GRIFF TIP! Many sellers find product in the most unusual places, for example, unclaimed merchandise from self-storage bins. The owners of self-storage companies hold auctions to liquidate unclaimed or abandoned storage bin contents. (They also liquidate the contents of bins whose renters have become seriously delinquent in rent payments.) Buyers usually cannot look through or examine the contents of the bins—they must bid for the stuff "blind"—a risky proposition but one that can pay off handsomely if the contents turn out to be treasure.

FINDING PRODUCT SOURCES ON THE INTERNET

Yes, it is still possible to find great sources of product on the Internet. In fact, you can find product to sell on eBay . . . on eBay. eBay now provides a new top-level category called Wholesale. It's available from the eBay home page:

Many eBay sellers find products to sell by browsing the Wholesale category. More and more wholesalers and liquidators are listing bulk quantities of items in this category: DVDs, home building supplies, business and industrial equipment, health and beauty items, cell phones, jewelry, computers, consumer electronics . . . the eBay Wholesale category is chock-full of potential inventory for resale on eBay.

DROP SHIPPERS

Many sellers offer items on eBay that are drop-shipped to the buyer. That is, the seller has made an arrangement with a wholesaler or manufacturer to purchase items for which they actually never take possession. Instead, the seller lists the items on eBay, and the wholesaler or manufacturer drop-ships the item directly to the winning buyer. Although there are many obvious advantages to a drop-shipping arrangement (no warehousing of inventory, no fulfillment and shipping tasks, etc.), there are also many potential pitfalls as well. Any seller entering into a drop-shipping arrangement must be fully aware of the possible downsides.

Finding Reliable Drop Shippers

Literally thousands of sellers are searching out undiscovered or underutilized drop shippers around the world. This is not to say that you won't find a good drop shipper—just be prepared for a potentially long hunt. A few well-known drop-shipping-resource Web sites offer to help connect a seller with a drop shipper. Searching Google using *drop shipper* brings up over one hundred thousand sites. In addition, many businesses that offer drop-shipping services have joined the eBay Solutions Directory. You can reach the directory by clicking the "services" link on the top of any eBay page. Then on the Services page click eBay Solutions Directory.

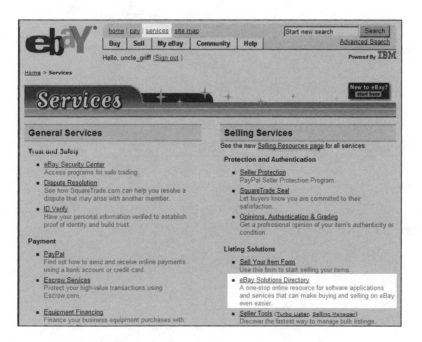

This will take you to the Solutions Directory. Scroll down toward the bottom of the page and click Sourcing.

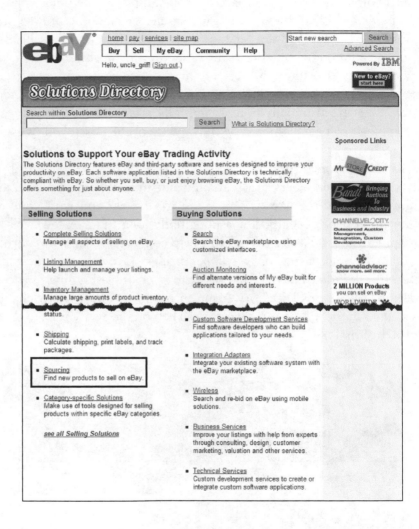

The Sourcing page displays all the certified eBay Solutions providers that provide drop shipping or other sourcing solutions. Click each company link to visit their Web page and explore their services.

We've covered a lot of information in this chapter. Again, don't be over-whelmed to the point of inaction. If you don't have product to sell, go grab an unwanted item from your attic or basement and start listing it on eBay. Many eBay sellers start off this way. In fact, eBay seller Tim Burnett started out with only four items!

My wife and I were trying to work a way of increasing our income, so we decided to try our hand at selling on eBay. We looked for suitable products we could get at a reasonable price that we could ship easily and would possibly not be widely available. We started off on eBay on a shoestring budget of $15 with four products. We listed our items on eBay for the princely sum of $2.65 (at the time we didn't have a scanner, so we had to scan our pictures at the local Kinko's for $2.10). Out of the four products, one got six bids and sold much higher than we had guessed, one sold at a reasonable profit, and the other two didn't sell at all. So we had found our market, art supplies.

At that time the only mode of transport we had was a 1969 VW camper bus, which my wife would drive twenty miles each way to work. This left me with a two-mile walk each way to the local post office, which I trudged three times a week to make sure our shipments went out on time. It's now less than six months down the line, and we are buying our products direct from the manufacturer, and our eBay sales are going toward building our business. We are planning to introduce many new products in the near future, and it's all thanks to eBay!

If we can start up on a total outlay of less than $20, you can do it too!

In my tenure at eBay I have seen just about anything you can imagine offered for sale. Art supplies, new and vintage clothing, old computers, new kitchenware, auto parts, golf clubs, time-shares, homemade crafts, brand-new electronic equipment, domain names . . . the list is endless.

There are even eBay businesses that offer fresh-baked goods custom-made and shipped overnight to your location.

With a little ingenuity and research, you may just find available sources of interesting or unusual products right in your own neighborhood—products you can then turn around for a potential profit on eBay.

If after giving it a lot of thought you still cannot come up with a product yourself, maybe you should consider selling items for others on consignment. That's were the eBay Trading Assistants program might help.

Trading Assistants

Trading Assistants are eBay sellers who sell for others on a consignment or fee basis. Selling on consignment at eBay can be a terrific business opportunity. Lots of folks have heard of eBay. Many of them may have things they would like to sell on eBay, but either the process is too overwhelming for them or they don't have the time to list their items themselves. That's where you, as a Trading Assistant, fit in.

To become a Trading Assistant, you must meet the following requirements:

- You've sold at least four items in the last thirty days.
- You have a feedback score of 50 or higher.
- Ninety-seven percent or more of your feedback is positive.
- Your eBay account is in good standing.

To remain in the Trading Assistants Directory, you need to meet the following requirements:

- You've sold at least one item in the last thirty days.
- You have a feedback score of 50 or higher.
- Ninety-seven percent or more of your feedback is positive.
- Your eBay account is in good standing.

If you meet those requirements, you can create a Trading Assistant account by clicking the "Become an Assistant" link from the Trading Assistants Directory.

Your eBay User ID will then be added to the Trading Assistants Directory and will be searchable via your region or location.

Folks in your region who want to sell an item on eBay but are not set up for selling can locate you by searching the Trading Assistants Directory. They then contact you and make arrangements for you to sell their item for them on eBay.

Joining the directory is a privilege, not a right, and eBay can remove you from the directory. This might happen, for example, if clients started complaining about your service as a Trading Assistant.

Including yourself in our Trading Assistants Directory is a lot like running a classified ad for your services. Trading Assistants are not employees or independent contractors of eBay. Nor does eBay endorse or approve them. Each Trading Assistant runs his or her own independent business free from any involvement by eBay.

As a Trading Assistant, you are free to run your business as you see fit. You may set your own fee schedule, and you may limit the types and quantities of items you are willing to sell on consignment. All sales at eBay are under your Seller's Account. You are charged all eBay fees but are free to pass these fees on to your clients as you see fit. All negotiations are between you and your clients.

You can learn more about the Trading Assistant program on the eBay Web site. Click the "services" link on the eBay Navigation Bar. The link for Trading Assistants can be found on the Services page.

Your Business Location

You have selected your business structure and you've a pretty good idea of what types of items you are going to sell on eBay. Now it's time to locate a place for your selling.

SELLING FROM YOUR HOME

Home-based selling has several advantages over separate retail-location selling, the most obvious being cost savings of not having to rent and run a separate location. There are also tax advantages. In most cases, you will be able to deduct a percentage of your regular home expenses (rent or mortgage, heat, electricity) as business expenses. You can work in your bathrobe and slippers. You can take coffee and cigarette breaks when you like. Best of all, if you are a stay-at-home parent, you can keep an eye on the little ones while you work (and once the little ones are able, you can recruit them into your home business workforce).

The disadvantages of selling from your home will grow exponentially as your eBay business starts to take off. It may become impossible to keep the physical parts of your business from commandeering all of the space in your home.

If you don't have the luxury of a second building, select one area of your home for eBay selling. It doesn't have to be much—a spare bedroom or basement or garage. If you cannot give over a complete room, then use a part of a room. For most eBay selling, you will find that a space roughly four feet deep by eight feet long will be more than adequate. Here is a real-life example of an eBay seller home office sent in by eBay seller Anita (beachbadge). Notice how well organized Anita keeps her home office.

Within your home office space, designate separate areas for your computer, for digital photography, for item storage, and for packing and shipping. The key is organization. If you keep your eBay office space strictly organized, you'll be better prepared for any growth of your business, and your business will run more efficiently.

Keep pace with your business. Don't cram your growing successful business into a space too small to contain it, else your business will suffer. If you are selling from your home and your eBay business is growing in leaps and bounds, you will know when it is time to move your eBay home business to a separate and bigger location.

GRIFF TIP! Don't set up your eBay business where there are smokers. Nothing turns off a buyer like opening a package and having stale cigarette smoke come wafting up from the box. If you or anyone in your household smokes, you should designate a well-ventilated, smoke-free room for the storage and packing of your eBay items.

ITEM STORAGE

Whether you are selling knickknacks or airplanes, merchandise takes up space. Depending on the type, size, and volume of merchandise you plan on selling, you will need an appropriate means of storage. In most cases, simple metal, plastic, or wooden shelving will do (airplanes will need hangar space, of course).

Label and mark all items with an identifying number. This will help prevent mix-ups later.

Avoid wasted storage space. Adapt your shelving or storage system to suit your needs. For example, if your store-bought shelving has shelves spaced every twelve inches and your items are only three inches tall, add more shelves. eBay User beachbadge keeps her smaller items on a set of hardware shelves.

eBay seller Karen Gray keeps her fabric items in sealed plastic bins.

Your Office Equipment

There isn't much to say about office equipment that isn't obvious, except maybe that good new equipment isn't cheap, so consider used if budget is a concern. New or used, here is a checklist of the basic equipment you will need for your eBay business.

A computer with an Internet connection. Although you can get by using a four-year-old or older computer, it is best to have the most up-to-date system you can afford. If you can afford it and it is available, get a high-speed Internet connection.

A printer to print out invoices, listing pages, shipping labels, etc. Again, if you can afford it, purchase two printers—a black-and-white and a color bubble jet. Print out your listing pages on the color printer and everything else with the black-and-white.

A digital camera. Buy the best you can afford. I suggest 2.1 megapixels or higher, and make sure it has a macro feature for extreme close-ups. Refer to Section Two, chapter 3, for more information on digital cameras.

A flatbed scanner. You may not use it all the time, but when you do need it, you will be glad you have one. Sellers of flat items like comic books, postcards, coins and stamps, etc., simply must have one. Refer to Section Two, chapter 3, for more information on scanners.

A good desk and chair. Pretty obvious, but I cannot tell you how many eBay seller homes I have been in where the desk was something like an old door on milk crates set too low or too high and the chair was a hard stool—neither item coming close to anything that could be considered ergonomically sound. If you are selling on eBay, you will be sitting in front of a computer for long stretches. Don't harm yourself by sitting incorrectly. Obtain a good desk and the best chair you can afford.

A filing cabinet. Two drawers at least. What with listing pages, invoices, letters . . . you are going to have a lot of paper to file. Keep it organized right from the start.

Good lighting for both the office space and for taking digital pictures.

The other various office necessities like printer paper, labels, and pens are obvious. You can get great deals for office equipment and supplies of all types at . . . hmmm, I wonder where?

Bookkeeping

One of the most common and, in some ways, distressing questions I field from both new and seasoned eBay sellers goes something like this: "I sell on eBay primarily as a hobby, so I don't have to keep books, right?"

Wrong.

Whether you're a sole proprietor or multinational corporation—you must keep accurate records of your business activity. As I wrote earlier, you cannot manage what you cannot measure, and no business can survive and thrive without management. Your eBay business is no exception.

Now, don't you wish you had paid better attention during Accounting 101? Not to worry. Several excellent bookkeeping software programs are available that will not only help you track your business but are actually fun to use.

Two popular applications for small businesses are Intuit's QuickBooks and Microsoft's Money. Both applications are excellent tools that allow you to record costs and income, track and manage expenses and accounts receivable, print invoices, and create custom reports to show the state of your business. Most important, come April 15, both applications will help you determine your tax liabilities.

In addition, for the budget conscious, there are also many free and shareware accounting applications. You can find some by going to *www.tucows.com* and searching their application library using the word *accounting*.

If you sell even one item at eBay, you should create and keep a record of the sale by at the very least saving:

A printout of the item page taken immediately after the listing closes.

A photocopy of the check or money order used to pay for the item (or if you are using an online payment service to accept credit cards, a printout of the payment page).

A receipt showing your purchase price or cost for the item.

The e-mail and mailing address of the buyer.

GRIFF TIP! As of this writing, eBay had just released a beta version of their brand new Accounting Assistant tool which works with QuickBooks to help sellers download and organize all their eBay selling data. Best of all, Account Assistant is free to all Stores Sellers and subscribers of Selling Manager, Selling Manager Pro, Seller's Assistant Basic, or Seller's Assistant Pro.

To download Accounting Assistant, go to *pages.eBay.com/ accountingassistant/*

and follow the instructions from there.

WHY KEEP RECORDS? THREE REASONS

Reason #1: Taxes. Even though you might not actually owe taxes on the proceeds of an eBay sale, you are obliged to report the income. Thus for your own peace of mind and to make sure you are in full compliance with all tax laws, create and save a complete record of every eBay sale as well as all your business expenses. They will come in handy in the event of a tax audit.

Reason #2: Access to business capital loans. If you decide to grow your business, you will need a record of your previous business activity when applying for business loans or establishing business lines of credit.

Reason #3: To grow your business, you have to have an accurate way of measuring it. Good bookkeeping will provide the blueprint for building your business plan from quarter to quarter, year to year.

WHICH BOOKKEEPING METHOD IS RIGHT FOR ME?

There are two basic methods of business accounting: cash and accrual.

The cash method of accounting is the simplest system. Every time you receive payment for an item or pay out an expense, you immediately record it (keep a ledger book or use accounting software). Using the cash method of accounting, most of your expenses and nearly all of your income are recorded the moment the cash for it is spent or received. The exceptions for expenses would be some capital expenditures for, say, office equipment (computers, printers, etc.) that need to be amortized or depreciated over time.

The accrual method of accounting is more complex than the cash method. In brief, when you use the accrual system, you record sales when they are made, not when the cash for them is actually received or spent.

If your business involves inventory, then you may be required to use the accrual method of accounting.

There are exceptions. If you sell services instead of items on eBay or if your eBay goods are custom-made or if you are an artist or photographer or writer who is selling his own work on eBay, then you might be able to use the cash method.

Either way, if you are in doubt or have questions, consult an expert accountant.

A few good online resources are the Business Owners Toolkit, *http://www. toolkit.cch.com/,* and of course, the IRS! *http://www.irs.gov/.*

In summary, if you plan on selling regularly on eBay, you really must set up a simple bookkeeping system both to adequately record your business activity and to help your business grow, and it bears repeating—I urge you to educate yourself about your tax and accounting responsibilities both on your own and through the services of a tax accountant or attorney.

Using Auction Management Tools

KEEPING TRACK OF YOUR LISTINGS

Once you get your eBay selling started, the processes for taking digital pictures and writing excellent descriptions become almost second nature. If you only sell a few items a week, then using the Sell Your Item form with a text-file template of your standard payment, shipping, and other terms is probably the easiest way to go. You can also keep track of your listings with "My eBay."

Using "My eBay"

In Section One, chapter 2, I outlined and described each section of "My eBay." The Selling, Account, and Feedback pages of your "My eBay" page are invaluable for managing your eBay listings.

The Selling tab shows you all of your items currently up for sale. It can also show all of your recent (past thirty days) closed listings.

The Account tab displays all of your eBay Seller's Account information including your last invoice and your to-date selling activity, with all fees displayed in a ledger form.

The Feedback tab allows you to view feedback left for you. More important, clicking a button on the "My eBay" Feedback page shows you all the feedback you need to leave for others.

For the low-volume seller, these "My eBay" features may be more than adequate to meet sales-tracking needs.

EBAY SELLER TOOLS

If you are listing ten or more items a week, you will want to employ a listing management tool to make listing easier. Listing management tools come in many types. eBay provides three basic listing management tools. They are:

- Turbo Lister
- eBay Selling Manager (Basic and Pro)
- eBay Seller Assistant (Basic and Pro)

Each of these tools provides various features that help eliminate as much repetitive data entry (typing) as possible and keep listings, invoices, e-mails, inventory, and accounts organized and manageable. Each tool is tailored to fit the needs of all types of eBay sellers.

TURBO LISTER

Turbo Lister is an auction management and bulk-uploading tool created by eBay. It is best suited for those sellers who list ten to one hundred items a week, but any seller can use it, even if listing only one item.

Turbo Lister helps you create a set of listings off-line that you can store as a collection for uploading to eBay at a later time. Turbo Lister also helps to eliminate most of the repetitive typing and feature selection one encounters when using the eBay Sell Your Item form.

Where do I get Turbo Lister?

Turbo Lister is available for download on the eBay Services pages. Click on "services" on the top of any eBay page. Scroll down the page and click Seller Tools, located under Listing Solutions.

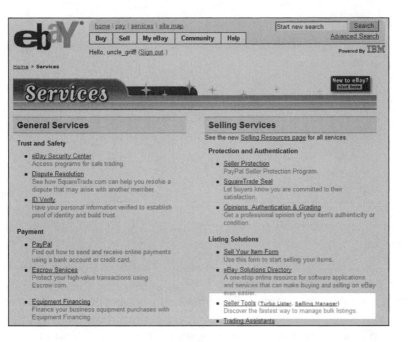

Turbo Lister is free to download and use.

Turbo Lister provides all of the following features:

- Preview listings before submitting
- Schedule when listings will start
- Easily create HTML descriptions with a WYSIWYG* interface (*What You See Is What You Get—no need to know HTML tags. You "draw" your description as you would create a text file in a word processor.)

Turbo Lister is easy to download, install, and use. Once you have the application installed, click the Turbo Lister icon on your desktop or task bar and follow the Wizard instructions.

SELLING MANAGER (BASIC AND PRO)

Selling Manager provides a comprehensive suite of listing management tools including e-mail management, invoicing, feedback alerts, payment status, and basic accounting tools as well as many other features tailor-made for the high-volume eBay seller.

Selling Manager is a subscription-based tool; that is, you pay a small monthly fee ($4.99 for Basic, $15.99 for Pro) to use it. All new subscribers receive their first month free.

There is nothing to download and install. Selling Manager works inside "My eBay," taking the place of the All Selling tab. Although it can be used as a stand-alone listing management solution, Selling Manager was designed to work in tandem with Turbo Lister. Together, they provide an excellent bulk-upload and listing-management solution for the full-time eBay seller.

Selling Manager comes in two versions, Basic and Pro. Both Selling Manager Basic and Selling Manager Pro have helpful features to make your selling experience easier and more enjoyable:

- Easy access from "My eBay." Selling Manager replaces the All Selling page view in "My eBay."
- Monitor your active listings in real time and keep up-to-date on all sales at a glance.
- Manage postsales activities. Send and track buyer e-mails, bulk relist sold and unsold items, mark which buyers have paid and left feedback, and print invoices and shipping labels and let buyers combine payments.

If you are selling a hundred items a week or more, you should give Selling Manager a try.

To subscribe to Selling Manager Basic or Pro, click the trusty "services" link on the top of any eBay page. Scroll down to Seller Tools under Listing Solutions. Click Selling Manager and follow the instructions for subscribing.

You can also subscribe to Selling Manager from the Selling tab on your "My eBay" page.

eBay Stores

In 2001, eBay introduced a new selling format called eBay Stores. eBay Stores offer the eBay seller an effective channel for growing a business on eBay. eBay Stores have various features to help sellers promote and market their eBay items to the rest of the world.

With an eBay Store you can:

- Create up to twenty custom categories in your eBay Store. Your eBay Store comes with its own search engine, which will only search for items in your eBay Store.
- Add your own business logo to your eBay Store pages or choose one of eBay's online images. In fact, eBay Stores are customizable using your own or eBay templates.
- Talk in depth about your business on your About My Store page.
- Market all your items across eBay by using the built-in cross-promotion tools that come as a part of your eBay Store.
- Receive monthly sales reports that provide a checkup on the effectiveness of your business.
- Access Store Traffic Reporting, which includes real-time data on page views and visitors for all of your listings and Store pages as well as information on search terms used by visitors in your Store.
- Create and send your own custom marketing e-mails directly to your buyers.

If you are a regular eBay seller, there are definite advantages to setting up an eBay Store, especially if you offer a large inventory of items. All of your eBay items—eBay Store, auction format, and fixed-price format—will display within your eBay Store, making it the ideal destination to send your eBay buyers.

Before you set up an eBay Store, you must:

- Have an eBay Seller's Account with a credit card on file.
- Have a minimum feedback rating of 20 or be ID Verified ($5 charge).
- Accept credit card payments via an online payment service such as PayPal or through a merchant account.

eBay Store fees are separate and different from those for regular eBay listings. eBay Stores are a subscription-based service. There are three levels of eBay Stores, each with their own suite of tools and features:

eBay Stores Basic—$15.95 per month
eBay Stores Featured—$49.95 per month
eBay Stores Anchor—$499.95 per month

Insertion fees for eBay Store items are significantly lower than regular eBay listing insertion fees. In brief, eBay Store format items are charged an insertion fee of two cents per thirty days, and a seller can opt for the eBay Store item to list for 30, 60, 90, or 120 days or "good until canceled."

An eBay Store is an attractively priced solution for a large number of listings or inventory. However, eBay Store format items do not show up in regular (non–eBay Store) categories. eBay Store items also do not appear by default in keyword search-result lists; however, eBay Store items will appear in eBay keyword search results under certain circumstances. If a keyword search returns only ten or less items, and there are matching eBay Store items, up to ten of the matching eBay Store items will appear below the regular eBay search results. If there are more than ten matching Store items, the link "see more matching Store items" will appear under the list of ten returned eBay Store results.

We covered browsing and buying through eBay Stores in Section One, chapter 3. Setting up an eBay Store is a snap. Go to the eBay home page and click on the link eBay Stores (located in the box on the top left-hand side of the page).

This will take you to the Stores home page.

On this page, click "Open a Store" on the top right-hand side of the page.

This takes you to Step 1 for setting up a Store. Follow each of the three easy steps. You can change any selection after your Store has been set up.

EBAY STORE SETUP TIPS

1. Pick a catchy, memorable name for your Store, preferably one that relates in some way to your business or the items you sell.
2. You will be asked to create a short description of your Store. This will ap-

pear under your Store name in the lists of Stores as well as at the top of your Store page, but more important, the words you supply in your description will be the words that search engines like Google use to pick up your eBay Store page. Thus, you should make sure your eBay Store description contains descriptive keywords that will help it show up in a Google search.

3. Create as many (up to twenty) customized categories as needed. Note that these categories are for your eBay Store only. Whenever you list an item at eBay—whether in your Store or as a regular listing—you will be prompted to select one of your eBay Store custom categories for your item.

Why the special search engine and customized categories? Some eBay Store sellers have thousands of items listed in their eBay Store. The personalized categories and personal search engine help their buyers find items more effectively in their eBay Store.

You can learn more about eBay Stores by going to the Stores page as described above and clicking on More FAQs.

GRIFF TIP! Items that you list exclusively in your eBay Store will not show up in a regular title search (although they do show up in a title search of eBay Stores). A trick that many sellers use is to list most of their inventory in an eBay Store and always have one or two similar items for sale in a regular (non–eBay Store) auction or Buy It Now. These sellers then cross-promote their eBay Store in their regular listings to help drive traffic to their store items.

EBAY CROSS PROMOTIONS TOOL

Many cool features come with an eBay Store, but a real favorite is known as eBay Cross Promotions. With Cross Promotions, you have the ability to create and manage specific cross-promotional marketing of your Store items so that these select items appear in key buyer locations such as on the bid confirmation and winning-buyer confirmation pages.

Here's an example of an active item listing page where the seller is using Cross Promotions to promote other items she has for sale.

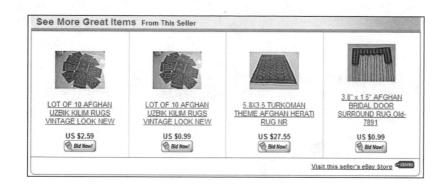

Cross Promotions can be a great boost for your eBay business. For example, say you are selling digital cameras at eBay and you also have digital camera accessories in your eBay Store. If someone bids on or buys one of your digital cameras, you can use Cross Promotions to have your digital camera accessories show up on the bid confirmation or winning-bidder or winning-buyer confirmation page, both to entice the buyer into purchasing more items from you (he might just need a digital camera bag) and to help lead him to your eBay Store.

To set up your eBay Store Cross Promotions, go to "My eBay." Click Manage Subscriptions, located under My Accounts.

Next, click Manage Your Store, under My Subscriptions on "My eBay."

On the Manage Your Store page, you'll find the link "Item cross-promotions."

Click Preferences to reach this page:

Make changes or edits to suit your promotional needs. Click Save Settings at the bottom of the page.

Navigate back to the Manage Your Store page and click "Default category settings" to reach this page:

Default Cross-Promotions

The settings below are used by default to cross-promote your items to buyers. When someone views, bids on, or buys one of your items, your other items from a particular category will be automatically promoted. You can change which categories are cross-promoted to maximize your sales. Learn more about how default settings are used.

For items in **Antiques:** (0 items) — Change categories
　　When someone **views an item**, first promote items from... Antiques (0 items)
　　When someone **bids** or **buys**, first promote items from... Antiques (0 items)

For items in **Oriental Rugs:** (0 items) — Change categories
　　When someone **views an item**, first promote items from... Oriental Rugs (0 items)
　　When someone **bids** or **buys**, first promote items from... Oriental Rugs (0 items)

For items in **Other Textiles:** (0 items) — Change categories
　　When someone **views an item**, first promote items from... Other Textiles (0 items)
　　When someone **bids** or **buys**, first promote items from... Other Textiles (0 items)

For items in **Pottery:** (0 items) — Change categories
　　When someone **views an item**, first promote items from... Pottery (0 items)
　　When someone **bids** or **buys**, first promote items from... Pottery (0 items)

For items in **Objet d'Art:** (0 items) — Change categories
　　When someone **views an item**, first promote items from... Objet d'Art (0 items)
　　When someone **bids** or **buys**, first promote items from... Objet d'Art (0 items)

For items in **Bizarre:** (0 items) — Change categories
　　When someone **views an item**, first promote items from... Bizarre (0 items)
　　When someone **bids** or **buys**, first promote items from... Bizarre (0 items)

For items in **Kitsch:** (0 items) — Change categories
　　When someone **views an item**, first promote items from... Kitsch (0 items)
　　When someone **bids** or **buys**, first promote items from... Kitsch (0 items)

For items in **Electronics:** (0 items) — Change categories
　　When someone **views an item**, first promote items from... Electronics (0 items)
　　When someone **bids** or **buys**, first promote items from... Electronics (0 items)

For items in **Digital Cameras:** (0 items) — Change categories
　　When someone **views an item**, first promote items from... Digital Cameras (0 items)
　　When someone **bids** or **buys**, first promote items from... Digital Cameras (0 items)

For items in **Clothing:** (0 items) — Change categories
　　When someone **views an item**, first promote items from... Clothing (0 items)
　　When someone **bids** or **buys**, first promote items from... Clothing (0 items)

For items in **Collectibles:** (0 items) — Change categories
　　When someone **views an item**, first promote items from... Collectibles (0 items)
　　When someone **bids** or **buys**, first promote items from... Collectibles (0 items)

For items in **Ephemera:** (0 items) — Change categories
　　When someone **views an item**, first promote items from... Ephemera (0 items)
　　When someone **bids** or **buys**, first promote items from... Ephemera (0 items)

For items in **Decorative Arts:** (0 items) — Change categories
　　When someone **views an item**, first promote items from... Decorative Arts (0 items)
　　When someone **bids** or **buys**, first promote items from... Decorative Arts (0 items)

For items in **Computers, Parts & Reference:** (7 items) — Change categories
　　When someone **views an item**, first promote items from... Computers, Parts & Reference (7 items)
　　When someone **bids** or **buys**, first promote items from... Computers, Parts & Reference (7 items)

For items in **Vintage Computers:** (0 items) — Change categories
　　When someone **views an item**, first promote items from... Vintage Computers (0 items)
　　When someone **bids** or **buys**, first promote items from... Vintage Computers (0 items)

For items in **Italian Villa Rental:** (25 items) — Change categories
　　When someone **views an item**, first promote items from... Italian Villa Rental (25 items)
　　When someone **bids** or **buys**, first promote items from... Italian Villa Rental (25 items)

For items in **Category 17:** (0 items) — Change categories
　　When someone **views an item**, first promote items from... Category 17 (0 items)
　　When someone **bids** or **buys**, first promote items from... Category 17 (0 items)

For items in **Category 18:** (0 items) — Change categories
　　When someone **views an item**, first promote items from... Category 18 (0 items)
　　When someone **bids** or **buys**, first promote items from... Category 18 (0 items)

For items in **Category 19:** (0 items) — Change categories
　　When someone **views an item**, first promote items from... Category 19 (0 items)
　　When someone **bids** or **buys**, first promote items from... Category 19 (0 items)

For items in **Other:** (1 item) — Change categories
　　When someone **views an item**, first promote items from... Other (1 item)
　　When someone **bids** or **buys**, first promote items from... Other (1 item)

Cross-promotion links
▶ View the status of all your cross-promotions in My eBay
▶ Change your cross-promotion preferences
▶ Customize your cross-promotion display

Let's change a cross-promotional relationship for the customized Antiques category in my eBay Store by clicking "Change Categories."

I now select one of my custom Store categories. I am heavily promoting a rental property in my Store, so I change options for both "When someone views an item . . ." and "When someone bids or buys . . ." so that my items in the Italian Villa Rental category appear at the bottom of the listings pages as well as the bid confirmation and winning-buyer confirmation screens.

Here is a preview of what my buyers will see when they view or bid on or buy an item from my Antiques category:

Italy Villa Vacation Rental Umbria 1st week of July

US $1,200.00
Buy It Now

Italy Villa Vacation Rental Umbria 2nd week of July

US $1,200.00
Buy It Now

Italy Villa Vacation Rental Umbria 3rd week of July

US $1,200.00
Buy It Now

Italy Villa Vacation Rental Umbria last week of July

US $1,200.00
Buy It Now

Visit this seller's eBay Store   stores

You can edit or delete any of these relationships between your items at any time by returning to the Manage Your Store page.

eBay Sales Reports

eBay sellers generate tremendous volume on the site. Millions of items sell every day. Tremendous sales volume generates stupendous amounts of sales data. Until recently, sellers had limited access to this data, and the format was not easy to plot into a graph. eBay sellers have enough on their hands without having to create, from scratch, comprehensive reports with graphs and charts showing their eBay selling activity.

With the recent introduction of eBay Seller Reports, sellers can now track and analyze all their eBay selling activity. Seller Reports compiles a seller's past activity by quarter and displays it in easy-to-read graphs, charts, and reports.

Why is this important? Remember our mantra: You cannot grow a business unless you can manage it effectively. You cannot manage a business effectively if you cannot measure it. As eBay's marketplace evolves, you'll need the most effective measuring tools available so you can identify new opportunities as they arise and plot a course to success.

eBay Seller Reports is the perfect business metrics for all your eBay selling activity. eBay Seller Reports comes in two flavors: a basic version called Seller Reports and an enhanced version named Seller Reports Plus.

SELLER REPORTS

Seller Reports is free by subscription to all eBay sellers. It provides data for:

- Sales
- Ended listings
- Successful listings (by percent)
- Average sale price
- eBay and Paypal fees

SELLER REPORTS PLUS

Seller Reports Plus includes all features of Seller Reports, plus:

- Metrics by category
- Metrics by format (auction, fixed price, store, etc.)

- Metrics by ending day or time
- Buyer counts
- Detailed eBay fees
- Unpaid Item credits requested

Seller Reports Plus costs $4.99 per month with a free thirty-day trial, but is free to all eBay Store sellers.

Seller Reports Plus provides four views: Sales Summary, Sales by Category, Sales by Format, and Archived Sales. The following screens show examples of each view.

Sales Summary

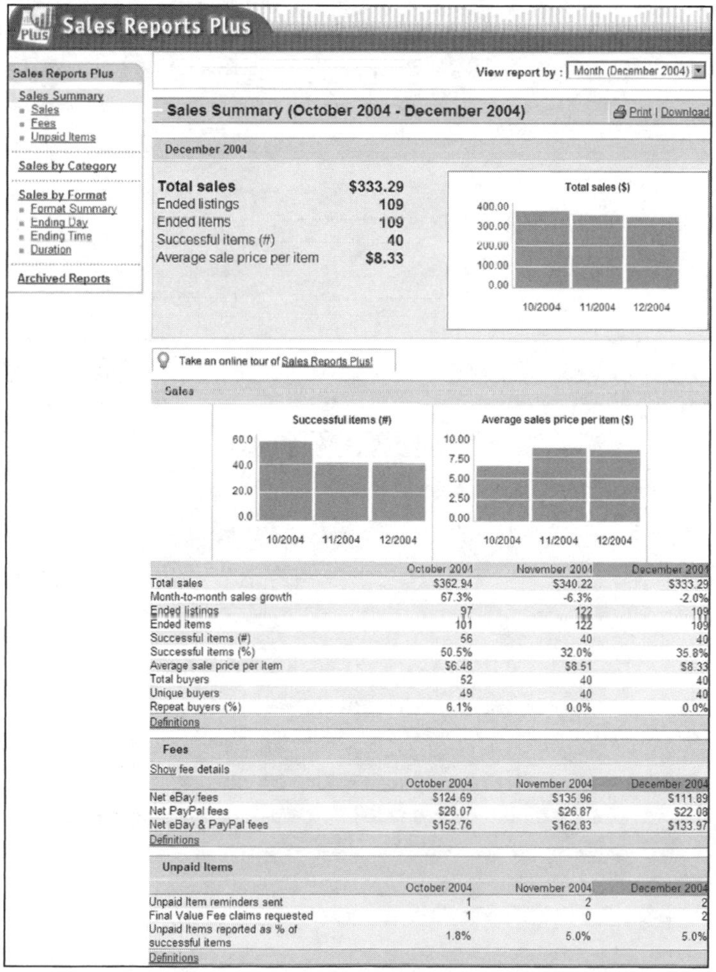

Sales by Category

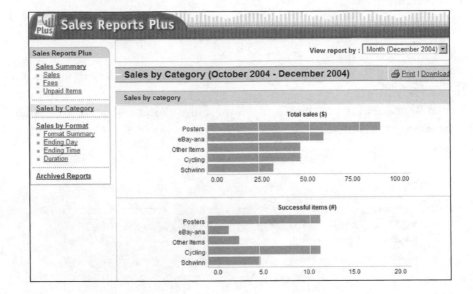

Sales by Format

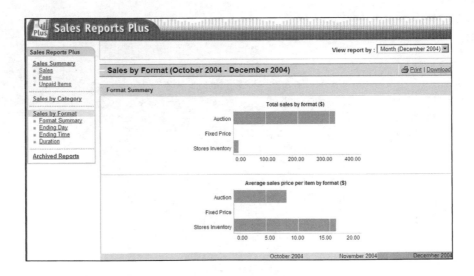

Archived Reports

Your Sales Report Plus will be available for 24 months after they have been generated.
they expire.

← Back to your current reports

Monthly Reports

2004

Sales Reports Plus, September 2004

Sales Reports Plus, October 2004

Sales Reports Plus, November 2004

Weekly Reports

2004

Sales Reports Plus, Week 10/24/04 - 10/30/04

Sales Reports Plus, Week 10/31/04 - 11/06/04

Sales Reports Plus, Week 11/07/04 - 11/13/04

Sales Reports Plus, Week 11/14/04 - 11/20/04

Sales Reports Plus, Week 11/21/04 - 11/27/04

Sales Reports Plus, Week 11/28/04 - 12/04/04

Sales Reports Plus, Week 12/05/04 - 12/11/04

Sales Reports Plus, Week 12/12/04 - 12/18/04

Sales Reports Plus, Week 12/19/04 - 12/25/04

Sales Reports Plus, Week 12/26/04 - 01/01/05

Subscribe to eBay Seller Reports by going to "My eBay" and clicking on Manage Subscriptions.

Select eBay Seller Reports from the list.

Manage Subscriptions

Available subscriptions

eBay Stores Learn more
eBay Stores is the best way for serious sellers to maximize their eBay business. Stores sellers receive powerful and easy-to-use tools that allow them to build their own brand on eBay and encourage buyers to buy more.

- Basic Store	Subscribe
- Featured Store	Subscribe
- Anchor Store	Subscribe

eBay Selling Manager Learn more
Selling Manager and Selling Manager Pro are eBay's Web-based sales management tools designed to help medium- to high-volume sellers manage sales more efficiently.

- Selling Manager	Subscribe
- Selling Manager Pro	Subscribe

eBay Seller's Assistant Learn more
Seller's Assistant Basic and Seller's Assistant Pro are eBay's desktop-based listing and sales management tools designed to save you time.

- Seller's Assistant	Subscribe
- Seller's Assistant Pro	Subscribe

Sales Reports Learn more
Sales Reports help you track key performance metrics that are critical to your business. These reports make it easier for you to make business decisions by identifying existing areas of growth and opportunities for improvement.

- Sales Reports	Subscribe
- Sales Reports Plus	Subscribe

eBay Picture Manager Learn more
Picture Manager is eBay's new, fully integrated online picture hosting solution. With Picture Manager, you can save money and attract bidders by adding multiple pictures to your listing without paying an extra fee. Choose the level of storage that's right for you (50MB to 300MB).

- Picture Manager (50MB)	Subscribe
- Picture Manager (125MB)	Subscribe
- Picture Manager (300MB)	Subscribe

Promoting Your eBay Business
with Your About Me Page

The About Me page is probably the most underused feature at eBay. I am constantly amazed at how many sellers do not take advantage of this excellent feature.

An About Me page is your eBay home page. Any eBay member can create and maintain an About Me page all on her own.

Building an About Me page is easy. To build yours, click the "services" link on the top of any eBay page. Then click "About Me page" under Member Reputation.

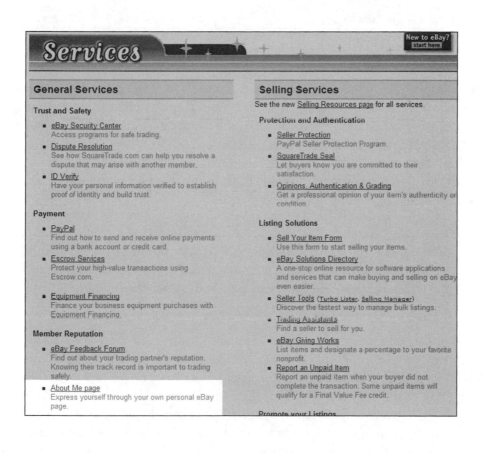

This brings you to the About Me hub page.

Follow the instructions from here. Note: You can change your About Me page at any time simply by returning to this page or by clicking Edit Your Page on the bottom of your About Me page.

You can select from the HTML templates eBay provides to simplify the process, or you can enter your own HTML in the text box provided. Learn more about HTML commands in the next chapter.

GRIFF TIP! If you are creating your own HTML-formatted text for your About Me page using a Web editor like FrontPage, only copy and paste the HTML between and excluding the <body> and </body> tags.

You can talk about practically anything you like on your About Me page. You can describe your business, and unlike the restrictions against linking to your Web site from your item page, you *can* link to your own Web site from your About Me page. You can talk about the items you sell (though you mustn't offer items for sale from your About Me page). You can even tell the world about your family, your favorite charities, your hobbies, and your collecting interests.

Once your About Me page is up, you can link to it from your item listing descriptions with a simple hypertext link along these lines: "Visit my About Me page to learn more about my eBay business."

eBay Keywords

If you shop on eBay, you've seen eBay Keywords promotions. They are the banner ads and promotion boxes that appear on the top of search result pages.

The eBay Keywords program, powered by adMarketplace and cobranded with eBay, provides an advertising solution for eBay sellers. Using eBay Keywords, eBay sellers can place advertisements for their eBay Store or product above the usual eBay listings in the form of a text box or banner ad. eBay sellers decide how much they are willing to pay per click per keyword and set their keyword campaign budget accordingly.

To set up your eBay Keywords campaign, click the "services" link on the top of any eBay page and scroll down to the Advanced Seller Services section. Click eBay Keywords.

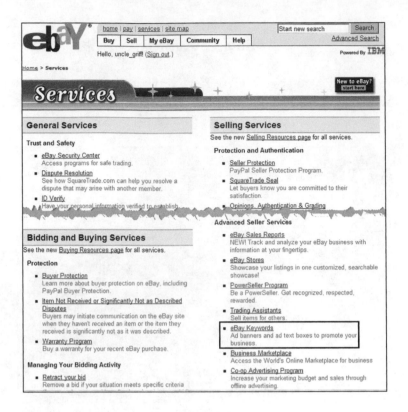

Click Get Started Now to register with eBay Keywords and begin creating your own ad campaign.

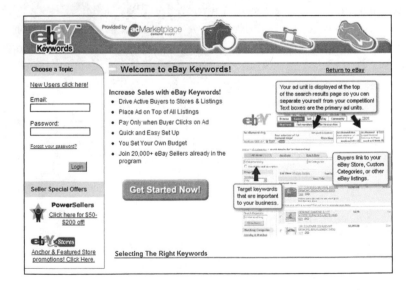

Growing Your eBay Business

You have done everything right so far and your eBay business is now thriving and growing. A growing business is usually most vulnerable once it starts to really take off. Often, an eBay seller will find a successful business strategy and will grab on to it tightly, sometimes so tightly that when the business climate changes, he doesn't. This inflexibility can be deadly to a business.

You can avoid these pitfalls by staying nimble in your business strategies and by always staying one step ahead of the market.

How? Research! Never take your eye off your competition. Learn what makes them successful—or not—and incorporate the lessons into your own business. Stay ahead of market trends for the items you list.

For example, it is the middle of June and you just got a great deal on a big lot of assorted batteries from a local store that is going out of business. Do you sell the lot off right away? Or do you hold on to it and sell it later? When do you think the demand for batteries is highest, on the Fourth of July or in December? You might have a hunch that your batteries will do better in December, but you may need to turn merchandise over sooner rather than later.

And there are other factors to consider. Who else is currently offering batteries at eBay? What are their starting prices? Are they aggressively marketing them in the middle of the summer? If not, maybe you could offer a portion of them now and reserve the rest of the lot for the upcoming holiday season.

A good business is never static. Stasis is the sure death of any business.

I met an eBay seller a few years ago who was offering a type of item that no other eBay seller had. Let's call this seller Pat. Pat was doing a great business. Pat had an extremely inexpensive source for these items and invested heavily in stocking up her inventory. Buyers interested in these items went to her listings, as she had the market cornered. All was profits and bliss until . . .

Eventually, another seller (let's call this seller Sam) discovered the market in these items simply by doing a little browsing in the eBay category where the items were listed. Sam did some research and discovered Pat's source. Sam began buying from the same source and offered the items at a slightly lower opening bid than Pat. That meant lower margins for Sam, but Sam was banking on making up for the lower margin of profit with a higher volume of sales.

Pat was suddenly faced with competition, and her sales started to slow. Pat faced a dilemma. If she lowered her opening bid prices, it would mean lower profits, but a higher volume of sales might offset this, just as Sam had gambled.

So what did Pat do? Nothing. Pat decided that lowering the prices of the items she had in inventory would be too big a risk, so she chose to wait out Sam's aggressive marketing attack, hoping that the market would expand enough to include both sellers. And it did, at least for a while, but within a few months, other sellers started moving into the same line of merchandise until there were several different sellers of the item.

This was great for buyers, who could now shop by price as well as by item. It was not good for the sellers, as they watched their gross sales drop.

An update: Sam saw the writing on the wall and unloaded his inventory of items for a small loss by dumping them on eBay for a penny opening bid each. Sam then took the cash and went searching for other wares—wares with not many sellers. Pat stuck it out, refusing to adjust prices or to expand the line of eBay merchandise, and was eventually out of business.

The moral of the story: If you choose to move ahead and make the wrong choice, you may fail—but you may also win. If you don't choose to move ahead but instead remain in place, you *will* fail.

The eBay PowerSeller Program

To recognize and reward with respect those sellers who generate a consistently high volume of sales, eBay created a program known as PowerSeller.

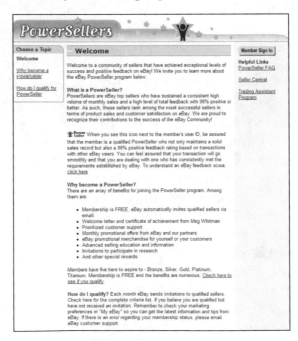

NOTE: You can reach the PowerSeller page above by clicking the PowerSeller link on the Services page. We'll assume that you know how to reach the Services page by now, but just in case . . . the "services" link is on the top of every eBay page.

The PowerSeller program is divided into five levels. Eligibility for each level depends on monthly gross merchandise sales (indicated below in parentheses next to the level name).

- Bronze ($1,000–$3,000)
- Silver ($3,000–$10,000)
- Gold ($10,000–$25,000)
- Platinum ($25,000–$150,000)
- Titanium ($150,000+)

There are benefits for those who join the PowerSeller program:

✔ Membership in the program is free.
✔ All PowerSellers receive a PowerSeller icon next to their User ID.

✔ Bronze PowerSellers: fast-track 24/7 e-mail support.
✔ Silver PowerSellers: Bronze benefits plus dedicated phone support during business days and hours (PST).
✔ Gold PowerSellers: Silver benefits with the addition of access to a pool of account managers.
✔ Platinum PowerSellers: Gold benefits plus 24/7 phone support as well as a dedicated Support account manager.
✔ Titanium PowerSellers: Platinum benefits plus initial phone contact from eBay for any listing issues or questions.
✔ The PowerSeller Portal and Forum, which lets all PowerSellers log in and network with other PowerSellers. PowerSellers also enjoy the benefits of a special recognition and rewards program.
✔ A banner-ad tool to create, target, and monitor their own eBay banner ads.
✔ Exclusive invitations to eBay-sponsored educational or special events.
✔ Monthly newsletters and program updates featuring new products, benefits, and policy updates.
✔ Exclusive PowerSeller Offers from eBay designed to help PowerSellers save time and money, for example, free eBay Keywords banner ads up to $200 per quarter.

You can find out more about the PowerSeller program requirements, levels, and benefits on the PowerSeller page.

Successful Business Practices—Treating Your Customers Like the Priceless Assets They Are

A time-honored golden rule of bricks-and-mortar business says, "The customer is always right." Actually, there are two rules of business. Rule number one: "The customer is always right." Rule number two: "When the customer is wrong, see rule number one."

eBay sellers with the most successful businesses all apply this rule to each and every customer. During my tenure at eBay Customer Support, I received many e-mails from sellers embroiled in disputes with their buyers, most of which stemmed from simple misunderstandings due to either an ambiguous e-mail or confusion over an item description or terms. Many, if not most, of these disputes usually result both in negative feedback for buyer and seller, as well as unnecessary additions to the world's already-too-large pool of ill will.

Here are my Seller Tips for nearly trouble-free eBay transactions:

BE EXPLICIT, POLITE, AND PROFESSIONAL IN YOUR LISTING TERMS

You cannot provide too much information in your item descriptions. Note every quality and every flaw of your item. If you don't have much information, do some research and provide what you find. State your payment and shipping terms with as much detail as possible, in neutral and polite language.

Nothing turns a potential buyer away from your listing faster than a list of harsh rules and regulations for bidders. Not that you shouldn't state your rules, only that you do so in polite and friendly language. Here's an example of text from an actual eBay listing followed by my rewording:

If you have any negative feedback, DO NOT BID! I will not accept any bids from a bidder with negative feedback, and I will cancel your bids AND I WILL CONTACT EBAY and you will be thrown off. So DON'T BID unless you UNDERSTAND THESE TERMS!

Makes one want to run and hide instead of bid. Wouldn't it sound better this way?

If you have any recent negative feedback, we still want your bid. However, please contact us via e-mail so we can discuss the reasons for the negative feedback before you bid. Thanks! We appreciate your cooperation!

DON'T TURN OFF POTENTIAL GOOD BIDDERS WITH HARSH REGULATIONS AND TERMS

Yes, you can use eBay's Bidder Management Tool to block the bids of an unwanted bidder, but unless you know the User ID of a bidder beforehand, you cannot block him in advance. Also, using negative feedback alone as a guide to a bidder's reliability or seriousness of intent can be misleading. Each case where negative feedback has been left is different. There may be extenuating circumstances. Give your bidders a chance to explain themselves if necessary. If you are unhappy with a bidder, quietly and without rancor cancel his bid, then add him to your item's blocked list.

PROVIDE A REFUND OPTION FOR YOUR BUYERS

Although eBay allows you as a seller to adopt an "all-sales-as-is, no-returns-or-refunds" policy, please don't do it. As efficient and fun as the eBay marketplace is, eBay buyers don't have the chance to examine items with their own hands and eyes until after they have paid for and received them. Even with the most explicit description and pictures, sometimes a well-meaning buyer simply isn't happy with the item once he has received it. Put yourself in a buyer's shoes. Would you want to be stuck with something you bought in good faith but find you don't like once you have received it? Of course not!

In the off-line world of retail, returns are an accepted way of life. If you want to succeed at eBay, offer a hundred-percent-satisfaction-guaranteed policy with no such conditions as "I'll take the item back this time, but don't ever bid on my items again!" In fact, if a bidder asks to return an item, not only should you cheerfully agree to take it back, but you should also encourage the bidder to come back and shop with you again. Your bidders will love you for it.

Those sellers who will not provide a hundred-percent-satisfaction-guaranteed policy should spell out their "no returns" policy in clear and concise language within the item description so that bidders are fully informed before they decide to bid—and, oh, best of luck. You'll need it.

NEVER GET ANGRY

Another fact of life in business is that you will now and then run into the "difficult" customer. I don't mean the nonpaying bidder. They are a separate problem dealt with in a separate way. By "difficult," I mean the customer who sends churlish or abrupt, demanding e-mail. We get them all the time at eBay Customer Support. We never respond in kind but instead always respond politely and professionally. We simply ignore any inappropriate or inflammatory language and focus only on the crux of the e-mail, responding to the complaint itself and not to its presentation—no matter how nasty or unpleasant.

You should always do the same. How you respond to an angry customer e-mail reflects directly on you. Think of yourself as the Customer Support for your eBay business. Do what you can to calm and placate an angry customer. If you are unable to satisfy him, in spite of offering a refund or kind, polite words, send a last e-mail with your regrets and offer of future assistance if needed.

If anyone sends you harassing e-mails—either in tone or in volume—contact the sender's Internet Service Provider (ISP) and forward them a copy of the e-mail with full headers attached. Then add the sender's e-mail address to your e-mail application's spam filter program. Remember, you are under no obligation to open, read, or respond to an e-mail sent to you. If all else fails, delete any and all e-mails from the sender without opening them.

"What if a customer sends me an e-mail threatening to come find me and do me bodily harm?"

We believe people are basically good. However, one might want to keep a closer eye upon some people out there. The lion's share of e-mail threats are hollow, but if someone threatens you with bodily harm, you may want to contact the local law-enforcement authorities in your and the sender's locale and alert them to the threat.

GO THE EXTRA MILE

Your customers are your most valuable business assets. Treat them like royalty. Always give at least a little more than expected. The most memorable experiences I have had at eBay as a buyer have been with those sellers who have sent refunds for unintentional overcharges for shipping or handling, or who have included some small but thoughtful "extra" with the item. Offer free gift wrapping and shipping directly to a gift recipient, and pay for a "confirmation of delivery" option. Again, your goal should be happy customers. Do whatever it takes to reach your goal. Here's what eBay seller Mike Ford has to say on going the extra mile:

"If you are selling an item that requires batteries, you can add a brand-new pack of batteries to the item and tell your potential buyers that in the auction! You can increase your sales just by including batteries. . . . You can get a brand-new pack of the batteries (any size) that item requires from top brands like Panasonic and Energizer for as low as $1 for a pack of four at most dollar stores! Be smart! Little things like this will give you the advantage over someone selling the exact same thing."

OFFER AUTHENTICATION SERVICES FOR YOUR ITEMS

If you plan on selling comic books, trading cards, Beanie Babies, stamps, coins, jewelry, sports autographs, or sports memorabilia, you should offer your items authenticated or graded by one of the recognized and trusted authentication or grading services on eBay's list of recommended vendors.

Authentication or grading will instill confidence in your bidders and establish a sense of security and trust that your item is genuine as described.

You can find a page of all the eBay-reviewed and -approved authentication and grading services by clicking the "services" link on the top of any eBay page.

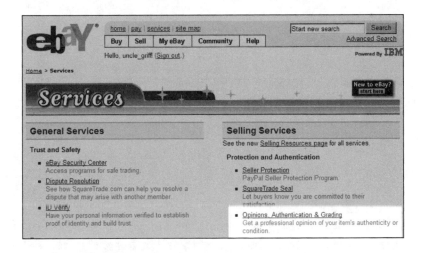

OFFERING ESCROW

If you are a brand-new seller and offering expensive items, you may want to provide an online escrow option for your bidders. Escrow acts like a trusted middleman between buyer and seller.

Once a listing has ended, the buyer sends payment to the escrow company, who verifies and holds the funds and then notifies the seller, who then sends the merchandise to the buyer. Once the buyer receives, inspects, and accepts the item, she notifies the escrow company, which then sends the payment to the seller.

If the buyer doesn't accept the item, she sends it back to the seller, who inspects the item and alerts the escrow company that the item has arrived in the same condition it was sent. The escrow company then refunds the funds to the bidder. Everyone is protected!

eBay's preferred and recommended escrow partner is Escrow.com.

The minimum fee is $22 plus a small percentage fee based on the final bid amount. It is customary for the buyer and the seller to split the fees.

Finally, here is what eBay seller Mikmartyka has to say about the road to successful eBay selling:

"Give your buyers more than they expect. Just an example in one area:

I've made quite a few purchases online with major retailers. You pay your money and they ship in seven to ten days.

I control all aspects of my small empire, so when a buyer pays me, they have their item in their hands in two to three days. They get their feedback immediately. They get a notice that the item is being shipped and the tracking number when it applies. Many of my feedback comments are from buyers surprised at how quickly they have their purchases."

There is nothing like a happy and satisfied customer.

PROMOTING YOUR BUSINESS OFF-LINE AND ON YOUR WEB SITE

Most eBay sellers have their own commercial Web sites. You can promote your eBay items on your Web site by including a link. eBay provides preapproved links and logos for users.

You can use the links and logos by going to the eBay Site Map and looking under the section Manage My Items for Sale for the link "Promote your listings with link buttons."

Special Selling Considerations

SELLING CARS, TRUCKS, BOATS, ETC., ON EBAY

eBay is becoming the destination of choice online for shoppers looking for new, used, and collector cars as well as trucks, motorcycles, and boats. Many used-car sellers have moved some or their entire inventory to eBay Motors.

Click the link eBay Motors on the eBay home page.

This will take you to the eBay Motors hub page.

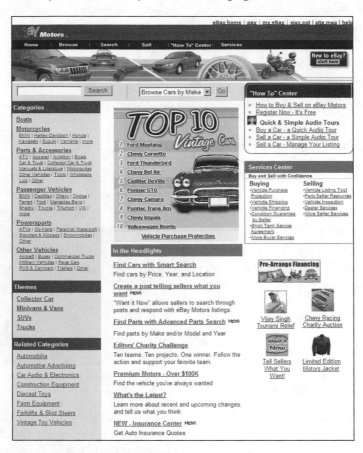

If you plan on selling a car or passenger vehicle, boat, or motorcycle, click the Sell link on the top of the eBay Motors hub page.

Selling a vehicle on eBay is similar to selling any other type of item, with a few extra concerns.

First, the fee schedule is different. The transaction service fee for all passenger vehicles and motorcycles is fixed. It costs $40 to list a passenger or other type of vehicle. It costs $30 to list a motorcycle.

In addition, if the item sells, there's a fixed $40 transaction services fee (similar to the eBay final value fee) for passenger vehicles and other vehicles; and a $25 transaction services fee for motorcycles. Again, this fee applies only if there is a successful high bid on the item.

All other fees are the same as for a standard eBay listing.

Some other tips for selling vehicles:

Take many photos. A car has many sides and facets—inside, outside, and underneath. Make sure that you have a digital image for all views of the vehicle, including both sides, front, back, inside trunk, under hood, front and back seats, dashboard, and undercarriage. Since eBay Picture Services limits you to six photos, you may want to supplement or use another hosting solution. (See Section Two, chapter 8, for more information on image hosting.)

Make sure the vehicle has a clear title and indicate this in the item description.

Be extra explicit in listing the details. Note and picture every imperfection. Include the blue-book values for the same car in conditions directly above and below the condition of your vehicle.

Be clear about your shipping terms. Most buyers of cars online understand that they will have to pay for shipping the car and that this can often cost several hundred dollars. Make sure to state this clearly in your listing.

When you list the item, you will be prompted to select a category for the vehicle that will also be the title of the item. You can provide a subtitle. Create your subtitle carefully! This is the text that is searched when using keywords, so remember to limit your eBay Motors item subtitle to only those keywords that relate to your vehicle. Try to avoid descriptive words like *choice* or *rare* or *must see*, etc. No one goes to eBay Motors and searches for all the *must see* items, and no one is actually impelled to open your listing because you have ordered them to do so. By using these useless words or phrases, you are wasting space. However, do feel free to use the subtitle for mention of miles on the odometer or maybe as a place to state "no reserve" if there is sufficient space after you enter your keywords (and the item is indeed a no-reserve item).

Selling to International Bidders

If you are going to sell on eBay, you have to decide right off whether you are going to welcome international eBay members to bid on or purchase your items. Let me try to help you make the right decision.

Sell to anyone, anywhere.

Wasn't that easy?

Yes, there are special considerations for selling, accepting payment, and shipping items internationally, but don't forget, you are doing business on eBay, the most vibrant and far-reaching marketplace mankind has ever created. eBay is a worldwide phenomenon. Millions of people around the world are ready to shop and buy, and you have to ask yourself, "Do I really want to cut out such a vast potential customer base?"

If my argument has failed to move you, then move on down a few paragraphs to the section "I Won't Sell Internationally."

The rest of you savvy businesspeople, follow me. . . .

Don't pay attention to those "fraidy" cats that I just sent on. Selling to international buyers on eBay isn't that difficult. Here is a list of tips and issues to keep in mind.

- Accept payment through an online payment service like PayPal. Currently, PayPal is accepted in forty-five countries. By accepting payment via PayPal, you are forgoing the need for cumbersome currency conversion (PayPal makes the conversion for you at the current rate of exchange), and you don't have to worry about clearing checks. In addition, you get paid fast, so you can ship the item fast—making for a happy seller and a happy buyer.
- Accept international money orders in lieu of checks or online payment from international buyers. However, you may want to consider limiting all international buyers to PayPal. In any event, never accept cash for any listing—domestic or international.
- Investigate all shipping options. Go to the USPS, FedEx, UPS, and DHL Web sites and learn how each one works for international shipping from the United States. Then, in your shipping terms, offer your international bidders a choice of those services that you have selected.
- For large or heavy items: Have a good estimate of the weight and dimensions of the item once it has been packed and post these in your item description. Include links to your preferred shipping services' Web sites' rate or postage calculators so that international bidders can calculate the approximate cost for shipping to their country *before* they bid.
- For smaller, lighter items: Use the built-in, free eBay Shipping Calculator, which offers international shipping services options.
- When you ship internationally, you will have to fill out a customs form. Familiarize yourself with the various forms (they aren't complicated), and if possible, keep a stack of them handy in your office. Note: Never deflate an item's value on a customs declaration when shipping internationally, no matter how hard the buyer insists. See the last tip below for more information on detailed payment and shipping terms for international buyers.
- Make insurance mandatory for all bidders and buyers.
- Use a packing list, invoice, and envelope as well as a shipping label. Make sure the invoice is complete.
- *Always* obtain a tracking number or use delivery confirmation. *Always* require a signature upon delivery.

- Finally, make your item description and terms for shipping, payment, and returns as explicit and detailed as possible for both international and domestic buyers—but even more so for international bidders.

Visit the eBay International Trading page for more tips and advice for selling to buyers around the world.

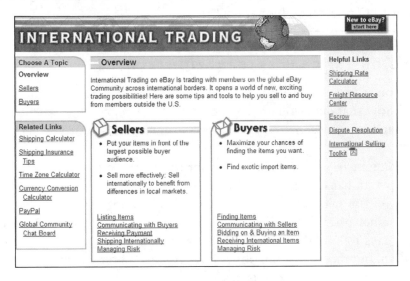

Click the "services" link on the top of any eBay page and look for International Trading, located under Tools.

I WON'T SELL INTERNATIONALLY

And no one can force you to do so. If you are not going to allow international buyers to spend their cash on your items, make sure you state your terms in clear, explicit language unavoidable to all.

In the first edition of this book, I stated, "Do keep in mind that eBay does not (and probably will never) provide a mechanism that automatically blocks international buyers from bidding or buying."

Well, I was wrong. eBay now provides a mechanism to block buyers in countries to which you will not ship from bidding on or purchasing your items. The feature, known as Buyer Requirements, was described in Section Two, chapter 4. Use it if you must; however, I strongly urge you to reconsider.

Even with Buyer Requirements set to block international buyers, you should still state your shipping terms in large, bold text in all your listing descriptions.

GRIFF TIP! If you decide to limit your sales to the United States only, make sure your terms of service do not offend! Use something along the lines of:

"We do not ship to locations outside the United States nor do we ship to an address that differs from the address a buyer has on his eBay registration contact information. "

SELLING ON THE EBAY INTERNATIONAL SITES

Most of you reading this are registered on the U.S. eBay site, *www.eBay.com*, but did you know that once you are registered on eBay, regardless of which site you used to register, you can list on any of the several eBay sites—U.S. or international?

There might be a time when you want to list on an international eBay site. For example, Italians are fanatic philatelists (they collect stamps; specifically Italian stamps). You may come across some Italian stamps someday, and you may realize a higher price if they are listed on the eBay Italian site, *www.eBay.it*. Of course, it pays to have some grasp of the language, and your description should be in Italian, but these are small obstacles if you use an online translation site like AltaVista's *http://babelfish.altavista.com/*.

NOTE: Online translators offer extremely rudimentary translations and do not take into consideration nuances and untranslatable idioms unique to each language. Thus, you should keep the descriptions for foreign-language listings as simple and basic as possible.

One more thing—when you list on an international site, you will be paid in the currency of that country. For the eBay Italian site, you would be paid in euros, and your Seller's Account will be charged fees based on euros (but converted to dollars), so your fees may be at the mercy of the conversion rate between the two currencies at the time the fees are charged.

Happy international selling!

We've now covered just about every aspect of selling on eBay that one can imagine. The rest of the chapters in this section cover lots of extra tips, tricks, and skills that can help make you a better eBay seller.

For example, advanced HTML . . .

7

HTML for eBay Sellers

This chapter covers several HTML tags that you will find useful in creating a professional eBay item description.

Even if you currently use a Web editor to create and format your item description text with HTML, I strongly suggest you read through this chapter. Understanding how HTML works from the bottom up will help you troubleshoot potential HTML snafus later.

Bob Bull (bobal) is a popular chat-board regular who has found great satisfaction teaching others about HTML. Bob, who is sixty-five, suffers from several serious disabilities.

"I was so lonely staying home alone while my wife, Alice, went to work every day. At one point, I didn't care if I lived or not."

But Bob did not give up, and in April of 1998 he discovered eBay. At first, he bought and sold small lots of items, always watching and learning from other savvy eBay members. Bob had a lot of questions about selling and began asking for help from other eBay members on the eBay chat boards. Over time, Bob asked so many questions and garnered so much helpful information that he became an HTML expert, answering newbie questions on the chat boards.

"I now live my life on eBay helping others. eBay has changed my life completely. When I can help a new user, I am on top of the world and I feel like my life is still worth living."

Today, Bob is a legend on the eBay chat boards and continues to help others figure out the ins and outs of selling. And he continues to make new friends every day. As he told me:

"No matter how many disabilities you have, you can help make a difference in someone's life."

GRIFF TIP! Hey, Mac owner. The Description Editor, which comes built into the Sell Your Item process, will not work for you. The information in this chapter will help you build your own simple, HTML-formatted item description.

Once you have finished this chapter, I guarantee that you will experience a great sense of accomplishment. Playing with HTML is fun!

WHAT IS HTML?

HTML (hypertext markup language) is the language of the Internet, specifically, that part of the Internet known as the World Wide Web (or "the Web" for short).

HTML was developed in 1990 by Tim Berners-Lee while working at the European Organization for Nuclear Research (known as CERN, the acronym of its old French name, Centre Européen pour la Recherche Nucléaire) in Geneva, Switzerland. I wonder if Tim ever imagined his little invention would literally change the world?

HTML is an easy-to-learn, universal formatting language that allows anyone to create text called Web pages, which, when placed on a Web server, can be viewed by anyone else on the Web using any type of computer and a web browser.

WHAT EXACTLY *ARE* WEB PAGES?

Web pages are text documents consisting of nothing but a simple text type called ASCII (American Standard Code for Information Interchange). Since all computer systems can read ASCII text, HTML documents can be created and viewed on any type of computer (IBM, Mac, Unix, Linux, etc.). This is what makes the Web accessible to anyone, regardless of what type of computer she uses.

WHAT IS THE WEB?

The Web, or World Wide Web, consists of a vast network of special computers called servers. Web servers are located across the planet in universities, ISPs, telephone companies, businesses, homes, and of course in huge private-industry complexes called server farms. These servers are all connected through various channels including regular phone lines, special phone lines, fiber-optic cables, and even, in some cases, microwaves or radio waves.

Although they are not technically the same thing, many people use the names *Internet* and *Web* interchangeably. Actually, the Web is only a part of the Internet, which includes many other parts, such as e-mail, FTP, IRC chat, etc.).

Anyone with a computer and a connection can access the Web.

There are basically two types of computers on the Web: the specially configured, aforementioned Web servers and "user" computers (for lack of a better word). Your user computer can be a Mac, a PC, a Unix computer, a laptop, a PDA, etc.

Web servers are where all Web pages are stored. Hundreds of thousands of Web servers are connected to the Web, containing millions and millions of Web pages. Millions of people like you across the globe are accessing the Web with their Mac or PC or Linux computer or handheld PDA or cell phone.

An extremely important feature of the Web bears emphasizing: For a Web page or picture to be seen by everyone on the Web, the page or picture *must* live on a Web server. The contents of your computer, unless it is a connected Web server, are not viewable on the Web! You can create Web pages or digital pictures on your computer and you can see them in your browser, but until you upload them to a Web server, no one will ever see them. *This includes your eBay pictures!*

GRIFF TIP! Anytime the address for a Web page looks like this—

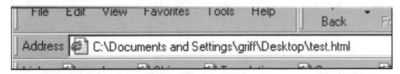

That is, the address starts with "C:\" (or sometimes "File|\\\"), you are viewing a file from your hard drive. No one else will be able to view it.

WHAT IS A WEB BROWSER?

A Web browser is a special type of application designed for viewing Web pages. The two most popular Web browsers are currently Internet Explorer and Netscape Navigator. All of our examples employ Internet Explorer but can easily be adapted to work with Netscape.

A Web browser has the built-in ability to read any text file with the extensions *htm, html,* and *txt.* Web browsers can also read picture files of the type *gif* and *jpg.* Using special "plug-ins," Web browsers can also read Word files, Adobe Acrobat files, and special multimedia files like Flash Graphics.

OH, COME ON, GRIFF. DO I REALLY NEED TO KNOW ALL THIS HTML STUFF TO SELL ON EBAY?

Honestly? No, you don't. Now that we have the handy eBay Description Editor built in to the Sell Your Item form, anyone with a PC can create a clean and professionally formatted item description without having to delve into HTML. However, the more knowledgeable you are about areas like HTML, the better prepared you will be for troubleshooting problems that might pop up later. Besides, you should really explore how HTML can make your listing description even more professional and dressy. At the least, it helps to know exactly what goes on behind a Web page, since your items will be viewed as Web pages. Plus, learning HTML can provide a lasting sense of accomplishment, as eBay seller Pat Fulton discovered:

Because I can't stand to leave things alone nor can I see any reason at all for anything to be just plain vanilla, I decided that if I was going to sell on eBay, my auction pages just had to be fancy! Having young males in the house can be very helpful when you want to learn such things, as their youthful minds obviously work in a totally different direction from that of their elderly parents. Of course, as a backup plan, I bought a book on HTML as, more often than not, I have no idea at all what the boys are saying when it comes to computer stuff.

Book in hand and son nearby, I bravely dove into HTML. Opening, closing, a <br> here and an <hr> there, tables, fonts, and colors. It was like I'd suddenly turned into Houdini doing magic tricks! Colors, lines, pictures! Amazing!

Of course there were mistakes here and there, and that's where the kid came in handy. "What's wrong with my creation? It's all weird." My son would scrutinize the page, fingers flying, clicking, shortcutting, and scrolling. "You didn't close the table" or "You put the line break in the wrong place again" was the frequent answer.

I finally got that very first item description all written up in HTML, and it had taken me days to do. Things went along very well, and as each item was listed, it sold!

Sound like fun? Let's try it and see!

CREATING AN HTML-FORMATTED EBAY DESCRIPTION FROM SCRATCH

You don't need special software to create an HTML page (or to format your eBay item description)—all you need is a text editor (in Windows, that would be Notepad. On a Mac, look for a program called Simple Text or TextEdit in your Applications folder), a Web browser, and some basic HTML. And basic HTML is easy!

GRIFF TIP! If you are a Mac user, you won't be able to use the Description Editor built into the Sell Your Item form. It only works for a PC. Given this limitation, Mac users will find this chapter extremely useful for creating well-formatted descriptions manually.

OPENING A TEXT EDITOR

PC users: To start, we open a blank Notepad file. Notepad can be started from the Windows Start menu at Programs: Accessories: Notepad:

MAC users: Look for and open a program on your hard drive called Simple Text or TextEdit. Follow along with us here, substituting either Mac text editor for Notepad.

Back to Windows . . . this will open an Untitled Notepad window:

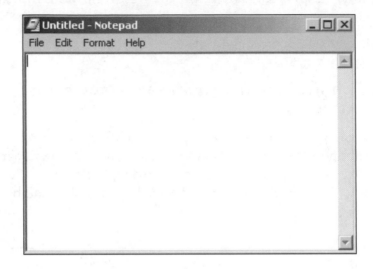

For the remainder of this chapter, you will type everything into this Notepad window.

Next, we open up a fresh new Internet Explorer (IE) browser window by clicking Start, Programs, and Internet Explorer or by clicking the Internet Explorer icon on your desktop or toolbar.

This will open a new IE window.

NOTE: I've have resized our browser window down for our purposes. Your IE window may be full-size. Also, I have typed "about: blank" into the Address window to show a blank (white) page.

This IE window is where we will view the text we input into our Notepad window. Think of it as our "view" window.

TYPING THE DESCRIPTION

Here we will use the same item description for the small pottery pitcher I photographed in Section 2, chapter 3. It describes the item by type, age, condition, and size. I also included detailed payment instructions and shipping terms and costs.

```
Untitled - Notepad                                          _ □ X
File  Edit  Format  Help  ⊘Send

Honiton Exton Small Pitcher

I was culling treasure from the china closet and found this Honiton pitcher, 4 1/2 inches
tall, circa 1950's. White clay. Exton shape. Pitcher is in excellent condition; no cracks,
breaks, chips or stains. Embossed mark on bottom: "Honiton Potteries Exton England" with a
black hand painted "t".

A Brief History of Honiton Pottery: Honiton Pottery was (and is) located in the town of
Honiton in Devon, England. The pottery was started by Foster and Hunt at the turn of the
19th/20th century. It was purchased by Charles Collard shortly after WWI. In 1947, Collard
sold the pottery to Norman Hull and Harry Barratt who ran it until 1961 when it was sold
to Paul Redvers. All production ceased in 1997 and the pottery was shuttered. The premises
were recently reopened as pottery and craft shop.

Payment Options:

Credit/debit card
Checks (item shipped immediately after check has cleared)
Money Orders


Shipping Terms:

I will ship this item anywhere to anyone. International bidders welcome. High bidder to
pay winning bid plus USPS priority or global priority shipping and insurance as shown
below.

US bidders: $5 USD
Canadian bidders: $8 USD
UK bidders: $10 USD
All others: $15 USD


Refunds, Returns, Regrets:

If you win this item and upon receiving it, are not 100% satisfied, you may return it to
me for a full refund of the winning bid and shipping. (Returning buyer pays for shipping
back to me.)
```

IMPORTANT! Notice that whenever I needed to create a new paragraph, I hit the Enter key on my keyboard twice to move down two lines.

SAVING THE DESCRIPTION AS A SPECIAL TEXT FILE

Now that the content of my description is finished, we want to view the description through Internet Explorer. Remember, for this HTML exercise, Notepad is the "input" window and Internet Explorer is the "output" window.

Viewing the text description through Internet Explorer will show us *exactly* how it will look on the eBay Item Description page when we list my item.

But, to view the text file containing the description in another application, we first must save it to our computer's hard drive. As it stands now, the file exists only in the computer's memory.

Why We Must "Save" First . . .

Computer memory or RAM (random-access memory) is divided into little sections using a special type of addressing plan. For example, when you open an application like Notepad, your computer assigns a block of addresses in its memory where the application loads and waits to do its job. For Notepad, that job is accepting input from your keyboard and displaying it on your computer monitor as words.

Once a set of addresses in RAM is filled with data, nothing else can read or write to those addresses. This is a built-in memory-protection mechanism used by all operating systems—Windows, Mac, Unix, etc. If this memory protection were not in place, any program could overwrite data in RAM at any time, making it impossible to use a computer securely.

Here's what happened when we opened Notepad: First, the computer code that makes up Notepad was loaded up from the hard drive into a section of RAM addresses that the computer assigned. Then, we typed in some data (our description), which was also loaded into addresses within the space the computer originally allotted to Notepad when we started it. That data is staring at us from the computer monitor.

We now want to read that data in Internet Explorer, but the rules of computer memory won't let any application read a memory address that is currently in use. The only application that can read the data is the one that loaded into that space: Notepad.

For another application to read the data from Notepad, we need to first save the data to the hard drive. Once it is saved safely on our hard drive, Internet Explorer can then read that same data by pulling it from the hard drive.

To create a computer file that Internet Explorer can read, we need to save the data to the hard drive by selecting "File, Save As . . ." from the Notepad toolbar.

FOLLOW THESE STEPS EXACTLY!

1. Select "File" and "Save As . . ." from the Notepad toolbar.
2. Choose a location on your hard drive for the new file. We will use the desktop.

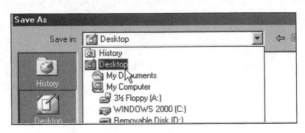

3. In the box "File name," type "test.html," and in the box "Save as type," click the arrow on the right of the drop-down box and select All Files. Ignore any box labeled Encoding.

4. Click Save.

NOTE: You have now saved a copy of this file to the hard drive. Note that I said "copy." There is a copy still in RAM. The copy on the hard drive is set in stone. The copy in RAM can be changed while it is open. Both copies have the same file name, in this case, "test.html."

By the way, you could name the part of this file before the "dot" anything you like. We chose "test." What is important is what comes after the dot. This must be "html" or our exercise will not work.

Let's open our "test.html" file in Internet Explorer—our "output" window.
Go to your fresh, new IE window. Click "File, Open . . ."

In the next box, click "Browse . . ."

This will bring up an "Open" box. In the box "Look in," click and select Desktop from the list of choices.

This will display a list of the files on your desktop, filtered so that only HMTL files are displayed. (You will notice that the box "Files of type" is set to HTML.)

Look for the file named "test" and double-click it.

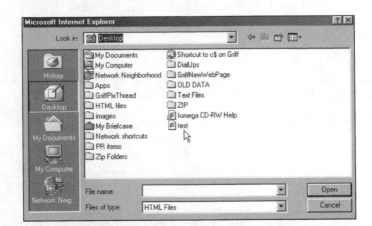

In the next box, click OK.

And here's our description, exactly as it would appear on an eBay Item Description page.

Notice something odd? All of the line and paragraph breaks we placed in our description are gone. If you go back and check the Notepad file, you will see that they are still there. So why are they missing from our description when it is viewed through a Web browser?

Web browsers are built to read all of the text characters on your computer keyboard. However, Web browsers do not recognize the Enter command used in Notepad to break to a new line, so they simply ignore it, running all the text together in one continuous line that breaks only when it reaches the right-hand side of the Web browser window.

Our description is still readable, but it certainly doesn't look professional or easy to parse.

How do we get the Web browser to recognize a line or paragraph break? We need to talk to it in its own language, HTML!

Tags

HTML is made up almost entirely of bits of text called tags. The simple syntax for an HTML tag looks like this:

<tag_name>

That's a "lesser than" character, a tag name, and a "greater than" character.

The tag name can be a letter, a combination of letters, or a word. The tag name is also case insensitive, which means it can be upper- or lowercase and still be read as the same tag. For visual consistency, we will use uppercase for all of our tag names.

The first tag we will use looks like this:

<P>

P is the tag name, and it stands for "paragraph." We need to type a <P> tag at every location in our description where we wish to insert a paragraph. The <P> tag will tell the browser, "Hey, browser, put a paragraph right here."

Let's type in a paragraph tag for each place in the "test.html" file where a paragraph appears.

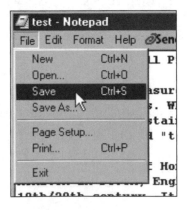

```
test - Notepad                                              _ □ X
File  Edit  Format  Help  Send
Honiton Exton Small Pitcher
<P>  ←
I was culling treasure from the china closet and found this Honiton pitcher, 4 1/2 inches
tall, circa 1950's. White clay. Exton shape. Pitcher is in excellent condition; no cracks,
breaks, chips or stains. Embossed mark on bottom: "Honiton Potteries Exton England" with a
black hand painted "t".
<P>  ←
A Brief History of Honiton Pottery: Honiton Pottery was (and is) located in the town of
Honiton in Devon, England. The pottery was started by Foster and Hunt at the turn of the
19th/20th century. It was purchased by Charles Collard shortly after WWI. In 1947, Collard
sold the pottery to Norman Hull and Harry Barratt who ran it until 1961 when it was sold
to Paul Redvers. All production ceased in 1997 and the pottery was shuttered. The premises
were recently reopened as pottery and craft shop.
<P>  ←
Payment Options:
<P>  ←
Credit/debit card
Checks (item shipped immediately after check has cleared)
Money Orders
<P>  ←

Shipping Terms:
<P>  ←
I will ship this item anywhere to anyone. International bidders welcome. High bidder to
pay winning bid plus USPS priority or global priority shipping and insurance as shown
below.
<P>  ←
US bidders: $5 USD
Canadian bidders: $8 USD
UK bidders: $10 USD
All others: $15 USD
<P>  ←
Refunds, Returns, Regrets:
<P>  ←
If you win this item and upon receiving it, are not 100% satisfied, you may return it to
me for a full refund of the winning bid and shipping. (Returning buyer pays for shipping
back to me.)
```

We have inserted the <P> tag in all the right places in our description. To see what these tags "do" to our description when viewed through Internet Explorer, we must resave the file to the hard drive.

Click on File on the Notepad toolbar and then click Save.

Now go back to the Internet Explorer window and click the Refresh icon on the IE toolbar.

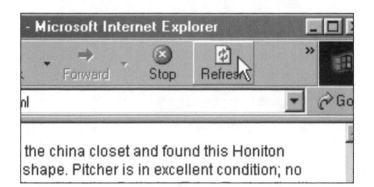

"Magically," where once there were no paragraphs, there are now several!

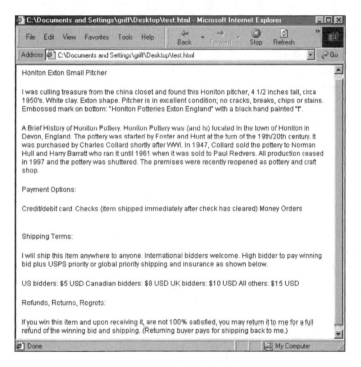

That's it. That's how HTML works. The <P> tag is just one tag out of many, but almost everything you need to know about HTML from here on is based on this simple exercise.

You could stop here and use only the <P> tag and your eBay item descriptions will be perfectly readable, if a bit plain. But I have a feeling you aren't satisfied with just the <P> tag.

Let's learn some more tags!

LINE BREAKS

The <P> tag works great for double line breaks, but what about those places where we only want to break to the next line? (For example, our list of payment options.)

> Payment Options:
>
> Credit/debit card Checks (item shipped immediately after check has cleared) Money Orders

Although it's readable, it would be much cleaner if each option item were on a separate line. The tag we need is the <BR> or "break" tag. Let's type one in after each of the payment options and the shipping costs in our Notepad file.

```
Payment Options:
<P>
Credit/debit card <BR>
Checks (item shipped immediately after check has cleared) <BR>
Money Orders
<P>

Shipping Terms:
<P>
I will ship this item anywhere to anyone. International bidders
pay winning bid plus USPS priority or global priority shipping
below.
<P>
US bidders: $5 USD <BR>
Canadian bidders: $8 USD <BR>
UK bidders: $10 USD <BR>
All others: $15 USD
<P>
```

Once we have typed in all of the <BR> tags we need, we must "Save" the changes in Notepad and "Refresh" the Internet Explorer window. From now on, I will refer to these two steps as "Save and Refresh," since we will be saving changes many times in the rest of this chapter.

Here's what our description looks like in Internet Explorer with the added <BR> tags:

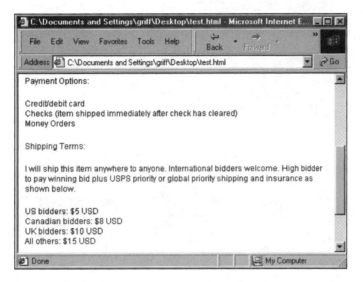

Our payment options and shipping costs are now a lot easier to understand. So, should we stop here or do you want to learn more tags?

I thought so.

BOLD

I like to emphasize titles and important words in my eBay listing descriptions. One way to do so is to use the <B> tag.

It stands for "Bold." Let's add it to the header line at the top of our description.

Save and Refresh! (Save in Notepad, Refresh in Internet Explorer.)

Here's what "bold" formatting using the <B> tag looks like:

Uh . . . so much for bold emphasis. We wanted only the top line of the description to appear bold, but now everything is bold, so nothing stands out! Why did this happen?

When you insert a text formatting tag into a text document, the Web browser that reads the document starts the formatting at the exact spot in the text where you placed the particular formatting tag, and it doesn't stop formatting until either it comes to the end of the document or you tell it where to stop.

Clearly, we need to tell the Web browser where to stop with the "bold." We do this by inserting a close tag. A close tag for a specific tag is the same tag with a forward slash before the name: </B>.

Let's type a "bold" close tag right after the word *Pitcher*.

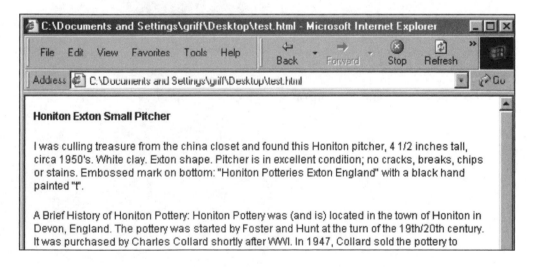

Save and Refresh!

Here's the result in Internet Explorer:

Exactly what we wanted!

Let's add "bold" tags to other important words in our description.

```
<P>
<B>Payment Options:</B>  ←
<P>
Credit/debit card
Checks (item shipped immediately afte
Money Orders
<P>

<B>Shipping Terms:</B>
<P>
I will ship this item anywhere to any
pay winning bid plus USPS priority or
below.
<P>
US bidders: $5 USD <BR>
Canadian bidders: $8 USD <BR>
UK bidders: $10 USD <BR>
All others: $15 USD
<P>
<B> Refunds, Returns, Regrets: </B>|
<P>
```

Save and Refresh!

Here's how our item description would look on our eBay listing:

```
C:\Documents and Settings\griff\Desktop\test.html - Microsoft Internet Explorer
File   Edit   View   Favorites   Tools   Help        Back  Forward   Stop  Refresh
Address  C:\Documents and Settings\griff\Desktop\test.html                    Go
```

Honiton Exton Small Pitcher

I was culling treasure from the china closet and found this Honiton pitcher, 4 1/2 inches tall, circa 1950's. White clay. Exton shape. Pitcher is in excellent condition; no cracks, breaks, chips or stains. Embossed mark on bottom: "Honiton Potteries Exton England" with a black hand painted "t".

A Brief History of Honiton Pottery: Honiton Pottery was (and is) located in the town of Honiton in Devon, England. The pottery was started by Foster and Hunt at the turn of the 19th/20th century. It was purchased by Charles Collard shortly after WWI. In 1947, Collard sold the pottery to Norman Hull and Harry Barratt who ran it until 1961 when it was sold to Paul Redvers. All production ceased in 1997 and the pottery was shuttered. The premises were recently reopened as pottery and craft shop.

Payment Options:

Credit/debit card
Checks (item shipped immediately after check has cleared)
Money Orders

Shipping Terms:

I will ship this item anywhere to anyone. International bidders welcome. High bidder to pay winning bid plus USPS priority or global priority shipping and insurance as shown below.

US bidders: $5 USD
Canadian bidders: $8 USD
UK bidders: $10 USD
All others: $15 USD

Refunds, Returns, Regrets:

```
Done                                                    My Computer
```

Now our description is starting to look like something. Still, there is so much more we can do to dress it up. For other different emphasis, we can use the <U> and <I> tags ("underline" and "italics").

```
<B>Payment Options:</B>
<P>
Credit/debit card<BR>
Checks (item shipped <U>immediately</U> after chec
Money Orders<BR>
<P>
<B>Shipping Terms:</B>
<P>
I will ship this item <I> anywhere </I> to anyone.
welcome. High bidder to pay winning bid plus USPS
```

Save and Refresh.

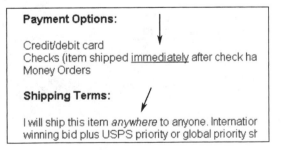

Payment Options:

Credit/debit card
Checks (item shipped <u>immediately</u> after check ha
Money Orders

Shipping Terms:

I will ship this item *anywhere* to anyone. Internation
winning bid plus USPS priority or global priority sh

Here is what the <I> and <U> tags do in Internet Explorer.

Our description is looking more and more professional. What? You want more? Then more you shall have!

LIST TAGS

One tag comes in handy when composing an eBay item description. Actually, it's a set of tags that work together to create lists. They are, of course, called the list tags:

<UL> </UL>
<LI>

Let's use them for our payment options. We will first need to remove the <BR> tags we typed in earlier. Then we place an opening <UL> tag before the items on the list of payment options and a closing </UL> tag after the last payment option on the list. Finally, we place a <LI> tag before each option on the list.

```
<UL>
<LI>Credit/debit card
<LI>Checks (item shipped <U>immediately</U> after check has cleared)
<LI>Money Orders
</UL>
```

Save and Refresh!

Here's what our list will look like in our item description:

Payment Options:

- Credit/debit card
- Checks (item shipped <u>immediately</u> after check has cleared)
- Money Orders

THE FONT TAG

Up to now, the tags that we have used in our item description have consisted of a name between lesser-than and greater-than characters. Some tags have more than just a name inside the lesser- and greater-than characters. One of them is the <FONT> tag.

The <FONT> tag is used to change either the size, color, or typeface of text. To make these changes, there needs to be more information inside the brackets than just the name FONT. This information is added after the name using the following syntax:

<name attribute=value>

Looks a little like algebra, but don't panic—it's not complicated. An attribute is some aspect of the name; for example, in HTML, FONT has a few common attributes. Two of the most commonly used are "size" and "color." A value is assigned to an attribute using the "=" equals sign in order to change that particular attribute.

The first attribute we will change using the <FONT> tag is SIZE. In HTML, the attribute for SIZE can take as a value any number from 0 to 7.

<FONT SIZE=6>

To close out the FONT tag, we use a closing tag:

</FONT>

Note that the closing <FONT> tag does not include the attribute value pair SIZE=6. Attribute/value pairs are only indicated in the opening tag, never the closing tag.

Let's add it to the title on the top of our item description.

To make it clearer, I have placed the tags above and below the line to be formatted. Let's Save and Refresh and view the change in our Web browser.

Amazing, isn't it? Well, there's more! Not only can we change the size, we can change the color of the font as well!

The attribute is COLOR and the value can be one of two types. The simplest type of values to use for COLOR are common color names like *red, blue, green, orange, yellow, purple, white, black,* etc. Note that some not-so-common color names like *maroon* and *fuchsia* will work, as will some combination words like *lightblue* or *lightgreen.* Uncommon names like *bruise, oatmeal,* and *monkeyspit* won't. There is another type of value that uses hexadecimal numbers, which I will tell you more about shortly. For now, we will use a common color name for a value. I'll use *yellow,* which will show up gray in our black-and-white illustration.

```
<FONT SIZE=6 COLOR=yellow>
</FONT>
```

Note that a tag can have more than one attribute value pair. When adding attribute value pairs, make sure that there is one space and only one space between them. More than one space will "break" the tag and it won't work. Let's add this attribute value pair for COLOR to our item description.

```
text.html - Notepad
File  Edit  Format  Help  ✐Send

<FONT SIZE=6 COLOR=yellow>

<B>Honiton Exton Small Pitcher</B>

</FONT>
```

Save and Refresh . . .

. . . to view the changes in Internet Explorer.

```
C:\Documents and Settings\griff\Desktop\text.html - Microsoft Internet Explo
File   Edit   View   Favorites   Tools   Help        Address  ents and Setti
⇐ Back  •  ⇒  • ⊗ ⊠ ⌂ | ⊗Search ⊠Favorites ⊛Media ⊗ | ⊠ • ⊿
Links  ⊠Banknorth Vermont  ⊠iweb  ⊠Business Travel Center  ⊠contact support
```

Honiton Exton Small Pitcher

I was culling treasure from the china closet and found this Honiton
1950's. White clay. Exton shape. Pitcher is in excellent condition; r
stains. Embossed mark on bottom: "Honiton Potteries Exton Engla
"t".

This is the easiest way to indicate a color, but it limits us to a narrow range of colors. There is, however, another type of value for the COLOR attribute that provides literally thousands of colors. It involves a special type of number called *hexadecimal*. Let's talk a little about hexadecimal numbers before we see them in action as a color value.

Our everyday number system is based on a *decimal* system; that is, a numbering system based on 10 (most likely because we have five fingers on each hand to work with when counting).

1 2 3 4 5 6 7 8 9 0

A *hexadecimal* number system is one based on 16. (Imagine if humans evolved with eight fingers on each hand. We would most definitely be using a hexadecimal number system instead of the decimal system we have always used.)

Since our decimal numbering system only has enough number symbols (10) to accommodate a decimal numbering system, we have to borrow other symbols to make up the difference. Our hexadecimal numbering system uses the digits 0 through 9, plus it "borrows" the first six letters of our alphabet:

0 1 2 3 4 5 6 7 8 9 A B C D E F

The type of hexadecimal system we will use as a value for our COLOR attribute has six places, for example:

34C8BA

We use a six-place hexadecimal number with a pound sign before it as a COLOR value, for example:

<font color=#FF33EE>

This number, #FF33EE, will give you a particular shade and hue of a color. The hexadecimal numbers for a color value are not random, though. Here is how they work:

The six-place hexadecimal color value number can be pictured as three separate two-place values, for example:

FF 33 EE

The three parts of the six-place numbers represent three values for colored light indicated as RGB (red, green, blue).

The value FF represents the strength of the red component of light, the 33 represents the strength of the green component of light, and the EE represents the strength of the blue component of light.

The values of the two-place hexadecimal numbers increase in strength from 00 (no value) up to FF (highest value). Here is an abridged scale from 00 to FF

00 01 02 03 04 05 06 07 08 09 0A 0B 0C 0D 0E 0F 10 11 12 13 14 15
16 17 18 19 1A 1B 1C . . . and on up to . . . 98 99 9A 9B 9C 9D 9E
9F AF BF CF DF EF FF

An interesting fact about light color: Equal amounts of full-strength red, green, and blue light produce white light. A zero value of red, green, and blue light equals black (no light). Therefore:

<font color=#FFFFFF> equals the color white
<font color=#000000> equals the color black

With all the other thousands and thousands of colors in between! Many Web pages on the Internet display color charts with each color's respective hexadecimal numbers. To find them, go to *www.google.com* and search on the words *HTML color chart*.

HTML Character Entities

Many folks e-mail or ask me at eBay University how to go about inserting a special symbol like ™ into their Item Description pages or About Me page. It's easy! Nothing complicated, it's all done with character entities.

A character entity is a small set of keyboard characters that make up special numeric or text code that stands for a special symbol. When a Web browser parses these sets of characters, it will display a related special symbol or character not found on your computer keyboard. For example, to insert a ™ into your listing description, you would type:

™

That's an ampersand, followed by a pound sign, then a 1, a 5, a 3, and finally a semicolon.

Here are some other popular character entities that rely on numeric codes:

¢ = ¢ (cent sign)
£ = £ (pound sterling)

¥ = ¥ (yen sign)
© = © (copyright)
® = ® (registered trademark)

Some character entities utilize ISO Latin 1 codes instead of numeric codes. Here is a good example using the ISO Latin code for "nonbreaking space."

If you type more than one space between words or objects into an HTML document, all Web browsers will ignore any spaces after the first one. For example, if I type

word   word

with six spaces between each *word*, the Web page will still display

word word

To add the extra spaces, we need to insert a special character entity for the "nonbreaking space." It looks like this:

If we type five of these character entities between each *word*—

word   word

—we get this:

word   word

Another good use of ISO character entities is for displaying actual HTML formatting tags on a Web page.

Let's say you wanted to show someone on one of eBay's chat boards how to create a hyperlink using HTML. You might type the following into your chat board post:

<A href=http://www.eBay.com> Visit eBay! </A>

But, of course, when others viewed your post, they would see

Visit eBay!

instead of the actual HTML. That's because the viewers' Web browsers parse and format the text based on the tags you provided. To display the actual HTML link tags within a Web browser, you would need to substitute character entities for the "lesser than" and "greater than" tags. Those character entities look like this:

< (which equals the "<" character)

That's an ampersand followed by the lowercase letter *l,* the lowercase letter *t,* and finally a semicolon.

> (which equals the ">" character)

That's an ampersand followed by the lowercase letter *g,* the lowercase letter *t,* and finally a semicolon.

By substituting these character entities, you effectively "break" the ability of the Web browser to parse and display the HTML as an actual link. This is good since your intention is not to create a link, but to *display* the HTML needed to create a link!

With the character entity substitutions, you would type

<A href=http://www.eBay.com> Visit eBay! </A>

and the Web browser would parse this and display it as

<A href=http://www.eBay.com> Visit eBay! </A>

QUIZ QUESTION!

When I was a regular on the eBay chat forums, I would use this character entity trick to display HTML tags for users who had questions about how to create a link. Other users would notice that I had effectively displayed HTML tags without the tags being parsed by the Web browser. They would ask me, "How did you do that?" I would then show them how. Again, note that if I type what I typed to create the "inactive" HTML link—

<A href=http://www.eBay.com> Visit eBay! </A>

—the following would display:

<A href=http://www.eBay.com> Visit eBay! </A>

What would one type into an HTML text document to display the following text inside a Web browser?

<A href=http://www.eBay.com> Visit eBay! </A>

(HINT! It involves a character entity substitution for one of the characters within the character entities *<* and *>*.)

Can you figure it out?

The answer:

To display the actual character entity without the Web browser parsing the entity and displaying the character, you substitute a character entity for one of the characters inside the original entity. In this case, we substituted the character entity for ampersand—*&*—for the *&* character. This could go on forever in an endless regression of nested character entities, but I will assume you got the point and will spare you the tedium of actually printing out an endless regression of nested character entities, but I will assume you got the point and will spare you the tedium of actually printing out an endless regression of nested character entities, but I will assume you got the point and will spare you the tedium of actually printing out an endless regression of nested character entities, but I will assume you got the point and will spare you the tedium of actually printing out an endless regression of nested character entities, but I will assume you got the point and will spare you the tedium of actually printing out an endless regression of nested character entities. . . .

Character entities also come in handy when you need to insert special non-English-alphabet characters into your text, for example, *ä* or *ö* (*a* and *o* umlaut).

You can find many complete lists of other numeric code and ISO Latin 1 HTML character entities by going to any good search engine (such as my favorite, *www.google.com*) and searching on the phrase *character entities*.

You probably never thought you could do so much with a description. You're learning fast!

So far, we've been formatting text. HTML can do much more.

Hyperlinks

One of the most important features of the Web is the ability to click a text link to "go" to another Web page. The Web would be almost impossible to navigate without these links (imagine having to type in a Web address for every page on the Web you wanted to visit).

Links, or more properly, *hyperlinks,* are easy to add to your item description. The tag for creating a hyperlink is the <A> tag.

The *A* stands for "anchor." The <A> tag never stands alone—it always contains an attribute=value pair where the attribute is href and the value is a *URL**
to a file somewhere on the Internet. The opening and closing <A> tags surround some text that you have selected to be the actual clickable link.

<A HREF=*some URL*> type text here that will be the clickable link </A>

Let's add a link to the item description. This link will take our bidders to our other eBay listings.

Click on Advanced Search on the top of any eBay page. Then on the left click "Items by Seller." Finally, enter your User ID into the box provided.

Click Search.

This takes us to the list of current listings by uncle_griff.

---

*URL stands for "uniform resource locator"—computer geek-speak for "Web address."

Thirty-three listings are currently open for uncle_griff, but even if there were no current listings, it wouldn't matter. All we need is the URL for this page and the trick will still work.

Find the Address box on the IE menu bar. Click once inside the box to highlight the entire URL (address). Keeping your mouse cursor over the highlighted URL, click the right button on your mouse and select Copy from the pop-up menu.

This copies the complete URL in the Address box to the Windows clipboard.

Go back to the item description in the Notepad file. At the end of the second paragraph of our description, before Payment Options, we'll add the following line of HTML formatted text:

<A href=> Visit my other eBay Items! </A>

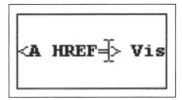

Once you have typed the line of HTML text into the description, place your mouse cursor so that it blinks right between the = and the > after *HREF.*

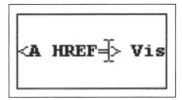

Now, without moving the cursor, click the right mouse button and select Paste from the pop-up menu.

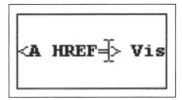

This will paste the entire Search URL into the appropriate space in the <A> tag:

```
text.html - Notepad
File  Edit  Format  Help  Send

<A
HREF=http://cgi6.ebay.com/aw-cgi/eBayISAPI.dll?ViewSellersOtherItems&userid=u
ncle_griff&completed=0&sort=3&since=-1&include=0&page=1&rows=25> Visit my
other eBay Items!</A>
```

Save and Refresh!

Go to the Internet Explorer window to view the link in the item description.

Honiton Exton Small Pitcher

I was culling treasure from the china closet and found this Honiton pitche
1950's. White clay. Exton shape. Pitcher is in excellent condition; no cra
stains. Embossed mark on bottom: "Honiton Potteries Exton England" w
"t".

A Brief History of Honiton Pottery. Honiton Pottery was (and is) located i
Devon, England. The pottery was started by Foster and Hunt at the turn c
was purchased by Charles Collard shortly after WW1. In 1947, Collard s
Hull and Harry Barratt who ran it until 1961 when it was sold to Paul Redy
ceased in 1997 and the pottery was shuttered. The premises were rece
pottery and craft shop.

Visit my other eBay Items!

Payment Options:

- Credit/debit card
- Checks (item shipped immediately after check has cleared)
- Money Orders

A FEW IMPORTANT CONSIDERATIONS ABOUT LINKS

eBay does not allow links from your item description to your personal or commercial Web page. This is an excerpt from the eBay site regarding links policy:

> **The eBay item page** can contain no URLs or links to, or promotional information about, any off-eBay Web page, including Web sites of the seller or any third party.
>
> There are two exceptions to this general rule—the eBay item page may contain a link to information related specifically to that item that:
>
> > Gives acknowledgment to a company that provided services related to that listing (such as counters, auction management tools, or payment and mediation services). This acknowledgment may contain both a logo (88 x 33 pixels) and up to ten words of text (HTML font size 3), but only one of those may be clickable.
> >
> > Points interested buyers to another Internet page that contains only more information (such as pictures, product specifications, or detailed terms and conditions) about eBay items listed by that seller

Just look at our eBay item description. We've gone from a single block of text to a professional-looking layout with a link in just a few minutes!

And you thought this was going to be hard. But wait! There's more. . . .

The Image Tag

In the previous chapters, when we actually listed our item live on eBay, we relied on eBay Picture Services, since it's a quick, no-fuss way to place digital pictures on your listing.

Still, it's important to know just how digital pictures are "placed" onto an eBay item page.

All Web page graphics—JPEGS, GIFS, pictures, icons, etc.—are embedded onto a Web page using the <IMG> tag.

The <IMG> tag does not have a closing tag. It does not format text; it "does" something, that is, it tells the Web browser to go fetch a copy of a digital picture file somewhere on the Internet. Here's how the <IMG> tag works.

The <IMG> tag, like the <FONT> tag, cannot live on its tag name alone. It needs an attribute-value pair. For the <IMG> tag, this attribute-value pair looks like this:

<IMG SRC=*url*>

where *url* is a valid URL that points to either a JPEG or GIF file.

Here is a URL that points to a picture of someone you might know:

http://www.unclegriff.com/images/feb-19-02-headshot05.jpg

Let's use it for our listing. Here is the complete URL.

<IMG SRC=http://www.unclegriff.com/images/feb-19-02-headshot05.jpg>

We will place it at the very bottom of our item description in Notepad, Save and Refresh, and check to see the results.

Save and Refresh!

And here's our description with a shot or yours truly:

If you know the URL to a picture, you can link to it using the <IMG> tag. The linking is the easy part. Placing a digital picture file on a Web server is a bit harder but not impossible. Again, we will use eBay Picture Services when we list our item in the next chapter. I will show examples of using other options for digital picture hosting at the end of the next chapter.

A NOTE ABOUT "BORROWING" PICTURES

As I mentioned earlier, if you know the URL for an image file, you can embed it into a Web page (such as your eBay Item Description page) by using the <IMG> tag. That means it's technically possible to link to any image on the Web. However, this doesn't mean that it's OK to do so without permission.

Never link to another person's or company's images or graphics without first asking their permission. This is especially important on eBay.

Table Tags

Tables are simply grids made up of one or more cells. Here is a typical (non-HTML) four-celled table created in Microsoft Word.

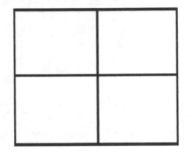

In Web pages (and especially in eBay item descriptions), HTML tables come in handy for creating layouts for text and pictures. We can place tables in our item description by using the <TABLE> tag set.

<TABLE> tags never act alone—they are used in sets just like list <UL> tags. The other tags that <TABLE> needs to do its job are <TR> (table row) and <TD> (table data).

HTML table cells can contain text, links, or images. HTML tables can also have visible or invisible borders. Here is an example of the HTML formatting used to create a four-celled table. Each cell contains the word *eBay:*

```
<TABLE BORDER=1>
<TR> <TD>eBay</TD> <TD> eBay</TD> </TR>
<TR> <TD >eBay</TD> <TD> eBay</TD> </TRB>
   </TABLE>
```

The above HTML, when we copy it into our "test.html" document, save the changes, and then refresh our browser, creates the following table:

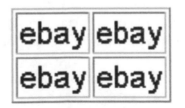

Every HTML table starts with a <TABLE> tag and ends with a </TABLE> tag. THIS IS EXTREMELY IMPORTANT! If you use tables in your item description and do not close them with the proper number of </TABLE> tags, your item description will not appear in some types of Web browsers!

The <TABLE> tag may include an attribute=value pair for BORDER=value. A value of 0 will make the border invisible. Any other value will show a border of increasing size. We will use a value of 1.

Every row in our table is indicated by <TR> and </TR> tags. (Again, TR stands for "table row.")

Within every set of table row tags, table cells are created by inserting <TD> and </TD> tags for each cell. (To repeat, TD stands for "table data.")

TEXT PLACEMENT USING TABLE TAGS

Tables can be useful for laying out text as data in cells. For example, our various shipping costs per location will look better if we place the data in a table. Here's how that section of our eBay item description looks now:

```
US bidders: $5 USD
Canadian bidders: $8 USD
UK bidders: $10 USD
All others: $15 USD
```

We have four rows of data for each location. Each row contains two parts: one for location and one for cost. Thus, we need a table of four rows with two columns for a total of eight cells. I like to type out the table tags first before typing in the data. Each row starts with an opening <TR> tag and ends with a closing </TR> tag. In between the <TR> and </TR> for each row, there are two sets of table data tags <TD> </TD>—one for each cell. (Remember, we need two cells for each row.) I am also going to add a fifth row for our headers: "location" and "shipping costs."

```
<TABLE BORDER=1>
<TR> <TD> </TD> <TD> </TD> </TR>
<TR> <TD> </TD> <TD> </TD> </TR>
<TR> <TD> </TD> <TD> </TD> </TR>
<TR> <TD> </TD> <TD> </TD> </TR>
<TR> <TD> </TD> <TD> </TD> </TR>
</TABLE>
```

Let's fill in the data for each cell. We *carefully* type it in between each <TD> and </TD> tag:

```
<TABLE BORDER=1>
<TR><TD>Ship To Location</TD> <TD>Shipping (USD)</TD> </TR>
<TR> <TD>US </TD> <TD>$5 </TD> </TR>
<TR> <TD>Canada </TD> <TD>$8 </TD> </TR>
<TR> <TD> UK </TD> <TD> $10 </TD> </TR>
<TR> <TD>All Others </TD> <TD>$15 </TD> </TR>
</TABLE>
```

I say *carefully* because if you type the data in the wrong place, your table will be a mess.

We now type this set of table tags with data into our eBay item description in our Notepad file in place of the original shipping costs.

```
<TABLE BORDER=1>
<TR> <TD>Ship To Location</TD> <TD>Shipping (USD)</TD></TR>
<TR> <TD>US </TD> <TD>$5 </TD> </TR>
<TR> <TD>Canada </TD> <TD>$8 </TD> </TR>
<TR> <TD> UK </TD> <TD> $10 </TD> </TR>
<TR> <TD>All Others </TD> <TD>$15 </TD> </TR>
</TABLE>
```

Save and Refresh!

Here's what our new tabled shipping costs look like viewed through Internet Explorer:

Shipping Terms:

I will ship this item *anywhere* to anyone
shipping and insurance as shown belo

Ship To Location	Shipping (USD)
US	$5
Canada	$8
UK	$10
All Others	$15

Refunds, Returns, Regrets:

If you win this item and upon receiving i

Data like our shipping costs is much easier to read when it is displayed in a table.

Creating tables bigger or fancier than a few rows and columns is difficult to do "by hand" without making simple errors created by mistyping a tag name or leaving off a closing tag. If you create HTML tables by hand for your eBay listing description (and I urge you to do so), keep them simple. Two columns and two to five rows should be easy to handle.

PICTURE PLACEMENT USING TABLE TAGS

The following HTML shows an example of how to use a simple two-celled table to align two images in an eBay item description. Between each <TD> and </TD> tag, there is a complete <IMG SRC> tag for a valid digital picture file. (These are digital pictures of our item that I uploaded to a Web server—*www.sover.net*—back in my old home state of Vermont. How to upload digital pictures to a server is covered in the next chapter.)

```
<TABLE BORDER=1>
<TR>
<TD> <IMG SRC=http://www.sover.net/~jimgriff/images/
    honiton03.jpg> </TD>
<TD> <IMG SRC=http://www.sover.net/~jimgriff/images/
    honiton04.jpg> </TD>
</TR>
</TABLE>
```

Let's Paste the above HTML formatting into our item description before the brief history section. Bidders like to see pictures ASAP!

Save and Refresh . . . and here's our item description viewed in Internet Explorer:

There is a big advantage to embedding digital image files into a table as opposed to without.

When a Web browser gets to an <IMG> tag, it stops loading the rest of the page as the pictures download. For fast Internet connections, this is not a big issue, but for those with slow dial-up connections, the wait can be annoying. Placing your image URLs in an HTML table helps to remedy this problem. Web browsers will load the table and keep loading the rest of the item page while the pictures load into the table cells, allowing the potential bidder to read the rest of the contents of the item description while the pictures download.

Other HTML Tags

CENTER

To center text or a picture on a Web page, use the <CENTER> tags:

```
<CENTER>
</CENTER>
```

Let's use the <CENTER> tag to center my picture on the item description page:

```
<P>
<CENTER>
<IMG SRC=http://www.sover.net/~jimgriff/images/feb-19-02-headshot05.jpg><BR>
Thanks for shopping with Uncle!
</CENTER>
```

Save and Refresh!

View the changes in Internet Explorer:

THE HORIZONTAL RULE TAG

The <HR> tag places a horizontal rule into the Web page. It comes in handy for separating sections of a Web page or eBay Item Description page.

Let's slip one in our item description to see what it does.

Save and Refresh!

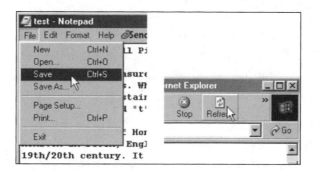

Ta da! A horizontal rule!

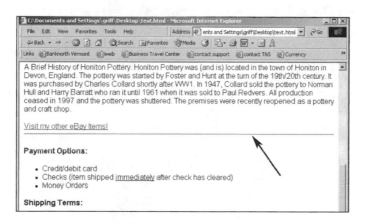

Using simple HTML tags, we've turned a boring, hard-to-read block of text into a polished and professional-looking eBay item description.

There's an additional benefit to creating our eBay item description in a separate text file. We can now save this file and use it over and over again as a template for future eBay listings, effectively avoiding endless retyping of our payment options or shipping and return policies. Saving the description also preserves our layout for future use.

That wasn't so difficult, was it? I told you HTML would be a snap. Now that we've finished this chapter, I have to fess up.

Few sellers actually work through HTML they way we just did. Most sellers rely on the Description Editor, which is built into the eBay Sell Your Item form. Many eBay sellers purchase predesigned templates with fancy borders, backgrounds, and shapes and simply fill in their text for each listing. Some eBay sellers use specialized applications called Web editors to create their item descriptions.

Web editors are like word processors for Web pages. They allow you to create a Web page without typing a single HTML tag.

So why did I put you through this HTML tutorial? Because, if you know how the HTML behind Web pages and specifically, eBay Item Description pages, works, you'll be better prepared to troubleshoot problems as they might arise.

Plus, you have to admit—this has been fun! You've accomplished something solid and useful that you can immediately put to use in your eBay listings.

GRIFF TIP! In the beginning of this chapter, we named our file "test.html." This file can be saved for use as a template for future eBay listings. One problem: If we save and close this file and then subsequently click on it to reopen it, it will open in either Internet Explorer or Netscape (depending on which browser you use), not Notepad. We can only make changes in this file when it is open in Notepad. If we open it in Internet Explorer, we won't be able to edit it since IE is an "output" window and doesn't accept "input."

In Windows, to force our "test.html" file to open in Notepad, we need to follow these steps:

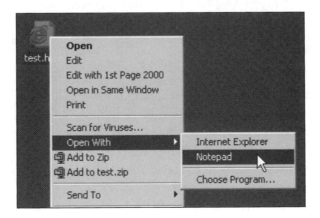

Go to your desktop, hover the mouse cursor over the icon for "test.html," and click the mouse's right-hand button to display a pop-up menu containing special commands.

Select Open With, and then select Notepad from the pop-up menus. This will open the "test.html" file in Notepad.

8

Advanced Image Hosting Solutions

Four years ago, Chris Spencer was a publicist and personal manager for actors.

"I had a very stressful job working twelve- to fourteen-hour days for unappreciative clients who would whine because they were only making $12,000 a week. I was miserable and unhappy."

Four years ago, Chris decided to take charge of his life. He started out eBay-selling antiques and collectibles.

"I know virtually nothing about antiques and I don't own any inventory. I work with very honorable and reputable dealers in the L.A. area who provide me with accurate, honest descriptions for the items that I take on consignment. Last year, I sold over $400,000 worth of antiques and collectibles on eBay."

Today, Chris is not only a Gold-level eBay PowerSeller (borntodeal), he's also a regular instructor at eDay University seminars.

"I like to teach others how to use the site so that they can make their business better and see the money I am seeing. It is a really fun life!"

eBay Listings and Digital Pictures—Advanced Solutions

For the first-time eBay seller, eBay Picture Services is invaluable. In our earlier example listings, we relied on eBay Picture Services to "host" (upload, store, and display) our digital-pictures in our eBay listing. As a digital-picture hosting option, eBay Picture Services is simple, fast, and, most important, automatically and seamlessly places our pictures on our listing page.

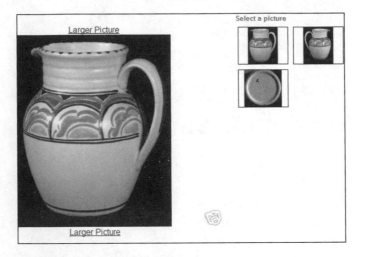

You can employ other digital-picture hosting solutions either in place of or in combination with eBay Picture Services.

These hosting solutions have solid advantages: You can add more than six pictures to a listing; you have more options regarding the placement and layout of your images; and if you are a subscriber to an Internet Service Provider, it may not cost you anything extra.

PICTURES ON A WEB PAGE—HOW DOES THAT WORK?

Before we explore other digital-picture hosting solutions, we need to examine a few Internet and digital-pictures basics.

eBay item pages are Web pages that contain text and images.

To our eyes, the text and images on an eBay item page make up one complete Web page computer screen, and in fact though they do "live" together as a single Web page in our Web browser, they didn't start off that way.

Usually, the two major components of a Web page—text and pictures—start out as separate files stored in separate locations on the Internet. That is, the text for the Web page is stored on one Web server while the digital-picture files may be stored on another Web server (which could be halfway around the world!).

It's the job of your Web browser to collect copies of all these components and put them together on your computer screen for you to view as one complete page.

I put up a simple Web page to illustrate how displaying a Web page with images works. If you are near a computer connected to the Internet, go to *http://www.xmission.com/~jimgriff/book/bookexample.html* and follow along. (Make sure you type in the tilde character before the user name *jimgriff*.)

The Web page at the end of the URL above is a single file called "bookexample.html."

It looks like this:

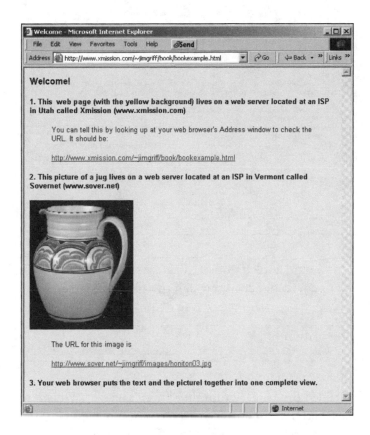

The Web page is actually a simple text file almost exactly like the one we created in the last chapter. (It has a few added HTML tags that are necessary for making a true Web page.)

Here is a copy of the text file I created in Notepad. It contains the HTML-formatted text that makes up our little yellow Web page.

```
bookexample[1] - Notepad                                    _ |□| X
File  Edit  Format  Help   Send
<html>
<head>
<title>Welcome</title>
</head>

<body vlink="#551a8b" alink="#ff0000" link="#0000ee"
text="#000000" bgcolor="#F8F1A5">
<p><font size="4"><b>Welcome!</b></font> </p>
<p><b>1. This  web page (with the yellow background) lives on
a web server
located at an ISP in Utah called Xmission
(www.xmission.com)</b></p>
<blockquote>
<p>You can tell this by looking up at your web browser's Address
window to check
the URL. It should be:</p>
<p><a
href="http://www.xmission.com/~jimgriff/book/bookexample.html"
target="_blank">http://www.xmission.com/~jimgriff/book/bookexample
.html</a></p>
</blockquote>
<p><b>2. This picture of a jug lives on a web server located at an
ISP in Vermont called Sovernet (www.sover.net)</b></p>
<p><img border="0"
src="http://www.sover.net/~jimgriff/images/honiton03.jpg"
width="189" height="236"></p>
<blockquote>
<p>The URL for this image is</p>
<p><a href="http://www.sover.net/~jimgriff/images/honiton03.jpg"
target="_blank">http://www.sover.net/~jimgriff/images/honiton03.jp
g</a></p>
</blockquote>
<p><b>3. Your web browser puts the text and the picture together
into one
complete view.</b></p>
</body>

</html>
```

Some of this should look familiar. There are <P> and <B> tags as well as some new tags not covered. Scroll through the file to find the <img> tag:

```
ISP in Vermont called Sovernet (www.sover.net)</b></p>
<p><img border="0"
src="http://www.sover.net/~jimgriff/images/honiton03.jpg"
width="189" height="236"></p>
```

I have underlined the URL within the <img> tag: *http://www.sover.net/~jim-griff/images/honiton03.jpg*.

The complete HTML tag is <img border="0" src="http://www.sover.net/~jimgriff/images/honiton03.jpg" width="189" height="236">.

There are attributes inside this <img> tag for border, width, and height, as well as the familiar *src*.

The URL after *src* points to a picture file called "honiton03.jpg,"

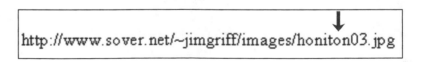

which "lives" in a folder called "images,"

http://www.sover.net/~jimgriff/images/honiton03.jpg

which is nested inside a folder called "~jimgriff,"

http://www.sover.net/~jimgriff/images/honiton03.jpg

which lives on a Web server called www.sover.net.

http://www.sover.net/~jimgriff/images/honiton03.jpg

The www.sover.net Web server is physically located at an ISP called Sovernet, which is nestled in the beautiful green mountains of Vermont.

I have an ISP account with Sovernet. As part of that account, I have "space" set aside in my user name for storing files. I moved ("uploaded") a copy of the "honiton03.jpg" picture from my computer, over the Internet, to the sover.net Web server using a special type of application on my computer known as an FTP client. (More on FTP later in this chapter.)

Once I uploaded a copy of the picture file to www.sover.net, I then uploaded a copy of the text file "bookexample.html" to another Web server called Xmission, which is located in Salt Lake City, Utah. I also have an account with Xmission.

I needed to upload a copy of this text file to make it a Web page that can be accessed by anyone on the Internet (like you, if you navigated to it earlier as part of this exercise). Again, we'll explore "uploading" in depth later in this chapter.

The URL for my little yellow Web page is *http://www.xmission.com /~jimgriff/book/bookexample.html*.

The HTML file "bookexample.html" "lives" inside a subfolder called "book," which is nestled inside another folder called "~jimgriff," which is located on the www.xmission.com Web server.

All my components are in place. The picture file lives on a server in Vermont. The little yellow Web page lives on a server in Utah.

Here's what happened when you opened the link *http://www.xmission.com/ ~jimgriff/book/bookexample.html* in your Web browser.

1. Your Web browser immediately sent a request through the Internet for the file name located at the end of the URL.
2. The Web server at Xmission, on which the requested file resides, then sent a copy of the HTML file back to your computer, and it opened up in your Web browser.
3. The browser then started to "parse" (scan) and convert the HTML-formatted text in the file into viewable text, which is displayed in the Web browser's window.
4. While parsing the HTML file, the Web browser came across the <IMG> tag for the picture file located in Vermont. The Web browser read the URL.
5. The computer then sent a request for a copy of the picture file to the location indicated by the URL in the <IMG> tag.
6. The Web server back in Vermont received and granted the request for a copy of "honiton03.jpg" and sent a copy of the digital picture back to your computer.
7. The computer hands the copy of the digital picture to the Web browser, which "embeds" the copy of the digital picture file into the exact place on the page where the original <IMG> tag lives.

You have a complete Web page with text and picture in your Web browser!

Every time you open a Web page in your Web browser, this same process occurs. If there are no pictures or files embedded into the page, then only one request is made—for the Web page HTML file itself. For each image file embedded in the HTML text file, your computer needs to make a request out to the Internet for a copy of the file. This is why a page with several pictures located in different physical locations can sometimes take a while to display completely.

Now that you have a better understanding of how digital pictures are retrieved from the Internet and displayed in your Web browser window, we can explore other digital picture options besides eBay Picture Services.

Digital Picture Hosting (Image Hosting)

First, some definitions:

Digital picture hosting (otherwise known as image hosting) is the moving (uploading) of a copy of your digital picture file from your computer to a remote

Web server on the Internet, where it is stored (hosted) for retrieval by any other Internet user.

The digital picture is then displayed on an item page by typing (embedding) the digital picture Internet address (URL or "uniform resource locator") into the item text. The embedded URL is said to "reference" the actual image file.

eBay Picture Services is an automatic image-hosting service. You only need to point to a picture on your hard drive and eBay Picture Services does the rest (upload the file to a Web server, host the file, embed the URL for your picture at the bottom of your listing, and display the picture file on your item page).

As I mentioned earlier, there are definite advantages to hosting image files using solutions other than eBay Picture Services. To repeat: You can host more than six pictures; you can place the images wherever you choose inside your item text; and it may not cost you, since you may be paying for the hosting service already!

Hosting an image file is a three-part process:

1. Acquiring hosting space on a Web server.
2. Moving copies of your picture files to a Web server.
3. Embedding copies of these picture files in your eBay Item Description text by using special HTML to go get the picture file and display it in the item page.

The first step is to find hosting space on the Internet.

1. ACQUIRING HOSTING SPACE ON A WEB SERVER

Your ISP

If you are paying an Internet Service Provider (ISP) to access the Internet, you most likely have file hosting space set aside for your use as a part of your service package. For example, if you are an AOL user, you automatically have twelve megabytes set aside on the AOL Web servers for your exclusive use.

I use an ISP in Vermont called Sovernet. As part of my monthly dial-up access plan, Sovernet provides me with several megabytes of Web server space where I can store my image files.

Most every local-based ISP will provide hosting space. Contact your ISP for more information.

Other Hosting Services

Many online companies provide image hosting services. Most charge a small fee.

You can view a vast list of them by going to *www.google.com* and searching on *image hosting*.

2. MOVING COPIES OF YOUR PICTURE FILES
TO A WEB SERVER

Once you have acquired space for image hosting, the next step is to upload copies of your digital pictures from your computer to this image hosting space. Moving copies of your digital picture files from your computer to a Web server is called file transfer protocol, or FTP. Note these two terms—I will use them frequently in the next few pages.

For some ISPs, you will need a special FTP application to move copies of digital picture files from your computer to your Web server space.

Other ISPs (such as AOL) have FTP software embedded within their own software, so you don't need a separate FTP application.

You can download one of several popular freeware and shareware FTP client applications from any of the download sites on the Internet.

Try *www.tucows.com* and type in *FTP* as a search for programs to download.

I downloaded and installed an FTP application called WS_FTP from the *www.tucows.com* site. I start the application by clicking its icon on my Start menu. This is the "application interface" for the most recent version of WS_FTP:

Most FTP applications look something like this. FTP applications usually have two windows. The one on the left shows the contents of my computer's hard drive. The one on the right is empty now, but once I connect to Sovernet, it will show the contents of my personal Web server space there.

To connect, I click Connect on the bottom left-hand corner of the application window:

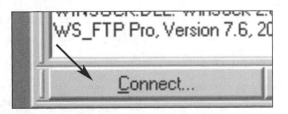

This brings up a dialog box where I can enter a new "site" connection. Sover-net's Web site has all the information I need for establishing an FTP connection.

GRIFF TIP! Your ISP will post on their Web site all the information you need for configuring the FTP connection to your Web server space.

I select the folder MySites, then click "Create Site . . ."

On the following screens, I enter the requested information in the spaces provided. I enter a name—Sovernet—for the new profile and opt to have it placed in the folder MySites.

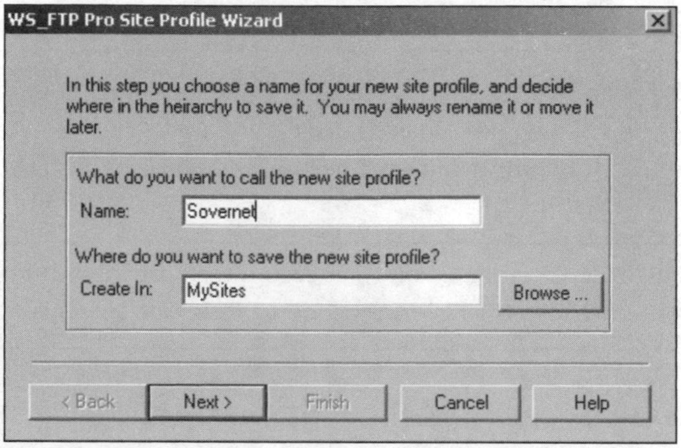

I click Next, and in the next screen, I enter the host name (as provided to me by the folks at Sovernet. Again, you must obtain your host name from your ISP).

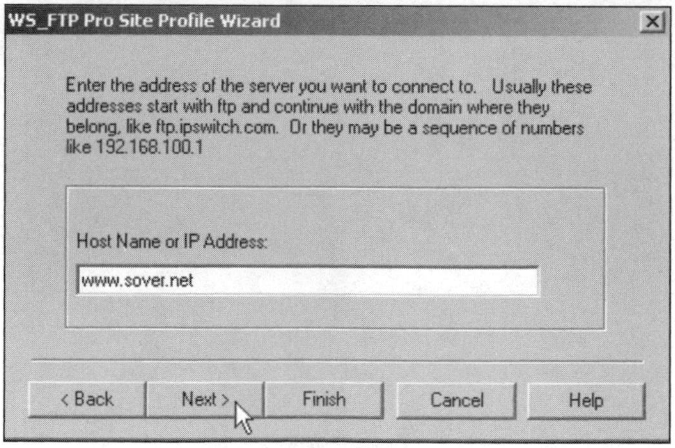

I again click Next to move to the next screen, then enter my User ID and Password. (Your ISP will tell you if you need an "account.")

I click Next to select the server type, which in most cases will be FTP, and then I click Finish.

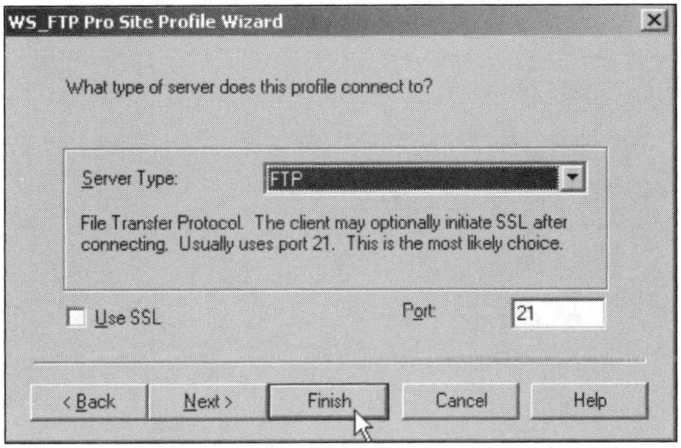

My connection profile is now recorded for quick future access. To connect to my FTP space at Sovernet, I click Connect.

Since I didn't provide my password when I created my profile for Sovernet, the system will prompt me for one before it will complete the connection.

Click Connect and the right-hand FTP window will display the file contents of the remote Web server back in Vermont.

Using this FTP application, I can now create folders or delete folders or files on my Web server space *almost as if it were a separate hard drive on my own computer!* I can also move files back and forth from one window to the other. To move a copy of an edited digital picture of my eBay Item from my computer to my Web server space, I locate the file on my hard drive in the left-hand window and either drag and drop it or highlight it and click the right arrow between the windows. I first have to make sure the source directory on my computer and the target directory or folder at sover.net are both open in their windows.

Now I can upload a copy of any file on my computer to my Web server space at Sovernet.

First, in the left-hand window, I locate the file on my computer I wish to upload (by clicking through the folders and/or using the green arrow to move up one level in the folder hierarchy on my hard drive). I am looking for a picture file called "honiton03.jpg." I find and then highlight the file.

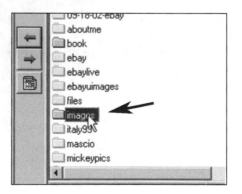

C:\Documents and Settings\griff\Desktop

Name	Size	Type
Tiff Files		File Folder
AOL Instant Messenge...	1KB	Shortcut
arrow4_black.gif	2KB	Binary file
bookexample.html	2KB	HTML Documen
ebay_links.htm	1KB	HTML Documen
EPSON Digital PhotoL...	2KB	Shortcut
Graphic Workshop.lnk	1KB	Shortcut
honiton.txt	2KB	Text Document
honiton03.jpg	23KB	Binary file
imagelink.html	1KB	HTML Documen
IrfanView.lnk	1KB	Shortcut
itemtext.txt	2KB	Text Document
Kana Power Client.lnk	1KB	Shortcut

1 object(s) selected   22KB

226 Transfer complete.
Transfer request completed with status: Finished

Disconnect   Cancel

Next I must navigate to the folder into which I want to place the copy of "honiton03.jpg." In the right-hand window, I locate and double-click the "images" folder to open it.

Once the "images" folder is open, I can click the right-hand arrow to move a copy of the "honiton03.jpg" file from the left-hand window to the right-hand window.

📁 Tiff Files		File Folder	1C				
👤 AOL Instant Messenge...	1KB	Shortcut	6/		anthonypooltable01.jpg	35KB	Binary file
arrow4_black.gif	2KB	Binary file	1C		bigballs01.jpg	191KB	Binary file
bookexample.html	2KB	HTML Document	1C		bluechinese-back01.jpg	68KB	Binary file
ebay_links.htm	1KB	HTML Document	1C		bluechinese-gallery.jpg	13KB	Binary file
EPSON Digital PhotoL...	2KB	Shortcut	1C		bluechinese-large01.jpg	303KB	Binary file
Graphic Workshop.lnk	1KB	Shortcut	1C		bluechinese01.jpg	110KB	Binary file
honiton.txt	2KB	Text Document	9/		brokenhandle-01.jpg	30KB	Binary file
honiton03.jpg	23KB	Binary file	1C		brokenhandle-02.jpg	28KB	Binary file
imagelink.html	1KB	HTML Document	1C		brookemural.jpg	125KB	Binary file
IrfanView.lnk	1KB	Shortcut	1C		cslogo3.gif	3KB	Binary file
itemtext.txt	2KB	Text Document	9/		cylinder01.jpg	37KB	Binary file
Kana Power Client.lnk	1KB	Shortcut	5/		cylinder02.jpg	36KB	Binary file

(Buttons: MkDir, View, Execute, Rename, Delete, Refresh, DirInfo, Upload)

This will tell the FTP application to send a copy of the selected file through the Internet to the "images" folder in the "~jimgriff" directory on the sover.net Web server. A status window shows the progress of the file transfer:

Transfer Manager					
File View Transfer Help					
Transfers	History				
Source	Status	Transferred	Rate (K...	Size	Time Left
⊞ 🖧 C:\Docu...	⬆	0	0.00	22,898	

Once the transfer is complete, a copy of the "honiton03.jpg" file now lives on the sover.net Web server and is accessible to the entire Internet using the unique URL or address to locate it. In this case, the URL is:

http://www.sover.net/~jimgriff/images/honiton03.jpg

the web server address — my folder — the images folder — the specific filename

I can also check the URL to make sure it is valid by typing it into my Web browser and hitting Enter.

If the image displays, then the URL is correctly typed and valid. It is a good habit to check your picture URLs in a Web browser. Better to correct mistakes in a URL before you list the item than to have to revise the item after it is listed.

Using Internet Explorer as an FTP Client

A little-known feature of the latest version of Internet Explorer is that it can be used as an FTP client!

If you have FTP space somewhere (check with your Internet Service Provider) and you have a User ID and password, you can use your Internet Explorer Web browser along with a Windows Explorer window to move files to and from your computer and a remote FTP location.

1. Open Internet Explorer.

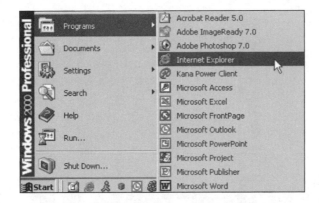

2. Type the following into the Address window, substituting your actual user name and password for *username* and *password* and your ISP's domain name for *domain.name*.

ftp://username:password@ftp.domain.name

Here is an example: ftp://jimgriff:**********@ftp.sover.net.

(No, I won't tell you my password, thankyouverymuch.)

3. Open Windows Explorer.

4. Position the two windows so that you can drag and drop files back and forth from either window.

5. You can create and delete directories (folders) on your remote FTP space by using the File, New command on the Internet Explorer menu bar.

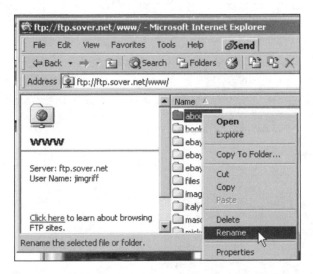

6. You can also rename, move, and delete files on your FTP space.

If you are an eBay seller, or if you are planning on selling at eBay, the next chapter is an absolute must.

Hosting Digital Picture Files at AOL

First, you'll need to have an AOL account! Many eBay sellers already do, but the majority of them are unaware that along with their monthly AOL access and AOL e-mail, they are also paying for twelve megabytes of AOL Web space. Twelve MBs of server space can come in real handy for hosting eBay image files.

The steps for uploading your digital pictures onto your space at AOL are easy to find. (1) Open your AOL software and search on keywords *my ftp space* to bring up the My FTP Space box.

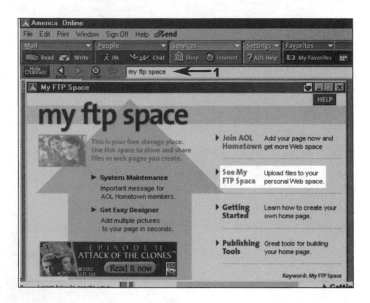

This is AOL's built-in FTP application. (Note: You don't need to download and install an application like WS_FTP when using your AOL account for hosting.)

(2) Click on See My FTP Space to see the current contents of your AOL FTP space.

NOTE: AOL's built-in FTP application has only one window.

Using this window, you can create new directories (folders) and you can upload files from your computer to AOL by clicking the Upload icon. Let's click Upload to start.

Next, you have to type a name for the file. This is an unusual procedure and not how most other FTP applications work. With AOL's FTP procedure, you are in effect creating an empty file on the AOL server and giving the empty file a name into which the file on your computer will be placed once you begin the uploading. It's confusing. To prevent any mix-ups, I usually type in the same name as the file on my hard drive I want to upload. I suggest you do the same.

I type in the name "honiton03.jpg," and then click Continue. In the Upload File window that pops up, I click the Select File icon to choose a file on my hard drive:

This brings up an Attach File window. I navigate through my hard drive to the file I wish to upload.

Once I have located the file, I double-click it to open it. The path of the file will show up in the File box on the Upload File window. Next, I click the Send icon:

The file will upload to your FTP space at AOL. A message will alert you when the transfer is complete. Click OK and you are nearly done.

To check if the file was successfully uploaded into the proper directory, I click on the "images" directory to find the file.

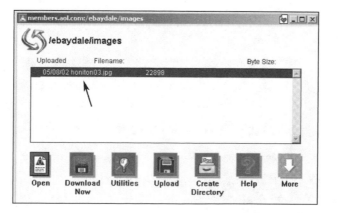

There it is!

Whenever I use AOL to host images or files, I like to double-check that they were uploaded correctly, so I always recheck the directory into which they were uploaded.

Now, let's test the image in a browser and get its URL. Go to any Web browser, type in the following—*http://members.aol.com/* and put your AOL user name after the last forward slash. Here's mine: *http://members.aol.com/ebaydale* (see below).

If you haven't previously set up an actual AOL member's hometown Web page, the URL with your AOL user name will display the contents of your AOL FTP space.

If I click the link for the "images" folder, I should see my file "honiton03.jpg." And there it is:

If I click the image name, it should display the actual digital picture . . .

. . . and it does.

GRIFF TIP! You can usually view the file contents of any Web folder *if* the folder does not contain a file named "index.html." Some Web servers (such as *www.xmission.com*) are set up so that the contents of a user's Web folders are not ever readable, even if they do not contain an "index.html" file.

This ability to read the contents of a Web folder can come in handy should you need to troubleshoot one of your own URLs.

---

3. EMBEDDING DIGITAL PICTURE FILE URLS IN YOUR EBAY ITEM DESCRIPTION

You have uploaded your item pictures to your own Web server space and you have the URLs (addresses) for each.

The last step in the process is to embed your digital pictures in your item description. You do this by typing into the item description the URL for each digital picture you uploaded in step 2. Each URL is placed inside an HTML <IMG> tag.

In the previous step, I uploaded a file to my Web server space at Sovernet. Here is the URL for that digital picture: *http://www.sover.net/~jimgriff/images/ honiton03.jpg.*

Here is how the URL looks when used as the value for the attribute src inside an <IMG> tag: *<IMG src=*http://www.sover.net/~jimgriff/images/honiton03.jpg>.

Let's review what happens when the Web browser gets to an <IMG> tag with a URL as the value for an src attribute.

Our URL shows the address location for the file "honiton03.jpg," which lives in a directory or folder called "images/," which in turn lives inside a directory folder called "~jimgriff/," which in turn lives on a Web server called "*www. sover.net.*"

GRIFF TIP! Think of any URL as a letter's mailing address, only in reverse. In a mailing address, the most specific final destination—the name of the recipient of the letter—is always on the top of the address:

> Mr. Honiton03 JPG
> Image Street
> Jimgriff, sover.net, www

However, in a URL, the final destination—the file name—is always at the end of the address: *http://www.sover.net/~jimgriff/images/ honiton03.jpg.*

When the browser gets to the "<IMG" part of the <IMG> tag, it knows that special instructions will follow.

The browser looks next for the src attribute and reads, from left to right, the URL after the equals sign. The URL tells the browser where on the Internet it needs to send a request for a file. Again, the actual file name is always at the very end of the URL. So reading from left to right, the browser tells the computer to go to a Web server called "sover.net" and ask if there is a file named "honiton03.jpg" in a subdirectory called "images" in a next-level directory called "~jimgriff," and, if there is such a file in such location, would the Web server be so kind as to send a copy of the file back through the Internet to your computer?

If the URL is correct, the Web server "serves" a copy of the digital picture named "honiton03.jpg" through the Internet back to your computer, which passes the file to your Web browser, which then displays the copy of the digital picture by "embedding" it within the Web page at the very spot in the HTML document behind the page where the <IMG> tag appears.

ANOTHER GRIFF TIP! You can quickly find the URL for any picture on the Web by using a special feature in Internet Explorer along with your right mouse button.

Find a picture on the Web. Hover your mouse over the picture and click the right-hand button on your mouse. Select Properties from the pop-up menu:

In the Properties box, there is a field for Address: (URL). Highlight the URL by holding down your left mouse button and dragging the mouse cursor over the URL itself. Once it is entirely highlighted, click the right mouse button and select Copy.

The URL for the picture is now copied to your Windows (or Mac) Clipboard, ready to paste into any text document. Using the "Save Picture As . . ." menu option in the same pop-up window,

you can save a copy of the digital picture somewhere on your computer!

ANOTHER GRIFF TIP! For consistency, create all your file names in lowercase. "honiton03.jpg" and "honiton03.JPG" are two different files as far as a Web browser is concerned, and one cannot be used to reference the other.

eBay's Picture Manager

eBay recently introduced an eBay-based image hosting solution called Picture Manager. You can subscribe to Picture Manager from "My eBay," Manage Subscriptions:

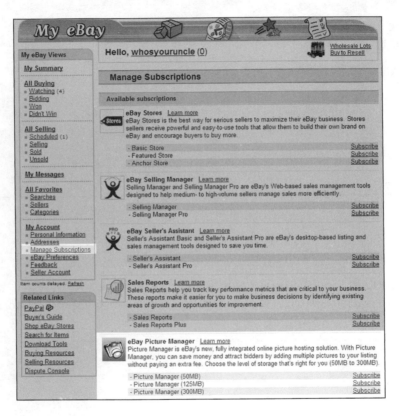

Once you subscribe to Picture Manager, you can add multiple pictures to all of your listings without paying any extra fees. Picture Manager offers three levels of storage space:

- 50 MB for $9.99 per month
- 125 MB for $19.99 per month
- 300 MB for $39.99 per month

Your monthly subscription fee is automatically added to your eBay account and will appear on your monthly invoice.

All Store sellers receive one megabyte of storage free with their Store subscription to host their Store logo and Store layout pictures. Featured and Anchored Store sellers also can benefit from the following discounted pricing:

Featured Store Sellers
- 50 MB for $4.99 per month
- 125 MB for $14.99 per month
- 300 MB for $34.99 per month

Anchored Store Sellers
- 50 MB free per month
- 125 MB for $4.99 per month
- 300 MB for $14.99 per month

I subscribe to Picture Manager. Here is what the interface looks like:

With Picture Manager, you can add, name, and edit folders, upload images from your computer, and move and rename them. One feature, Web Links, comes in handy. Here's how it works.

Check the images for which you need to obtain URLs and click the Web Links button.

This pops up a window containing the URL for that image, which you can then copy and paste into your listing description using the <IMG> tag that we learned about in the previous chapter on HTML.

In addition, you can add Picture Manager photos into your item description via eBay Picture Services. I strongly recommend Picture Manager as the best integrated photo hosting solution on eBay.

9

Help!

Our last chapter covers all aspects of obtaining help for a myriad of potential eBay situations. Let's start off with Trust and Safety.

Trust and Safety for Sellers

Selling on eBay can be great fun as well as potentially profitable. I hope this book proves to be of some help on your path to successful eBay selling. However, before you start out, there is one area of selling that many sellers don't give due consideration, even after they have been selling on eBay for months or years.

THE RULES

Yes, Virginia, there are rules for selling on eBay, and all eBay sellers are expected to become fully acquainted with the rules before they start selling.

As of this writing, "the rules" are better known on eBay as Trust and Safety. We will cover the most common topics of eBay Trust and Safety as they relate directly to sellers. I strongly suggest that you visit the site as soon as possible and read them all in greater detail.

Not all the rules are obvious! There are procedural ins and outs to eBay selling. It would be foolish for any eBay seller to assume she knows and understands all the rules without reading them carefully.

So, unless you don't mind having your listings ended, receiving warnings for prohibited activity, or having your registration on eBay suspended, possibly forever, then this chapter is an absolute must.

EBAY TRUST AND SAFETY—A HISTORY AND OUTLINE

In 1997, we in eBay Customer Support created a special department called Safe-Harbor. SafeHarbor's mission was to explain and apply the rules, processes, and policies governing all eBay members' activity on the eBay site. In the very beginning, the SafeHarbor team had jurisdiction over all potentially prohibited site activity, from bidding and feedback offenses to prohibited items.

In 1999 eBay entered its most frenetic period of explosive growth, and with this growth came whole new areas of prohibited activities and items. The number of new offenses, such as feedback abuse and spam, rose along with the exploding number of new users who registered on eBay each day. It soon became apparent to all of us in Customer Support and on eBay in general that one department alone could not adequately handle these increasingly complex issues and their attendant questions. Thus, in early 1999, a decision was made to split SafeHarbor into four separate departments—SafeHarbor, Community Watch, Fraud, and VeRO.

These separate teams have grown and changed since 1999, but they are still staffed by specially trained eBay Customer Support reps who have experience with all the rules governing activity on the eBay site, and certain eBay member activity off the eBay site. All four of the teams now live under the umbrella of the customer-support meta-team Trust and Safety.

QUESTIONABLE OR PROHIBITED PRACTICES AND ACTIVITIES

All eBay community members—buyers and sellers alike—are expected to adhere to certain standards of business conduct when using eBay. However, since the typical eBay transaction usually has the buyer sending payment to the seller before goods are shipped, eBay sellers bear a larger share of responsibility when it comes to staying within the rules.

Most of the rules pertaining to eBay selling are based on good old common sense. Before you initiate some action at eBay—writing out an item description, constructing terms of service for your buyers, etc.—ask yourself this question: "Will my action provide my listings or my online business with an unfair advantage over other sellers?" If the answer is yes or even maybe, then you need to check the list of policies and offenses on the eBay Rules and Safety page (navigation road map below).

For example, you might think that a great way to promote your business would be to link to your Web site directly from your eBay Item Description page. After all, why shouldn't you take advantage of the traffic that your eBay item is bound to receive? With potentially hundreds of visitors to your eBay listing, a link to your Web site would indeed be to your benefit. However, linking to your Web Site from your eBay listing description is strictly prohibited. You may not have realized this, but ignorance will be little comfort when all of your offending listings are ended early by eBay.

Your best protection against having all of your eBay listings ended is to *know the rules!* Safeguard the time and effort you put into listing your items at eBay by reading through all of the eBay selling rules and selling policies before you list an item for bid or sale.

GRIFF TIP! You can navigate to any of the Trust and Safety "Rules for Sellers" pages by following these steps:

Click the Help link on top of any eBay page (sign in if required). On the Help page, look for "Rules and Policies" toward the bottom of the topics.

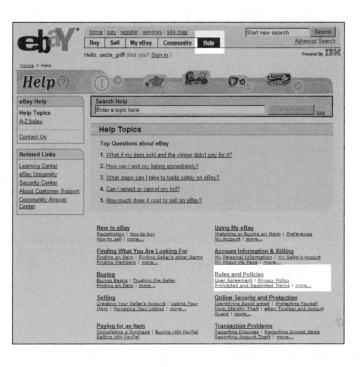

Click "Rules for Sellers."

Review the topics and their contents by clicking on each one and reading them carefully.

You will need this page in the future. Remember where it is. Bookmark it for safekeeping.

A Few of the Rules

The Trust and Safety team handles reports of selling abuses or seller rule violations including, but not limited to, the following areas:

> Bidding offenses
> Feedback
> Unpaid Items (aka UPIs)
> Listing violations

BIDDING OFFENSES—SHILL BIDDING

Simply put, sellers are not allowed to inflate the bid for their items by employing second accounts or agents to bid on their items. This activity is known as shill bidding. Not only is shill bidding strictly prohibited on eBay, but since it may include violations of local, state, or federal laws, you could find yourself in need of a good bail bondsman.

You can get a fairly good picture of the seriousness of shill bidding by going to *www.google.com* and typing in *shill bidding*. Read some of the archived news articles about past shill bidders who are now punching out license plates instead of eBay listings.

FEEDBACK

Certain activities are prohibited within the Feedback Forum. For example, you may not post another member's contact information—in part or in whole—within a feedback comment or, for that matter, anywhere else on eBay. This includes, but is not limited to, the other party's first name, phone number, e-mail address, city, or state.

Also, you may not leave profanity or obscenities in another person's feedback file. And using altered spellings or substituting punctuation marks does not excuse the offense, so *as**ole* is as unacceptable as the same word fully spelled out. Besides, rules and policies aside, your words reflect your character. You should choose them with the utmost care as they are going to tell the world who you are. You may believe the other party in a transaction to be an *as**ole*, but don't think for one minute that anyone reading your comment isn't going to say to herself, "Hmmm . . . sounds like this seller is the *real* as**ole."

Finally, if the other party reports such a comment to eBay, we will remove the entire comment and serve a warning to the poster of the offending remark.

The upshot? Leave feedback that you would have others leave for you.

UNPAID ITEMS

Buyers are obligated to follow through with their purchases after a listing has closed. The vast majority of bidders are basically good. Sometimes a buyer bids on or purchases an item and a real-life crisis takes him away, often to a place where he is unable to make contact with you or pay for the item. It happens.

Other times, a buyer may have intended to pay for the item if she won, but she suddenly found herself in unexpected dire financial straits. This doesn't automatically excuse the buyer from her obligation to follow through on her purchase, but you might work out a payment schedule or some other solution.

The point? Always give Unpaid Item buyers the benefit of the doubt. If they don't respond to your e-mails, try calling them. You can obtain their contact information by clicking on the Advanced Search link on the top of any eBay page and then clicking the Find Members link in the left-hand column. Scroll down and enter the buyer's User ID in the box marked Contact Information.

On occasion, a new member will traipse around the site, randomly and frivolously bidding away on things he has no intention of buying. You try to contact him and he ignores your e-mail or you attempt to phone him and he doesn't answer his phone or, worse, the line has been disconnected. These deliberately frivolous bidders are not welcome on eBay.

We cannot hold these bidders upside down and shake the funds out of them. We cannot force them to pay for your item. However, we can show them the exit—but only with your help.

You can help rid eBay of these nuisance bidders by reporting them to eBay through the Unpaid Item process. Simply follow the instructions on the Unpaid Item page:

1. Go to "My eBay."
2. Click Selling.
3. Scroll down to Selling-Related Links.
4. Click "more . . ." if necessary, to expand the list of links.
5. Look for Unpaid Item Process. Click it and follow the instructions.

Each Unpaid Item alert is recorded on the buyer's eBay account. On the third report, the buyer is automatically suspended from the eBay site.

Note that the process has built-in safeguards to prevent sellers who are not basically good (they aren't reading this book, remember) from abusing it. Thus, if you should ever have to use this process, you must take specific steps before you can file an Unpaid Item report, such as attempting to contact the bidder via e-mail, waiting a fair amount of time for a reply, etc.

You may be impatient to file your report ASAP, but we are certain that if the shoe should ever be on the other foot, you would want these safeguards to prevent you being the subject of a hastily filed UPI report that could result in the suspension of your eBay registration.

LISTING VIOLATIONS

The Trust and Safety team also fields all reports of listing violations. These include items that are prohibited or restricted on eBay, and reports of such activities as "keyword spamming" (the inclusion of words or phrases into a listing title or description intended to provide unfair advantage to the listing in search results), links to a seller's Web site included in item pages, payment surcharges, etc.

Not all otherwise legal items can be listed on eBay, so don't assume yours is OK. For example, although it is perfectly legal to sell a bear rug in the rest of the U.S.A., it is not legal in California. eBay headquarters are located in California;

thus we (and, by association, you) are bound by the California state laws prohibiting the sale of bears or bear parts.

Trust and Safety also has jurisdiction over the contents of an item description. On the same page as above, you will find the link "Listing policies," which contains a list of all eBay listing policies and prohibited listing activities.

Note that practically all reports of prohibited listings or listings with prohibited activities are sent to eBay by other eBay members.

All activities that eBay considers reportable to Trust and Safety can be found on the eBay Security & Resolution Center, whose link is on the bottom of every eBay Web page.

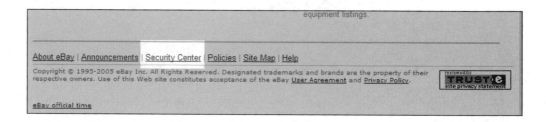

This takes you to the Security & Resolution Center.

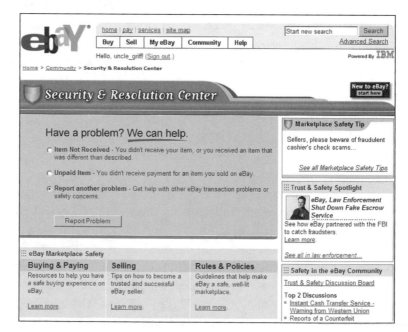

Read through the Security & Resolution Center at least once.

EBAY AND PAYPAL BUYER PROTECTION

We (eBay and the eBay community of your fellow buyers and sellers) believe you are basically good. Give yourself a hearty pat on the back. Or a hug.

How do we know that you are basically good? For nearly a decade, you have proven your goodness and honesty by speeding an item to your buyer once she has submitted payment. Despite what the cynics predicted, you have shown the world day after day, year after year, that people are indeed basically good. In fact, we are dead certain of it. How can we be so certain? Because you are an honest and considerate seller whose primary concerns—in order—are:

- Happy, satisfied buyers
- Your sterling eBay reputation (as exhibited by your feedback)
- The viability and continued success of your eBay business

You, like all basically good sellers, only have the best of intentions for your customers. They come first! You, like all basically good sellers, want to avoid disputes with your buyers. Sometimes, this becomes extremely difficult to do. Sometimes, an item is damaged or lost in the mail. Other times you might mistakenly have described an item as one thing when it was, unbeknownst to you, quite another thing entirely. No big sin. You didn't mean it. You really thought it was solid gold when it was, in fact, plated. We are all only human and we are all prone to the rare error in attribution. That's why you always immediately take back that gold-plated-but-mistakenly-sold-as-solid-gold item and quickly and cheerfully refund the buyer's money.

If any of these unfortunate mishaps should happen to you and your buyer, we are sure that you are going to bend over backward to make it right.

But then there are some other sellers. (They are not reading this book, so we can talk behind their backs.) They are not numerous. In fact, they make up less than .001 percent of all eBay sellers. But no matter—these sellers are sadly, tragically, *not* basically good. Oh, they were good once. They tried, really they did. But somewhere along the line they decided being basically good wasn't worth all the diligence, the excellent feedback, the happiness of their customers, or the eventual long-term success of their businesses. These sellers, who are not you, who are not basically good, go for the quick return with no concern at all for their buyer's satisfaction or to the consequences. These sellers say, "Your item was damaged in shipping? Too bad for you. It's not my problem. Your package never arrived? Blame it on the mailman. It's not really solid gold after all? The ad said 'as is' so tough cookies."

Oh, these poor, sad sellers. They have no idea what tragic fate awaits them.

Outraged and angry buyers who have tried to get some satisfaction from these sad sellers usually quickly alert eBay by filing for either eBay Standard Purchase Protection or PayPal Buyer Protection.

The eBay Standard Protection Program provides coverage up to $200 of the final bid value for the item (less a $25 fee for processing the claim). PayPal Buyer Protection covers buyers up to $1,000 as long as they have purchased the item from a seller displaying the PayPal Buyer Protection icon in his Seller Information box. Both protection plans cover buyers if they:

1. Paid for an item and never received it, or
2. Received an item that is less than what was described—such as winning a solid-gold necklace but receiving a plated one instead.

If a buyer is awarded payment from either protection program, the seller at fault runs the risk of immediate suspension from eBay. Thus it behooves any seller to do whatever it takes to satisfy a filed complaint, including refunding the buyer's money or exchanging the plated-gold item with a sold-gold example.

You can learn more by visiting the eBay Security & Resolution Center and following the links there for "Selling, Rules & Policies" and the brand-new Item Not Received process.

THE EBAY VERO PROGRAM (VERIFIED RIGHTS OWNERS)

Offering items that infringe upon an owner's trademark, copyright, or other intellectual property rights is strictly prohibited on eBay.

Believe it or not, some sellers (again, not you, of course) find sources for infringing items and offer them on eBay. For example, chic handbags with the Fendi brand name and trademark that are not genuine Fendi. Or a wristwatch that was made offshore somewhere but is inaccurately and dishonestly labeled Rolex.

Important note! These items, if not manufactured by the trademark holder, are infringing on the trademark holder's rights, and the seller of said infringing items can be suspended from eBay for offering them. In addition, sellers of infringing items run the serious risk of civil or criminal prosecution.

When I first started on eBay back in 1996, I would occasionally field reports from concerned eBay members about fake Rolex watches on the site. They were easy to spot. The sellers of such items would use words like *faux* (French for "false") or *not* in their titles. I would quickly remove these items from the site and send the sellers a stern warning about the consequences of future activity of this sort.

More times than not, the offending sellers would respond with surprise that what they were doing was in any way wrong. "But I was not being dishonest! I stated that they were fakes/knockoffs/copies/reproductions! I demand that you reinstate my listing."

At which point I would reply that our decision is final, but they were free to contact the trademark holder (in this case, Rolex) and ask them for their opinion.

Property rights are not limited to trademarks or name brands. Copyrights cover all sorts of intellectual property, including but not limited to video, film, music, software, and books.

If you are a trademark or copyright holder, you may want to join the VeRO Program yourself! Learn more about the VeRO Program. Click the Help link on the top of any eBay page and follow the links for Online Security and Protection > Protection Programs > Protecting Intellectual Property > eBay's Verified Rights Owner.

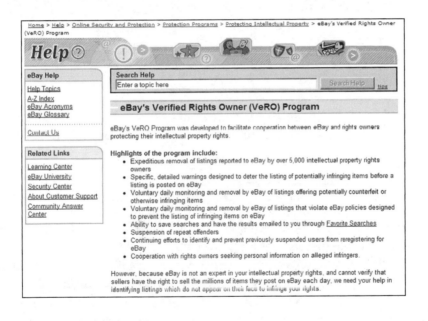

DISPUTE RESOLUTION

Some buyer and seller disputes are, to a great extent, no-fault disputes; that is, no real fraud was intended on the part of either the seller or the buyer. Something just went terribly, horribly wrong. This is where dispute resolution comes in handy.

eBay's third-party partner of choice for dispute resolution (at the time of this writing) is SquareTrade: *http://www.squaretrade.com/*.

SquareTrade is an independent service that provides a neutral place where a buyer and a seller can work out their dispute online efficiently and effectively.

HOW TO GET ASSISTANCE AT EBAY

Although this book should prove to be useful in using eBay, there is a seemingly infinite number of topics and potential issues regarding how to use eBay, and it would be impossible for one book to cover them all in detail.

Not to despair! The eBay Web site is a virtual treasure trove of valuable information, tips, answers, and clarifications. However, just as with any treasure, one has to hunt a little to find it. I hope that this last section will serve as a handy road map for finding answers to nearly any question, issue, complaint, or concern you might have about eBay.

Here are a few starting points for finding help, information, and general eBay knowledge right on the eBay Web site.

ON-SITE

You can find the answers to most common eBay procedure and policy questions quickly and easily by clicking Help, on the top of most eBay pages.

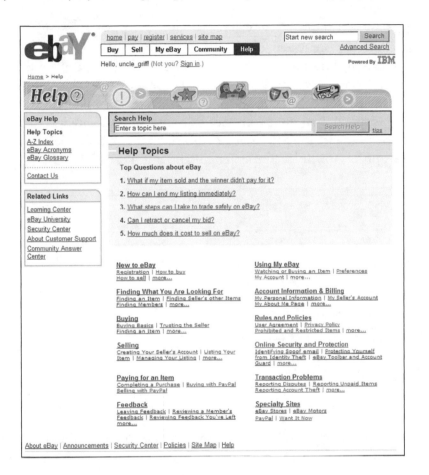

On the Help portal page, you can type into the box one or more keywords that relate to your query or scroll and click through the list of Help topics. Either way provides a treasure trove of help, answers, and explanations of policies and procedures. In fact, I use the eBay Help pages myself whenever I am stumped for an answer.

The keyword method of searching Help will search the entire Help database for matches and return a list of links with the most relevant first.

The topic method of searching Help allows you to drill down an intuitive pathway, starting with high-level topics down to detailed subtopics.

CLICK HERE TO "LEARN MORE"

The eBay Web site is chockablock with reams and reams of helpful information, tips, knowledge, clarifications, explanations, tutorials, etc. The key, of course, is finding this information.

A quick perusal of any eBay Web page, especially those pages where one can "do" something like register, search, list an item for sale, bid, etc., will show small links, usually but not always labeled "Learn more," sprinkled throughout the page. I am constantly amazed at how little use these valuable links receive.

If you are anywhere on eBay and are confused or unsure about how to proceed, look for the "Learn more" or "See example" links related to that topic or question. For example, the Sell Your Item form has "See example" links next to each of the options for Bold, Border, Highlight, and Featured.

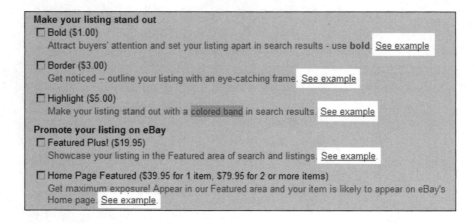

Clicking one brings up a window with more information about the format.

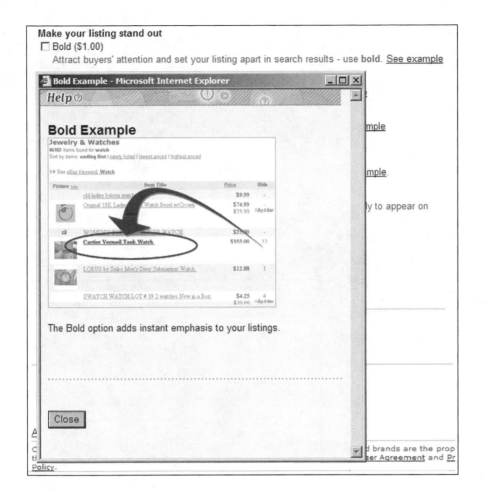

"See example" links cover practically any and every eBay-related topic you could imagine. Take the time to click these helpful links whenever you have a question about a particular topic or feature.

"MY EBAY"

Your "My eBay" All Buying, All Selling, Favorites, and Account pages each contain lists of related links at the bottom of the left-hand column. For example, the bottom left-hand side of the Selling page has the box Selling Links, with selling-related links covering nearly every aspect of selling on eBay.

Click the "more . . ." link to expand the view to the complete list of selling-related links.

If you have a selling, buying, account, or preferences-related question, check the bottom of the appropriate page in "My eBay" before sending an e-mail to Customer Support or contacting Live Help.

OTHER MEMBERS

eBay members are an invaluable source of eBay-related knowledge. Lucky for us, most expert eBay members are eager to dispense their wisdom, free of charge!

I have mentioned the chat boards in previous chapters, but it bears repeating here that the smartest eBay members in the world hang out on one or more of the many eBay chat boards.

You can find the chat boards under Community, and Talk on the eBay Navigation Bar.

Click on Discussion Boards to begin. This displays the various Community help boards and category specific Discussion boards.

I will select Packing and Shipping.

This displays the page of threaded discussions for the topic, Packing and Shipping.

Each "title" is a separate thread started by either an eBay member or, in some cases, an eBay employee. Anyone—registered eBay member or not—can read the contents of any of the threads. Only registered members can start a thread or post responses to a thread. To start a thread or post a response, a member must first log in with her registered eBay User ID and password.

To read a thread, simply click on its title. Let's check out the thread for A Buyer's Tutorial to Shipping and Handling (Sellers should read also).

This opens the thread for reading and posting.

Note the "Sign in to the community boards" link in the upper left-hand corner. If you want to post a query or answer, you need to click this link and log in first. Follow the instructions from there.

The members that hang out on these topic-specific chat boards provide a great service to other members. It's a subject near and dear to my heart, since I got my start at eBay by answering questions on the first eBay chat board. The tradition continues!

LIVE HELP

eBay Customer Support recently initiated a project called Live Help to quickly respond to new-customer queries. Live Help works similarly to an instant-messenger service. You—the brand-new eBay member—look for and click the Live Help icon, which brings up a messaging window. For those unfamiliar with the instant-messaging format, the concept is simple. You type your query into the window, and within moments an expert eBay support representative is assigned to your case. Then the two of you conduct an online conversation using text in real time.

eBay Live Help is intended primarily as a resource for new eBay buyers and sellers with questions about registration, bidding, and selling, along with some basic computer and Internet technical questions. However, the expert specialist reps on staff for Live Help can often assist with questions regarding Community Watch, account security, eBay policies and procedures, user-to-user disputes, or the eBay VeRO Program.

Here's the process step-by-step.

1. Locate a Live Help icon. One can usually be found on those pages frequented by new users, such as the eBay home page, the Registration form, and the Sell Your Item form.

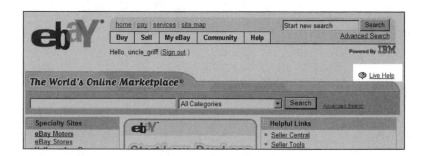

2. Depending on how your Web browser is configured, you may see an alert to accept a cookie. If so, you must accept this cookie to use Live Help. (If your Web browser is configured to reject cookies, see the section "Fine Tuning Your Web Browser for eBay" in Section Two, chapter 4.)

3. In the next window, you type in a "chat" name. It can be just about anything. You also select a topic from the drop-down list.

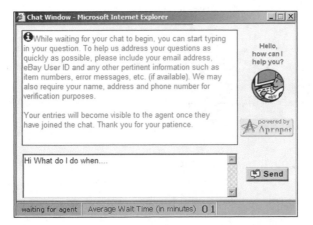

I have selected the topic "Other" for other questions. Click Send to begin the chat session.

4. Type your question into the box at the bottom of the next window. Once a support rep is free, he or she will respond.

5. You can then continue to chat until your question is answered to your satisfaction.

CONTACTING EBAY CUSTOMER SUPPORT

If the information provided through the eBay site, eBay Live Help, or eBay members doesn't adequately answer your question, you should send an e-mail to eBay Customer Support—but only after exhausting all the above options.

It can sometimes take twenty-four to forty-eight hours to receive a response to an e-mail. For many questions, you can find an answer on the site in less than a few minutes.

Click the Help link on the top of any eBay page and then click Contact Us under eBay Help.

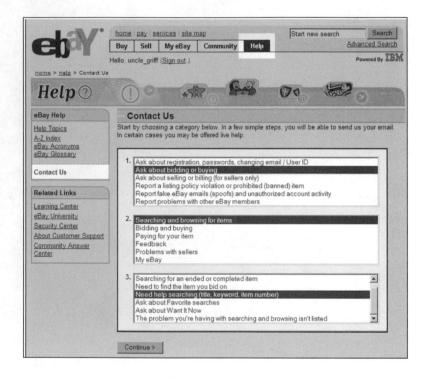

Select the appropriate topics and subtopics. If your particular query doesn't quite fit the list of topics, select one that most closely matches. In the third box, you will be able to select a subtopic for "topic isn't listed" otherwise known as "other."

On the next page, you can opt for one more look at a related Help page or e-mail. Select "e-mail."

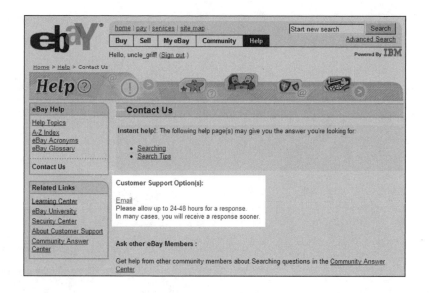

Include a detailed report in your own words and click the Send E-mail button.

GLOSSARY

About Me: A page you can create on eBay that tells other members about you and your eBay business. You'll see the icon next to the User ID of anyone who has an About Me page.

Administrative Cancellation: The cancellation of a bid by eBay due to administrative circumstances, such as when a bidder becomes unregistered.

Account Guard: The security feature of the eBay Toolbar: the Account Guard feature identifies when toolbar users are on an eBay or PayPal Web site, and warns them when they are on a potentially fraudulent (spoof) Web site.

Announcement Boards: Special pages where eBay posts current news and information. You'll find announcements about new features and promotions, policy changes, special event information, and notices about system issues. (Click Community on the top of any eBay page.)

Answer Center: Special pages where you can ask questions and get help with using eBay from other members of the eBay community.

Auction-Style Listing (Online Auction Format): The basic, most common way to sell an item on eBay—listing the item for sale, collecting bids for a fixed length of time, and selling the item to the highest bidder.

Authentication Services: Provided by third-party companies, authentication services offer everything from opinions to certified authentication and grading for items like jewelry, books, stamps, coins, comic books, and trading cards. (Click the Services link on the top of any eBay page.)

Bid Cancellation: The cancellation of a bid by a seller during an auction-style listing. In general, you should not cancel bids in your listings. However, you might cancel a bid if you are unable to verify the identity of the bidder. Once a bid is canceled, it cannot be reinstated by the seller. However, the bidder may bid again. (Click My eBay > All Selling > Seller-Related Links)

Bid Increment: The amount by which a bid must be raised in order for it to be accepted in an auction-style listing. For example, if the current bid for an item is $5.00, and the bid increment is $0.50, the next bid must be at least $5.50. The bid increment is automatically determined based on the current high bid.

Bid Retraction: The cancellation of a bid by a buyer during an auction-style listing. In general, a retraction may be allowed only under special circumstances. For example, if you accidentally enter the wrong bid amount (entering $99.50 rather than $9.95), you may retract it and enter the right bid amount as long as you do so immediately. (Click My eBay > All Buying > Buyer-Related Links)

Bidder Search: A search for all the items that a member of eBay has placed bids on. You can use this feature to see what another member has bid on during the last thirty days. All you need is the member's User ID.

Block Bidders/Buyers: A feature that lets you create a list of specific eBay members who are not allowed to bid on or buy items you list for sale. People on the list will be blocked from participating in all of your items until you take them off the list. (Click My eBay > All Selling > Seller-Related Links)

Buy It Now: A listing feature that lets a buyer purchase an item immediately for a price the seller has set. Items with this feature will display the icon and the Buy It Now price in the seller's listings.

Buyer Requirements: Special preferences any seller can set through My eBay that will block a buyer from bidding on your item based on four criteria: location, feedback score, unpaid item strikes, and PayPal. (Click My eBay > All Selling > Seller-Related Links)

Category Listings: The set of categories by which items are organized on eBay, such as Antiques, Books, Computers, Sporting Goods, etc.

Changed User ID Icon: Indicates that the member has chosen a new User ID within the past thirty days. (Click My eBay > Accounts > Personal Information)

Completed Litings (Search): A search for items that have ended over the last fifteen days. (Click Advanced Search)

Discussion Boards: Special pages where members can post messages to the eBay community about various topics. (Click Community on the top of any eBay page)

Dispute Console: Accessible through My eBay, the Dispute Console helps buyers and sellers manage, track, and take action on disputes related to their transactions, such as the Unpaid Item process and the Item Not Received process.

Dutch Auction (Multiple-Item Auction): A listing in which a seller offers multiple identical items for sale. For example, 500 pens, each at a starting price of $0.99.

eBay Anything Points: A unique program that allows buyers to pay for eBay items with a new promotional currency called eBay Anything Points when they pay using their PayPal account. In addition, eBay sellers can use their points to pay for their eBay seller fees when they make a payment to eBay with their PayPal account. You can earn Anything Points from program partners, special offers, and sellers who offer Anything Points. (Click the Services link on the top of any eBay page.)

eBay Keywords: Powered by adMarketplace, eBay Keywords offers eBay sellers the ability to place advertisements for their eBay Store or product above the usual eBay listings in the form of a text box or banner ad. (Click the Services link on the top of any eBay page.)

eBay Picture Services: An effective and easy-to-use picture-uploading tool available through the eBay Sell Your Item form. (Available in the Sell Your Item form)

eBay Sales Reports: Helps sellers track and record their selling activity quarter-to-quarter. Metrics include listings and sales by category and format, average sales price, conversion rates, and more. (Click the Services link on the top of any eBay page.)

eBay Shop: A Web site offering officially licensed, quality merchandise with the eBay logo. eBay Shop offers great items for you to purchase—from apparel to office accessories to cool collectibles.

eBay Stores: Special pages on eBay featuring all the items offered by an individual seller, including Buy It Now items not available in regular eBay listings. (Click the eBay Stores link on the eBay home page)

eBay Time: The official time of day at eBay headquarters in San Jose, California, in the United States. This location is in the Pacific time zone.

eBay Toolbar: A free eBay buying tool that you can add to your Web browser, which tracks items you're bidding on or watching, alerts you when listings are about to end, and offers simple yet powerful ways to search for items. (Click the Services link on the top of any eBay page.)

Escrow: A procedure in which a third party holds a buyer's payment in trust until the buyer receives and approves the item from the seller. Escrow is recommended for purchases of $500 or more. eBay recommends that you use Escrow.com as your escrow company. If a seller suggests a different company, please use caution. (Click the Services link on the top of any eBay page.)

Feedback: A system that eBay members use to rate their buying or selling experience with other eBay members. The feedback system helps you build your reputation on eBay and helps you check the reputation of other members of the community.

Feedback Score: A number used to measure a member's reputation on eBay. After a listing is completed, the buyer and seller can leave a rating (positive, neutral, or negative) for each other. Members receive points as follows:

+1 point for a positive rating

0 points for a neutral rating

−1 point for a negative rating

The feedback score is the sum of all the ratings a member has received from unique users. Every member of eBay has a feedback score. You'll find it in parentheses next to the User ID. Click on the feedback score to see that member's entire feedback profile.

Feedback Star: Indicates that an eBay member has achieved a certain feedback score. The star will vary according to the feedback score of the member:

Yellow Star: 10 to 49
Blue Star: 50 to 99
Turquoise Star: 100 to 499
Purple Star: 500 to 999
Red Star: 1,000 to 4,999
Green Star: 5,000 to 9,999
Yellow Shooting Star: 10,000 to 24,999
Turquoise Shooting Star: 25,000 to 49,999
Purple Shooting Star: 50,000 to 99,999
Red Shooting Star: 100,000 or higher

Final Value Fee: A fee or commission that eBay charges to a seller when a listing ends. This fee is based on the "final value" of the item, which is the closing bid or sale price.

Fixed Price Format: A selling format that lets you list an item for an unchanging, set price, with no auction-style bidding.

Gift Services: A listing option that lets you promote the item you're selling as something that would make a great gift. When you use this feature, an eye-catching gift box icon appears next to your listing on search and browse result lists. You can also promote gift-related services, such as gift wrapping and shipping to the gift recipient.

Giving Works: eBay Giving Works is the dedicated program for charity listings on eBay. List an item through eBay Giving Works and donate 100% of the final sale price to a member nonprofit organization, and eBay will donate the insertion fee and the final value fee to the nonprofit selected in the listing. (Click the Services link on the top of any eBay page.)

ID Verify: Indicates that the identity of a seller has been confirmed, giving buyers an extra measure of security. To ID-verify a seller, a third-party company works with eBay to cross check the seller's contact information across consumer and business databases. (Click the Services link on the top of any eBay page.)

Insertion Fee: The fee that eBay charges to a seller for listing an item. This fee varies by the type of listing and is nonrefundable. Please see the Fees page to learn more about how the insertion fee is determined in different types of listings.

Item Not Received: eBay's new online tool for resolving transaction disputes, problems, or miscommunication. Use this process when you've paid for an item but didn't receive it, or when you've paid for and received an item, but it was significantly different from the item's description.

Learning Center: eBay Education's hub page containing links to eBay University, online tours and tutorials, and the eBay Education Specialist program.

Member Profile: A page showing all of a member's feedback information, including ratings and comments from others who have bought or sold with that person before. To see a member's profile, just click on the feedback score in parentheses, next to the User ID.

Merge Accounts: To combine your eBay accounts when you have more than one. If you've created two eBay accounts (with two User IDs) during the time you've used eBay, merging them can simplify your buying and selling activities.

Multiple Item Auction (see Dutch Auction)

My eBay: A central place on eBay where you can manage all of your activities, including buying, selling, feedback, and general account preferences.

New Listing Icon: Indicates that the item has been listed within the last 24 hours. If you search or browse for the same kind of items repeatedly, this icon helps you spot items you may not have seen before.

New Member/User Icon: Indicates that the user has been a registered member of eBay for thirty days or less.

Online Auction Format (see Auction-Style Listing)

PayPal: A fast, easy, secure payment method offered by most eBay sellers for purchasing items. When you use PayPal, your payment is sent from your credit card or bank account without giving your account information directly to the seller.

PayPal Buyer Protection: A buyer-protection program that offers up to $1,000 of free coverage for buyers who pay with PayPal on qualified listings. Listings are qualified if the seller has a feedback score of 50 (98% positive) and meet other transaction-related requirements. Items that qualify for PayPal Buyer Protection are denoted by the PayPal Buyer Protection shield on the View Item page.

Picture Icon: Indicates that the listing has a picture of the item in its description. This icon appears in browse and search result lists.

Picture Manager: eBay's own picture-hosting service, available to all sellers at a low monthly subscription price. Works in conjunction with eBay Picture Service.

PowerSeller: A seller on eBay who has maintained a 98% positive feedback score and provided a high level of service to buyers. (Click the Services link on the top of any eBay page.)

Pre-Approve Bidders/Buyers: A feature that lets you create a list of specific eBay members who are allowed to bid on or buy an item you're listing for sale. Each pre-approved list applies to only one item, so you can restrict bidding or buying on one of your listings without changing the others.

Private Auction Listing: A listing in which the User IDs of bidders are not displayed to others. When a private auction listing ends, the seller and high bidder are notified through e-mail.

Proxy Bidding: The feature of an auction-style listing in which eBay automatically bids on your behalf, up to the maximum amount you set.

Real Estate Advertisement Format: A listing format to advertise real estate to eBay's audience without having to hold an auction-style listing or conduct the sale on eBay. There is no bidding with this format—interested buyers provide their contact information to the seller through the listing.

Registered Member/User: A person who has registered with eBay by providing basic contact information.

Relisting: Listing an item for sale again after it did not sell the first time.

Reserve Price: The lowest price at which you're willing to sell your item in an auction-style listing. When you list your item, you can set a secret reserve price. If the highest bid does not meet your reserve price, then you're under no obligation to sell the item to the bidder.

Second Chance Offer: A feature that lets you make an offer to a non-winning bidder when either the winning bidder has failed to pay for your item, or you have a duplicate of the item.

Secure Server: A special server used for processing credit card and other sensitive information that you submit. This server uses Secure Sockets Layer (SSL) encryption to keep your information private and safe.

Secure Sockets Layer (SSL): An industry-standard encryption protocol that is used to transmit users' personal or credit card information securely and privately over the Internet. eBay uses this technology to keep your information safe.

Security and Resolution Center: The central location on the eBay site for members to report problems, as well as for members to learn how to stay safe on eBay and online. (Click the Security Center link on the bottom of any eBay page.)

Sell Similar Item: A feature that lets you list a new item based on the information you've previously entered for another item.

Seller's Return Policy: A feature in the Sell Your Item form that enables sellers to specify their product return policy. This feature includes a set of pre-formatted policies from which the seller can choose.

Seller Search: A search by User ID for a specific seller on eBay.

Seller's Assistant: An advanced eBay selling tool that helps frequent sellers create professional listings in bulk, track them at eBay, and manage customer correspondence. (Click the Services link on the top of any eBay page.)

Selling Manager: An advanced eBay selling tool that lets you perform all of your listing- and sales-related activities from one location in My eBay. (Click the Services link on the top of any eBay page.)

Selling Manager Pro: An eBay selling tool that has all the features of Selling Manager, but has additional capabilities to track inventory, list items in bulk, send feedback and e-mails in bulk, and generate profit-and-loss reports. (Click the Services link on the top of any eBay page.)

Shill Bidding: The deliberate placing of bids to artificially raise the price of an item. This practice is not permitted on eBay. Family members, friends, and individuals living together, working together, or sharing a computer should not bid on one another's items.

Shipping Calculator: Free seller tool that provides accurate, calculated shipping amounts to buyers based on parcel originating and destination zip codes.

Sniping: Placing a bid in the closing minutes or seconds of an auction-style listing. Any bid placed before the listing ends is allowed on eBay.

SquareTrade: Third party vendor that offers dispute resolution and identity verification services for all eBay members. (Click the Services link on the top of any eBay page.)

Starting Price: The price at which you want bidding for your item to begin in an auction-style listing.

Store Inventory Format: A selling format that eBay Store sellers can use to list items in their Store for a fixed price.

Title Search: A method of finding items on eBay by entering keywords that match the title of the items.

Trading Assistants: Trading Assistants are experienced eBay sellers who will sell your items on eBay for a fee. Find them in the Trading Assistants directory at www.ebay.com/ta. (Click the Services link on the top of any eBay page.)

Turbo Lister: An advanced, free desktop-based eBay selling tool that helps you create multiple eBay listings quickly and easily offline from your computer. (Click the Services link on the top of any eBay page.)

Unpaid Item Process: The dispute resolution process used by sellers when they have not been paid for their item. The Unpaid Item Process provides sellers with a method for obtaining a refund for a Final Value Fee credit from eBay. (Click Help and A–Z index)

User Agreement: The terms under which eBay offers registered members access to eBay services. (Click Help and A–Z index)

User ID: The "nickname" you choose to identify yourself to other eBay members. You choose a User ID when you register on eBay.

VeRO: eBay's Verified Rights Owner (VeRO) program facilitates cooperation between eBay and rights owners who wish to protect their intellectual property rights. (Click Help and A–Z index)

Want It Now: eBay's place where buyers can tell sellers exactly what they want. Buyers post a message to Want It Now with a description of what they'd like to buy. Sellers can review these posts and respond to buyers with items they are selling on eBay. (Click Help and A–Z index)

INDEX